INITIA AMHARICA

INITIA AMHARICA

An Introduction to Spoken Amharic

BY

C. H. ARMBRUSTER, M. A.
Sudan Civil Service;
Late of H.M. Administration, British Central Africa;
sometime Minor Scholar of King's College, Cambridge

PART I
GRAMMAR

GYAN

Published by

GYAN

Gyan Publishing House
5, Ansari Road
Daryaganj, New Delhi-110002
Phone: 011-47034999, 9811692060
E-mail: books@gyanbooks.com

Distribution Network
gyanbooks.com
India, USA, Canada, UK, Australia, France

ISBN : 978-81-212-4433-6 (Set)
ISBN : 978-81-212-4863-1 (PB)
First Published, 1910

2nd Impression 2020

Printed at: Gyan Press, Delhi.

Initia Amharica
Author: C. H. Armbruster

INITIA AMHARICA

An Introduction to spoken Amharic

BY

C. H. ARMBRUSTER, M.A.

Sudan Civil Service;
late of H.M. Administration, British Central Africa;
sometime Minor Scholar of King's College, Cambridge.

PART I
GRAMMAR

CAMBRIDGE:
at the University Press
1908

ἐμοὶ δὲ παρὰ πάντα τὸν λόγον ὑποκέεται ὅτι τὰ λεγόμενα ὑπ' ἑκάστων ἀκοῇ γράφω.

HEROD. II. 123.

To

a Friend

PREFACE.

THE words and phrases in this work have been taken down from the mouth of natives[1]. As many as possible of the phrases are such as have been said spontaneously, i.e. are not the products of cross-examination. The Abyssinian, like other members of partially civilised peoples, or uneducated individuals of highly civilised races, does not always speak naturally when questioned by a stranger. If he has had no education of any kind he experiences the same difficulty in answering enquiries concerning the language he unreflectingly uses as would, in similar circumstances, an uncultured European. Those, on the other hand, who have any smattering of learning tend to supply one with 'fine language'[2], which may or may not be idiomatic, instead of the ordinary conversational expressions current among themselves. In any case it is of course incompatible with the position of the white man that natives should address him in the style in which they address one another. I have, therefore, paid more attention to what I have heard natives say to each other than to

---

[1] While the language of all sorts and conditions of men, from wherever they come, has been noted, it is hardly necessary to say that care has been taken to avoid as informants individuals speaking Tigrịñña, Agaûñña, Gallịñña, Arabic, etc., and knowing Amharic only as an acquired tongue.

[2] cp. the so-called عربي عالي and نحوي.

what they have said to me, and have not excluded words or modes of expression on account of their so-called vulgarity[1]: the object in view being to give some description not so much of what, in the opinion of learned Europeans and natives, Abyssinians ought to say as of what in point of fact they do say.

In dealing with a spoken language I have not hesitated to use colloquial English.

Those who wish to pursue their acquaintance with Amharic beyond this 'Introduction' I would refer to the writings of Guidi, my indebtedness to which I desire to acknowledge most gratefully. In his magnificent 'Vocabolario', a work indispensable to serious students of the language, there is a brief bibliography of Amharic and kindred subjects.

In the few cases where I have differed from Guidi in regard to the meaning of words[2] it has been with diffidence, and only after repeated verification. Differences as regards form are of more frequent occurrence, as I have concerned myself with the spoken rather than the written word.

The publication of this series has been rendered possible by the financial assistance of the Egyptian Government, as advised by Lord Cromer, and by the liberal attitude of the Syndics of the Pitt Press.

---

[1] Quot homines, tot sententiae: e.g. Mondon-Vidailhet, Gram. p. 201 **እንትን፡** 'Cette façon de parler passe aujourd'hui pour vulgaire': yet I heard this useful word employed repeatedly by Dejjazmach Gassasa, a man of great courtesy and refinement.

[2] In cases like **እዚያ** or **እዝያ** = there, Guidi's 'quello là' (Vocab. p. 487) may be the original meaning: I give the one I find in use.

Preface.

I wish to express my cordial thanks, for valuable information supplied and for assistance rendered in many ways, to Maj.-Gen. Sir F. Reginald Wingate, K.C.B. etc., Sirdar and Governor-General, Lt.-Col. E. B. Wilkinson, Maj. W. S. R. May, Capt. R. C. R. Owen, C.M.G., A. L. Butler, Esq. and J. Grieve, Esq., of the Sudan Government: to Lt.-Col. Lord Edward Cecil, D.S.O. and Capt. the Hon. C. James, of the Egyptian Government: to Capt. R. B. Black, Capt. C. Garvice, D.S.O. and El Mulazim Awwal Mustafa Effendi Izzeddin, of the Egyptian Army: to H. Farnall, Esq., C.B. etc., of the Caisse de la Dette, to F. B. Wynch, Esq., of the National Bank of Egypt, to W. B. Heard, Esq., late H.M. Vice-Consul at Addis Abeba, to Dr E. A. Wallis Budge, of the British Museum, and to Prof. F. C. Burkitt, Dr M. R. James, George Wherry, Esq., M.A. etc., R. T. Wright, Esq., M.A., A. R. Waller, Esq., M.A. and J. Clay, Esq., M.A., of Cambridge: እንግዲህ ፡ ላፌ ፡ ወርቅ ፡ ልጅ ፡ ለወልደ ፡ ማሯም ፡ የሚባል ፡ ሰው ፡ ዘወትር ፡ ብዙ ፡ የረዳኝ ፡ ስራ ፡ ጨርሼ ፡ እግዚአብሔር ፡ ይስጥልኝ ፡ እላለኍ ።

Notices of errors and suggestions for improvements will be thankfully received, and should be addressed to me

c/o The Sudan Agent,
War Office,
Cairo.

C. H. ARMBRUSTER.

KHARTOUM,
January, 1908.

CONTENTS.

b 2

[1] In alphabetical order, as most convenient for beginners.

ABBREVIATIONS.

abbr. abbreviated, abbreviation.
acc. accusative.
act. active.
adj. adjective, (-val, -vally).
adv. adverb, (-bial, -bially).
Am. Amharic.
an. animate.
approx. approximate(ly).
Ar. Arabic.
art. article.
aux. auxiliary.
card. cardinal.
caus. causative.
comp. compound.
compos. composition.
conj. conjunction, (-tive).
conjug. conjugation.
conn. connected.
constr. constructed, (-tion).
cont. contingent (mood).
cp. compare.
dat. dative.
dem. demonstrative.
dist. distributive.
e.g. for instance.
emph. emphasis, (-atic).
encl. enclitic.
Eng. English.
esp. especial(ly).
Eth. Ethiopic.
Eur. European.
f. feminine.
fin. final.
Fr. French.
G. Gojjám.
Gall. Gallı̥ññа.
gen. general(ly).
Ger. German.
Gr. Greek.
i. intransitive.
i.e. that is.
imp. imperative.
imperf. imperfect.
impers. impersonal(ly).
inan. inanimate.
ind. indicative.
indecl. indeclinable.
indef. indefinite.
inf. infinitive.
inter. interrogative.
interj. interjection.
iron. ironical(ly).
It. Italian.
juss. jussive.
lit. literal(ly).
m. masculine.
mil. military.
neg. negative.
nom. nominative.
num. numeral.
obj. object.

onom. onomatopoetic.
ord. ordinal.
p. page, passive.
part. participle.
perf. perfect.
pers. person (-al, -ally).
pl. plural.
plup. pluperfect.
pol. polite, the form for addressing superiors.
poss. possessive.
pref. prefix(ed).
pron. pronoun (-nominal).
prop. properly.
prov. proverb.
prp. preposition.
q.v. which see (in vocabularies).
r. reflexive.
rad. radical.
s. substantive.
s.v. under the word (in vocabularies).
sg. singular.
simp. simple.
subj. subject.
subst. substantive (-val, -vally).
suff. suffix(ed).
Š. Šə̂ua (Shoa).
t. transitive.
T. Tįgrįñña.
v. verb.
vet. veterinary.
vocab. vocabularies.
1st, 2nd, 3rd: the respective persons.

√ root or stem.
– long.
⌣ *very* short.
⏑̄ sometimes long, sometimes short.
ʹ stress accent; words marked with two accents usually have the first when final, the second before another word (§ 8).
† not in general use.
* theoretical form.
= amounts to, is equal to, the same as.
§ refers to the paragraphs of the Grammar (Part I.).

USE OF BRACKETS AND HYPHENS.

In English

(*a*) Inclusive :

dirt, s. (-ty, adj.) = dirt, s. and dirty, adj. (for which Amharic uses the same word).

He (it) is = he is ; also : it is.

(*b*) Explanatory :

Disposition (character) = disposition in the sense of character.

In Amharic

i̥d(i̥)f = i̥di̥f and i̥df.

tí̥q(i̥š)šã = tí̥qi̥ššã and tí̥qšã.

[የ]ትም[ህ]ርት = የትምህርት, also ትምህርት, የትምርት and ትምርት.

sḁbábbḁrḁ (-ỵá-, -är-) = sḁbábbḁrḁ ; also sḁỵábbḁrḁ, sḁ-bábbärḁ and sḁỵábbärḁ, (see § 7*d*).

In English the masculine is intended unless the feminine is specified, and 'you' and similar words are singular unless marked plural.

In the phrases the Eng. verbs in the 2nd pers. are sg. ; pol., pl., after the translation of a phrase = the same phrase with the *subject* in the pol. or pl.

Try it : —— pol. = try (pol.) it.
pl. = try (pl.) it.

Give him something to eat : —— pl. = give (pl.) him etc.

ABBREVIATIONS OF WORKS REFERRED TO.

Afevork, Gram. Grammatica della lingua amarica, di G. J. Afevork, Roma, 1905.

Cust, Lng. Afr. A Sketch of the Modern Languages of Africa, by R. N. Cust, London, 1883.

Guidi, Coniug. Sulle coniugazioni del verbo amarico. Di I. Guidi, in the Zeitschrift für Assyriologie, VIII.

Guidi, Gram. Grammatica elementare della lingua amariña, 2nd edition, Roma, 1892.

Guidi, Redupl. Sulla reduplicazione delle consonanti amariche, di I. Guidi, in the Supplementi Periodici all'Archivio Glottologico Italiano, Roma, 1895.

Guidi, Vocab. Vocabolario Amarico-Italiano, compilato da I. Guidi, Roma, 1901.

Isenberg, Gram. Grammar of the Amharic Language, by the Rev. C. W. Isenberg, London, 1842.

Lepsius, St. Alph. Standard Alphabet for reducing unwritten languages and foreign graphic systems to a uniform orthography in European letters, by C. R. Lepsius, 2nd edition, London, 1863.

Ludolf, Lex. Æth. I. Ludolfi Lexicon Æthiopico-Latinum, editio secunda, Francofurti ad Moenum, 1699.

Mondon-Vidailhet, Gram. Grammaire de la langue abyssine (amharique), par C. Mondon-Vidailhet, Paris, 1898.

Munzinger, Vocab. Vocabulaire de la langue tigré, par W. Munzinger, Leipsic, 1865.

Praetorius, Am. Spr. Die Amharische Sprache, von F. Praetorius, Halle, 1879.

Praetorius, Gram. Æth. Grammatica Æthiopica, scripsit Dr F. Praetorius, Carlsruhe, 1886.

Reinisch, Wört. Beḍ. Wörterbuch der Beḍauye-Sprache, von Leo Reinisch, Vienna, 1895.

Vollers and Burkitt, Gram. A Grammar of the Modern Egyptian Dialect of Arabic, by K. Vollers and F. C. Burkitt, Cambridge, 1895.

CORRIGENDA.

Page	line	for	read
3	6, 7	ሐ = ح = ח, ኀ = خ	ሐ = ح, ኀ = خ = ח
9	28	ዢ ži̥, ž,	ዢ or ዥ ži̥, ž,
15	11	alsḁ́ṭṭḁnn	alsḁ́ṭḁnn
17	27	ya͡í̥däll	yá͡i̥däll
18	11	bi̥lí̥č̣lič̣	bi̥lí̥č̣li̥č̣
18	20	di̥ṿli̥qlíqq	di̥ṿli̥qlí̥qq
22	8	nḁ́ggḁsa	nḁ́ggḁsḁ
31	11	ā́lh	ā̃lh
31	12	h^{w}ónh	h^{w}onh
34	12	ደኅና ፡	ደኅና ፡
35	15	ṣḁ́ha͡i	ṣḁ́ha͡i̥
37	9	yā́ṿárāl	yā́ṿḁ́rāl
44	11	zḁtḁná	zḁṭḁná
57	18–20	-ā-	-ā́-
59	11	^{w}o	-^{w}o
60	23–25	-ā-	-ā́-
60	26	to him (him, pol.)	(to him, him, pol.)
62	19	ai̥nḁgrā́č(č)͡ḁum	a͡i̥nḁgrā́č(č)͡ḁum
68	16,17	this is (that's)	that is
81	15	í̥ra	ṭí̥ra
83	26	i̥mḁtállḁ͡u^{h}	i̥mḁṭállḁ͡u^{h}
90	13	kḁ-lḁ́-kkḁ-la	kḁ-lḁ́-kkḁ-lḁ
91	22	-ṿa	-ṿḁ
91	23	lḁsḁ́llḁsa	lḁsḁ́llḁsḁ
95	22	yi̥lḁ́qm	yi̥lḁ́q(ĭ̥)m
96	16	lḁ́qqḁma	lḁ́qqḁmḁ

Page	line	for	read
103	11	"the conjunction -ም"	"a conjunction such as -ም"
112	24	-gāč(č)yuhāl	-gā́č(č)yuhāl
120	25	ã̄tt(i̥)lḁ́qmu	ã̄tt(i̥)lḁ́qmu
123	10	እይደለህም	እይዶለህም
127	10	ā́ddä-	-ā́ddä-
134	17	sḁṭi̥č̣čā́llau̥[h]	sḁṭi̥ččā́llau̥[h]
135	7, 27	ā́ln	ã̄ln
138	24	čč	-čč
140	19	ĩ̄t	fĩ̄t
149	10	mḁiḁmmḁ́ryã̄	mḁjḁmmḁ́ryã̄
172	25	mḁ́ṭṭānāl	mḁ́ṭṭã̄nnāl
176	14	sow	sew
190	27	bí̥	bí̥-
208, 9	5	mḁ́ṭtŏ͡āl, mḁ́ṭtʷo	mḁ́ṭ(ĭ̥)tŏ͡āl, mḁ́ṭ(ĭ̥)tʷo
209	21	(mā́- § 8)	(mā́- ; § 8)
221	13, 14	(šā́-, -ā́ññ § 6)	(šā́- ; -ā́ññ § 6)
238	22	yi̥mmã̄́ttā̃l	yi̥mmã̄́ttāl
242	5 (end)	(-ärā́-)	(-ärā-)
243	16	ሺ.-	-ሺ.
243	19 (end)	tā́-	tä-
252	27	(-äsā́-)	(-äšā́-)
255	8	(-äsā́-)	(-äšā́-)
263	6	ññ	-ññ
297	28	nḁ́srʷȭt	nḁ́srʷṓt (§ 8)
378	24	tā́-	ṭā́-

ADDENDA.

Page	line		add
14	14	… …	"but የለምን ። yállämi̥n?, is he (it) absent?"
63	2	"sg. 3rd f.;"	"and after sg. 2nd f. (§ 43*b*) ending in resultants in § 7*b*; e.g. ክፈይው፡ ki̥fḁi̥u, pay (f.) him; divide (f.) it; ስጭኝ፡ si̥č̣i̥ñ, give (f.) me;"
132	12	ቍሟል …	Š. ቆሟል qʷŏ́mŏ͡āl
„	19	ቍሞ …	Š. ቆሞ qʷŏ́mʷo
„	20	ጢሼ …	Š. ጤሼ ṭʸĕ́šš̌ʸe
„	20	ቍሜ …	Š. ቆሜ qʷŏ́mmʸe
157	1	… …	§ 54*e*
172	25	… …	"The simp. perf. is sometimes used to express an immediate future: e.g. እንግዲህ፡ ሄድን። ṅgdʸeh hắdnḁ, well, we are going."
209	5	nå͡i …	(nḁ͡i̥)
323	10	juss. ያስይዝ, imp. አስይዝ	"Š. also Isenberg's ያስያዝ, አስያዝ (Gram. p. 128), and in similar verbs forms corresponding with his አስማል (p. 118)."

AMHARIC GRAMMAR.

INTRODUCTION.

Field of the Language.

Amharic (አምኃርኛ or አማርኛ amār̥ñña) is the language most widely spoken and written in Abyssinia at the present day[1]. It is indigenous not only in Amhára, the district from which the name is taken, but over the greater part of Central Abyssinia. The ascendency of the Shoan race, whose mother-tongue it is, has established it as the official language of the Ethiopian Empire. As a language of commerce it is heard beyond the limits of Abyssinia proper in the Italian colony of Eritrea, the French Somali Coast protectorate, and the eastern provinces of the Sudan. § 1*a*

Dialects.

Two principal dialects of Amharic are distinguished, that of Gojjam (G.) and that of Shoa (Š.). The differences between them are, generally speaking, of a minor character, and barely warrant the use of the term 'dialect' in this connection. Forms marked G. are also in use in the country north and west of Gojjam and those marked Š. also to the south and east of Shoa. § 1*b*

---

[1] For other Abyssinian languages see Cust, Lng. Afr. pp. 87—140.

Place in the Semitic Family.

§ 2 The Ethiopian branch of the Semitic family is divided into two groups, northern and southern. The former is represented by the ancient Ethiopic (ግዕዝ g͡ịịz) with its modern descendants Tígrê or Khásа (الخاصية) and Tịgrịñña (ትግርኛ); while Amharic is the chief modern representative of the latter.

A considerable literature has been preserved in Ethiopic, which is still in use as the ecclesiastical language of Abyssinia; but of its sister language of the southern group, of which Amharic is a development, we have no written record.

Thus Amharic stands in the relationship of a niece[1] to Ethiopic, which would appear, moreover, to have exerted, either directly or indirectly, a marked influence on the younger language.

But if Amharic has in great measure assimilated the vocabulary and appropriated the grammatical forms of Ethiopic, it has done so with such independence[2] as to indicate extensive imitation rather than primitive affinity[3].

In its present state it is lacking in some most

---

[1] not a daughter: Praetorius, Am. Spr. p. 4, '... was schon Rödiger und Dillmann erkannt haben, dass die heutige amharische Sprache nicht die Tochter des Æthiopischen ist, sondern dass das Altamharische zum Æthiopischen nur in einem geschwisterlichen Verhältniss stand.'

[2] Guidi, Vocab. p. ix.

[3] Munzinger, Vocab. p. iv.

characteristic Semitic features, and those which it displays give one the impression of having been superimposed on an alien (possibly Hamitic) basis. As in Ethiopic, the strong and weak Semitic aspirates are confused, though the Ethiopic characters corresponding with each are retained: ሀ = ه = ה, ሐ = ح = ח, ኀ = خ, but ሀ ሐ ኀ are to-day all pronounced alike and interchanged in writing, or even omitted; similarly between አ = ا = א and ዐ = ع = ע the distinction, both in writing and in speech, has been lost. Many, too, of the consonantal modifications described in § 7 are not found in Ethiopic and are foreign to the spirit of Semitic enunciation. Again, in regard to the construction of the sentence, while Semitic languages co-ordinate phrases, Amharic subordinates them and, like Latin or German, readily encloses a whole period between subject and verb.

The exact place, then, of Amharic in a general classification of languages is open to discussion. Meanwhile, for practical purposes such as the arrangement of dictionaries and the exhibition of its accidence, it is treated as a Semitic language, a system from which I have seen no reason to depart.

PHONOLOGY.

Phonetic Alphabet.

§ 3 In order to designate the pronunciation of Amharic as far as possible without ambiguity I employ the following phonetic alphabet. The principle held in view is that one letter should never represent more than one sound, and one sound should not be represented by more than one letter[1]. In regard to the consonants this is a feasible system; but the fluctuating character of some of the short vowels precludes a strict adherence to it, which would involve the use of an impracticably large number of letters to represent variations of no essential importance. The indications, then, by means of examples taken from European languages of the value of the sounds which occur are, especially in the case of the vowels, only approximately exact.

With the exception of the 'explosive[2]' sounds represented by p̣, q, ṭ, č̣, ṣ, and the guttural χ (frequently pronounced k by Abyssinians themselves) the pronunciation of Amharic presents little difficulty to an Englishman.

---

[1] Lepsius, St. Alph. pp. 31, 32, 38.

[2] See end of this §.

Vowels.

All vowels are pronounced short unless marked
¯ = long, ¯̆ = long or short, ˘ = *very* short.

a	a in It. fatto.
ā	a in father.
ä	e in bet, but more open.
ǟ	e in send, but more open.
ḁ	a in formula, e in Fr. le.
ḁ̄	e in herd (or er when r has no consonantal value).
e	e in bet, but less open.
ē	e in send, but less open.
i	i in It. minuto.
ī	i in machine.
i̥	i in quick, but pronounced with the lips more closed.
ī̥	i̥ lengthened.
ü	u in Fr. absolument.
ω	a in was.
o	o in It. caro, but more open (not o aperto).
ō	o in It. padrone, but more open (not o aperto).
u	u in full.
ū	u in It. luna.

ä ḁ and ω represent the same vowel in Amharic (g͡i̥i̥z § 4). The above examples show, approximately, the commonest pronunciations of this variable vowel[1]. When ä ḁ ω are given as alternatives they represent a gradation of sounds from e in 'bet' through approx. u in 'but', eu in Fr. neuf, e in Fr. le, ö in Ger. Götter to a in 'was' (§ 7*d*).

---

[1] Guidi, Gram. § 4*b*, 'suono non ben determinato'; see Lepsius, St. Alph. p. 48, and cp. our varying pronunciations of e in 'offering', i in 'girl', u in 'occurrence.'

Diphthongs.

Diphthongs are merely their component vowels pronounced in rapid succession without any intervening hiatus. They are marked ͡ . The following approximations are fairly close:

á͡i̥	i in bite.
ä́͡i̥	ai in Ger. Waise.
á͡u	au in Ger. Haus.
ḁ́͡u	o in no.
ώ͡i̥	oy in boy.

Consonants.

χ	ch in Ger. noch.
h	h in he.
q	an explosive guttural pronounced a little further back than k[1]; the centre of the tongue is raised towards the palate.
k	k in kin.
g	g in go.
ṅ	ng in singing.
ṭ	tt in hottest, but pronounced with an explosion.
ṣ	sibilant ṭ, similar to ts in pots, but pronounced with an explosion.
č̣	ch in church, but pronounced with an explosion.
č	ch in cheese.
š	sh in she.
ž	j in Fr. je.

---

[1] but not as far back as Syrian ق.

j	j in jam, but the tongue comes nearer the teeth.
y	y in you.
ñ	ñ in Spanish señor.
t	dental t, as in Fr. tu.
d	dental d, as in Fr. de.
s	s in so.
z	z in prize.
l	l in let.
r	r in red.
n	n in no.
p	p in pot.
p̣	p pronounced with an explosion.
b	b in be.
f̣	bilabial f, (the teeth not touching the lips).
ṿ	bilabial v, b in Spanish arriba.
f	labio-dental, f in fan.
v	labio-dental, v in van.
w	w in went, but the lips are more open: u in It. uomo.

^{h}, ^{y}, ^{w}, are h, y, w, pronounced very slightly, ^{y} and ^{w} almost merged into the adjacent vowel (§ 7*d*), and ^{h} final tending to disappear. y and w may be regarded as the consonantal forms of i̥ and u respectively; after a vowel they often pass into those vowels and form diphthongs (cp. y in layer, w in lower): a + ya = a͡i̥a, a + wa = a͡ua; similarly i̥ and u when doubled (§ 6) become yy, ww (uw).

q, p̣, ṭ, ṣ, č̣ are pronounced with emphasis, and appear to be separated from a following vowel by a slight explosion of breath. They are quite distinct from k, p, t, s, č.

The Amharic Characters.

§ 4*a* Amharic employs the Ethiopic syllabary, with additional signs representing sounds not occurring in Eth. The characters are read from left to right. There are seven forms of each character, each representing the consonant followed by (and including) a different vowel. These seven classes are known by their Eth. names (of which the Am. pronunciation is given).

I.	ግዕዝ	gi̥i̥z, original, representing the consonant followed by		ḁ (ä, ω)
II.	ካዕብ	kai̥y̥, second,	„ „ „	ũ
III.	ሣልስ	sali̥s, third,	„ „ „	ĩ
IV.	ራብዕ	ray̥i̥, fourth,	„ „ „	ã
V.	ኃምስ	hami̥s, fifth,	„ „ „	^{y}ẽ
VI.	ሳድስ	sadi̥s, sixth,	„ „ „	i̥ or no vowel
VII.	ሳብዕ	say̥i̥, seventh,	„ „ „	^{w}õ

There is also a series of characters representing the consonant followed by w and a vowel; this w is often pronounced ŏ before ã.

gi̥i̥z		kai̥y̥		sali̥s		ray̥i̥		hami̥s		sadi̥s		say̥i̥	
ሀ	hã	ሁ	hũ	ሂ	hĩ	ሃ	hã	ሄ	h^{y}ẽ	ህ	hi̥, h	ሆ	h^{w}õ
ለ	lḁ	ሉ	lũ	ሊ	lĩ	ላ	lã	ሌ	l^{y}ẽ	ል	li̥, l	ሎ	l^{w}õ
ሐ	hã	ሑ	hũ	ሒ	hĩ	ሓ	hã	ሔ	h^{y}ẽ	ሕ	hi̥, h	ሖ	h^{w}õ
መ	mḁ	ሙ	mũ	ሚ	mĩ	ማ	mã	ሜ	m^{y}ẽ	ም	mi̥, m	ሞ	m^{w}õ
ሠ	sḁ	ሡ	sũ	ሢ	sĩ	ሣ	sã	ሤ	s^{y}ẽ	ሥ	si̥, s	ሦ	s^{w}õ
ረ	rḁ	ሩ	rũ	ሪ	rĩ	ራ	rã	ሬ	r^{y}ẽ	ር	ri̥, r	ሮ	r^{w}õ
ሰ	sḁ	ሱ	sũ	ሲ	sĩ	ሳ	sã	ሴ	s^{y}ẽ	ስ	si̥, s	ሶ	s^{w}õ

g͡ii̥z		kā̂i̥y		sā́li̥s		rā́vi̥		hā́mi̥s		sā́di̥s		sā́vi̥	
ሸ	šḁ, šä	ሹ	šū	ሺ	šī	ሻ	šā	ሼ	šʸē	ሽ	šḭ, š	ሾ	šʷō
ቀ	qḁ	ቁ	qū	ቂ	qī	ቃ	qā	ቄ	qʸē	ቅ	qḭ, q	ቆ	qʷō
በ	bḁ	ቡ	bū	ቢ	bī	ባ	bā	ቤ	bʸē	ብ	bḭ, b	ቦ	bʷō
ተ	tḁ	ቱ	tū	ቲ	tī	ታ	tā	ቴ	tʸē	ት	tḭ, t	ቶ	tʷō
ቸ	čä	ቹ	čū	ቺ	čī	ቻ	čā	ቼ	čʸē	ች	čḭ, č	ቾ	čʷō
ኀ	hā	ኁ	hū	ኂ	hī	ኃ	hā	ኄ	hʸē	ኅ	hḭ, h	ኆ	hʷō
ነ	nḁ	ኑ	nū	ኒ	nī	ና	nā	ኔ	nʸē	ን	nḭ, n	ኖ	nʷō
ኘ	ñä	ኙ	ñū	ኚ	ñī	ኛ	ñā	ኜ	ñē	ኝ	ñḭ, ñ	ኞ	ñō
አ	ā	ኡ	ū	ኢ	ī	ኣ	ā	ኤ	ʸē	እ	ḭ	ኦ	ʷō
ከ	kḁ	ኩ	kū	ኪ	kī	ካ	kā	ኬ	kʸē	ክ	kḭ, k	ኮ	kʷō
ኸ	χḁ	ኹ	χū	ኺ	χī	ኻ	χā	ኼ	χʸē	ኽ	χḭ, χ	ኾ	χʷō
ወ	wḁ, wω	ዉ	wū	ዊ	wī	ዋ	wā	ዌ	wʸē	ው	wḭ, wŭ, u	ዎ	wō
ዐ	ā	ዑ	ū	ዒ	ī	ዓ	ā	ዔ	ʸē	ዕ	ḭ,	ዖ	ʷō
ዘ	zḁ	ዙ	zū	ዚ	zī	ዛ	zā	ዜ	zʸē	ዝ	zḭ, z	ዞ	zʷō
ዠ[1]	žḁ, žä	ዡ	žū	ዢ	žī	ዣ	žā	ዤ	žʸe	ዥ	žḭ, ž	ዦ	žʷō
የ	yä	ዩ	yū	ዪ	yī	ያ	yā	ዬ	yē	ይ	yḭ, i, ḭ	ዮ	yō
ደ	dḁ	ዱ	dū	ዲ	dī	ዳ	dā	ዴ	dʸē	ድ	dḭ, d	ዶ	dʷō
ጀ	jä	ጁ	jū	ጂ	jī	ጃ	jā	ጄ	jʸē	ጅ	jḭ, j	ጆ	jʷō
ገ	gḁ	ጉ	gū	ጊ	gī	ጋ	gā	ጌ	gʸē	ግ	gḭ, g	ጎ	gʷō
ጠ	ṭḁ	ጡ	ṭū	ጢ	ṭī	ጣ	ṭā	ጤ	ṭʸē	ጥ	ṭḭ, ṭ	ጦ	ṭʷō
ጨ	c̣ä	ጩ	c̣ū	ጪ	c̣ī	ጫ	c̣ā	ጬ	c̣ʸē	ጭ	c̣ḭ, c̣	ጮ	c̣ʷō
ጰ	p̣ḁ	ጱ	p̣ū	ጲ	p̣ī	ጳ	p̣ā	ጴ	p̣ʸē	ጵ	p̣ḭ, p̣	ጶ	p̣ʷō
ጸ	ṣḁ	ጹ	ṣū	ጺ	ṣī	ጻ	ṣā	ጼ	ṣʸē	ጽ	ṣḭ, ṣ	ጾ	ṣʷō
ፀ	ṣḁ	ፁ	ṣū	ፂ	ṣī	ፃ	ṣā	ፄ	ṣʸē	ፅ	ṣḭ, ṣ	ፆ	ṣʷō
ፈ	fḁ	ፉ	fū	ፊ	fī	ፋ	fā	ፌ	fʸē	ፍ	fḭ, f	ፎ	fʷō
ፐ	pḁ	ፑ	pū	ፒ	pī	ፓ	pā	ፔ	pʸē	ፕ	pḭ, p	ፖ	pʷō

[1] also ዠ žḁ, žä, ዡ žū, ዣ žā, ዤ žʸē, ዥ žḭ, ž, ዦ žʷō.
ጚ = ግ + ዚ.

gı͡iz	sālis	rāyi	hāmis	sādis	rāyi
		ሏ lwā, lŏā			
		ሟ[1] mwā, mŏā			
		ሯ rwā, rŏā			ፘ[2] ryā
		ሷ swā, sŏā			
		ሿ šwā, šŏā			
ቈ qwω	ቊ qwī	ቋ qwā, qŏā	ቌ qwē	ቍ qwi̥, qwŭ	
		ቧ bwā, bŏā			
		ቷ twā, tŏā			
		ቿ čwā, čŏā			
ኈ hwḁ, hwω	ኊ hwī	ኋ hwā, hŏā	ኌ hwē	ኍ hwi̥, hwŭ	
		ኗ nwā, nŏā			
ኰ kwω	ኲ kwī	ኳ kwā, kŏā	ኴ kwē	ኵ kwi̥, kwŭ	
		ዃ χwā, χŏā			
		ዟ zwā, zŏā			
		ዷ dwā, dŏā			
ጐ gwω	ጒ gwī	ጓ gwā, gŏā	ጔ gwē	ጕ gwi̥, gwŭ	
		ጧ ṭwā, ṭŏā			
		ጯ č̣wā, č̣ŏā			
		ጿ ṣwā, ṣŏā			
		ፏ[3] fwā, fŏā			

[1] also ፙ, ሟ.

[2] used for rwā, rŏā, by those who reject ሯ; native opinion on the point is divided.

[3] also ፚ.

Value of Characters.

In the traditional Ethiopic pronunciation the vowels of all the classes except gi̊i̊z and sádi̥s are considered long; but in spoken Amharic they are all constantly shortened (§ 7*d*). § 4*b*

The vowel of gi̊i̊z differs from that of rā́yi̥ not so much in quantity (rā́yi̥ often being short) as in quality, in which it varies (§ 3) in different words. But in ሀ ሐ ኀ አ ዐ[1] it is of the same quality[2] as rā́yi̥. The above are its commonest values after the various consonants; but ለ lä, lω, and ቸ čḁ, čω also occur. For this and other variations in pronunciation see § 7*d*.

Some characters which represented different sounds in Eth. are now pronounced the same and are interchangeable in writing:

ሀ = ሐ = ኀ ha
ሠ = ሰ sḁ
አ = ዐ a
ጸ = ፀ ṣḁ

ሌ is also written ሊየ, ሜ = ሚየ etc., and ሬ = ርየ or ሪየ.

አ and ዐ (§ 2) contain no consonant, but are vowels and as such may be blended with an adjacent vowel (§ 7*a*)[3].

---

[1] gi̊i̊z in these 5 letters as in the rest is theoretically short, and is usually pronounced so unless the accent (§ 8) falls on it when it is often pronounced long.

[2] hḁ, hä occur as pronunciations of ከ ኸ.

[3] ያለ (for የ- + አለ § 7*a*) sometimes sounds yäállä, i.e. the crasis is not always complete; but no hiatus occurs between ä and á in any way comparable with ء.

Punctuation.

§ 4*c* ፡ marks the end of a word.

፤ corresponds to a semicolon.

። „ „ full stop.

፨ marks the end of a paragraph.

Doubling of Consonants.

§ 5 In English we pronounce doubled consonants as if they were single, only one f being heard in offer, stiffer, etc. In Amharic doubled consonants are pronounced double: ff as -ff f- in 'off fur' (pronounced without any hiatus between the words) or ff in Italian goffo; ṭṭ as -t t- in 'hot tea', etc.

The Amharic characters represent not only single but also double consonants with a following vowel: ለ = lḁ or llḁ.

Thus since ተ = t, ti̥, tt or tti̥

ነ = n, ni̥, nn or nni̥

ሸ = š, ši̥, šš or šši̥,

ትንሽ tí̥nni̥š, small, might be transliterated in 64 different ways.

There are no means of indicating by Amharic characters whether a consonant is doubled or not, or whether the consonant of a character in column VI of the syllabary (sắdi̥s) is followed by a vowel or not: and in both cases both alternatives are equally common:

አመመ ắ-mmḁ-mḁ, it ached.

እመም í̥-mḁ-m, pain.

ቅልጥም qí̥-l-ṭi̥-m, marrow.

ንግግር ni̥-gí̥-ggi̥-r, pronunciation.

ምድር ḿ-di̥-r, ground.

ክፍት ki̥-f-t, open.
ይክፈት yí̥-k-fḁ-t, let him open.
ልክ li̥-kk, measurement.
እንልክላችኋለን i̥-nni̥-li̥-ki̥-llā-čči̥-hwá-llä-n, we send to you (pl.).

This defect of Amharic orthography has involved the designation by the same characters of words with different pronunciations and meanings:

አለ	(*a*)	ā́lḁ,	he said,
	(*b*)	állä,	he is present;
አልገባም	(*a*)	algḁ́ẏām[1],	I will not enter,
	(*b*)	algḁ́bbām[2],	he has not entered;
ይመታል	(*a*)	yi̥mḁ́tāl,	he will strike,
	(*b*)	yi̥mmḁ́ttāl,	he will be struck.

A knowledge of the accidence, especially that of the verb (§ 21, § 7*c*), enables one to tell to a certain extent when a consonant is single and when double, and of what significance the doubling may be; but in a great many cases the exact form of a word cannot be gathered from its representation in Amharic characters, but must be learned by experience.

Doubling of Final Consonants.

The remarks in § 5 refer to the general question as to whether any component consonant of an isolated word is single or double. But when words are augmented by suffixes or combined with other words in § 6

---

[1] I have not heard the pronunciation given by Isenberg, Gram. p. 153, note: አልመጣም alĕmat'am, I do not come.

[2] For ẏ and bb see § 7*d*.

a sentence a further question arises[1], that of the variation of a final consonant between being single or double or either.

Certain final letters are doubled before a vowel at the beginning of a suffix or of a following word before which there is no pause or break in the sense, but otherwise remain single:—

-ል -l, see -ኽ, -ወይ, አይዶለም below; cp. § 32*a*.

-ም -m, suff. attached to indef. pron. (§ 16) and to neg. verb (§ 37), also conj. = and, even, also, (§ 48*b*):

ምንም ፡ ከዚህ ፡ አልነበር ። mí̥ni̥m käzzíh alnḁ́bbḁr, there wasn't anything here,

ምንም ፡ አልነበር ። mí̥ni̥mm alnḁ́bbḁr, there wasn't anything;

-m is also occasionally doubled before በ and የ, especially when y becomes ʸ (§ 7*d*):

ምንም ፡ ቢሆን ፡ mí̥ni̥mm[2] bí̥hʷon, whatever may be the case, on any account,

ምንም ፡ የለ ። mí̥ni̥mm yállä (-mmʸál-), there isn't anything,

ሁሉም ፡ ያዘ ። húllumm yázḁ, he seized everything;

-ች -č, (i) in the pl. ending -ʷō ች (§ 10*b*):

ፈረሶች ፡ መጡ ። fḁ́rḁsʷōč̣ mḁ́ṭṭu, (the) horses have come,

ፈረሶቹ ፡ fḁrḁsʷṓčču, the horses,

ፈረሶች ፡ አመጡ ። fḁ́rḁsʷōčč amḁ́ṭṭu, they have brought some horses;

---

[1] Guidi, Redupl., discusses the first but not the second of these questions.

[2] also -i̥m.

(ii) the f. suff. -ች -č (§ 24):

ነበረች ። nḁ́bbḁräč, she was,

አልነበረችም ። alnḁ́bbḁräčči̥m, she was not,

እርሷ ፡ ነበረች ፡ አለ ። i̥rso͡á nḁ́bbḁräčč ā́lḁ, he said it was she;

-ን -n, the pers. suff. (§ 12*c*) us, to us:

አሉን ። ā́lun, they told us,

አላሉንም ። alā́lunni̥m, they did not tell us,

ይሉናል ። yí̥lunnāl, they will tell us,

ሰጠን ። sḁ́ṭṭḁn, he gave us,

አልሰጠን ፡ አለ ። alsḁ́ṭṭḁnn ā́lḁ, he refused to give us;

-ኝ -ñ, (i) the pers. suff. (§ 12*c*) me, to me:

ሰጠኝ ። sḁ́ṭṭäñ, he gave me,

አልሰጠኝም ። alsḁ́ṭṭäññi̥m, he did not give me,

አልሰጠኝ ፡ አለ ። alsḁ́ṭäññ ā́lḁ, he refused to give me;

(ii) standing for -ኒ -ni (§ 7*b*) of the part. (§ 31, § 36, § 42):

ለማኝ ፡ lḁ́mmāñ, a beggar,

ለማኞች ፡ lḁmmā́ññōč, beggars,

ለማኝ ፡ ነበር ። lḁmmā́ñ nḁ́bbḁr, he was a beggar,

ለማኝ ፡ አለ ። lḁmmā́ññ állä, there is a beggar;

(iii) in some parts of verbs with last rad. ኝ :

አግኝ ። ā́gi̥ñ, find,

አግኘው ። ā́gi̥ññä͡u, find him,

አግኝ ፡ አለኝ ። ā́gi̥ññ ā́läñ, he told me to find;

(iv) in certain words:

ኩፍኝ ፡ kúffi̥ñ, small-pox,

ኩፍኝ ፡ አይደለም ። kúffi̥ññ a͡i̥dálläm, it is not small-pox;

-ጥ -ṭ in certain words:

መጠጥ ፡ mḁ́ṭḁṭ, something to drink,

መጠጥ ፡ አለ ። mḁ́ṭḁṭṭ állä?, is there something to drink?

-ይ -i̥, (i) standing for -ሊ -li (§ 7*b*) of the part. (§ 31, § 36, § 42), is single or doubled when nothing follows or before a consonant, doubled before a vowel:

ቀይ ፡ qḁ́͡i̥ or qḁyy (§ 3), red (part. of ቀላ qḁ́llã),

ቀይ ፡ ነው ። qḁ́͡i̥ (qḁyy) nḁ͡u, it is red,

ቀዩ ፡ qḁ́yyu (§ 11) the red one,

ቀይ ፡ አይደለም ። qḁyy a͡i̥dállām, it is not red;

(ii) in parts of verbs with last rad. የ is usually single when nothing follows or before a consonant, doubled before a vowel:

ይቈይ ። yí̥qwω͡i̥, let him wait,

ይቈይ ፡ ነበር ። yi̥qwώ͡i̥ nḁ́bbḁr, he was waiting,

ይቈየኝ ። yi̥qwώyyäñ, let him wait for me,

አትቈይ ፡ አሉኝ ። atti̥qwώyy ḁ́luñ, they told me not to wait.

The inter. suff. -አ -ā́ and -ወይ or -oይ (sáyi̥ + ይ) -wḁ́͡i̥ (-wώ͡i̥, -wí̥) double certain consonants when they are attached to them:

-ል -l, of the aux. -አል -āl (§ 32):

ይበቃል ። yi̥yḁ́qāl, it is enough,

ይበቃላ ። yi̥yḁ́qāllá?, ይበቃልወይ ። yi̥yḁ́qāllwώ͡i̥?, ይበቃሎይ ። yi̥yḁ́qāllwí̥?, is it enough?

-ም -m (as above):

አይደለህም ። a͡i̥dállähi̥m, you are not (§ 40),

አይደለህሞይ ። a͡i̥dállähi̥mmwí̥?, are you not?

-ች -č in certain words:

ድንች ፡ dịnnịč, potato,

ድንቻ ፡፡ dịnnịččá?, potato?

The w of -wá̜i̜ (-wώ̜i̜, -wί̜) is doubled after a vowel:

መጣወይ ፡፡ má̜ṭṭawwί̜?, has he come?

-ን -n in certain words is single when nothing or a consonant follows, single or doubled before a vowel:

ማን mān?, who? (§ 15),

ማን ፡ ያውቃል ፡፡ mān yáuqāl?, who knows?

ማን ፡ አለህ ፡፡ mān (-nn) ā́läh?, who told you?

ምንድን mί̜ndi̜n?, what? (§ 15),

ምንድን ፡ መጣ ፡፡ mί̜ndi̜n má̜ṭṭa?, what came?

ምንድን ፡ አመጣ ፡፡ mί̜ndi̜nn amá̜ṭṭa?, what did he bring?

-ን -n in ይህን yί̜hā́n (acc.; § 8; § 13*a*) is single or double in any position:

ይህን ፡ ፈረስ ፡ አምጣ ፡፡ yi̜hā́n (-nn) fá̜ra̜s ánṭa (§ 7*d*), bring this horse,

ይህን ፡ አምጣ ፡፡ yi̜hā́n (-nn) ánṭa, bring this.

In analogy with the above variations the ll of አይደለም a̜i̜dá̜lläm (-dá- § 7*d*; § 40) becomes l when the -ም is dropped, unless a vowel follows, and -ኝ -ññ in parts of verbs with last rad. ኝ is pronounced single:

ደግ ፡ አይደለም ፡፡ dägg a̜i̜dállām, and

ደግም ፡ አይደል ፡፡ dá̜ggi̜mm ā́i̜däl, he is not good;

ያይደል ፡ እንደሆን ፡ yaί̜däll ί̜nda̜h^{w}on, if he is not;

bi̜ggá̜ñ for bi̜ggá̜ññ ቢገኝ ፡ if he is found.

The doubled final -ል -ll
-ቅ -qq
-ክ -kk
-ጥ -ṭṭ
-ጭ -č̣č̣

of adv. and interj. of more than one syllable constr. with ኣለ ā́lḁ (s.v. √በለ) usually become single before a consonant:

ብልጭልጭ ፡ ኣለ ፡ bı̥lí̥č̣lı̥č̣č̣ ā́lḁ, it lightened,

ብልጭልጭ ፡ ይላል ። bı̥lí̥č̣lı̥č̣ yí̥lāl, it is lightening,

ብልጭልጭ ፡ ሊል ፡ ነው ። bı̥lí̥č̣lič̣ lı̥l nḁ͡u, there is going to be lightning.

-qq, -kk are sometimes retained before y:

ስቅቅ ፡ ይላል ። sí̥qı̥qq yí̥lāl, it grates,

ሽክሽክ ፡ ይላል ። šḁkšḁ́kk yí̥lāl, it makes a slight rattling sound;

and sometimes before any consonant:

ድብልቅልቅ ፡ ኣለ ። dı̥ṿlí̥qlı̥qq ā́lḁ, it was in great confusion,

ድብልቅልቅ ፡ ይላል ። dı̥ṿlı̥qlíqq (§ 8) yí̥lāl, it is in great confusion,

ድብልቅልቅ ፡ ሲል ፡ dı̥ṿlı̥qlí̥qqı̥̆ (§ 7*d*) sı̥l, when it is in great confusion.

When such words are not constr. with ኣለ their final consonant may be single, and remain so before a vowel:

ድብልቅልቅ dı̥ṿlí̥qlı̥q, in great confusion,

ድብልቅልቅ ፡ ኣይደለም ። dı̥ṿlí̥qlı̥q a͡ı̥dállām, it is not in great confusion.

Monosyllabic adv. and interj. and those ending in consonants other than the above usually keep a doubled final consonant always doubled:

ዘው ፡ አለ ። zḁ́uw (§ 3) ā́lḁ, he entered unexpectedly,

ዘው ፡ ቢል ፡ zḁ́uwĭ̥ (§ 7*d*) yi̥l, if he enters unexpectedly;

ጎፈፍ ፡ አለ ። gʷófḁff ā́lḁ, he was very stout,

ጎፈፍ ፡ የሚል ፡ ሰው ፡ gʷófḁff yämmi̥l sḁu, a very stout man.

Crasis or Contraction of Adjacent Vowels. § 7*a*

When the formation of words, grammatical inflexion, or the application of other prefixes or suffixes involves the meeting of certain vowels, the following contractions and modifications occur:

gi̥̥i̥z + gi̥̥i̥z = ráyi̥, ḁ (ä) + ã (§ 4*b*) = ã	e.g. ያለ yállä, which exists, for የ- yä- + አለ állä;
gi̥̥i̥z + ráyi̥ = ráyi̥, ḁ (ä) + ã = ã	e.g. ባመት bā́mḁt, by the year, for በ- bḁ- + ዓመት ā́mḁt;
gi̥̥i̥z + sā́di̥s = gi̥̥i̥z, ḁ (ä) + i̥ = ḁ (ä)	e.g. የርሱ yársǘ, of him, his, for የ- yä- + እርሱ i̥rsǘ;
ráyi̥ + gi̥̥i̥z = ráyi̥, ã + ã = ā	e.g. ይመጣል, yi̥mátāl, he is coming, for ይመጣ yi̥mátã + -አል -āl (§ 32);
ráyi̥ + ráyi̥ = ráyi̥ ã + ā = ā	e.g. ጌታቸው gʸētáččḁu, their master, for ጌታ gʸétã + -áቸው -áččḁu (§ 12*b*);

sā́di̥s + gí̥i̥z = rā́vi̥, e.g. ላምጣ lánṭã (§ 7*d*)?, shall I
i̥ + ã = ã bring?, for ሌ- li̥- + አምጣ ánṭã;

sā́di̥s + sā́di̥s = sā́di̥s, e.g. ስሄድ si̥hā́d, when I go,
i̥ + i̥ = i̥ for ስ- si̥- + እሄድ i̥hā́d;

sā́di̥s + ያ = sā́li̥s + ያ[1] e.g. ሲያመጣ siyāmáṭã (si̥ãm-,
i̥ + yã = i(i̥ § 7*d*) + yã syãm-), when he brings, for ስ- si̥- + ያመጣ yãmáṭã;

sā́di̥s + ይ = sā́li̥s, e.g. ሲመጣ sĩmáṭã (si̥m-), when
i̥ + yi̥ = ĩ (i̥ § 7*d*) he comes, for ስ- si̥- + ይመጣ yi̥máṭã.

የ may arise from sā́li̥s:

sā́li̥s + gí̥i̥z = sā́di̥s + ያ, e.g. ትለቅምያለሽ ti̥lḁqmyā́lläš,
ĩ + a = (the consonant) + yã you (f.) are picking, for ትለቅሚ ti̥lḁ́qmi + አለሽ álläš (§ 32*a*).

የ may arise from hā́mi̥s:

hā́mi̥s + gí̥i̥z = sā́di̥s + ያ[2], e.g. ለቅምያለሁ lḁqi̥mmyā́llḁu^{h}
ʸẽ + ã = (the consonant) + yã (§ 7*d*), I have picked, for ለቀሜ lḁ́qi̥mmʸe + አለሁ állа̥u^{h} (§ 32*a*);

hā́mi̥s + rā́vi̥ = sā́di̥s + ያ[2], e.g. በርያቸው bḁryā́ččḁu, their
ʸẽ + ā = (the consonant) + yā bull, for በሬ bḁ́rʸe + ā́ቸው -ā́ččḁu.

---

[1] This is a point of orthography rather than of phonology; the common pronunciation is syãm-.

[2] If the consonant in sā́di̥s is one of the resultants in § 7*b* it may become rā́vi̥, absorbing ያ: e.g. አይችያለሁ ai̥ččyā́llḁu^{h} or አይቻለሁ ai̥ččā́llḁu^{h}, I have seen, for አይቼ ā́i̥ččʸe + አለሁ állḁu^{h}.

ወ may arise from kā́i̥ỵ or sā́ỵi̥:

kā́i̥ỵ + rā́ỵi̥ = sā́di̥s + ዋ, e.g. ሰጧቸው (= ሰጥዋቸው § 4*b*)
ŭ + ā̆ = (the consonant) + wā̆ — saṭṭwā́ččau̥, they gave them, for ሰጡ sḁ́ṭṭu + -á ቸው -áččau̥;

sā́ỵi̥ + gí̥i̥z = sā́di̥s + ዋ, e.g. ለቅሟል (= ለቅምዋል § 4*b*)
ʷō̆ + ā̆ = (the consonant) + wā̆ (ŏā̆) — lḁ́qmŏāl, he has picked, for ለቅሞ lḁ́qmʷo + -ኣል -āl (§ 32*a*).

Modification of Consonant by following Vowel. § 7*b*

When, in the same circumstances, especially in the formation of parts of the verb (§ 43), l, s, t, n, z, d, ṭ, ṣ are followed by i, y or e in the same word, they are thus modified:

ሊ	li, ልይ ly	become	ይ	i̥ (yy § 6).
ሌ	l^{y}e	„	ዬ	ye or ያ yä.
ሢ, ሲ	si, ሥይ, ስይ sy	„	ሽ	š.
ሤ, ሴ	s^{y}e	„	ሼ	š^{y}e or ሻ šä.
ቲ	ti, ትይ ty	„	ች	č.
ቴ	t^{y}e	„	ቼ	č^{y}e or ቻ čä.
ኒ	ni, ንይ ny	„	ኝ	ñ (ññ § 6).
ኔ	n^{y}e	„	ኜ	ñe or ኛ ñä.
ዚ	zi, ዝይ zy	„	ዥ	ž.
ዜ	z^{y}e	„	ዤ	ž^{y}e or ዣ žä.
ዲ	di, ድይ dy	„	ጅ	j.
ዴ	d^{y}e	„	ጄ	j^{y}e or ጃ jä.
ጢ	ṭi, ጺ, ፂ ṣi, ጥይ ṭy, ጽይ, ፅይ ṣy	„	ጭ	č̣.
ጤ	ṭ^{y}e, ጼ, ፄ ṣ^{y}e	„	ጬ	č̣^{y}e or ጫ č̣ä.

If the original consonant was doubled (§ 5) the resultant consonant is doubled also:

e.g. with the model

ለቀመ lḁ́qqḁmḁ, pick, ger. sg. 1st ለቅሜ lḁ́qịmmʸe,
part. ለቃሚ lḁqā́mi,

cp. ሰቀለ sḁ́qqḁlḁ, suspend, ger. sg. 1st ሰቅዬ sḁ́qịyye,
part. ሰቃይ sḁ́qā́i̥ (-ā́yy § 6),

ነገሠ nḁ́ggḁsa, reign, ger. sg. 1st ነግሼ nḁ́gḁ̣ššʸe,
part. ነጋሽ nḁ́gā́š,

ከፈተ kḁ́ffḁtḁ, open, ger. sg. 1st ከፍቼ kḁ́fịččʸe,
part. ከፋች kḁ́fā́č.

In the part. of bilitteral verbs (§ 42)

ሚ, ሲ also becomes ሺ ši,
ቲ „ „ ቺ či, etc.

E.g. ላሰ lā́sḁ, lick, part. ላሽ lāš or ላሺ lā́ši, for *ላሲ lā́si,
ቀጣ qḁ́ṭṭā, punish, part. ቃጭ qḁč̣ or ቃጪ qḁ́č̣i, for *ቃጢ qḁ́ṭi.

Exception:

አነጠ ánnḁṭḁ, fashion, ger. አንጭጬ ánnịč̣č̣ʸe, but part. አናጢ an(n)ā́ṭi.

Cp. also

ጀመረ jḁ́mmḁrḁ, begin, መጀመሪያ (§ 7*a*) mḁjḁmmḁ́ryā, initial,
and
ጨረሰ č̣ā́rrḁsḁ, end, መጨረሻ mḁč̣ärrḁ́šā, final,
ቀነተ qḁ́nnḁtḁ, girth up, መቀነቻ mḁqḁnnḁ́čā, girth.

This modification does not occur invariably

throughout the accidence; e.g. the pers. suff. -ʸe, my (§ 12*b*), does not cause it, and pref. like ስ- s(i̥)-, when (§ 45), are not susceptible of it.

Assimilation of Consonant by following Consonant.

The assimilation of adjacent consonants is comparatively infrequent; the following occur in the verb: § 7c

ል l in the neg. pref. አል- al- (§ 37, § 38), is assimilated by, and in writing disappears before, the following letters, which with the exception of y are then doubled (§ 5) in pronunciation, (a- often being lengthened):

r, e.g. አረሳም ãrrḁssãm, he did not forget, for *አልረሳም alrḁssãm;

t, in the pref. ት- ti̥- of the sg. 3rd f., 2nd m., f., and pl. 2nd (§ 26, § 27):

e.g. አትርሳ ãttí̥rsã, do not forget, for *አልትርሳ altí̥rsã;

n, in the pref. እን- i̥nn(i̥)- of the pl. 1st (§ 26, § 27):

e.g. አንረሳም ãnn(i̥)rḁ́sãm, we shall not forget, for *አልንረሳም al(i̥)nn(i̥)rḁ́sãm;

y (§ 7*b*), in the pref. ይ- yi̥- of the sg. 3rd m., pl. 3rd (§ 26, § 27), አልይ- alyi̥- becoming አይ- a͡i̥-:

e.g. አይረሳም a͡i̥rḁ́sãm, he will not forget, for *አልይረሳም alyi̥rḁ́sãm.

ት t, of the reflexive or passive pref. ተ- tḁ- (§ 22*a*, § 41*a*) is assimilated by any following consonant, which is doubled (§ 5)[1] in pronunciation, ት disappearing in writing:

e.g. ይለቀማል yi̥llḁ́qqḁmāl, it will be picked, for *ይትለቀማል yi̥tlḁ́qqḁmāl,

ይቈረጣል yi̥qqwώrrḁṭāl, it will be cut, for *ይትቈረጣል yi̥tqwώrrḁṭāl.

§ 7*d* *Variations and Anomalies of Pronunciation.*

The pronunciation of Amharic varies not only in the mouth of individuals of different districts, but also, as in English[2], in that of the same individual on different occasions, according as he speaks slowly or fast, carefully or carelessly, to a superior or to a companion.

A native, too, that has any knowledge of reading, is inclined on occasion to pronounce words as they are written, there being many gradations of the extent to which this is done.

---

[1] But if this assimilating consonant is itself followed by another consonant it is usually pronounced single:

ይንቀጠቀጣል yi̥ṅqḁṭḁ́qqḁṭāl, he is trembling, from ተንቀጠቀጠ tḁṅqḁṭḁ́qqḁṭḁ;

or either single or double:

ይርገበገባል yi̥r(r)gḁṿḁ́ggḁṿāl, it is waving, from ተርገበገበ tḁrgḁṿḁ́ggḁṿḁ.

[2] Cp. our use of 'sha'n't', 'don't', 'won't', etc.; such words might well prove unintelligible at first hearing to a foreigner knowing 'shall not', etc.

An exhaustive treatment of the subject of variation in pronunciation would be beyond the scope of this work; but the following instances will give some indication of its nature and the extent of its prevalence.

Vowels.

Those marked ‿̄ are commonly pronounced short unless accented (§ 8):

e.g. መጣ ፡ mḁ́ṭṭã, he came, usually mḁ́ṭṭa:

ይህ ፡ የመጣ ፡ ነው ። yí̥he yämḁṭṭắ nḁ͡u, this is he who came.

But they often remain short even when accented, unless the accent is received from an enclitic; and ã generally remains short in ã́͡u, ã́͡i̥.

gí̥͡i̥z, ḁ, ä, *ω* (§ 3): for value after consonants and with no consonant preceding see § 4; often ä before h, l, r, t, č, č̣, š, ž, j, ñ, especially when they are final or followed by i or i̥, and before any single consonant followed by i:

ሰጠ sḁ́ṭṭḁ, he gave,

ሰጠኝ sḁ́ṭṭḁñ or sḁ́ṭṭäñ, he gave me,

part. ሰጪ sḁč̣ or säč̣ (§ 7*b*), giver;

ሰፋ sḁ́ffã, (*a*) he sewed, (*b*) it was broad;

part. ሰፊ (*a*) sḁ́fi or sắfi, tailor,

(*b*) sḁ́ffi, broad;

ä followed by u gen. forms ḁ͡u:

የለም yắlläm, there is none,

የለውም yắllḁ͡um, he has none;

usually ω after w:

ወንድ wωnd, male,

ወምበር wώmbḁr (-är), chair,

ቈየ qwώyyä, he waited.

kḁ̄i̯y, ŭ: final u is generally weak, sometimes very short:

ብርቱ፡ bi̥rtŭ, strong;

and the u of -ሁ -hu (or -ኩ -ku, see ሀ below) in the verb when it (the vowel u) is final approaches ŭ:

ሰማሁ s̥ámmāhu, I heard, approaches s̥ámmāhŭ, and is also written ሰማኍ s̥ámmāhwŭ, s̥ámmāhw.

The u of ሁ hu is often displaced, i.e. precedes instead of following h:

(i) in the sg. 1st ending -ሁ of the simp. perf. (§ 25), especially in verbs retaining the vowel of the last rad. (§ 42*a*, *b*, § 32) or with last rad. a guttural:

lḁ́qqḁmuh for lḁ́qqḁmhu ለቀምሁ, I picked,

s̥ámmau͡h for s̥ámmāhu ሰማሁ, I heard,

s̥ḁ́t̥t̥ḁu͡h for s̥ḁ́t̥t̥ḁhu ሰጠሁ, I gave,

állä͡uh, állḁu͡h, for állḁhu አለሁ, I am present,

እለቅማለሁ i̥lḁqmállḁu͡h, I am picking,

አደግሁ áddaguh, I was brought up.

This ending is also written -ኍ hwŭ, which becomes -uh; and by a similar displacement ኋ hwā becomes uhā:

bḁu͡hālā for bḁhwālā በኋላ, after.

(ii) in the pron. suff. (§ 12 *b*, *c*) and 2nd pl. ending (§ 25) -āችሁ -ā̆č(č)yuh, for -ā̆č(č)i̥hu (see ወ below):

አገራችሁ agḁrā̆č(č)yuh, your (pl.) country,

ለቀማችሁ lḁqqḁmā̆č(č)yuh, you (pl.) picked.

But before a suff. other than the aux. -አል -āl (§ 32, § 12*c*) this displacement does not occur:

ለቀማችኋል lḁqmā̆č(č)yuhāl for lḁqmā̆č(č)i̥hwāl, you (pl.) have picked,

but ለቀማችሁት lḁqqḁmā̆č(č)i̥hut[1], you (pl.) picked it,

ሰማሁህ sḁ́mmahuh, I heard you,

ሰጠሁት sḁ́ṭṭḁhut, I gave him,

የለሁም yā́llḁhum, I am not present,

ያደግሁበት yáddḁghubbḁt, in which I was brought up.

A similar displacement occurs in

áurʸe for árwʸe አርዌ, beast,

lŭ́gám for li̥gwám ልጓም, bridle,

and cp. mḁ́ʷωq (máʷωq) መወቅ for mā̆qʷo (mʸḗqʷo) ሚቆ, oribi,

tώkkosḁ for tḁ́kkʷωsḁ ተኰሰ, scorch,

ŭ́kkul for i̥kkul እኩል, half.

sā́li̥s, ī: often i̥, especially when not accented:

ሲመጣ sīmḁ́ṭa or si̥mḁ́ṭa, when he comes;

sometimes when accented:

ሒድ hi̥d, go.

---

[1] occasionally -ā̆č(č)ŭhut.

For sā́li̥s before -ያ -yā̃ see § 7*a*: it is pronounced as sā́di̥s + yā̃:

 መለኪያ mḁlḁ́kkyā̃, measure.

rā́yi̥, ā̃: occasionally ä in the ending -ያ -ya when unaccented (§ 8):

መሳሪያ mḁssárya or -ryä, tool,

but መሳሪያ ፡ ነው ። mḁssaryá nḁu͡, it is a tool.

hā́mi̥s, ^{y}ē̃: the ^{y} is most noticeable when ^{y}ē̃ is accented, and in ሬ r^{y}ē̃́;

ē in ሌላ lḗla, other;

ḁ̄̃, ā̃̈ in ሔደ hā̃̈dä (hḁ̄̃́-, -dḁ, less commonly h^{y}ē̃́-) he went.

sā́di̥s, i̥:

often ŭ after w, and sometimes, if accented, ū̆:

ውስጥ wŭsṭ, interior,

ውብ wŭẏ, beautiful,

ውበት wŭ́ẏät (wū̆́-), beauty;

ü in

ክፉ kí̥fu, kŭ́fu or kǘfu, bad,

ክፍት ki̥ft (kŭ́ft), open, ክክ ki̥kk (kükk), coarse-grained;

ḁ in

እንስሳ (i̥)nsḁ́sa, domestic animal,

ጥር ṭḁrr (ṭi̥rr), January,

እረግ ḁ́rḁg!, nonsense!

ä, e, in

ይህ yí̥he (yähe), this.

sấdi̥s, i̥ tends to disappear in rapid speech, even though accented by a slower speaker:

የመጣውን ፡ እቃ ፡ ፍታው ። yämaṭṭáu͡n íqā fi̥táu͡ becomes yämaṭṭáu͡n qaftáu͡, undo the baggage that has come;

ይሻዩ ፡ እቃ ፡ yäšáju͡ i̥qa becomes yäšáu͡qa, the tea-things.

Unaccented i̥ is dropped when the word is easily pronounced without it, as often becomes the case when a suff. is added:

ነብር nấvi̥r, leopard,

ነብሩ nấvi̥ru, or nấvru, the (his) leopard;

ቢመስል bi̥mási̥l, if it seems,

ቢመስለው bi̥más(i̥)lau͡, if it seems to him.

Initial i̥ disappears after a preceding vowel:

እስከዚህ i̥skấzzih, as far as this,

መጡ ፡ እስከዚህ ። maṭṭu skấzzih, they came as far as this.

In words beginning with i̥n-, i̥ṅ-, i̥m- the i̥ is often omitted, the n, ṅ or m forming a syllable by itself[1]:

እንኳን ńkwān, indeed,

እምቢ ፡ አለ i̥mbi̥ ấlḁ or ḿbi̥ ấlḁ, he refused;

but after a consonant the i̥ is heard:

ልጅ ፡ እምቢ ፡ አለ ። li̥j i̥mbi̥ ấlḁ, the child refused.

sấdi̥s without a vowel, on the other hand, is often slightly vocalised in a word ending in two consonants or in one doubled (§ 6) consonant

---

[1] as in Bantu ḿtu (⏊⏑), etc.

when it is followed by one beginning with a consonant, especially an enclitic (§ 8):

ስምንት sí̥mmi̥nt, eight,

ስምንት ፡ ብር ፡ sí̥mmi̥ntĭ̥ yi̥rr, eight dollars;

ውድ wŭdd, expensive,

ውድ ፡ ነው ። wŭ́ddĭ̥ nḁu͡, it is expensive;

ዝም ፡ በል ። zi̥mm bäl, and zí̥mmĭ̥ yäl, be quiet.

i̥, ĭ̥ is often prefixed to initial r, and sometimes to n(i̥), which then lose a following i̥:

እረዳ ĭ̥rḁ́dda for ረዳ rḁ́dda, he helped,

imp. ርዳ rí̥da or እርዳ í̥rda, help;

ነካ nḁ́kka, he touched,

imp. ንካ ni̥ka or እንካ í̥n̈ka (ńka), touch.

sáyi̥, ʷŏ: the ʷ is most noticeable when ʷŏ is accented, and in ሮ rʷŏ;

ḁ, ä in አይደለም a͡i̥dḁ́lläm (-dá-), he is not, no, (§ 40).

Consonants.

(In discussing a letter under this heading gi̥͡i̥z is used as the simplest and original form without reference to its inherent vowel.)

ሀ, ሐ, ኀ: final h after a vowel is weak, and after a diphthong tends to disappear (see ka͡i̥y above):

áyya͡uʰ አየሁ, I saw.

Initial h is often lost:

ăgḁr አገር for hágḁr ሀገር, country;

i̥lm እልም for hi̥lm ሕልም, dream,
áttḁmḁ አተመ for háttḁmḁ ኀተመ, he sealed.

h is displaced in
mḁhā́tḁm for máhtḁm ማኅተም, seal,
bhā́ri for báhri ባሕሪ, character.

h after a consonant interchanges with k,
in the ending -ሁ -hu (§ 25), also written -ኩ:
lḁ́qqḁmku ለቀምኩ for lḁ́qqḁmhu ለቀምሁ, I picked,

and with k, χ,
in the ending -ህ -h (§ 25, § 12 *b*, *c*):
ãlχ, ãlk, for ã́lh ኣልህ, you said,
hʷonχ, hʷonk, hʷoṅk, for hʷṍnh ሆንህ, you have become,
rā́sχi̥n, rāski̥n, for rā́shi̥n ራስህን, your head (acc.).

This -h or -k is sometimes assimilated to or assimilates an adjacent guttural, which is then doubled (§ 6), g becoming kk:
á͡uwωqq for á͡uwωqh አወቐህ, you knew, you have understood,
adḁ́rrḁkkḁ͡u for adḁ́rrḁghḁ͡u አደረግሀው, you did it,
fḁ́llḁkk for fḁ́llḁgh ፈለግህ, you wanted.

መ: m sounds n in
ánṭã for ámṭã ኣምጣ, bring.

ረ: see sā́di̥s above.

ሰ: s sounds z in
mḁzf for mḁsf መስፍ, anvil.

ቀ: q in Š. is pronounced like hamza[1] ء in Arabic: (cp. the Cairene pronunciation of ق):

ç̣ạrḁ́ʾã for ç̣ạrḁ́qã ጨረቃ, moon,

ʾị́y̥ʸe for qị́y̥ʸe ቅቤ, butter.

በ: when doubled always bb; beginning a sentence usually, and after m always, b; otherwise b or ṿ:

ይበላል yịbbálāl, it is said,

በቅሎ ፡ ነበር ። bḁ́qlʷo nḁ́bbär, it was a mule,

occasionally, ṿḁ́qlʷo nḁ́bbär,

ወምበር wώmbär, chair,

ተበለ tạbálạ or tạṿālạ, it was said,

ይህ ፡ በቅሎ ፡ yị́he bḁ́qlʷo (ṿḁ́-), this mule.

ንበ varies between nb, mb, nṿ:

አንበሳ anbḁ́ssa, ambḁ́ssa and anṿḁ́ssa, lion.

በ is often f̣ in

ከብት kạf̣t or kạṿt, property,

ገብስ gạfs (-ṿs, -bs), barley.

ቾ: č occasionally sounds almost yy in G.:

sʸétʷōyy for sʸétʷōč ሴቶች, women.

ነ: see sḁ̄dis above;

final n is often weak after ʸe, ʷo, u, and is dropped in

qwḁ̄gmʸe for qwḁ̄gmʸen ቋግሜን, part of September,

ā́wω, ā́͡uω, for ā́wωn አወን, yes,

(ị)ntʷō እንቶ for (ị)ntʷōn እንቶን, what's-hiṣ-name (§ 16).

---

[1] Vollers and Burkitt, Gram. § 2 B. 1, "a simple suspension or catching of the breath......in Fr. the h in 'la honte' is a true hamza."

n before gutturals often (but not always) becomes ṅ:

dḭngạt or dḭṅgạt ድንገት, perhaps,

ጭንቅ č̣ḭṅq, difficult.

n before b may become m: see በ above.

ኝ: ñ affects preceding ạ, see gḭ̂ḭz above;

final ñ sometimes becomes ḭ:

nā̂ḭ for näñ ነኝ, I am (§ 13*b*),

ámā̂ḭ for ámā́ñ አማኝ, loyal.

ከ: k interchanges with h, χ, see ሀ above:

ያህል yahl, about, nearly, is a cont. (§ 26) of

አከለ ákkạlạ (q.v.), to amount.

G. has hạ- for kạ- ከ-, in, from,

hā́zzih for kā́zzih ከዚህ, here,

hạ́mdḭr for kạ́mdḭr ከምድር, on the ground.

ኽ: χ interchanges with h, k, see ሀ above;

pronounced h in

ጮኸ č̣ʷóhạ, he shouted.

ወ: for w and u see § 3.

ው wḭ, wŭ (see sā́dḭs above), ʷu, becomes u after ạ,

ä, ã, ē, ḭ and forms diphthongs with them, ḭu becoming yu:

ውጣ wḭ́ṭa and wŭ́ṭa, come out,

አውጣ âuṭa, take out.

ዘ: z is sometimes s before h (χ, k, see ሀ):

yāsh for yāzh ያዝህ, you took,

yāsχ for yāzχ ያዝኽ, = ያዝህ

yāsk for yāzk ያዝክ, = ያዝህ

sometimes assimilated to following š:
yãšš for yãzš ያዝሽ, you (f.) took.

ዠ: see ጀ; ž arising from zi, z^ye (§ 7*b*) does not interchange with j.

የ: for y and i̥ see § 3.

ይ yi̥ following ḁ, ä, ω, ã becomes i̥ and forms diphthongs with them:

ይሁን yí̥hun, let him be,

አይሁን á͡i̥hun, let him not be;

initial ይ- yi̥- may do this with the final vowel of the preceding word:

ደኅና ፡ ይደሩ ። dähná͡i̥däru !, good-night ! (pol.).

In the mouth of many individuals yy between vowels tends to become i̥, and i̥ to become ^{y} or disappear altogether:

ያስታያል ። yastáyyāl, yastá͡i̥āl, he lets (something) be seen,

ሀያ há^{y}ã, há͡ã (Š.), twenty,

አያልፍም ። a͡i̥álfi̥m, a^{y}álfi̥m, a͡ál-, he will not pass.

Similarly initial y becomes ^{y}:

ክፉም ፡ የለ ። kí̥fumm yállä, -mm^{y}áll-, there isn't any bad.

ደ: d before other consonants often becomes r:

qárm^{w}o for qḁ́dm^{w}o ቀድሞ, formerly,

li̥hárnäñ for li̥hád näñ ልሔድ ፡ ነኝ ። I am going,

hárku for hádku ሔድኩ I went,

wώssärku for wώssḁdku ወሰድኩ, I removed,

አድርገው ádri̥ga͡u̥ becomes árga͡u̥, do it.

ጀ: initial j interchanges with ž in Š.:

ጅግራ j̥gra or ዥግራ ž̥gra, guinea-fowl;

when this variation occurs in a verb it continues throughout its derivatives:

ጀመረ jḁ́mmḁrḁ (ዠ- žḁ́-), begin,

ተጀመረ tḁjḁ́mmḁrḁ (ተዠ- tḁžḁ́-), be begun,

መጀመሪያ mḁjḁmmárya (መዠ- mḁžḁ-), beginning;

sometimes when final: ልዥ li̥ž, for ልጅ li̥j, child.

j arising from di, dʸe (§ 7*b*) does not interchange with ž.

ጭ: sometimes almost yy before t:

afwáyyt͡ŏal for afwáč̣t͡ŏal አፏጭቷል, he has whistled.

ጸ, ፀ: ṣ is ṭ out of G.:

ጣፈ ṭáfḁ, and ጻፈ ṣáfḁ (G. and 'learned'[1]), write,

ጠሐይ ṭḁ́ha͡i̥, and ፀሐይ ṣḁ́ha͡i̥ (G. and 'learned'), sun.

ፈ: f or v in

ነፍስ nḁfs or nḁvs, soul.

Accent.

By accent is meant stress accent, and by the accent of a word the principal stress that falls on it: thus the accent of 'cab-proprietor' is on the 'a' or the syllable of which 'a' is the vowel. § 8

(The sentence accent, by which an emphatic word in a sentence receives more stress than other words,

---

[1] i.e. used elsewhere by those with some knowledge of Ethiopic; in G. it is a genuine survival.

and intonations indicating a question, surprise, a menace, etc., are similar to those of English.)

Accent must be carefully distinguished from quantity (§ 7*d*):

ይጫን ። yį̊́ç̌ān, let him put the saddle on.

Quantity may influence accent:

በዛብኝ bą̊́zzabbį̊ñ, it is too much for me, also bą̊zzā́bbį̊ñ.

For the influence of accent on quantity see § 7*d* and enclitics below.

The stress accent in Amharic is in general much less marked than in English. Amharic speech, like French, runs with an almost even distribution of stress on each syllable. This is one of the reasons why to the beginner, who finds it difficult to distinguish the separate words in a phrase, a native appears to speak much faster than he actually does: and why, even to a practised ear, it is a matter of difficulty in many cases to detect where the principal accent of a particular word lies[1].

Secondary Accent.

Before and after a doubled consonant (§ 5, § 6), or two consecutive consonants, though the principal accent may lie elsewhere, there is often a marked secondary accent, (as on the i in 'cab-proprietor'), which is sometimes almost equal to the principal accent:

---

[1] Guidi, Gram. § 6*b*, 'in generale l'accento non è sempre stabile e chiaro.'

አበሉብኝ ። ábbḁlḁbbi̥ñ, he lied to me, sounds to all intents and purposes ábbḁlḁ́bbi̥ñ,

ይልክልሃል ፡ yi̥lí̥ki̥lli̥hāl, he will send to you, yi̥lí̥-kí̥lli̥hāl,

ትመለሳላችሁ ። ti̥mmällḁsallä́ččyuh, you (pl.) will return, tí̥mmä́llḁsállä́ččyuh,

አግብቷል ። ā́gi̥ṿtŏ͡āl, he has taken in, ā́gí̥ṿtŏ͡āl,

ይሆናል ። yi̥h^{w}ónāl, he will be, yí̥h^{w}ónāl,

ያበራል ። yāṿḁ́rāl, he is lighting, yā́ṿárāl,

ጠለየ ። ṭḁ́llḁ͡i̥ä, he prayed, ṭḁ́llḁ́͡i̥ä.

In some words, such as

ተቀመጥ ። tḁqḁ́mḁṭ, sit down,

it is barely perceptible that the stress on the accented syllable is greater than that on either of the others.

The adequate pronunciation of doubled consonants and unaccented vowels is necessary to ensure syllables not marked with the accent receiving their due share of it.

Accentuation of the Verb.

The accent of the simplest form of the verb (§ 21) falls on the syllable preceding the doubled radical:

ገባ gḁ́bbā, he entered,

ለቀመ lḁ́qqḁmḁ[1], he picked,

መነዘረ mḁnḁ́zzḁrḁ[1], he changed,

---

[1] I cannot endorse Afevork's statement, Gram. § 17, 'sulla media radicale, ደገፈ degghéfe,' 'sulla penultima radicale, ገሰገሰ ghesegghése,' though there is often a perceptible secondary accent on these syllables.

ዘገየ zḁgḁ́yyä, he was late.

For the accentuation of the derived forms and the conjugations, see §§ 21–45.

The accent of the greater part of the conjugation of the verb is fixed, and as the verb usually comes at the end of the clause (§ 73*b*) its accent is less likely than that of other words to be disturbed by that of an enclitic.

Accentuation of Diphthongs.

An accented diphthong usually has the accent on the first vowel, but it may fall on the second:

ላይ lá͡i̥, above,

ሰው ፡ ነው ። sḁ́͡u nḁ͡u, it is a man ;

ቀሳውስት qʸesá͡ust, priests,

ቀሳውስት ፡ አሉ ። qʸesa͡úst álu, the priests said so.

Final i̥ *and* u.

The accent hardly ever rests on final i̥ or u: but ይህ ፡ ልጅ ፡ yi̥hé li̥j, or yí̥he li̥j, this child: (also written ይኸ).

Variation of Accent.

Enclitics. An enclitic is a word which is so closely connected both in sense and pronunciation with the preceding word as virtually to form part of it, throwing back, in many cases, its accent upon it, i.e. causing the preceding word, which may or may not preserve its original accent, to be accented on its last syllable. Many monosyllabic words in Amharic are of this nature.

E.g.

ነው nḁ͡u, he (it) is, ናት nāt, she is, etc. (§ 13*b*);

substantives like

ብር bi̥rr, dollar,

ቀን qḁn, day,

ልጅ li̥j, child,

ቤት b^yēt, house;

imperatives like

ና nã, come,

ዙር zur, go round,

ባል bḁl (bäl), say;

and the second part of composite prepositions (§ 47*b*)

በ-... ላይ bḁ-... lḁ͡i, upon.

ማለፊያ mālấfya, pleasant;

ማለፊያ ፡ ነው ፡፡ mālăfyấ (§ 7*d*) nḁ͡u[1], it is pleasant;

መቼ mḁ́čä?, when?

መቼ ፡ ነው ፡፡ mḁčấ nḁ͡u?, when is it?

ትንሽ tí̥nni̥š, small,

ትንሽ ፡ ናት ፡፡ ti̥nní̥š nāt, she (it) is small;

መልክተኛ mḁlaktấñña, messenger,

መልክተኛ ፡ ነህ ፡፡ mḁlaktäññấ näh?, are you a messenger?

አምሳ ámsa, fifty,

አምሳ ፡ ብር ፡ amsấ yi̥rr, fifty dollars;

እኩል ŭ́kkul (§ 7*d*), half,

እኩል ፡ ቀን ፡ ŭkkúl qḁn, noon;

---

[1] Cp. κρεῖττόν ἐστιν.

አንተ ántḁ, you,

አንተ ፡ ልጅ ። antá (§ 7*d*) li̥j!, you there! (calling a boy);

እቃ í̥qa, goods,

እቃ ፡ ቤት ፡ i̥qá y^{y}ēt, store;

ገንዘብ ፡ ይዘህ ፡ ግዛው ። gḁ́nzḁṿ yí̥zäh gí̥za͡u, take some money and buy it,

ገንዘብ ፡ ይዘህ ፡ ና ። gḁ́nzḁṿ yi̥zä́h na, bring some money;

ችኩል ፡ ችኩል ፡ በል ። čí̥kkul či̥kkúl ṿäl, make great haste.

The accent from an enclitic does not rest on final i̥ or u (see above), e.g. the article -ው -u (§ 11), but on the preceding syllable, or the first vowel of a diphthong formed by the article:

መንገዱ mḁ́ṅgḁdu, the road,

በመንገዱ ፡ ላይ ፡ bḁmḁṅgḁ́du la͡i̥, on the road;

ገበታው gḁ́ṿḁta͡u, the table,

ተገበታው ፡ ዙር ። tḁgḁṿḁtá͡u zur, go round the table.

Certain suffixes bring the accent to the vowel immediately preceding them:

e.g. the emphatic suff. -ው -u:

ይህ yí̥he, this,

ይሀው yi̥há͡u, this very one;

ከዚህ kä́zzih, here,

ከዚሁ käzzíhu, just here;

but ተዚያው tḁ́zzya͡u and tḁzzyá͡u, just there.

An enclitic does not throw back its accent across a pause, or on to a word with which it is not immediately connected by the sense:

> እቃ ፡ ቤት i̥qá ỵ^{y}ēt, store,
>
> ለዚሁ ፡ እቃ ፡ ቤት ፡ የለውም ። läzzíh í̥qa ỵ^{y}ēt yállạ͡um, there is no receptacle for these things;
>
> የሌባ ፡ ነው ። yäl^{y}ēṿá nạ͡u, he is a thief,
>
> የሌባ ፡ ደግሞ ፡ ነው ። yäl^{y}éṿa dắmm^{w}o nạ͡u, he is a thief, too.

The position of the accent may determine the sense, by showing what words are closely connected:

> የዬቷ ፡ ሴት ፡ ልጅ ። yäyetwắ-s^{y}et li̥j?, the child of which woman?
>
> yäyếtwa s^{y}ét-li̥j, of which daughter?

In some cases an enclitic may or may not throw back its accent, however closely connected with the preceding word[1]:

> አሥር ፡ ብር ፡ assí̥r ṿi̥rr, and ássi̥r ṿi̥rr, ten dollars;
>
> ብዙ ፡ ነው ። bi̥zú nạ͡u, and bí̥zu nạ͡u, it is a lot;
>
> ምንድር ፡ ነው ። mi̥ndí̥r nạ͡u?, and mí̥ndi̥r nạ͡u?, what is it?

When accented initial i̥ disappears (§ 7*d*) its accent falls on a preceding vowel; if no vowel precedes, a following n, ṅ, m takes the accent:

> አየች ፡ እንደው ። áyyäčč í̥ndạ͡u, she just looked;

---

[1] Both accentuations are common and apparently they do not differ in meaning: all inquiries on the point meet with the reply ሁሉ ፡ አንድ ፡ ነው ፡ እንዳነጋገር ፡ ነው ።

አየ ፡ እንደው ። ayyá ndau, he just looked ;

እንኳን ፡ አልመጣም ። ńkwān, almáṭṭām, no, he hasn't come.

The enclitic particle እንጂ (i)nji, oh, but..., indeed, retains its accent:

አምጣው ። ánṭau (§ 7*d*), bring him,

አምጣው ፡ እንጂ ። ánṭaunjí !, oh, but bring him !

The inter. suff. -ኣ and -ወይ (§ 6) do not throw back their accent:

አልቋል ። álqōāl, it is finished,

አልቋላ ። álqōāllá ?, is it finished ?

አይደለም ። aidállām, he is not,

አይደለሞይ ። aidállämmwį, is he not ?

Other suffixed particles sometimes affect the accent of the word to which they are attached and sometimes do not:

e.g. -ማ -mmã, as for,

ይህ yihe, this,

ይህማ yihámma, as for this;

ፈረሱ fárasu, the horse,

ፈረሱማ fárasumma, as for the horse.

Other variations of Accent.

Apart from the disturbance that may be caused by an enclitic, the accentuation of a word varies in many cases according to its position: according, that is, as it stands (*a*) alone or before a pause, or (*b*) before any other word with which it is connected by the sense; and many words exhibit further variations of accent in each of these positions[1]. The position (*a*) is called in this section 'final', and the position (*b*) 'connected'.

Note. Isolated words in the course of this work marked with two accents usually take the first, sometimes[2] the second, when final, the second when connected. But words with accented suffixes such as -ኦ -ā́, -ወይ -wḁ̄i̥ (-wǿi̥, -wí̥), marked with their own original accent as well, are pronounced with both accents.

Taking any letters ገ, ፊ, ሬ, ከ, with which to compose forms as types (without regard to differences in vowels or consonants immaterial in accentuation), the following variations are exhibited by certain forms according to their position:

ግፋ gi̥fā:

fin. gí̥fa:

ስራ sí̥ra, work;

conn. gí̥fa or gi̥fā́: in rapid speech the word loses its accent altogether:

ስራ ፡ በዛብኝ ፡፡ sí̥ra (si̥rā́, si̥ra) y̥azzábbi̥ñ, the work is too much for me.

---

[1] Afevork, Gram. § 15, 'Intorno all'accento...... l'Amarico non ne ha ancora, con regole e norme fisse, stabilito le leggi.' '...avviene che tante e tante parole si sentano pronunziate ora in un modo, ora in un altro...'

[2] Words of this type are to be heard accented on the last when final in questions: e.g., s.v. ማንን.

*ገፈሬ gḁfḁrā̃:

fin. gḁfḁ́ra, also gḁ́fḁra:

ነጠላ nḁṭḁ́la, open, also nḁ́ṭḁla,

ዘጠና zḁṭḁ́na, ninety, also zḁ́ṭḁna,

እንግዳ ṅgí̥da, stranger, also ṅ́gi̥da,

በሽታ bḁ́ši̥ta, disease;

conn. gḁ́fḁra, also gḁfḁrā̃́:

ነጠላ ፡ ጫማ ፡ nḁ́ṭḁla č̣ámma, slipper, also nḁṭḁlá č̣ámma,

ዘጠና ፡ ሞቱ ፡፡ zḁ́ṭḁna mʷótu, ninety died, also zḁṭḁná mʷótu,

እንግዳ ፡ መጣ ፡፡ ṅ́gi̥da mḁ́ṭṭa, a stranger has come, also ṅgi̥dá mḁ́ṭṭa,

በሽታ ፡ ነከው ፡፡ bḁ́ši̥ta nā́kkau͡, the disease attacked him, also bḁši̥tá nā́kkau͡.

*ገፈሬ gḁffḁrā̃:

fin. gḁffḁ́ra, occasionally gḁ́ffḁra:

ጨለማ č̣ällā́ma, darkness,

ደመና dḁmmḁ́na, cloud, occasionally dḁ́mmḁna,

ፍለጋ fi̥llḁ́ga, track;

conn. gḁ́ffḁra, also gḁffḁrā̃́:

ጨለማ ፡ ነበር č̣ällāma nḁ́bbḁr, it was dark, also č̣ällämá nḁ́bbḁr,

ደመና ፡ ብዙ ፡ ነው ፡፡ dḁ́mmḁna bí̥zu nḁu͡, it is very cloudy, also dḁmmḁná bí̥zu nḁu͡,

ፍለጋ ፡ የለም ፡፡ fí̥llḁga yállām, there is no track.

*ገፈር g̥af̥ar :

(prp. + substantive)

fin. g̥áf̥ar, also g̥af̥ár :

የበግ : yắv̥ag̥, of a sheep,

but የላም ፡ ነው ፡ የበግ ። yälắm n̥a͡u yäv̥ág̥ ?, is it a cow's or a sheep's ?

conn. g̥af̥ár :

የበግ ፡ ሥጋ : yäv̥ág̥ s̥íg̥a, mutton.

*ገፈር g̥aff̥ar :

fin. g̥áff̥ar :

ዬት ፡ ነው ፡ ወምበር ። yēt n̥a͡u wώmb̥ar ?, where is the chair ?

ወለድ wώll̥ad, interest,

እንደምን ፤ በወለድ ። ndắm̥in ? b̥a͡uώll̥ad ?, on what terms ? at interest ?

ክክ ፡ ነው ፡ ልዝብ ። kúkk̥ĭ n̥a͡u l̥ízzi̥v̥ ?, is it fine or coarse ?

ኩፍኝ kúff̥in̥, small-pox ;

conn. g̥áff̥ar and g̥aff̥ár :

ወምበር ፡ ተሰበረ ። wώmb̥ar t̥as̥ább̥ar̥a, the chair is broken,

በወለድ ፡ ተበደረ ። b̥a͡uωll̥ád t̥av̥ádd̥ar̥a, he borrowed at interest,

ልዝብ ፡ ዱቄት ፡ l̥izzív̥ dʷṓqʸet, fine flour, also l̥ízzi̥v̥ dʷṓqʸet,

ኩፍኝ ፡ የወጋው ፡ ነው ። kuffín̥ yäwωggá͡u n̥a͡u, he is pitted with small-pox.

*ገፈሮ gḁfḁr^{w}ŏ :

fin. gḁ́fḁr^{w}o, sometimes gḁfḁ́r^{w}o :

ገበሎ gḁ́ṿḁl^{w}o, gecko, sometimes gḁṿḁ́l^{w}o ;

conn. gḁ́fḁr^{w}o :

ገበሎ ፡ አየሁ ። gḁ́ṿḁl^{w}o áyyāu^{h}, I saw a gecko.

*ገፈር gḁf(f)ĭr :

fin. gḁ́f(f)ir, occasionally gḁf(f)ĭ́r :

ና ፡ ወዲህ ። na wώdih (occasionally wωdíh), come here,

ቆይ ፡ ከዚህ ። qwω͡i̥ kḁ́zzih (occasionally kḁzzíh), wait here;

conn. gḁf(f)ĭ́r :

ወዲህ ፡ አትምጣ ። wωdíh attí̥mṭa, don't come here,

ከዚህ ፡ አትቆይ ። kḁzzíh attí̥qwω͡i̥, don't wait here.

*ገፋር gḁffār :

fin. gḁ́ffār, sometimes gḁffā́r :

መልካም mḁ́lkām, excellent,

ሹራብ šúrrāṿ, sock, sometimes šurrā́ṿ,

መምጣት mḁ́mṭāt, to come;

conn. gḁffā́r :

መልካም ፡ ነበር ። mḁlkā́m nḁ́bbḁr, it was excellent,

ሹራብ ፡ አምጣ ። šurrā́ṿ ánṭa, bring some socks,

መምጣት ፡ እፈልጋለሁ ። mḁmṭā́t i̥fḁlli̥gállḁu^{h}, I want to come.

*ገፍራ gḁfrā̃ :

fin. gḁ́frā̃ :

ደኅና dā́hnā, well;

conn. gḁfrā́, also gḁ́frā :

ደኅና ፡ ገባ ፡፡ dähnā́ gḁ́bba, he arrived safely,

ደኅና ፡ ወጥ ፡ ይሰራል ፡፡ dā́hnā wωṭ yi̥sárāl, he cooks well.

*ጋፈራ gāfḁrā :

fin. gāfḁ́ra, sometimes gā́fḁra :

ማለዳ mālḁ́da, early, sometimes mā́lḁda,

ጎተራ gʷotḁ́ra, barn, sometimes gʷótḁra ;

conn. gā́fḁra, sometimes gāfḁrā́ :

ማለዳ ፡ ሔዱ ፡፡ mā́lḁda hā́du, they went early,

ማለዳ ፡ መጡ ፡፡ mālḁdá mḁ́ṭṭu, they came early,

ጎተራ ፡ ተቃጠለ ፡፡ gʷótḁra tḁqáṭṭḁlḁ, the barn was burnt.

*ግፍር gi̥fi̥r :

fin. gí̥fi̥r :

ትንኝ tí̥ni̥ñ, mosquito ;

conn. gí̥fi̥r, also gi̥fí̥r :

ትንኝ ፡ የለም ፡፡ tí̥ni̥ñ yā́lläm?, are there no mosquitoes?, also ti̥ní̥ñ yā́lläm?

*ገፈረክ gḁfḁrḁk :

fin. gḁ́fḁrḁk, occasionally gḁfḁ́rḁk :

አቀበት áqḁṿḁt, uphill, occasionally aqḁ́ṿḁt ;

conn. gḁ́fḁrḁk :

አቀበት ፡ ሲሔዱ ፡፡ áqḁṿḁt si̥hā́du, when they go uphill.

*ገፈረክ gḁffḁrḁk :

fin. gḁffḁ́rḁk :

ሰንሰለት sḁnsḁ́lḁt, chain,

ቍልቍለት qwŭlqwŭ́lḁt, downhill ;

conn. gḁ́ffḁrḁk, also gḁffḁrḁ́k :

ሰንሰለት ፡ ጠፋ ፡፡ sḁ́nsḁlḁt ṭḁ́ffa, the chain was lost,

ቍልቍለት ፡ ሔደ ፡፡ qwŭ́lqwŭlḁt hắdä, he went downhill,

ቍልቍለት ፡ ሲወርድ ፡ qwŭlqwŭlḁ́t si̥wώrd, when he goes downhill.

*ገፈራክ gḁfḁrāk :

fin. usually gḁfḁ́rāk, sometimes gḁ́fḁrāk or gḁfḁrā́k ;

መሰላል mḁsḁ́lāl, ladder, sometimes mḁ́sḁlāl or mḁsḁlā́l,

ደረታም dḁ́rḁtām, broad-chested, sometimes dḁrḁtā́m,

ውሸታም wŭšä́tām, false, sometimes wŭ́šätām or wŭšätā́m,

በክራይ bḁ́ki̥ra͡i̥, for hire, also bḁkí̥ra͡i̥ ;

conn. gḁfḁrā́k :

በመሰላል ፡ ወጣ ፡፡ bḁmḁsḁlā́l wώṭṭa, he mounted by a ladder,

ደረታም ፡ ፈረስ ፡ dḁrḁtā́m fḁ́rḁs, a broad-chested horse,

ውሸታም ፡ አይደለም ፡፡ wŭšätā́m a͡i̥dállām, he is not false,

በክራይ ፡ አሉ ፡፡ bḁki̥rá͡i állu, they are to be had for hire.

*ገፋራክ gḁfārāk :

fin. gḁfā́rāk, sometimes gḁfārā́k :

ዷያታም dwa͡i̥ātām, sickly, sometimes dwa͡i̥ātā́m ;

conn. g̥afārắk :

ዲያታም ፡ አይዶለም ። dwa͡i̥ātám a͡i̥dállām, he is not sickly.

*ገፍርክ g̥afi̥rk :

fin. gắfi̥rk :

አጥንት ắṭi̥nt, bone,

ንግሥት ni̥gi̥st, queen;

conn. gắfi̥rk and g̥afí̥rk :

አጥንት ፡ ተሰበረ ። ắṭi̥nt t̥as̥ábbăr̥a, the bone is broken, also āṭí̥nt t̥asắbbăr̥a,

ንግሥት ፡ ትበላለች ። ni̥gí̥st ti̥bbālállāč, she is called a queen.

Words in -ጌፍ -gʸēf, -ጎፍ -gʷōf :

fin. ´-gʸef, ´-gʷof :

ዶቄት dʷṓqʸet, flour,

በምን ፡ ይደረጋል ፤ በዶቄት ። b̥amí̥n yi̥ddárr̥agāl? b̥adʷṓqʸet?, what is it made with? flour?

ችሎት čí̥lʷot, government office,

ዬት ፡ ናቸው ፤ ተችሎት ። yēt nắčča͡u? t̥ačí̥lʷot?, where are they? in the office?

conn. ´-gʸēf, ´gʷōf, also -gʸḗf, -gʷṓf :

ዶቄት ፡ ሰጠው ። dʷṓqʸet sátta͡u, he gave him some flour, also dʷoqʸḗt sátta͡u,

ችሎት ፡ ሔዱ ። čí̥lʷot hắdu, they have gone to the office, also či̥lʷṓt hắdu.

-ጋፍ -gāf, -ጌፍ -gʸēf, -ጎፍ -gʷōf receive the accent when a suffix is attached to them :

ሰካር sákkār, drunkard,

ሰካሮች sḁkkā́rʷōč, drunkards,

ሰካሮቹ sḁkkārʷṓčču, the drunkards;

መሬት mḁ́rʸĕt, ground,

መሬቱ mḁrʸĕ́tu, the ground;

and there is a perceptible secondary accent on the penultimate in words like

መንገዱ mḁ́ṅgḁdu, the road,

ፋኑሱ fā́nusu, the lantern,

ሴቲቱ sʸĕ́titu (-i̥tu), the woman,

ትልቁ tí̥lli̥qu, the large one.

The adj. ending -ኛ -ññã has the accent on the syllable preceding it:

fin. and conn. አማርኛ amārí̥ññã, Amharic,

ምርኮኛ mi̥rkʷóññã, prisoner;

but when -ው is added the accent varies:

የትኛው fin. yĕ́ti̥ñña͡u, conn. yĕtí̥ñña͡u.

The general tendency in these variations is for the accent to come forward before a suffix or another word: but in some cases nothing but an enclitic brings it forward:

መለከት mḁ́lḁkḁt, bugle,

መለከቶች mḁ́lḁkḁtʷōč, bugles,

መለከት ፡ ነፋ ። mḁ́lḁkḁt nḁ́ffa, he sounded a bugle,

መለከቶችን ፡ ነፉ ። mḁ́lḁkḁtʷōččun nḁ́ffu, they sounded the bugles,

መለከት ፡ ነው ። mḁlḁkḁ́t nḁ͡u, it is a bugle.

ACCIDENCE.

THE NOUN.

The Substantive. § 9

Substantives are of two genders, masculine and feminine, have two numbers, singular and plural, and in addition to the nominative an accusative case.

Gender. § 9*a*

There is no special form of the substantive for either gender.

Number. § 9*b*

The pl. is formed by adding -^{w}ōች -^{w}ōč (-^{w}ōčč before a vowel § 6) to the last consonant of the sg.

ቤት b^{y}ēt, house, pl. ቤቶች b^{y}ét^{w}ōč.

ጌታ g^{y}étã, master, pl. ጌቶች g^{y}ét^{w}ōč.

ለማኝ lḁmmắñ (§ 8) beggar, pl. ለማኞች lḁmmắññ^{w}ōč (§ 6).

In some cases (see vocab.) -ያ -yã disappears:

ባሪያ bắryã, slave, pl. ባሮች bắr^{w}ōč;

and i is sometimes retained:

ሰፊ sḁ́fi, tailor, pl. ሰፎች sḁ́f^{w}ōč
and (not G.) ሰፊዎች sḁ́fi^{w}ōč.

Besides the pl. in -^{w}ōች some irregular plurals (Ethiopic forms) occur:

በቅሎ bḁ́ql^{w}o, mule, pl. በቅሎች bḁ́ql^{w}ōč,

also አበቊልት abắqwi̥lt (aỵ-, -qwŭ-, -ቍ- -qi̥-),

and አበቊልቶች abắqwi̥lt^{w}ōč (aỵ-, -qwŭ-, -ቍ- -qi̥-).

The irregular pls. more commonly in use are given in the vocab.; all nouns with irregular pl. also have the regular pl. in -ʷō̩ች.

§ 9c *Case.*

The accusative is formed by adding -ን -n to the nominative (of which final sádi̥s receives i̥):

nom.	ቤት	bʸēt,	acc.	ቤትን	bʸéti̥n.
„	ጌታ	gʸétā̃,	„	ጌታን	gʸétā̃n.
„	ለማኝ	lḁ́mmāñ,	„	ለማኙን	lḁmmáññi̥n (§ 6).
„	ቤቶች	bʸétʷōč,	„	ቤቶችን	bʸētʷóčči̥n (§ 6).

-ን comes after the art. (§ 11) and pers. suff. (§ 12*b*), but before other suff.:

ቤቱን	bʸétun,	the house,
ሴቲቱን	sʸéti̥tun,	the woman,
ቤቴን	bʸétʸen,	my house,
ቤቷን	bʸétwān,	her house,
ቤታችንን	bʸētáčči̥ni̥n,	our house.
ቤቱንም	bʸétuni̥m,	and his (the) house.

The Ethiopic Accusative.

§ 9d The Ethiopic accusative in -ḁ survives in some cases, in which the form but not necessarily the meaning is acc.[1]: the effect in Amharic is generally to give an objective sense to a following noun:

---

[1] 'Status constructus.' Praetorius, Gram. Æth. § 125, 'Quoad formam status constructi nihil refert num nomen in eo positum nominativi sensum habeat an genitivi an accusativi.'

ንጉሥ ni̥gūs, king,

ንጉሠ ፡ ነገሥት ፡ ni̥gúsḁ nḁ́gḁst, king of kings, emperor;

ባል bāl, master,

ባለቤት bālḁỵ^{y}ét, master of the house.

But in some phrases the form in -ḁ has the objective sense (§ 67*c*):

ነገር nḁ́gḁr, word,

ነገረ ፡ ሰሪ ፡ nḁ́gḁrḁ sắri, (maker of words), slanderer.

The Adjective.

The adjective does not differ in accidence from the substantive: § 10

sg. nom. ደግ dḁgg (dä-), good, ክፉ kí̥fu (kú̆-, kú̈-), bad,

acc. ደግን dḁ́ggi̥n, ክፉን kí̥fun,

pl. nom. ደጎች dḁ́gg^{w}ōč (-čč § 6), ክፎች kí̥f^{w}ōč (-čč § 6),

acc. ደጎችን dḁgg^{w}ṓčči̥n. ክፎችን ki̥f^{w}ṓčči̥n.

For irregular (Eṭh.) pls. see vocabulary; all adj. with these form the regular pl. as well.

There is no special form of the adj. for either gender.

The Article.

The definite article 'the' is expressed by the suffixes: § 11

sg. m. -u, written -ው after a vowel[1],

f. -ቱ -itu (-i̥tu), written -ይቱ after a vowel,

pl. m. & f. -u.

---

[1] i.e. after any class of letter but sắdi̥s (§ 4*a*).

Š. has sg. f. -ዋ -wã.

All the above form the acc. in -ን -n.

ቤት bʸēt, house, ቤቱ፡ bʸétu, the house, acc. ቤቱን bʸétun.

ጌታ gʸéta, master, ጌታው gʸéta͡u, the master, acc. ጌታውን gʸéta͡un.

ሴት sʸēt, woman, ሴቲቱ፡ sʸétitu (-i̥tu), the woman, acc. ሴቲቱን sʸétitun (-i̥tun).

ቤቶች bʸétʷōč, houses, ቤቶቹ፡ bʸētʷṓčču, the houses, acc. ቤቶቹን bʸētʷṓččun.

ፈረስ fḁ́rḁs, horse, mare (§ 9*a*),

Š. ፈረሷ fḁ́rḁswã, the mare, acc. ፈረሷን fḁ́rḁswãn.

The article may be attached to a noun sub. or adj. or to the rel. + verb (§ 14).

When it is attached to a verb ending in a consonant, the form -ው is used, connected by the vowel ḁ (gi̥͡i̥z § 4*a*; cp. the mode of connecting the pron. suff. -ው § 12*c*). The f. ending -ች -č (-čč § 6) takes -ው without the connecting ḁ, and in G. -ቱ፡ -itu (-i̥tu).

After a verb ending in -u the art. takes the form -ት -t or -ቱ፡ -tu.

E.g. የሞተ፡ yämʷótḁ, who died,

የሞተው፡ ሰው፡ yämʷotḁ́͡u (§ 8) sḁ͡u, the man who died.

የሚወርድ፡ yämmi̥wώrd, that (rel.) descends,

የሚወርደው፡ ዝናብ፡ yämmi̥wώrdḁ͡u zi̥nāḅ, the rain that descends.

የሞተች፡ yämʷótäč, who (f.) died,

የሞተችውን ፡ ሴት ፡ yämʷotáččyun (§ 6) sʸēt, the woman (acc.) who died, G. -ቺቱን -ččitun (-i̥t-).

የተገደሉት ፡ ሰዎች ፡ yätagáddalut sáuʷōč, the men who were killed,

የተገደሉቱን ፡ አየ ። yätagáddalutun áyyä, he saw those who were killed,

የመጡቱ ፡ ናቸው ። yämáṭṭutu ṇáččau, they are those who came.

There is no form for the indef. art. in Amharic.

The Pronoun.

The Personal Pronoun.

The personal pronouns are of two kinds, disjunctive (the emphasizing and distinguishing forms), which stand alone, and conjunctive, which cannot stand alone, but are suffixes attached to nouns, verbs, etc. § 12

Disjunctive Personal Pronouns.

The disjunctive personal pronouns are: § 12a

sg. 1st — እኔ í̥nʸé (§ 8), I.

2nd m. — አንተ ántḁ (-tä)[1], you.

2nd f. — አንቺ ánči[2], you.

3rd m. — እርሱ i̥rsǘ (§ 8)[3], he, it.

3rd f. — እርሷ i̥rsŏá (§ 8)[4], she, it.

---

[1] or አንት ant, (see vocab.)

[2] አንች anč, „ „

[3] or እሱ i̥ssǘ, (see vocab.), which is generally used of inanimate objects.

[4] or እሷ i̥ssŏá.

pl. 1st እኛ i̥ññá (§ 8), we.

2nd እላንት i̥llánt (§ 8)[1], you.

3rd እርሳቸው i̥rsắč(č)ḁu[2], they.

The polite form of address is

sg. 2nd እርሰዎ i̥rsḁʷo[3] (§ 8), you, which is constr. with the verb in the pl. 3rd; pl. እላንት.

The polite form of reference is እርሳቸው, he, they (e.g. the Rās, the Rāses), with verb in pl. 3rd.

All the above form the acc. in -ን -n (§ 9*c*), may take the article (§ 11), and simple and composite prepositions (§ 47) may be constr. with them:

e.g. እኔን ፡ መታኝ ። i̥nʸén mḁttāñ, he (it) struck *me*, myself.

የኔን ፡ አምጣ ። yänʸén ánṭa (§ 7*d*), bring one of (some of) mine (የ + እ = የ § 7*a*).

የኔውን ፡ አምጣ ። yänʸéun ánṭa, bring mine.

ታንተ ፡ ጋር ፡ tantắ gār, with you (ተ + አ = ታ § 7*a*).

ለርሱ ፡ ነው ። lärsű nḁu, it's for him (ለ + እ = ለ § 7*a*).

በኛ ፡ ታች ፡ bäññá tāč, beneath us (as distinguished from others).

---

[1] or እላንተ i̥llántḁ (-tä), እናንት (i̥)nnánt (-ተ -tḁ, -tä), s.v. እነ-.

[2] or እሳቸው i̥ssắč(č)ḁu, which is generally used of inanimate objects,

or እነርሱ (i̥)nnḁrsű (-ná-), እነሱ (i̥)nnḁssű (-ná-), s.v. እነ-.

[3] or እርስዎ ፡ [እርሶ] i̥rsʷó, እሰዎ i̥ssḁʷo, እስዎ ፡ [እሶ] i̥ssʷó; in Š. also used as pol. form of reference.

እላንትን ፡ አልፈልግም ። i̥llántin̥ alfḁlli̥gi̥m, you (pl.) I don't want.

የናንተይቱ ፡ ናት ። yännantḁ́i̥tu (§ 8) nāt, she is yours (pl.).

እርሳቸውን ፡ አየኍ ። i̥rsáččḁun áyyäu[h], them I have seen.

Personal Pronouns conjunctive with Nouns. § 12b

The personal pronouns conjunctive with nouns, other pronouns (§§ 16—19), and some adverbs, rendering the possessive or genitive, are the following suffixes:

sg.	1st	-ʸẽ, after a vowel[1] -ዬ -yẽ (-i̥ẽ, ʸẽ)[2],	my.
	2nd m.	-ህ -h[3],	your.
	2nd f.	-ሽ -š,	your.
	2nd pol.	-ḁዎ -ḁʷo[4], after a vowel -ዎ -ʷo,	your.
	3rd m.	-u, after a vowel -ው -u,	his, its.
	3rd f.	-ዋ -wã (-ŏã),	her, its.
pl.	1st	-āችን -áč(č)i̥n,	our.
	2nd	-āችሁ -áč(č)i̥hu (-áč(č)yuh § 7d),	your.
sg. 3rd pol. and pl. 3rd		-āቸው -áč(č)ḁu,	their (his, pol.).

These all form the acc. in -ን -n.

---

[1] i.e. after any class of letter but sádi̥s (§ 4a).

[2] or -ያ -yä (-ʸä).

[3] or -ኽ -χ (-h), -ክ -k (§ 7d).

[4] or -ዎ -wo (-ʷo); Š. also sg. 3rd pol.

When -ሀ or -ሽ are attached to sắdi̥s (§ 4*a*) it has i̥, unless they have a further suff.

These suff. are attached as follows:

(*a*) to a consonant: ቤት b^{y}ēt, house.

ቤቴ	b^{y}ét^{y}e,	my	house.
ቤትህ	b^{y}éti̥h,	your (m.)	,,
ቤትሽ	b^{y}éti̥š,	your (f.)	,,
ቤትዎ	b^{y}étḁ͡^{w}o,	your (pol.)	,,
ቤቱ	b^{y}étu,	his (its)	,,
ቤቷ	b^{y}étwa,	her (its)	,,
ቤታችን	b^{y}ētáč(č)i̥n,	our	,,
ቤታችሁ	b^{y}ētáč(č)i̥hu (-č(č)yuh),	your (pl.)	,,
ቤታቸው	b^{y}ētáč(č)ḁ͡u,	their (his, pol.)	,,

acc.

ቤቴን	b^{y}ét^{y}en,
ቤትህን	b^{y}éti̥hi̥n (-thi̥n),
ቤትሽን	b^{y}éti̥ši̥n (-tši̥n),
ቤትዎን	b^{y}étḁ͡^{w}on,
ቤቱን	b^{y}étun,
ቤቷን	b^{y}étwãn,
ቤታችንን	b^{y}ētáč(č)i̥ni̥n,
ቤታችሁን	b^{y}ētáč(č)i̥hun (§ 7*d*),
ቤታቸውን	b^{y}ētáč(č)ḁ͡un.

(*β*) to -ā̃ : ጌታ g^{y}ḗtā̃, master.

ጌታዬ	g^{y}ētā͡i̥^{y}e (-ā́^{y}e)[1],	my	master.
ጌታህ	g^{y}ḗtāh,	your (m.)	„
ጌታሽ	g^{y}ḗtāš,	your (f.)	„
ጌታዎ	g^{y}ētá͡^{w}o[1],	your (pol.)	„
ጌታው	g^{y}ḗta͡u,	his (its)	„
ጌታዋ	g^{y}ētá͡ua[1],	her (its)	„
ጌታችን	g^{y}ētā́č(č)i̥n (a + ā = ā § 7*a*),	our	„
ጌታችሁ	g^{y}ētā́č(č)i̥hu (-č(č)yuh),	your (pl.)	„
ጌታቸው	g^{y}ētā́č(č)ḁ͡u,	their (his, pol.)	„

(*γ*) to ^{w}o : በቅሎ bḁ́ql^{w}o, mule.

በቅሎዬ	bḁql^{w}ó͡i̥^{y}e (-l^{w}ó͡^{y}e)[2],	my	mule.
በቅሎህ	bḁ́ql^{w}oh,	your (m.)	„
በቅሎሽ	bḁ́ql^{w}oš,	your (f.)	„
በቅሎዎ	bḁql^{w}ó͡^{w}o (-l^{w}ṓ)[2],	your (pol.)	„
በቅሎው	bḁ́ql^{w}o͡u,	his (its)	„
በቅሎዋ	bḁql^{w}ó͡ua[2],	her (its)	„
በቅሏችን	bḁqlŏ͡ā́č(č)i̥n,	our	„
በቅሏችሁ	bḁqlŏ͡ā́č(č)i̥hu (-č(č)yuh),	your (pl.)	„
በቅሏቸው	bḁqlŏ͡ā́č(č)ḁ͡u,	their (his, pol.)	„

---

[1] fin. (§ 8), but conn. g^{y}ḗta^{y}e : ጌታዬ ፡ መጣ ። g^{y}ḗta^{y}e mḁ́t̥t̥a, my master has come. Similarly, conn. g^{y}ḗta͡^{w}o, g^{y}ḗta͡ua.

[2] fin. (§ 8); conn. bḁ́ql^{w}o͡^{y}e, bḁ́ql^{w}ō, bḁ́ql^{w}o͡ua.

The genders and numbers given above refer to the possessor, not to the object qualified:

e.g. ምስትህ mi̥sti̥h, your wife,

ባልሽ báli̥š, your husband,

በቅሎቼ bḁqlʷóččʸe, my mules.

With adv.:

በታቻችን bḁtāččāč(č)i̥n, beneath us (as distinguished from e.g. above us).

§ 12c *Personal Pronouns conjunctive with Verbs.*

The personal pronouns conjunctive with verbs[1], rendering the dative and accusative, are the following suffixes, also used as infixes:

			connecting vowel
sg. 1st	-ኝ -ñ (-ññ § 6),	to me, me.	ḁ (ä)
2nd m.	-ህ -h[2],	to you, you.	i̥ and ḁ (ä)
2nd f.	-ሽ -š,	to you, you.	i̥
2nd pol.	-ዎ -ʷo[3],	to you, you.	ḁ and none
3rd m.	-ው -u,	to him, him, (to it, it).	ḁ
	-ት -t after o, u,	„ „ „	none
3rd f.	-āት -āt,	to her, her, (to it, it).	none
pl. 1st	-ን -n (-nn § 6)[4],	to us, us.	ḁ (ä)
2nd	-āችሁ -āč(č)i̥hu (-āč(č)yuh § 7*d*),	to you, you.	none
sg. 3rd pol. & pl. 3rd	-āቸው -āč(č)ḁu,	to them, them; to him (him, pol.)	none

[1] also with በ-, ለ-, when joined to a verb (§ 47*a*); also with እነሆ q.v. [2] or -ኽ -χ, -k, (§ 7*d*).
[3] or -ዎት -ʷot; S. also sg. 3rd pol. [4] or -ና -nnḁ.

These suff. are attached to all parts of the verb (§ 34) except the infin. and part. which, as nouns, take the suff. given in § 12*b*.

The connecting vowel joins them to a verb ending in a consonant.

They are inserted between the verb and the aux. **አለ** (§ 32) or another suff., such as the neg. suff. -**ም** (§ 37).

E.g.:

(*a*) after a consonant:

ይንገር yí̥ṅgḁr (-är), let him tell.

ይንገረኝ	yí̥ṅgḁrḁñ (-ärä-),	let him tell me.		
ይንገርህ	yí̥ṅgḁri̥h (-är-),	„	„	you (m.)
ይንገርሽ	yí̥ṅgḁri̥š (-är-),	„	„	you (f.)
ይንገረዎ	yí̥ṅgḁrḁ͡ʷo (-är-)[1],	„	„	you (pol.)
ይንገረው	yí̥ṅgḁrḁ͡u (-är-),	„	„	him.
ይንገራት	yí̥ṅgḁrāt (-är-),	„	„	her.
ይንገረን	yí̥ṅgḁrḁn (-ärä-)[2],	„	„	us.
ይንገራችሁ	yi̥ṅgḁrā́č(č)i̥hu (-är-, -ā́č(č)yuh),	„	„	you (pl.)
ይንገራቸው	yi̥ṅgḁrā́č(č)ḁ͡u,	„	„	them (him, pol.)

ይነግራል yi̥nǻgrāl, he tells.

ይነግረኛል	yi̥nǻgrḁññāl (-äñ-),	he tells me.		
ይነግረሃል	yi̥nǻgrḁhāl (-äh-)[3],	„	„	you (m.)

---

[1] or **ይንገርዎት ፡** [-**ሮት**] yí̥ṅgḁrʷot (-är-).

[2] or **ይንገረና** yí̥ṅgḁrḁnnḁ (-är-).

[3] or -**ኻል** -χāl.

ይነግርሻል	yi̥nḁ́gri̥šāl,	he tells		you (f.)
ይነግረዎአል	yi̥nḁ́grḁ͡ʷoāl[1],	„	„	you (pol.)
ይነግረዋል	yi̥nḁ́gr͡ḁuāl,	„	„	him.
ይነግራታል	yi̥nḁ́grātāl,	„	„	her.
ይነግረናል	yi̥nḁ́grḁnnāl,	„	„	us.
ይነግራችኋል	yi̥nḁgrā́č(č)i̥hwāl (-č(č)yuhāl)	„	„	you (pl.)
ይነግራቸዋል	yi̥nḁgrā́č(č)͡ḁuāl,	„	„	them (him, pol.)

አይነግርም a͡i̥nḁ́gri̥m, he will (does) not tell.

አይነግረኝም	a͡i̥nḁ́grḁññi̥m (-rä-),	he will not tell me.		
አይነግርህም	a͡i̥nḁ́gr(i̥)hi̥m[2],	„	„	you (m.)
አይነግርሽም	a͡i̥nḁ́gri̥ši̥m,	„	„	you (f.)
አይነግረዎም	a͡i̥nḁ́grḁ͡ʷom[3],	„	„	you (pol.)
አይነግረውም	a͡i̥nḁ́gr͡ḁum,	„	„	him.
አይነግራትም	a͡i̥nḁ́grāti̥m,	„	„	her.
አይነግረንም	a͡i̥nḁ́grḁnni̥m (-rä-)[4],	„	„	us.
አይነግራችሁም	a͡i̥nḁgrā́č(č)i̥hum,	„	„	you (pl.)
አይነግራቸውም	ai̥nḁgrā́č(č)͡ḁum,	„	„	them (him, pol.)

---

[1] or -ረዎታል -rḁ͡ʷotāl, -ርዎታል ፡ [-ሮታል] -rʷotāl.

[2] or -ኽም -χi̥m.

[3] or -ግርዎትም ፡ [ግሮትም] -grʷoti̥m.

[4] or -ነም -nnḁm.

(β) after the ending -ች -č (-čč § 6) of the simp. perf. sg. 3rd f.; the connecting vowel, if there is one, is always i̥ (ĭ̥ y):

ሰጠች sḁ́ṭṭäč, she gave.

ሰጠችኝ	sḁ́ṭṭäčči̥ñ,	she gave	me.
ሰጠችህ	sḁ́ṭṭäčči̥h,	„ „	you (m.)
ሰጠችሽ	sḁ́ṭṭäčči̥š,	„ „	you (f.)
ሰጠችዎ	sḁ́ṭṭäččĭ̥ʷo[1],	„ „	you (pol.)
ሰጠችው	sḁ́ṭṭäččyu,	„ „	him.
ሰጠቻት	sḁ́ṭṭäččāt,	„ „	her.
ሰጠችን	sḁ́ṭṭäčči̥n[2],	„ „	us.
ሰጠቻችሁ	sḁṭṭäččā́č(č)yuh (§ 7*d*),	„ „	you (pl.)
ሰጠቻቸው	sḁṭṭäččā́č(č)ḁu͡,	„ „	them (him, pol.)

(γ) after -ḁ (gi̥͡i̥z):

ነገረ nḁ́ggḁrḁ, he told.

ነገረኝ	nḁ́ggḁrañ (-äñ),	he told	me.
ነገረህ	nḁ́ggḁräh,	„ „	you (m.)
ነገረሽ	nḁ́ggḁräš,	„ „	you (f.)
ነገረዎ	nḁ́ggḁrḁ͡ʷo[3],	„ „	you (pol.)
ነገረው	nḁ́ggḁrḁu͡,	„ „	him.
ነገራት	nḁ́ggḁrāt,	„ „	her.
ነገረን	nḁ́ggḁrḁn (-än)[4],	„ „	us.
ነገራችሁ	nḁggḁrā́č(č)yuh (§ 7*d*),	„ „	you (pl.)
ነገራቸው	nḁggḁrā́č(č)ḁu͡,	„ „	them (him, pol.)

---

[1] or ሰጠችዎት sḁ́ṭṭäččĭ̥ʷot.

[2] or ሰጠችና sḁ́ṭṭäčči̥nnḁ.

[3] or ነገረዎት nḁ́ggḁrḁ͡ʷot.

[4] or ነገረና nḁ́ggḁrḁnnḁ (-ännḁ).

አልነገረም alnḁ́ggḁrḁm, he did not tell.

አልነገረኝም alnḁ́ggḁrḁññi̥m (-rä-), he did not tell me.
አልነገረህም alnḁ́ggḁrähi̥m[1], „ „ you (m.)
አልነገረሽም alnḁ́ggḁräši̥m, „ „ you (f.)
አልነገረዎም alnḁ́ggḁrḁ͡ʷom[2], „ „ you (pol.)
አልነገረውም alnḁ́ggḁr͡ḁum, „ „ him.
አልነገራትም alnḁ́ggḁrāti̥m, „ „ her.
አልነገረንም alnḁ́ggḁrḁnni̥m (-rä-)[3], „ „ us.
አልነገራችሁም alnḁggḁrā́č(č)i̥hum, „ „ you (pl.)
አልነገራቸውም alnḁggḁrā́č(č)͡ḁum, „ „ them (him, pol.)

(δ) after -ū (ká͡i̥y):

ነገሩ nḁ́ggḁru, they told.

ነገሩኝ nḁ́ggḁruñ, they told me.
ነገሩህ nḁ́ggḁruh, „ „ you (m.)
ነገሩሽ nḁ́ggḁruš, „ „ you (f.)
ነገሩዎ nḁ́ggḁruʷo[4], „ „ you (pol.)
ነገሩት nḁ́ggḁrut, „ „ him.
ነገሯት nḁ́ggḁrwāt, „ „ her.
ነገሩን nḁ́ggḁrun[5], „ „ us.
ነገሯችሁ nḁggḁrwā́č(č)yuh, „ „ you (pl.)
ነገሯቸው nḁggḁrwā́č(č)͡ḁu, „ „ them (him, pol.)

---

1 or -ኽም -χi̥m.
2 or -ረዎትም -rḁ͡ʷoti̥m.
3 or -ነም -nnḁm.
4 or ነገሩዎት nḁ́ggḁruʷot.
5 or ነገሩነ nḁ́ggḁrunnḁ.

(ε) after -ī (sā́li̥s):

ብትነግሪ bi̥tti̥nḁ́gri, if you (f.) tell.

ብትነግሪኝ	bi̥tti̥nḁ́griñ (-i̥ñ),	if you (f.) tell	me.
ብትነግሪው	bi̥tti̥nḁ́gryu,	„ „	him.
ብትነግርያት	bi̥tti̥nḁ́gryāt,	„ „	her.
ብትነግሪን	bi̥tti̥nḁ́grin (-i̥n)[1],	„ „	us.
ብትነግርያቸው	bi̥tti̥nḁgryā́č(č)ḁu͡,	„ „	them.

(ζ) after -ã (rā́y̥i̥):

ሰማ sḁ́mmã, he heard.

ሰማኝ	sḁ́mmāñ,	he heard	me.
ሰማህ	sḁ́mmāh,	„ „	you (m.)
ሰማሽ	sḁ́mmāš,	„ „	you (f.)
ሰማዎ	sḁ́mma͡ʷo[2],	„ „	you (pol.)
ሰማው	sḁ́mma͡u,	„ „	him (it).
ሰማት	sḁ́mmāt,	„ „	her.
ሰማን	sḁ́mmān[3],	„ „	us.
ሰማችሁ	sḁmmā́č(č)yuh,	„ „	you (pl.)
ሰማቸው	sḁmmā́č(č)ḁ͡u,	„ „	them (him, pol.)

---

[1] or ብትነግሪነ bi̥tti̥nḁ́grinnḁ (-i̥n-).

[2] or ሰማዎት sḁ́mmaʷot.

[3] or ሰማነ sḁ́mmānnḁ.

(η) after -^{y}ĕ (hắmi̥s):

ሰጥችያለሁ sḁṭi̥ččyállḁu^h or ሰጥቻለሁ sḁṭi̥ččāllḁu^h, [= ሰጥቼ ፡ አለሁ ፡ § 32*a*], I have given.

ሰጥቼሃለሁ	sḁṭi̥čč^{y}ehállḁu^h [1],	I have given to		you (m.)
ሰጥቼሻለሁ	sḁṭi̥čč^{y}ešállḁu^h,	„	„	you (f.)
ሰጥቼዎአለሁ	sḁṭi̥čč^{y}e^{w}oállḁu^h [2],	„	„	you (pol.)
ሰጥቼዋለሁ	sḁṭi̥čč^{y}ewállḁu^h,	„	„	him.
ሰጥችያታለሁ	sḁṭi̥ččyātállḁu^h [3],	„	„	her.
ሰጥችያችኋለሁ	sḁṭi̥ččyāč(č)yuhállḁu^h [4] (§ 7*d*),	„	„	you (pl.)
ሰጥችያቸዋለሁ	sḁṭi̥ččyāč(č)ḁuállḁu^h [5],	„	„	them (him, pol.)

(θ) after -^{w}ŏ (sắvi̥):

ነገሯል ፡ [ነገሮአል ፡] nḁgrŏāl, he has told.

ነገሮኛል	nḁgr^{w}oññāl,	he has told		me.
ነገሮሃል	nḁgr^{w}ohāl [6],	„	„	you (m.)
ነገሮሻል	nḁgr^{w}ošāl,	„	„	you (f.)
ነገሮዎአል	nḁgr^{w}o^{w}ŏāl [7],	„	„	you (pol.)
ነገሮታል	nḁgr^{w}otāl,	„	„	him.
ነገሯታል	nḁgrŏātāl,	„	„	her.
ነገሮናል	nḁgr^{w}onnāl,	„	„	us.
ነገሯችኋል	nḁgrŏāč(č)yuhāl,	„	„	you (pl.)
ነገሯቸዋል	nḁgrŏāč(č)ḁuāl,	„	„	them (him, pol.)

---

[1] or ሰጥቼኻለሁ sḁṭi̥čč^{y}eχállḁu^h.

[2] or ሰጥቼዎታለሁ sḁṭi̥čč^{y}e^{w}otállḁu^h.

[3] or ሰጥቻታለሁ sḁṭi̥ččātállḁu^h.

[4] or ሰጥቻችኋለሁ sḁṭi̥ččāč(č)yuhállḁu^h.

[5] or ሰጥቻቸዋለሁ sḁṭi̥ččāč(č)ḁuállḁu^h.

[6] or -ኻል -χāl. [7] or ነገሮዎታል nḁgr^{w}o^{w}otāl (-r^{w}ōt-).

The Demonstrative Pronoun. §13*a*

The demonstrative pronouns are, for near objects:

sg. nom. m. **ይህ** yı̥he (yi̥h, yấhe)[1] this, that,

f. **ይህች** yı̥hi̥č (-čč) or **ይች** yi̥č (yi̥čč)[2],

acc. m. **ይህን** yı̥hän (-nn § 6) or **ይህንን** yi̥hánnän,

f. **ይችን** yı̥čči̥n,

pl. nom. **እነዚህ** (i̥)nnḁzzíh (-ấz-, -ı̥h; § 8)[3] or **እኔህ** (ı̥)nnʸếh[4] (§ 8),

acc. **እነዚህን** (i̥)nnḁzzíhi̥n (-äz-, -ı̥h-), **እኔህን** (i̥)nnʸếhi̥n.

For distant or absent objects:

sg. nom. m. **ያ** yã, that, that other,

f. **ያች** yăč (-čč),

acc. m. **ያን** yãn or **ያንን** yánnän,

f. **ያችን** yấčči̥n.

pl. nom. **እነዚያ** (i̥)nnḁ́zzyấ (-ấz-; § 8)[5], or **እኒያ** (ı̥)nnyấ (§ 8),

acc. **እነዚያን** (i̥)nnḁ́zzyấn (-ấz-; § 8), or **እኒያን** (ı̥)nnyấn (§ 8).

---

[1] § 7*d*; also written **ይኸ**; G. **እሄ** ı̥hʸe.

[2] G. **እሂች** ı̥hičč (-i̥čč), ʸi̥čč, i̥čč.

[3] or **እለዚህ** i̥llḁ́zzíh (-ấz-, -ı̥h; § 8).

[4] or **እሌህ** ı̥llʸếh, **እኒህ** (ı̥)nníh (-ı̥h; § 8), **እሊህ** ı̥llíh (-ı̥h).

[5] or **እለዚያ** i̥llḁ́zzyấ (-ấz-), **እሊያ** ı̥llyấ.

After prefixes

ይህ	becomes	-ዚህ	-zzih (-zi̥-).
ይህች	„	-ዚች	-zzi̥č (-čč).
ያ	„	-ዚያ	-zzyā̆[1].
ያች	„	ዚያች	-zzyā̆č (-čč).

[የ]ወዲህኛው (yä)wωdihi̥ññáu (-di̥h-; § 8), the nearer (of two), nearest (of several),

[የ]ወዲያኛው (yä)wωdyā́ññáu (-ωdā́- Š.; § 8), the further (of two), furthest (of several);

in these forms -ው is inflected like the article (§ 11).

All the above refer to animate or inanimate objects, and may be used substantivally or adjectivally.

ያ- may be prefixed to its noun.

E.g. ይህ ፡ ይበቃል ። yi̥he yi̥vā́qāl, this is enough.

ያች ፡ ምስቱ ፡ ናት ። yáčči̥ (§ 7*d*) mi̥stu nāt, this is (that's) his wife.

ይህ ፡ ፈረስ : yi̥he fḁ̈rḁs, this horse, that (near) horse.

ያዛፍ : yázāf, that (distant) tree.

ያን ፡ ዛፍ ፡ አትቍረጠው ። yan zāf atti̥qwúrḁṭḁu, don't cut that other tree down (that tree we saw, were speaking about, etc.).

እኔህ ፡ መጣፎች ፡ የማን ፡ ናቸው ። nnʸēh mḁṭáfʷōč yämán náččau?, whose are these books?

እነዚህ ፡ ይበልጣሉ ፡ ተነዚያ ። nnäzzi̥h yi̥vḁlṭállu ṭḁnnázzya (§ 7*a*), these are more than those (others).

---

[1] but ተያ tḁ́yā́ (§ 8) or ተዚያ tḁ́zzyā́ (§ 8), from, than, in or on that; there.

ስለዚሁ : si̥lázzi̥h (§ 8), because of this, therefore.

የዚች : ሴት : yäzzi̥čči̥ (§ 7d) sʸēt, of this woman.

እስከዚያ : i̥skḁ́zzyā́ (§ 8), as far as that, up to there.

ይሀ : ይሻላል : ተዚያ ። yi̥he yi̥ššālāl tā́zzya, this is better than that other.

የወዲሀኛው : ፈረስ : yäwωdi̥hi̥ññáu fḁ́rḁs, the nearer (-est) of those horses.

የወድያኛይቱ : ናት : yäwωdyāññái̥tu nāt, she is the further (-est) of those.

ነው

The demonstrative particle *ነ- nḁ- (nä-), look!, § 13b see! (not found alone), takes the pers. suff. conjunctive with verbs (§ 12c), and expresses the present tense of the verb 'to be' (§ 40):

sg.	1st	ነኝ	näñ (nái̥ § 7d),	I am.
	2nd m.	ነህ	nḁh (näh),	you are.
	2nd f.	ነሽ	näš,	you are.
	2nd pol.	ነዎ	nḁ́ʷo,	you are.
	3rd m.	ነው	nḁ́u,	he (it) is.
	3rd f.	ናት	nāt,	she (it) is.
pl.	1st	ነን	nän,	we are.
	2nd	ናችሁ	nā́č(č)i̥hu (nā́č(č)yuh),	you are.
	3rd	ናቸው	nā́č(č)ḁu,	they are, he (pol.) is.

The monosyllables above are enclitics (§ 8) and cause a preceding word to be accented on the last syllable.

E.g. እኔ ፡ ነኝ ። i̥nʸé näñ, it is I.

አንተ ፡ ማን ፡ ነህ ።[1] ántä mān näh?, who are you?

የኔ ፡ ነው ። yänʸé nḁ͡u, it's mine.

ራስ ፡ ደኅና ፡ ናቸው ። rās dähnā́ nā́ččḁ͡u?, is the Rās well?

§ 14 *The Relative Pronoun.*

The relative pronoun, which is always prefixed to a verb (§ 34), is, for all numbers, genders, cases and persons:

የ- yä- pref. to simp. perf. (§ 25), የም- yämm- or እም- i̥mm- pref. to cont. (§ 26)	who, which, what; see § 62.

የም- is yämmi̥- and እም- is i̥mmi̥- before a consonant (which, if t, becomes tt, § 5); እም- is mm(i̥)- after a vowel.

አለ állä (§ 32), he is present, there is, and the neg. የለም (§ 39), አይደለም (§ 40) take የ-, making

ያለ yállä (§ 7*a*), he who is present, that which there is,

የሌለ yälʸállä, he who (that which) is absent,

ያይደል yái̥däl (§ 7*a*, -ll § 6), he who (that which) is not.

The neg. pref. አል- al- (§ 37) comes between the rel. and the verb.

The relative refers to animate and inanimate objects.

The antecedent, if expressed, usually follows the

---

[1] also written ማንህ ። mā́nnäh?

verb to which the relative is attached. If no antecedent is expressed the rel. implies one of any number, gender, case or person, according, if it is in the nom., to that of the verb to which it is attached.

The rel. + verb, being tantamount to a noun, may take the -ን -n of the acc. (§ 9*c*) and the article (§ 11)[1].

E.g. የመጣ ፡ yämḁ́ṭṭa, he who (that which) came.

የመጣ ፡ ሰው ፡ yämḁṭṭā́ (§ 8) sḁ͡u, a man who came.

የመጣህ ፡ yämḁ́ṭṭāh, you who came.

የምንመጣ ፡ yämmi̥nni̥mḁ́ṭa, we who are coming.

የሚመጣ ፡ ሰው ፡ yämmi̥mḁṭā́ (§ 7*a*; § 8) sḁ͡u, a man who is coming.

የምትመጡ ፡፡ yämmi̥ttmḁ́ṭu, you (pl.) who are coming.

እርሱ ፡ ነው ፡ እሚመጣ ፡፡ i̥rsū́ nḁ͡u mmi̥mḁ́ṭa, it is he who is coming.

አንተ ፡ ነው ፡ እምትመጣ ፡፡ antā́ nḁ͡u mmi̥ttmḁ́ṭa ?, is it you who are coming?

ያለ ፡ ይበቃል ፡፡ yā́llä yi̥vḁ́qāl, what there is is enough.

የማልፈልገው ፡ ፈረስ ፡፡ yämmalfḁ́lli̥gḁ͡u (§ 7*a*) fḁ́rḁs, the horse which I do not want.

---

[1] Occasionally, especially in G. and Wallo, a pl. in -ʷōች (§ 9*b*) of the rel. + verb is heard:

የሔዶች ፡ ናቸው ፡፡ yähā́dʷōč nā́ččḁ͡u, they are those who went, = የሔዱ ፡ ናቸው ፡፡ yähā́du nā́ččḁ͡u.

የሚሔዶች ፡ ናቸው ፡፡ yämmi̥hā́dʷōč nā́ččḁ͡u, they are those who are going, = የሚሔዱ ፡ ናቸው ፡፡ yämmi̥-hā́du nā́ččḁ͡u.

የመጣን ፡ አየህ ። yämḁ́ṭṭan áyyäh?, have you seen who (what) came?

የመጣው ፡ ሰው ፡ yämḁṭṭá͡u sḁ͡u, the man who came.

የመጣውን ፡ ሰው ፡ አየሀው ። yämḁṭṭá͡un sḁ͡u áyyähḁ͡u?, have you seen the man who came?

ያለን ፡ ስጠኝ ። yállän si̥ṭäñ, give me what there is.

የመጡ ፡ yämḁ́ṭṭu, they who (those which) came.

የመጡት ፡ ፈረሶች ፡ yämḁ́ṭṭut fḁ́rḁsʷōč, the horses which came.

የመጡቱ ፡ ናቸው ። yämḁ́ṭṭutu náččḁ͡u, they are those who (which) came.

የሚመጡቱን ፡ አየህ ። yämmi̥mḁ́ṭutun áyyäh?, have you seen those who (which) are coming?

ያለበትን ፡ አላውቅም ። yallábbḁti̥n alá͡uŭqi̥m, I don't know (α) who (what) is in it, (β) the place in which he (it) is.

ያለችበቲቱ ፡ ሴት ፡ yalläčči̥bbḁtitu sʸēt, the woman who is in it.

The Interrogative Pronoun.

§ 15 The interrogative pronouns are,

referring to persons:

sg. nom. ማን mān (-nn § 6)?, who?,

acc. ማንን mánnän?,

pl. nom. ማን mān (-nn § 6)?, or እነማን (i̥)nnḁmán?[1] (-nn § 6; § 8),

acc. ማንን mánnän?, or እነማንን (i̥)nnḁmánnän?

---

[1] or እለማን i̥llḁmán? (-nn § 6; § 8)

Referring to inanimate[1] objects:

sg. nom. & acc. ምን mi̥n?, what?,
pl. nom. ምኖች mí̥nʷōč? (-čč § 6),
acc. ምኖችን mi̥nʷṓčči̥n?

ምን may take the m. art. (§ 11), and the pers. suff. conjunctive with nouns (§ 12*b*).

sg. nom. & acc. ምንድር mí̥ndi̥r?[2], what?,
pl. nom. ምንድሮች mí̥ndi̥rʷōč?[3] (-čč § 6),
acc. ምንድሮችን mi̥ndi̥rʷṓčči̥n?

ምንድር may take the m. art. (§ 11).

A pl. of ማን and ምን is also formed by repeating them with the conj. -ና -nnã = and:

pl. nom. ማንናማን mān(ni̥n)nã́mā́n?[4] (-nn; § 8), who?,
acc. ማንናማንን mān(ni̥n)nãmā́nnän?[4],
pl. nom. & acc. ምንናምን mi̥ni̥nnā́mi̥n?, what?;

these forms when used substantivally may be constr. with a pl. or sg. verb.

---

[1] also to animals and occasionally to persons:
ምን ፡ ሰው ። mi̥n sḁ͡u?, what man?
ምን ፡ ሆንህ ። mi̥n hʷonh?, what is the matter with you? (lit. what have you become?).
ፈረሲቱ ፡ ምንድን ፡ ሆነች ። fḁ́rḁsi̥tu mí̥ndi̥n hʷónäč?, what has become of (happened to) the mare?

[2] or ምንድን mí̥ndi̥n? (-nn § 6).

[3] or ምንድርኖች mí̥ndi̥rnʷōč?, ምንድኖች mí̥ndi̥nnʷōč?, (-čč § 6).

[4] The -ni̥n- is dropped in rapid speech.

Referring to animate and inanimate objects:

sg. m. nom. **ማናቸው** mānnáč(č)ḁ͡u?[1], which? (of two or more), acc. **-ቸውን** -ččḁ͡un,

f. nom. **ማናቾይቱ** mānnáč(č)ʷo͡i̥tu?, acc. **-ቱን** -tun,

pl. nom. **ማናቸዎች** mānnáč(č)ḁ͡uʷōč?[2] (**-ቾዎች** -ččʷoʷōč; -čč § 6), acc. **-ችን** -ččḭn.

sg. m. nom. **ዮቱ** yĕ́tu?[3], which? (of two or more), acc. **-ቱን** -tun,

f. nom. **ዮቷ** yĕ́twā̃?[4], acc. **-ቷን** -twā̃n,

pl. nom. **እኔቱ** (i̥)nnʸĕ́tu?[5], acc. **-ቱን** -tun.

---

[1] or **ማንላቸው** mānni̥lláččḁ͡u?, f. **ማንላቾይቱ** mānni̥lláččʷo͡i̥tu?, etc.

[2] or **ማናቾቹ** mānnāččʷŏ́čču?, **ማንላቾቹ** mānni̥llāččʷŏ́čču?, acc. **-ቹን** -ččun,

or **ማኖቻቸው** mānnʷōččáččḁ͡u?,

ማንሎቻቸው mānni̥llʷōččáččḁ͡u?,

ማናቻቸው mānnāččáččḁ͡u?,

ማንላቻቸው mānni̥llāččáččḁ͡u?,

ማናቾቻቸው mānnāččʷōččáččḁ͡u?,

ማንላቾቻቸው mānni̥llāččʷōččáččḁ͡u?,

all with acc. **-ቸውን** -ččḁ͡un.

[3] also written **የቱ** etc., G. **ሀቱ** hḁtu?

[4] or **የቲቷ** yĕ́titwā̃? (-ti̥t-). G. **ሀቲቱ** hḁtitu?, **ሀቷ** hḁtwā̃?

[5] or **እኔቶች** (i̥)nnʸĕ́tʷōč? (-čč; **-ቶቹ** -tʷŏ́čču), acc. **-ቶችን** -tʷŏ́ččḭn (**-ቶቹን** -tʷŏ́ččun);

G. **ሀቶች** hḁtʷōč? (-čč), acc. **-ቶችን** -tʷŏ́ččḭn, or **እነሀቱ** (i̥)nnḁhḁtu? acc. **-ቱን** -tun.

ዬትኛው yĕti̥ññau?[1] (§ 8), which?, what kind of?, of which -ው is inflected like the art. (§ 11)[2].

ስንት si̥nt?, how much?, how many?, is indecl., and usually constr. with a sg. noun or verb, sometimes with the pl.

All the above are used substantivally or adjectivally, except ምንድር, ማንናማን and ምንናምን, which are only used substantivally.

E.g. ማን ፡ ነው ። mān nḁu?[3], who is it?

ማነን ፡ አየህ ። mánnän áyyäh?, whom did you see?

ለማን ፡ ሰጠህ ። lḁmán sḁ́ṭṭäh?, whom did you give it (them) to?

ማን ፡ ሰው ፡ ነው ፡ እሚያደርገው ። mān sḁ́u nḁu mmyādḁ́rgḁu?, what man is it that will do it? (who is the man that ...?).

እነማን ፡ ናቸው ። nnḁmán náččḁu?, who are they?

ማን ፡ ናችሁ ። mān náččyuh?, who are you (pl.)?

ማን ፡ አሉ ። mānn állu?, who are present?

ማንናማን ፡ መጣ ። mānni̥nnāmán (§ 8) mḁ́ṭṭa? (or መጡ mḁ́ṭṭu), who have come?

ማንናማነን ፡ አየህ ። mānni̥nnāmánnän áyyäh?, what persons did you see?

ምን ፡ አለ ። mi̥n állä?, what is there?

ምን ፡ አለ ። mi̥n álḁ?, what did he say?

---

[1] also written የትኛው

G. ሀትኛው hḁ́ti̥ññau? (§ 8).

[2] it may be dropped in the pl. የትኞች yĕti̥ññōč (-čč)?, acc. -ኞችን -ññóččči̥n.

[3] also written ማነው.

ምን ፡ ጊዜ ፡ ላምጣው ። mi̥ṅ gí̥z^{y}e lā́nṭa͡u? (§ 7*d*), what time shall I bring it?

ይህ ፡ ለኔ ፡ ምኔ ፡ ነው ። yí̥he lḁn^{y}é mi̥n^{y}é nḁ͡u?, what use is this to me?

ምኑን ፡ ላምጣ ። mí̥nun lā́nṭa?, what shall I bring?

ምንድር ፡ ነው ። mi̥ndí̥r (§ 8) nḁ͡u?, what is it?

ምንድን ፡ ነበር ። mí̥ndi̥n nḁ́bbḁr?, what was it?

ምንድን ፡ አየህ ። mí̥ndi̥n áyyäh?, what have you seen?

ምንድሮችን ፡ አየህ ። mi̥ndi̥r^{w}ŏčči̥n áyyäh?, what objects did you see?

ገበያ ፡ እሔዳለኍ ፤ ምንናምን ፡ ልግዛ ። gḁ́vḁ͡i̥a i̥hädállḁ͡u^{h}: mi̥ni̥nnámi̥n lí̥gza?, I am going to market: what things shall I buy?

የማናቸው ፡ ፈረስ ፡ ነው ። yämānnáččḁ͡u (§ 47*a*) fḁrḁ́s (§ 8) nḁ͡u?, which man's horse is it?

ማንላቸው ፡ ፈረስ ፡ mānni̥lláččḁ͡u fḁ́rḁs?, which horse?

ማናቾይቱ ፡ በቅሎ ፡ ናት ። mānnāčč^{w}ó͡i̥tu yḁql^{w}ŏ (§ 8) nāt?, which (she-) mule is it?

ዮቱ ፡ ነበር ። yĕ́tu nḁ́bbär?, which was it?

የቱ ፡ ሰው ፡ ነበር ። yĕ́tu sḁ́͡u nḁ́bbär?, which man was it?

የየቷ ፡ ሴት ፡ ልጅ ፡ ነው ። yäyētwá̄ (§ 8) s^{y}ēt li̥j nḁ͡u?, which woman's child is it?

ቤቱ ፡ ዮትኛው ፡ ነው ። b^{y}ĕ́tu yeti̥ññá͡u (§ 8) nḁ͡u?, which is his house?

የትኛው ፡ ፈረስ ፡ yetí̥ñña͡u (§ 8) fḁ́rḁs?, which horse?, what kind of horse?

ስንት ፡ አለ ። si̥nt állä?, how much is there?

ስንት ፡ አሉ ። si̥nt állu?, how many are there?

ስንት ፡ ገንዘብ ፡ ነበር ። si̥nt gḁ́nzḁy nḁ́bbḁr?, how much money was there?

ስንት ፡ ፈረስ ፡ መጣ ። si̥nt fḁ́rḁs mḁ́ṭṭa?, or

ስንት ፡ ፈረሶች ፡ መጡ ። si̥nt fḁ́rḁsʷōč mḁ́ṭṭu?, how many horses have come?

ምንኛ mi̥ní̥ññā?, prop. what kind of?, is generally used as an intensive adv., how! ምን may also be used in this way (§ 77; s.v. አከለ):

e.g. ምንኛ ፡ ሞኝ ፡ ነው ። mi̥ní̥ñña mʷóññi̥ nḁu!, how foolish he is!

ምን ፡ ትልቅ ፡ ነው ። mi̥n ti̥llí̥q nḁu!, how big it is!

The Indefinite Pronoun.

The indefinite pronouns are, § 16

referring to animate objects:

sg. nom. ማንም mḁ́nni̥m (-mm § 6), some(-body), any (-body),

acc. ማነንም mḁ́nnäni̥m (-mm),

pl. nom. እነማንም (i̥)nnḁmḁ́nni̥m (-mm),

acc. እነማነንም (i̥)nnḁmḁ́nnäni̥m (-mm).

Referring to persons:

sg. nom. እንተን (í̥)ntḁn (-än)[1], what's-his-name,

acc. እንተነን (í̥)ntäni̥n[2],

pl. nom. እንተኖች (í̥)ntḁnʷōč (-tä-; -čč § 6)[3],

acc. እንተኖችን (i̥)ntḁnʷōčči̥n (-tä-);

these forms may take the art. (§ 11).

---

[1] or እንቶ (í̥)ntʷō, እንቶን (í̥)ntʷōn.

[2] or እንቶን (í̥)ntʷōn.

[3] or እነንተን (i̥)nnḁ́ntḁn (-än), with art. -ኑ -nu, acc. እነንተነን (i̥)nnḁ́ntäni̥n, with art. -ኑን -nun; this pl. is also used of inanimate objects.

sg. nom. እገሌ i̥g̥ál̥^{y}e[1], so-and-so,

acc. እገሌን i̥g̥ál̥^{y}en,

pl. nom. እነገሌ (i̥)nnḁg̥ál̥^{y}e[2],

acc. እነገሌን (i̥)nnḁg̥ál̥^{y}en.

Referring to inanimate objects:

sg. nom. & acc. ምንም mi̥ni̥m (-mm § 6), anything,

" " ምንምን mi̥nímmi̥n, anything at all.

sg. nom. & acc. እንትን (í̥)nti̥n, what's-its-name,

pl. nom. እንትኖች (i̥)nti̥n^{w}ōč (-čč § 6)[3],

acc. እንትኖችን (i̥)nti̥n^{w}ṓčči̥n;

these forms may take the art. (§ 11).

Referring to animate or inanimate objects:

sg. nom. ማናቸውም mānnắč(č)ḁ͡um (-mm § 6)[4], some (-body), any(-body), one of the,

acc. ማናቸውንም mānnāččḁ́͡unni̥m (-mm),

pl. nom. ማናቾችም mānnāčč^{w}ṓčči̥m (-mm),

acc. ማናቾችንም mānnāčč^{w}ṓčči̥ni̥m (-mm).

The pl. of this form is constr. with a sg. or pl. noun.

---

[1] G. የከሌ yäkál̥^{y}e, acc. -ን -n; የ- (q.v.) is dropped after a prp.

[2] G. እናከሌ (i̥)nnākál̥^{y}e, acc. -ን -n.

[3] or nom. & acc. እንንትን (i̥)ní̥nti̥n.

[4] or ማንላቸውም mānni̥llắč(č)ḁ͡um (-mm), etc.

sg. nom. & acc. አንዳች ándắč (-čč § 6; § 8)[1], some (-body); any (-body); one of the.

sg. nom. አንዳቸው andắč(č)ḁu[2], some (-body); any (-body); one of the,

acc. አንዳቸውን andắč(č)ḁun.

sg. nom. & acc. አንዳንድ ándánd (§ 8), some, a few, several,

pl. nom. አንዳንዶች andánd^{w}ōč (-čč § 6),

acc. አንዳንዶችን andand^{w}ṓččịn.

sg. nom. አያሌ ayyál^{y}e[3], several; much, a good deal, a great many; what a lot!, how many!

acc. አያሌን ayyál^{y}en,

pl. nom. አያሎች ayyál^{w}ōč (-čč § 6),

acc. አያሎችን ayyāl^{w}ṓččịn.

አያሌ is constr. with a sg. or pl. noun.

sg. nom. & acc. ሌላ lélă, other, another, different,

pl. nom. ሌሎች lél^{w}ōč (-čč § 6),

acc. ሌሎችን lēl^{w}ṓččịn;

with the art. (§ 11), ሌላው lélau, the other.

---

1 or አንዳችም andắččịm (-mm § 6).

2 or አንዲላቸው andịllắč(č)ḁu, acc. -ቸውን -č(č)ḁun,
አንዳቸውም andắč(č)ḁum (-mm), acc. -ቸውንም -č(č)ắunnịm (-mm),
አንዲላቸውም andịllắč(č)ḁum (-mm), acc. -ቸውንም -č(č)ắunnịm (-mm).

3 or አያል áyyál (§ 8).

ሁሉ- hull-, all, every,
with the pers. suff. (§ 12*b*), in addition to which it may take -ም -m (-mm § 6);
with -u it may be constr. with pl. noun; it generally follows a noun it qualifies.

Of the above,

እንተን, እገሌ, ምንም, ምንምን, እንትን are used substantively,

እያሌ is used adjectivally,

and the rest are used in either way.

እንዳች, እንዳቸው and the forms in -ም are generally (ምንም, ምንምን always) followed by a neg. verb (§ 37), which drops its own final -ም, if the pron. has one.

E.g.

ለማንም ፡ ስጥ ። ḽamānnḽm (§ 8) sḽṭ, give it to somebody.

ማንም ፡ የለ ። mánnḽmm yállä (-mmʸállä § 7*d*), there isn't anybody.

ማንም ፡ ፈረስ ፡ አይሒድ ። mánnḽm fḁrḁs ái͡ḥḽd, no horse is to go, (lit. any horse let-it-not-go).

ማንንም ፡ አላየህ ። mánnänḽmm aláyyäh?, didn't you see anybody?

ምንም ፡ አላየሁ ። mḽnḽmm aláyyä͡uʰ, I didn't see anything.

ምንምን ፡ አልነበር ። mḽnḽ́mmḽn alnḁ́bbär, it (there) wasn't anything at all.

እንትን ፡ አምጣ ። ńṭḽn ánṭa, fetch a what's-its-name, (e.g. something for the name of which one does not know the Amharic).

ለገሌ ፡ ስጥ ። lḁgḁl^{y}e (§ 7*a*) sḭṭ, G. ለከሌ ፡ ስጥ ። lḁkḁl^{y}e sḭṭ, give it (them) to so-and-so.

ለማናቸውም ፡ አትስጥ ። lḁmānnáččḁ͡umm áttḭsṭ, don't give it (them) to anyone (of them).

ማንላቸውንም ፡ አላየሁ ። mānnḭllāččá͡ḁunnḭmm aláyyä͡u^{h}, I didn't see anyone (of them).

ማንላቾችንም ፡ ፈረሶች ፡ [or ፈረስ ፡] አላየሁ ። mānnḭllāč-č^{w}óččḭnḭm fḁrḁs^{w}ōčč (or fḁrḁs) aláyyä͡u^{h}, I didn't see any of the horses.

ለማናቸውም ፡ አሽከር ፡ ስጥ ። lḁmānnáččḁ͡umm aškär (§ 8) sḭṭ, give it (them) to one of the servants.

አንዳች ፡ አላየሁም ። andáčč aláyyähum, or

አንዳችም ፡ አላየሁ ። andáččḭmm aláyyä͡u^{h}, I didn't see any.

አንዳቸውን ፡ ጥሩ ። andáččḁ͡un ḭra, call one of them.

አንዳቸውን ፡ አሽከር ፡ ጥሩ ። andáččḁ͡un áškär ṭḭra, call one of the servants.

አንዳንድ ፡ ሰው ፡ andánd sḁ͡u, a few people.

አንዳንድ ፡ አየሁ ። andánd áyyä͡u^{h}, I saw some.

አንዳንዶች ፡ ሴቶች ። andánd^{w}ōč s^{y}ét^{w}ōč, several women.

እያሌ ፡ እቃ ፡ ayyál^{y}e ḭqa, a good deal of baggage.

እያሌ ፡ ሰዎች ፡ ናቸው ። ayyál^{y}e sḁ͡u^{w}óč náččḁ͡u, they are a good many men, what a lot of men there are!

ሌላ ፡ ጥሩ ። léla ṭḭra, call another.

ሌላውን ፡ ጥሩ ። léla͡un ṭḭra, call the other.

ሌላ ፡ ፈረስ ፡ አሳዩኝ ። léla fḁrḁs asáyyäñ, show me another horse.

ሌላውን ፡ ፈረስ ፡ አምጣ ። lé̥la͡un fḁrḁs ánṭa (§ 7*d*), bring the other horse.

ሁሉ ፡ húllu, all of it.

ሁሉም ፡ húllum, everything.

ይህ ፡ ሁሉ ፡ ነው ። yi̥he húllu nḁ͡u, this is all.

ተሁሉም ፡ አገር ፡ ነው ። tḁhúllumm agä́r nḁ͡u, it is everywhere, (in every part of the country).

ሁሉን ፡ አልፈልግም ። húllun alfḁlli̥gi̥m, I don't want it all.

ሁሉንም ፡ አልፈልግ ። húlluni̥mm alfḁlli̥g, I don't want any of it.

ሁሉን ፡ ስጠው ። húllun sí̥ṭa͡u, give him all of it.

ሁሉንም ፡ ስጠው ። húlluni̥m sí̥ṭa͡u, give him everything.

ገንዘቡ ፡ ሁሉ ። gḁ́nzḁvu húllu, all the money.

ሳጥኖችን ፡ ሁሉ ፡ አምጣ ። sāṭi̥nʷőčči̥n húllu ánṭa (§ 7*d*), bring all the boxes.

ሁላችን ፡ አለን ። hulláčči̥n állän, we are all here.

ሒዱ ፡ ሁላችሁ ። hí̥du hulláččyuh, go away, all of you.

ወታደር ፡ ሁሉ ፡ ሔደ ። wωttáddär húllu hä́dä, or

ወታደር ፡ ሁሉ ፡ ሔዱ ። wωttáddär húllu hä́du, or

ወታደሮች ፡ ሁሉ ፡ ሔዱ ። wωttáddḁrʷōč húllu hä́du, or

ወታደሮች ፡ ሁላቸው ፡ ሔዱ ። wωttáddḁrʷōč hulláččḁ͡u hä́du, all the soldiers have gone.

The Reflexive Pronoun.

For the reflexive pronoun the words § 17

ራስ rās, lit. head,

ነፍስ nḁfs (nä-, -vs), lit. soul,

ባለቤት bālḁb^{y}ét (-ḁy̥-), lit. householder,

ሰውነት sḁ͡unnḁt (-ät), lit. person,

and the phrase

በገዛ ፡ እጅ ፡ bḁgḁzzájj (§ 8), lit. with what the hand has in its power (s.v. ገዛ)

are used with the pers. suff. (§ 12*b*) to express 'self', when it is not expressed with sufficient clearness or emphasis by the reflexive form of the verb (§ 21).

The above refer only to persons, and are used substantivally or adjectivally:

e.g.

ራሱን ፡ ገደለ ። rásun gáddḁlḁ, he killed himself.

የሀነንስ ፡ እርስዎ ፡ ራስዎ ፡ ይፈልጉታል ። yi̥hánnäni̥ss i̥rsḁ́^{w}o rásḁ^{w}o yi̥fálli̥gutāl, but you (pol.) will want this yourself.

ይሀ ፡ ለራሳችን ፡ ነው ። yi̥he lḁrāsāččin (§ 8) nḁ͡u, this is for us ourselves.

ነፍሴን ፡ እላጫለሁ ። náv s^{y}en i̥lāččállḁ͡u^h, I shave myself, (or ሰውነቴን ፡ እላ- sḁ͡unnät^{y}en i̥lā-).

ራስ ፡ ባለቤታቸው ፡ አልነበሩም ። rās y̥ālḁy̥^{y}ētáččḁ͡u alnábbḁrum, the Rās himself wasn't there.

በገዛ ፡ እጄ ፡ እመጣለሁ ። bḁgḁzzájj^{y}e i̥mḁtállḁ͡u^h, I will come myself.

በገዛ ፡ እጃቸው ፡ አደረጉት ። bḁgḁzzajjáččḁu adḁ́rrḁgut, they did it themselves.

በገዛ ፡ እጅ- is perhaps an emphatic personal rather than a true reflexive pronoun.

The Distributive Pronoun.

§ 18 The distributive pronouns are:

አንዳንድ ándánd (§ 8), indecl., each, one by one, (cp. § 83*a*),

እየ-...-u, iyyä-[1]...-u (written -ው after a vowel), indecl., each; -u is dropped after numerals, or may be replaced by pers. suff. (§ 12*b*).

The above refer to animate or inanimate objects; they are used adjectivally[2]; they may take the pers. suff. of the 1st and 2nd pl. (§ 12*b*, -u disappearing), in which case አንዳንድ may be used substantivally. They do not always logically refer to the noun with which they are constructed.

E.g. ለሁሉ ፡ አንዳንድ ፡ ብር ፡ ስጣቸው ። lḁhúllu andándi̥ (§ 7*d*) yi̥rr si̥ṭáččḁu, give them all a dollar each.

ላንዳንድ ፡ ወታደር ፡ አምሳ ፡ ጥይት ፡ አካፍል ። landánd (§ 7*a*) wɷttáddär ámsa ṭíyyi̥t akkáfi̥l, distribute fifty cartridges to each soldier.

አንዳንዳችንን ፡ ጠየቁን ። andandáčči̥ni̥n ṭáyyäqunnḁ, they questioned each of us.

አንዳንዳችሁ ፡ ሒዱ ። andandáččyuh hi̥du, go one at a time.

---

[1] also written ኢየ-

[2] i.e. in constr.: logically they may be substantival.

እየቤቱ፡ iyyäỵʸétu, each house.

እየራሱ፡ በቅሎውን፡ ያምጣ። iyyärásu ỵḁ́qlʷo͡un yámṭa, each is to bring his mule himself.

እየሴቱ፡ ልጅዋን፡ ታንሣ። iyyäsʸétu lí̥jwān tánsa, let each woman take up her child.

እየሳጥኑ፡ ከፈተ። iyyäsáṭi̥nu kḁ́ffḁtḁ, he opened each box.

በየስሙ፡ ይመልስ። bḁyyási̥mu (§ 7*a*) yi̥málli̥s, or

በየስማቸው፡ ይመልሱ። bḁyyäsi̥máččḁ͡u yi̥málli̥su, let each answer to his name.

አሥር፡ በየሶስት፡ ብር፡ ássi̥r ỵḁyyäsʷőstɨ̥ ỵi̥rr, ten at three dollars each.

እየቤታችሁ፡ ሒዱ። iyyäỵʸētáččyuh hí̥du, each of you go to his (own) house.

The Reciprocal Pronoun.

The reciprocal pronoun is § 19

እርሳ በርስ- í̥rsḁ[1] bḁrs-[2] (ỵḁ-, -ärs-), with the pl. pers. suff. (§ 12*b*), each other.

This pron. refers to animate or inanimate objects, and is used substantivally or adjectivally.

The pl. of the disjunctive pers. pron. (§ 12*a*) or the dem. pron. (§ 13*a*) repeated, with በ- bḁ- pref. to the second pron., is used in the same sense.

E.g. እርሳ፡ በርሳችን፡ ተጣላን። í̥rsḁ ỵärsáčči̥n tḁṭállān, or እኛ፡ በኛ፡ ተጣላን። i̥ññá ỵäññá tḁṭállān, we have quarrelled with each other.

---

[1] or እርስ i̥rs, እሳ í̥ssḁ, እስ i̥ss.

[2] or በስ- bḁss- (ỵḁ-, -äss-).

እርስ ፡ በርሳችሁ ፡ አተጣሉ ። i̥rs ỵärsáččyuh attḁṭálu, don't quarrel with each other.

ሳጥኖች ፡ እርሰ ፡ በርሳቸው ፡ ይጋጫሉ ። sáṭi̥nʷōčč i̥rsḁ bärsáččḁu yi̥ggāč̣č̣állu, the boxes knock against each other.

እነዚህ ፡ በነዚህ ፡ ተጋብተዋል ። nnäzzí̥h ỵḁnnäzzíh tḁgáỵtḁuāl, these and those are connected with each other by marriage.

The Numeral.

The Cardinal Numeral.

§ 20*a* The cardinal numerals are:

Cypher		
፩	አንድ and[1],	1.
፪	ሁለት húlḁtt (-ätt),	2.
፫	ሶስት sʷōst,	3.
፬	አራት árā́tt (§ 8),	4.
፭	አምስት ámmi̥st,	5.
፮	ስድስት sí̥ddi̥st,	6.
፯	ሰባት sḁbā́t (-ḁ́ỵ-; § 8),	7.
፰	ስምንት sí̥mmi̥nt,	8.
፱	ዘጠኝ zḁ́ṭḁñ (-ā́ṭä-),	9.
፲	አሥር ássi̥r,	10.
፲፩	አሥራ ፡ ሐንድ asrāhánd[2],	11.
፲፪	አሥራ ፡ ሁለት asrāhúlḁtt (-ätt),	12.
፳	ሀያ hḁ́ʸā (hḁ́ā)[3],	20.

[1] f. አንዲት ándi̥t.

[2] or አሥራንድ asrā́nd.

[3] Š. ሀያ háʸa, háā, ሃ hā.

፳፩	ሀያ፡ሐንድ hḁʸahánd[1],	21.
፴	ሠላሳ sḁlā́sã,	30.
፵	አርባ árbã (-ry̥-),	40.
፶	አምሳ ámsã,	50.
፷	ስልሳ sí̥lsã[2],	60.
፸	ሰባ sḁ́bã (-ḁ́y̥-),	70.
፹	ሰማንያ sḁmā́nyã,	80.
፺	ዘጠና zḁṭḁ́nã (zä-; § 8),	90.
፻	መቶ mḁ́tʷõ,	100.
፪፻	ሁለት፡መቶ húlḁtt mḁ́tʷo,	200.
፲፻	ሽህ ši̥h[3],	1000.
፼	እልፍ i̥lf,	10,000.
፲፼	አሥር፡እልፍ ássi̥r i̥lf,	100,000.
፻፼	መቶ፡እልፍ mḁ́tʷo i̥lf,	1,000,000.

ተ- tḁ- may be used to join numbers above 99:

መቶ፡ታንድ[4] mḁ́tʷo tand or መቶ፡አንድ[5] mḁ́tʷo and, 101.

መቶ፡ተስልሳ mḁ́tʷo tḁsí̥lsa or መቶ፡ስልሳ mḁ́tʷo sí̥lsa, 160.

The cardinals are used substantivally or adjectivally.

With animate objects they take the sg. or pl. from 2 to 99, usually the sg. above 99; with inanimate

---

[1] or ሀያ፡አንድ hḁʸaánd, (-ʸā́nd).

[2] or, occasionally, the T. forms ስድሳ sí̥dsã, ስሳ sí̥ssã.

[3] or ሺ ši̥. [4] or ተሐንድ tḁhánd. [5] or ሐንድ hand.

objects the sg. or pl. from 2 to 9, usually the sg. above 9:

e.g. ሁለት ፡ ፈረስ ፡ húlätt fḁ̊rḁs, or ሁለት ፡ ፈረሶች ፡ húlätt fḁ̊rḁsʷōč, 2 horses.

ሁለት ፡ ልጅ ፡ አላት ። hulắtt (§ 8) li̥j állāt, she has two children.

ስልሳ ፡ ሰው ፡ si̥lsā́ (§ 8) sḁu͡, or ስልሳ ፡ ሰዎች ፡ sí̥lsa sḁ́u͡ʷōč, 60 men.

መቶ ፡ በቅሎ ፡ mḁ́tʷo ɣḁ́qlʷo, 100 mules.

አምስት ፡ ሳጥን ፡ ámmi̥st sā́ṭi̥n, or አምስት ፡ ሳጥኖች ፡ ámmi̥st sā́ṭi̥nʷōč, 5 boxes.

አምሳ ፡ ሳጥን ፡ ámsa sā́ṭi̥n, 50 boxes.

The Ordinal Numeral.

§ 20*b* The ordinal numerals are formed from the cardinals by the suffix -ḁ̊ኛ[1] -ḁ̊ññã (-ā́ññã):

e.g. ሁለተኛ hulḁttḁ́ññã (-lä-, -ā́ñ-)[2], 2nd,

ሶስተኛ sʷōstḁ́ññã (-ā́ñ-), 3rd,

ሀያኛ hḁʸáññã[3], 20th, etc.

1st is ፊተኛ fitḁ́ññã (fi̥-, -ā́ñ-), or

መጀመሪያ mḁjḁmmḁ́ryã (-ā́r-); but

አሥራ ፡ ሐንደኛ asrahandḁ́ññã (-ā́ñ-), 11th.

In compound numbers only the last takes the ordinal form:

e.g. ሠላሳ ፡ አምስተኛ sḁlása ammi̥stáññã, 35th.

---

[1] or -ኛ -ññã.

[2] or ሁለትኛ hulḁttí̥ññã (-lä-), ሶስትኛ sʷōstí̥ññã, etc.

[3] or ሀየኛ hḁʸáññã.

All ordinals commonly take the art. (§ 11), and **ፊተኛ** and **መጀመሪያ** also the pref. **የ-** yä-:

e.g. **የፊተኛው ፡ ሰው ።** yäfi̥täññáu (§ 8) sḁu, the first man.

የመጀመሪያው ፡ ነበር ። yämḁjḁmmáryau nḁ́bbär, he (it) was the first.

Another ordinal form is in **-ያ** -(í̆)yyã[1]:

ሁለትያ hulḁttíyyã (-lä-), 2nd, etc.

The Fraction.

Fractions are expressed by the ordinals, usually § 20c
by the form in **-ያ**:

e.g. **ሁለት ፡ ሶስትያ**[2]: húlätt sʷōstíyyã, 2/3.

1/2 is **እኩል** í̥kkul (ŭ́k-), usually adj., or

እኩሌታ i̥kkulʸétã (ŭk-), s.

1/4 is **ሩብ** rub (ruv̩), or **አራትኛ** arãttí̥ññã.

Fractions are joined to whole numbers by **ተ-**:

e.g. **አንድ ፡ ተኩል** and tḁ́kkul, 1 1/2.

THE VERB.

Primitive Form of Verb (Root).

The primitive verb in its simplest form, which is § 21
the third person singular of the past[3], consists in three radicals or root-letters[4]:

---

[1] or sắli̥s + **ያ** (§ 7*a*), **ሁለቲያ**, etc. [2] or **-ቲያ.**

[3] called simple perfect (§ 24).

[4] using 'letter' in the Am. sense of a consonant, single or double (§ 5), with its following vowel (§ 4*a*).

ለቀመ lḁ́-qqḁ-mḁ[1], to pick[2], gather.

ፈለገ fḁ́-llḁ-gḁ, to seek, want.

The consonant of the 2nd[3] radical is doubled (§ 5). In some verbs (type A § 34) it remains single in certain parts of their conjugation; in others (type B § 35) it is doubled throughout[4].

Some verbs, e.g. መሰለ, follow both types, but with a different meaning in each case; others, e.g. ተቀመጠ, follow either type without change of meaning.

The triliteral is the commonest root-form, but there are also quadriliteral verbs[5]:

መነዘረ mḁ-nḁ́-zzḁ-rḁ, to change,

ከለከለ kḁ-lḁ́-kkḁ-la, to hinder,

with 3rd rad. doubled: and numerous biliteral verbs,

---

[1] corresponding in form but not in force with Ar. قتّل. A perf. corresponding with قتل does not occur in Amharic, unless in such biliterals as ዞረ zʷōrḁ (for *ዘወረ zḁ́wḁrḁ) to revolve, which has caus. ዘወረ zḁ́wwḁrḁ (zḁ́͡uwḁrḁ), to cause to revolve. See Guidi, Coniug. pp. 246—251.

[2] lit. 'he picked'; this root-form being, so to speak, the 'name' of the verb is conveniently represented by our infinitive, which is the Eng. 'name' of a verb.

[3] rarely the 3rd: ዘገየ zḁgḁ́yyä, to be late.

[4] There is nothing, on the face of it, to show which type a verb follows in its conjugation; type B is commonly transitive (Guidi, Coniug. p. 247); type A may be either transitive or intransitive.

[5] A few verbs have more than four radicals,

e.g. አውደለደለ a͡udḁlḁ́ddḁlḁ, to be idle.

most of which are triliteral roots which have lost a rad.:

ጣፈ ṭá-fḁ, to write, (cp. Eth. ጸሐፈ.),

መጣ mḁ́-ṭṭã, to come, (cp. Eth. መጽአ),

ሰማ sḁ́-mmã, to hear, (cp. Eth. ሰምዐ).

Derived Forms of Verb.

From the primitive form others are derived[1], of § 22a
which the commonest are:

(α) Passive or Reflexive, formed by prefixing ተ- tḁ-[2]:

ተለቀመ tḁlḁ́qqḁmḁ, to be picked,

አጠበ áṭṭḁbḁ (-ỵḁ), to wash, ታጠበ táṭṭḁbḁ (-ỵḁ; § 7a), to be washed, wash oneself,

ተመነዘረ tḁmḁnḁ́zzḁrḁ, to be changed,

ተጣፈ tḁṭḁ́fḁ, to be written,

ተሰማ tḁsḁ́mmã, to be heard.

(β) Causative formed by prefixing አ- a-, expressing causation or effectuation of the action or state of the primitive verb:

አለቀመ alḁ́qqḁmḁ, to take (animals) to pasture;

from ቀረበ qḁ́rrḁbḁ (-ỵḁ), to be near,

አቀረበ aqḁ́rrḁbḁ (-ỵa), to bring near;

from ለሰለሰ lḁsḁ́llḁsa, to be soft,

አለሰለሰ alḁsḁ́llḁsḁ, to render soft;

አመጣ amḁ́ṭṭã, to fetch, bring.

---

1 No single verb occurs in all the possible derived forms; some verbs occur only in certain derived forms, the primitive form not occurring.

2 Cp. تقتّل.

(γ) Causative formed by prefixing አስ- as-, expressing causation, effectuation, or permission of the action or state, usually by the employment of other persons (§ 68):

አስለቀመ aslḁ́qqḁmḁ, to cause or allow to pick or be picked, have (a thing) gathered;

አስከለከለ askḁlḁ́kkḁlḁ, to cause or allow to hinder or be hindered;

አስመጣ asmḁ́ṭṭã, to cause or allow to come, import.

The causative of verbs with 1st rad. አ is formed by አስ-:

አለፈ állḁfḁ, to pass,

አሳለፈ asállḁfḁ, to cause or allow to pass.

Less Common Derived Forms of Verb.

§ 22b (δ) A form with ã preceding the doubled rad.[1]:

ዳመጠ dámmḁṭḁ, to gin (cotton);

ቀለቀለ qḁlḁ́qqḁlḁ, and

ቀላቀለ qḁlã́qqḁlḁ, to mix;

ላጨ lã́čči, to shave.

(ε) Passive or reflexive of (δ): this often has a relative or reciprocal force[2]:

ተዳመጠ tḁdámmḁṭḁ, to be ginned;

ወደደ wǽddḁdḁ, to like,

ተዋደዱ tḁwáddḁdu[3], to like each other, agree;

ተቀላቀለ tḁqḁlã́qqḁlḁ, to be mixed;

---

[1] Cp. قَاتَلَ; but in Am. this form has a primitive not a derived force; see Guidi, Coniug. p. 252.

[2] Cp. تَقَاتَلَ. [3] pl. (§ 34), as commonly used.

ተላጨ taḻáčča, to be shaved, to shave oneself;

or indicates a habit:

ነከሰ naḻkkaḻsa̱, to bite,

ተናከሰ ta̱nǟkka̱sa̱, to have or acquire the habit of biting.

(ζ) Causative (γ) of (δ) in አስ- of which s is assimilated to the next consonant: often with relative or distributive force:

አላቀመ allǟqqa̱ma̱[1], pick with others, help to pick;

ከፈለ ká̱ffa̱la̱, to divide,

አከፈለ akkǟffa̱la̱[2], to divide among others, distribute;

ሰነበተ sa̱ná̱bba̱ta̱, to remain,

አሰናበተ assa̱nǟbba̱ta̱, to dismiss[3].

(η) Reiterative, (and thence Intensive or the reverse), formed by interposing the single consonant of the doubled rad., with the vowel ǟ, before that rad.:

ለቃቀመ la̱qǟqqa̱ma̱, to pick a little here and there, pick out, select;

ፈላለገ fa̱lǟlla̱ga̱, to make a slight search for;

ሰበረ sá̱bba̱ra̱, to break,

ሰባበረ sa̱bǟbba̱ra̱ (-a̱yǟ-), to break to pieces, smash;

ገለበጠ ga̱lá̱bba̱ta̱, to turn over,

ገለባበጠ ga̱la̱bǟbba̱ta̱ (-a̱yǟ-), to turn right over, turn over and over;

---

[1] for አስላ- aslǟ-. [2] for አስከ- askǟ-.

[3] here, as in other cases, the connection between the forces of the primitive and derived forms is not clear.

ፈጀ fą̊jjä, to destroy,

ፈጃጀ fąją̈jjä, to destroy utterly.

(θ) Passive or reflexive of (η):

ተለቃቀመ tąląqą̈qqąmą, be picked out here and there, selected,

ተሰባበረ tąsąbą̈bbąrą (-ąyą̈-), be broken to pieces, smashed,

ተገለባበጠ tągąląbą̈bbątą (-ąyą̈-), be turned over and over, completely disarranged.

(ι) Causative of (η) in አ-:

አለቃቀመ aląqą̈qqąmą, cause to pick a little, send to pasture.

(κ) Causative of (η) in አስ- of which s is assimilated to the next consonant; cp. (ζ), to which this form is often equivalent:

አለቃቀመ alląqą̈qqąmą, pick with others, help to pick,

አገለባበጠ aggąląbą̈bbątą (-ąyą̈-), to cause or allow to be completely disarranged, (§ 68).

(λ) Causative of passive or reflexive[1], usually in verbs with 1st rad. 'a' or 'ha':

አወቀ áuwωqą, to know,

አስታወቀ astáuwωqą, to inform.

(μ) A form (usually quadriliteral) with pref. አን- an- (active):

አንጠለጠለ antąlą́ttąlą, to suspend.

---

[1] Cp. إِسْتَقْتَلَ but see Guidi, Coniug. pp. 259, 260.

(ν) Reflexive or passive (usually of quadriliteral root), in ተን- tḁn-:

ተንጠለጠለ tḁnṭḁlḁ́ṭṭḁlḁ, to be suspended.

Voice.

There are no special forms for the voices other than the derived forms given in § 22. § 23*a*

If an English transitive verb is rendered by an Amharic verb in its primitive form, a passive is supplied by the derivative in ተ- (§ 22*a*, α); if the Am. verb is in a causative form (§ 22*a*, β), a passive may generally be supplied by its primitive form:

e.g. to seek: ፈለገ fḁ́llḁgḁ,

to be sought: ተፈለገ tḁfḁ́llḁgḁ;

to bring: አመጣ amḁ́ṭṭā,

to be brought: መጣ mḁ́ṭṭā.

Mood.

The verb in all its forms, primitive and derived, has the following moods: § 23*b*

Indicative (stating):

ይለቅማል yi̥lḁ́qmāl, he is picking.

Contingent[1] (supposing):

ይለቅም yi̥lḁ́qm, (if, when, etc.) he picks, picked, or will pick.

---

[1] called the simple imperfect by Guidi because of its form; but Isenberg's term 'contingent', considering the use of this form, seems more appropriate. It does not distinguish any tense, but is used to express both perf. and imperf.

Jussive (ordering):

ይልቀም yí̥lqḁm, let him pick.

Imperative[1] (ordering):

ልቀም lí̥qḁm, pick.

It also has the:

Gerund (a dependent clause in itself):

ለቅሞ lḁ́qmʷo, he·picking, he having picked.

Infinitive (the action):

መልቀም mḁ́lqḁm, to pick, picking.

Participle (the agent):

ለቃሚ lḁqā́mi, one that picks, picker.

Tense.

§24*a* Tenses are distinguished in the indicative only, which has the following:

Perfect:

(*α*) Simple[2]: ለቀመ lḁ́qqḁma, he picked or has picked.

(*β*) Compound[2]: ለቅሟል lḁ́qmŏ͡āl, he has picked.

Imperfect:

(*α*) Simple[2], only in the neg.[3]: አይለቅምም a͡i̥lḁ́q-mi̥m, he is not picking.

(*β*) Compound[2]: ይለቅማል yi̥lḁ́qmāl[4], he is picking.

---

[1] The imperative and jussive are the same mood; I have retained the time-honoured term imperative for the 2nd person of the jussive.

[2] referring to the form.

[3] this is the cont. with neg. pref. and suff. (§ 37); also expresses: he does not pick, he will not pick.

[4] also expresses: he picks, he will pick.

Composite Tenses.

By means of auxiliaries the following tenses are § 24*b*
formed from the contingent and gerund:

Pluperfect:

ለቅሞ ፡ ነበር ፡ lḁ́qmʷo nḁ́bbḁr[1], he had picked.

Past Imperfect:

ይለቅም ፡ ነበር ፡ yi̥lḁ́q(ĭ̥)m nḁ́bbḁr[2], he was picking.

Similarly

ለቅሞ ፡ ይሆናል ፡ lḁ́qmʷo yi̥hʷónāl, he would pick[3].

ይለቅም ፡ ይሆናል ፡ yi̥lḁ́q(ĭ̥)m yi̥hʷónāl, he may pick[4].

The Regular Triliteral Verb.

Formation and Inflexion of Parts.

The number, person and gender are shown by § 25
adding the following prefixes and suffixes to a stem, which is in the indicative simple perfect the root, in the contingent, jussive and imperative a modification of the root.

---

[1] also expresses: he would have picked.

[2] also expresses: he used to pick, he would pick, he ought to have picked.

[3] or: he must have picked.

[4] or: he probably will pick.

Indicative Simple Perfect.

Stem: ለቀመ lḁ́-qqḁ-mḁ (§ 34), or ፈለገ fḁ́-llḁ-gḁ (§ 35).

Suffixes:

sg.	3rd m.	— (stem),	all three radicals	gi̥͡i̥z (§ 4*a*)
	3rd f.	— ች -č[1]	„ „	gí̥͡i̥z
	2nd m.	— ህ -h[2]	last radical	sádi̥s[6]
	2nd f.	— ሽ -š	„ „	sádi̥s[6]
	1st	— ሁ -hu[3]	„ „	sádi̥s[6]
pl.	3rd	— u	„ „	ká͡i̥y
	2nd	— ኣችሁ -áč(č)i̥hu[4]	„ „	ráyi̥
	1st	— ነ -nḁ[5]	„ „	sádi̥s[6].

§ 26

Contingent.

Stem, type A (§ 34) *ለቅም lḁ́-q-m[7],
type B (§ 35) *ፈልግ fḁ́-lli̥-g.

Prefixes and suffixes:

sg.	3rd m.	ይ —	yi̥ —
	3rd f.	ት —	ti̥ —
	2nd m.	ት —	ti̥ —
	2nd f.	ት — i	ti̥ — i
	1st	እ —	i̥ —
pl.	3rd	ይ — u	yi̥ — u
	2nd	ት — u	ti̥ — u
	1st	እን —	i̥nni̥ —[8].

---

[1] -čč (§ 6). [2] also pronounced -ኽ -χ, -ክ -k, (§ 7*d*).

[3] or -hŭ, -uh (§ 7*d*, ká͡i̥y), -ኍ -hwŭ, -uh, -ኩ -ku, -kŭ.

[4] or -áč(č)yuh (§ 7*d*). [5] or -ን -n.

[6] except in verb with last rad. doubled, which

For the modification of these prefixes by other pref. see § 45.

The vowel i̥ of these pref. coalesces with initial a- to form ã- (§ 7*a*):

e.g. **አጠበ** áṭṭḁvḁ (-bḁ), to wash,

cont. stem ***አጥብ** a-ṭ-v,

cont. sg. 3rd m. **ያጥብ** yã́ṭ(ĭ̥)v, (if, etc.) he washes.

The sg. 1st is written **አጥብ** ã́ṭ(ĭ̥)v, not ***አጥብ** (§ 4*b*).

[So in caus. conjug. (§ 41*d, e*) cont. sg. 1st **አለቅም** ãlḁ́q(ĭ̥)m, (if, etc.) I take to pasture, **አስለቅም** ãslḁ́qqi̥m, (if, etc.) I cause to pick or be picked.]

The suff. -i (sáli̥s § 4*a*) of the sg. 2nd f. modifies certain preceding consonants (§ 7*b*):

e.g. **ከፈተ** kḁ́ffḁtḁ, to open,

cont. stem. ***ከፍት** kḁft,

cont. sg. 2nd f. **ትከፍች** ti̥kḁ́fč, (if, etc.) you (f.) open.

In all cases the form given for pl. 3rd is also used for the polite form of the sg. 2nd and sg. 3rd (§ 12*a*).

The above prefixes and suffixes and those of the ger. and inf. given below (§§ 29, 30) are applied to all verbs, primitive and derived alike.

---

retains its vowel: e.g. **ዘገየህ** zḁgḁ́yyäh, you were late: and see § 42*a, b*, § 44*b*.

[7] The 2nd rad. sometimes has ĭ̥ in slow speech, lḁ́qĭ̥m, in cases which can hardly be pronounced without it, e.g. when the word ends with the two consonants.

[8] or i̥nn —.

§ 27 *Jussive.*

Stem, type A (§ 34): *ልቃም l-qḁ-m,

type B (§ 35): *ፈልግ fḁ́-lli̥-g (same as cont.).

The pref. and suff. are the same as those of the cont. (§ 26).

The 2nd person is only used in the formation of the neg. imperative (§ 37), and the sg. 1st not without pref. ል- (§ 48*a*).

The vowel i̥ of the pref. coalesces with initial i̥ to form i̥ (§ 7*a*):

e.g. እጠበ, juss. stem *እጠብ í̥ṭḁṿ,

juss. sg. 3rd m. ይጠብ yí̥ṭḁṿ, let him wash.

§ 28 *Imperative.*

Stem, type A: ልቃም lí̥-qḁ-m,

type B: ፈልግ fḁ́-lli̥-g.

The suff. are the same as those of the cont. (§ 26). There are no pref.[1]

In the neg. (§ 38) the corresponding persons of the juss. are used for the imp.

---

[1] Verbs with 1st rad. ረ or ነ are sometimes pronounced, especially in the imp., with an initial እ; but this is not confined to the imp. See § 7*d*, under sā́di̥s.

Gerund. § 29

Stem, type A (§ 34): *ለቅም l̥aqm, sg. 1st lḁ́qi̥mm,
type B (§ 35): *ፈልግ fḁ́lli̥g, sg. 1st fḁ́lli̥gg.

Suffixes:

sg. 3rd m. — ʷo
3rd f. — ã
2nd m. — ḁሀ -ḁh (-äh)[1]
2nd f. — äሽ -äš
1st — ʸe
pl. 3rd — ḁው -ḁu͡
2nd — ā́ችሁ -ā́č(č)i̥hu (-ā́ččyuh)
1st — ḁን -ḁn (-än).

The suff. -ʸe of the sg. 1st modifies certain preceding consonants (§ 7*b*):

e.g. ከፈተ
ger. sg. 1st stem *ከፍት kḁ́fi̥tt,
ger. sg. 1st ከፍቼ kḁ́fi̥ččʸe.

Infinitive. § 30

Stem, type A: *ለቀም lqḁm,
type B: *ፈለግ fḁ́llḁg.

Prefix: መ— mḁ—.

The inf. is a substantive, and as such may take the -ን of the acc. (§ 9*c*), the art. (§ 11), and the pers. suff. (§ 12*b*):

e.g. መፈለጋችሁን ፡ አላውቅም ። mḁfḁllḁgā́čči̥hun alá͡uŭqi̥m, I am not aware of your (pl.) seeking.

---

[1] or -ḁሽ -ḁχ, -äχ (§ 7*d*).

§ 31 *Participle.*

Stem, type A: *ለቃመ lḁqām,

type B: *ፈላግ fḁllāg.

Suffix: -i (sál̥is § 4*a*), which modifies certain preceding consonants (§ 7*b*):

e.g. ከፈተ

part. stem, *ከፋት kḁfát,

part. ከፋች kḁ́fāč (§ 8), one that opens.

The part. is a noun, and as such may take the -ን of the acc. (§ 9*c*) the art. (§ 11), and the pers. suff. (§ 12*b*), and forms a pl. in -ʷōች (§ 9*b*).

§ 32a *Compound Tenses.*

Compound Perfect and Imperfect; አለ állä.

The auxiliary verb አለ állä, to be, is attached to the ger. (§ 29) to form the compound perfect, and to the cont. (§ 26) to form the compound imperfect.

አለ, though imperf. (present) in sense, is in form a simp. perf. (§ 25, note 6; § 42*b*), and is conjugated thus[1]:

sg.	3rd m.	አለ	állä, he (it) is.
	3rd f.	አለች	álläč[2], she is.
	2nd m.	አለህ	älläh, you are.
	2nd f.	አለሽ	älläš, you are.
	1st	አለሁ	állḁuʰ[3], I am.
pl.	3rd	አሉ	állu, they are.
	2nd	አላችሁ	allā́čči̥hu (-ā́ččyuh § 7*d*), you are.
	1st	አለን	állän, we are.

---

[1] አለ only occurs in this tense. [2] -čč (§ 6).

[3] § 7*d*, under kḁ́iy; also written አለኍ.

In all the persons of the comp. perf. except the sg. 3rd f. and sg. 1st, and also in the sg. 3rd m. of the comp. imperf. the aux. is shortened to -āል -āl.

Thus

ለቅሟል lḁqmŏ͡āl[1], he has picked,

= ለቅሞ lḁ́qmʷo + -āል -āl (§ 7b);

ትለቅምያለሽ ti̥lḁqmyā́lläš, you (f.) are picking,

= ትለቅሚ ti̥lḁ́qmi + አለሽ ā́lläš (§ 7b).

A single word is formed by verb and aux., between which, however, a pronominal pers. suff. (§ 12c), alone or with a preposition (§ 47a), or the conjunction -ም (§ 48b) may be interposed:

e.g. ለቅሞታል lḁ́qmʷotāl, he has picked it;

ለቅሞለታል lḁ́qmʷollḁtāl (§ 8), he has picked it for him;

ለቅሞማል lḁ́qmʷommāl, and he has picked.

In the comp. imperf. § 32b

pl. 3rd ይለቅማሉ yi̥lḁqmā́llu, they are picking,

pl. 2nd ትለቅማላችሁ ti̥lḁqmallā́ččyuh, you are picking,

the suff. -u of the cont. (§ 26) disappears.

But when anything is interposed between verb and aux. -u reappears, and -ā́ሉ -ā́llu is shortened to -āል -āl:

e.g. ይለቅሙልኛል yi̥lḁ́qmulli̥ññāl, they are picking for me;

ትለቅሙታላችሁ ti̥lḁqmutallā́ččyuh, you (pl.) are picking it.

---

[1] also written ለቅምዋል (§ 4b).

Alternative Form of Compound Perfect.

§ 32*c* An alternative form of the comp. perf., common in G., consists in the simp. perf. (§ 25) with the suff. -ናል -nnāl[1] for all numbers and persons, the pers. suff. (§ 12*c*), etc. being interposed between verb and aux. as in § 32*a*:

e.g.

ለቀመናል lḁ́qqḁmḁnnāl, [= **ለቅሟል**] he has picked;

ለቀመችናል lḁ́qqḁmäččị̥nnāl (§ 6 ; § 8), [= **ለቅማለች** lḁqmā́l-läč,] she has picked;

ለቀመውናል lḁ́qqḁmḁ͡unnāl, [= **ለቅሞታል**] he has picked it;

ለቀመለትናል lḁ́qqḁmḁllḁtị̥nnāl, [= **ለቅሞለታል**] he has picked it for him;

ለቀመምናል lḁ́qqḁmḁmmị̥nnāl, [= **ለቅሞማል**] and he has picked.

Independent Use of **አለ** *állä.*

§ 32*d* **አለ** állä when used independently, i.e. not as an aux., means to exist, be present[2], rather than to be, which is rendered in this tense (present) by **ነው** nḁ͡ú (§ 13*b*):

ውሃ ፡ አለ ። wǘha állä ?, is there any water?

ውሃ ፡ ነው ። wŭhā́ (§ 8) nḁ͡u ?, is it water?

ወታደር ፡ አለ ። wωttáddär állä, there is a soldier, there are some soldiers.

ወታደር ፡ ነው ። wωttaddā́r nḁ͡u, he (it) is a soldier.

---

[1] a final consonant to which -ናል is attached receiving ị̥. [2] = il y a, es gibt, hay, c'è, vi è.

Composite Tenses.

The Past Imperfect; ነበረ nḁ́bbḁrḁ.

The aux. verb ነበረ nḁ́bbḁrḁ (-är-), or ነበር nḁ́bbḁr (-är), to be[1], following the cont. (§ 26) forms the past imperf., both affirmative (§§ 34–36) and negative (§ 38). § 33*a*

Either (*a*) both verb and aux. are conjugated or (*β*) ነበረ is impersonal and remains invariable, usually in the form ነበር:

e.g. እለቅም ፡ ነበርኍ i̥lḁ́q(ĭ̥)m nḁ́bbḁrhwŭ (-är-, -ruh § 7*d*),
or እለቅም ፡ ነበር i̥lḁ́q(ĭ̥)m nḁ́bbḁr (-är), I was picking, or, I used to pick.

The Pluperfect.

The pluperfect is formed § 33*b*

(*a*) in the affirmative by the ger. (§ 29) followed by ነበረ (varying as in § 33*a*):

ለቅመህ ፡ ነበርህ lḁ́qmäh nḁ́bbärh, or
ለቅመህ ፡ ነበር lḁ́qmäh nḁ́bbḁr (-är), you had picked;

(*β*) in the neg. (§ 38), and in the apodosis of a conditional sentence introduced by በ-, by the simp. perf. (§ 25) followed by ነበረ (varying as in § 33*a*):

አልለቀማችሁም ፡ ነበራችሁ allḁqqḁmắč(č)i̥hum nḁbbḁ-rắč(č)yuh (§ 7*d*),
or አልለቀማችሁም ፡ ነበር allḁqqḁmắč(č)i̥hum nḁ́bbḁr (-är), you (pl.) had not picked.

በለኝ ፡ በለቀምኍ ፡ ነበርኍ ። [ነበር ።] bắläñ, bḁlḁ́qqḁmuh (§ 7*d*) nḁ́bbḁruh (nḁ́bbär), if he had told me I should have picked.

---

[1] conjugated like ለቀመ (§ 25, § 34); only occurs in the simp. perf.

Other Composite Tenses.

§ 33c In the same way in similar tenses (§ 24b) formed by ይሆናል yi̥hʷónāl (comp. imperf. sg. 3rd m. of ሆነ hʷŏnḁ, to be, become, happen) the aux. may be conjugated or may be impersonal and remain invariable:

e.g. ይለቅሙ ፡ ይሆናሉ ። yi̥lḁ́qmu yi̥hʷonā́llu, or

ይለቅሙ ፡ ይሆናል ። yi̥lḁ́qmu yi̥hʷónāl, they may pick, or, they probably will pick;

ለቅመው ፡ ይሆናሉ ። lḁ́qmḁu yi̥hʷonā́llu, or

ለቅመው ፡ ይሆናል ። lḁ́qmḁu yi̥hʷónāl, they would pick, or, they must have picked.

Independent Use of ነበረ.

§ 33d ነበረ when used independently (i.e. not as an aux.) supplies a past both of ነው (§ 13b) and of አለ (§ 32d):

e.g. ውሃ ፡ ነበር ። wúha nḁ́bbär, (α) it was water, (β) there was some water.

ትናንት ፡ ነበር ፡ ዛሬ ፡ የለም ። ti̥nánt nḁ́bbär, zárʸe yál-läm (§ 39), yesterday he was present, to-day he is absent (yesterday there was some, to-day there is none).

ፊት ፡ የርሱ ፡ ነበር ፡ አሁን ፡ የኔ ፡ ነው ። fi̥t yärsú nḁ́bbär, áhun yänʸé nḁu, formerly it was his, now it is mine.

PARADIGM OF THE REGULAR TRILITERAL VERB.

TYPE A. § 34

ለቀመ lḁ́qqḁmḁ, to pick, gather.

Indicative.

Simple Perfect (§ 25)

sg. 3rd m.	**ለቀመ**	lḁ́qqḁmḁ,	he (it) picked or has picked.
3rd f.	**ለቀመች**	lḁ́qqḁmäč[1],	she picked, etc.
2nd m.	**ለቀምህ**	lḁ́qqḁmh[2],	you (m.) picked, etc.
2nd f.	**ለቀምሽ**	lḁ́qqḁmś,	you (f.) picked, etc.
1st	**ለቀምሁ**	lḁ́qqḁmhu[3],	I picked, etc.
pl. 3rd[4]	**ለቀሙ**	lḁ́qqḁmu,	they (you, he, pol.) picked, etc.
2nd	**ለቀማችሁ**	lḁqqḁmắč(č)ḭhu[5],	you (pl.) picked, etc.
1st	**ለቀምነ**	lḁ́qqḁmnḁ[6],	we picked, etc.

---

[1] -čč (§ 6).

[2] sometimes lḁ́qqḁmḭh; also **ለቀምኽ** lḁ́qqḁmχ, **ለቀምክ** lḁ́qqḁmk, (§ 7*d* under **ሀ**).

[3] (-hŭ) or lḁ́qqḁmuh, also **ለቀምኍ** lḁ́qqḁmhwŭ (-muh), **ለቀምኩ** lḁ́qqḁmku, (-kŭ) (§ 7*d*, under kā͡ḭy, **ሀ**).

[4] also sg. 2nd pol. and sg. 3rd pol. (§ 12*a*) in this and all tenses.

[5] or lḁqqḁmắč(č)yuh (§ 7*d*).

[6] or **ለቀምን** lḁ́qqḁmn.

Compound Perfect[1] (§ 32*a*)

sg.	3rd m.	ለቅሟል	lḁ́qmŏ͡āl, he has picked.
	3rd f.	ለቅማለች	lḁqmā́lläč[2],
	2nd m.	ለቅመሃል	lḁ́qmḁhāl[3],
	2nd f.	ለቅመሻል	lḁ́qmäšāl,
	1st	ለቅምያለሁ	lḁqi̥mmyā́llḁ͡uʰ[4],
pl.	3rd	ለቅመዋል	lḁ́qmḁ͡uāl,
	2nd	ለቅማችኋል	lḁqmā́č(č)i̥hwāl[5],
	1st	ለቅመናል	lḁ́qmḁnāl.

Compound Imperfect (§ 32*a*, *b*)

sg.	3rd m.	ይለቅማል	yi̥lḁ́qmāl, he is picking, picks, or will pick.
	3rd f.	ትለቅማለች	ti̥lḁqmā́lläč[6],
	2nd m.	ትለቅማለህ	ti̥lḁqmā́lläh,
	2nd f.	ትለቅምያለሽ	ti̥lḁqmyā́lläš,
	1st	እለቅማለሁ	i̥lḁqmā́llḁ͡uʰ[7],

---

[1] Alternative form in G. of comp. perf. (§ 32*c*):

sg.	3rd m.	ለቀመናል	lḁ́qqḁmḁnnāl, he has picked.
	3rd f.	ለቀመችናል	lḁ́qqḁmäčči̥nnāl,
	2nd m.	ለቀምህናል	lḁ́qqḁmhi̥nnāl,
	2nd f.	ለቀምሽናል	lḁ́qqḁmši̥nnāl,
	1st	ለቀምሁናል	lḁ́qqḁmhunnāl,
pl.	3rd	ለቀሙናል	lḁ́qqḁmunnāl,
	2nd	ለቀማችሁናል	lḁqqḁmā́čči̥hunnāl,
	1st	ለቀምንናል	lḁ́qqḁmni̥nnāl.

[2] -čč (§ 6). [3] or lḁ́qmähāl, -ኻል -χāl (§ 7*d*).

[4] § 7*d*, also written -ለኍ.

[5] or lḁqmā́č(č)yuhāl (§ 7*d*).

[6] -čč (§ 6). [7] § 7*d*, also written -ለኍ.

pl. 3rd ይለቅማሉ yi̥lḁqmã́llu,
2nd ትለቅማላችሁ ti̥lḁqmallã́č(č)yuh[1],
1st እንለቅማለን i̥nn(i̥)lḁqmã́llän.

Past Imperfect (§ 33*a*)

sg. 3rd m. ይለቅም ፡ ነበረ yi̥lḁ́q(ĭ̥)m nḁ́bbḁrḁ[2], or ይለቅም ፡ ነበር yi̥lḁ́q(ĭ̥)m nḁ́bbḁr[3], } he was picking, used to pick.
3rd f. ትለቅም ፡ ነበረች ti̥lḁ́q(ĭ̥)m nḁ́bbḁräč[4], or ትለቅም ፡ ነበር ti̥lḁ́q(ĭ̥)m nḁ́bbḁr[3], }
etc.

Pluperfect (§ 33*b*)

sg. 3rd m. ለቅሞ ፡ ነበረ lḁ́qmʷo nḁ́bbḁrḁ[2], or ለቅሞ ፡ ነበር lḁ́qmʷo nḁ́bbḁr[3], } he had picked.
3rd f. ለቅማ ፡ ነበረች lḁ́qmã nḁ́bbḁräč[4], or ለቅማ ፡ ነበር lḁ́qmã nḁ́bbḁr[3], }
etc.

CONTINGENT (§ 26)

sg. 3rd m. ይለቅም yi̥lḁ́q(ĭ̥)m, (if, when, etc.) he picks, picked, or will pick.
3rd f. ትለቅም ti̥lḁ́q(ĭ̥)m,
2nd m. ትለቅም ti̥lḁ́q(ĭ̥)m,
2nd f. ትለቅሚ ti̥lḁ́qmi,
1st እለቅም i̥lḁ́q(ĭ̥)m,
pl. 3rd ይለቅሙ yi̥lḁ́qmu,
2nd ትለቅሙ ti̥lḁ́qmu,
1st እንለቅም i̥nn(i̥)lḁ́q(ĭ̥)m.

---

[1] § 7*d*. [2] or -ärḁ. [3] or -är.
[4] -čč (§ 6), -är-.

JUSSIVE (§ 27)

			IMPERATIVE (§ 28)
sg.	3rd m.	ይልቀም y̥ílqḁm, let him pick.	
	3rd f.	ትልቀም t̥ílqḁm,	
	2nd m.	[*ትልቀም t̥ílqḁm,][1]	ልቀም l̥íqḁm, pick.
	2nd f.	[*ትልቀሚ t̥ílqḁmi,][1]	ልቀሚ l̥íqḁmi,
	1st	[*እልቀም ̥ílqḁm,][2]	
pl.	3rd	ይልቀሙ y̥ílqḁmu,	
	2nd	[*ትልቀሙ t̥ílqḁmu,][1]	ልቀሙ l̥íqḁmu.
	1st	እንልቀም i̥nn̥ílqḁm.	

GERUND (§ 29)

sg.	3rd m.	ለቅሞ	lḁ́qm^{w}o, he picking or having picked.
	3rd f.	ለቅማ	lḁ́qmā,
	2nd m.	ለቅመህ	lḁ́qmḁh[3],
	2nd f.	ለቅመሽ	lḁ́qmäš,
	1st	ለቅሚ	lḁ́qi̥mm^{y}e,
pl.	3rd	ለቅመው	lḁ́qmḁ͡u,
	2nd	ለቅማችሁ	lḁqmáč(č)i̥hu[4],
	1st	ለቅመን	lḁ́qmḁn[5].

INFINITIVE (§ 30)

መልቀም mḁ́lqḁm, to pick, picking.

PARTICIPLE (§ 31)

ለቃሚ lḁqámi, one that picks, picker.

---

[1] only used to form the neg. imperative (§ 38).

[2] only occurs with ል-l- (§ 48*a*) prefixed: ልልቀም l̥íl-qḁm, let me pick.

[3] or -äh, -መኽ -mḁχ, -mäχ, (§ 7*d*).

[4] or -áč(č)yuh (§ 7*d*). [5] or -än.

TYPE B.[1] § 35

ፈለገ fḁ́llḁgḁ, to seek, want.

INDICATIVE.

Simple Perfect (§ 25)

sg.	3rd m.	ፈለገ	fḁ́llḁgḁ, he (it) sought, has sought.
	3rd f.	ፈለገች	fḁ́llḁgäč[2],
	2nd m.	ፈለግህ	fḁ́llḁgh[3],
	2nd f.	ፈለግሽ	fḁ́llḁgš,
	1st	ፈለግሁ	fḁ́llḁghu[4],
pl.	3rd[5]	ፈለጉ	fḁ́llḁgu,
	2nd	ፈለጋችሁ	fḁllḁgä́č(č)i̥hu[6],
	1st	ፈለግነ	fḁ́llḁgnḁ[7].

---

[1] differing from type A in formation of stems but not in inflexion.

[2] -čč (§ 6).

[3] sometimes -gi̥h, also fḁ́llḁkk (§ 7*d*, under **ሀ**), ፈለግኽ fḁllḁgχ.

[4] or -ghŭ, fḁ́llḁguh, fḁ́llḁkku (-kŭ), also written ፈለግኍ, (§ 7*d* under kai̥y, **ሀ**).

[5] also sg. 2nd pol. and sg. 3rd pol. (§ 12*a*) in this and all tenses.

[6] or fḁllḁgä́č(č)yuh (§ 7*d*).

[7] or ፈለግን fḁ́llḁgi̥n.

Compound Perfect[1] (§ 32*a*)

sg.	3rd m.	ፈልጓል	fḁ́lli̥go͡āl, he has sought.
	3rd f.	ፈልጋለች	fḁlli̥gálläč[2],
	2nd m.	ፈልገሃል	fḁ́lli̥gḁhāl[3],
	2nd f.	ፈልገሻል	fḁ́lli̥gäšāl,
	1st	ፈልግያለሁ	fḁlli̥ggyállḁ͡uʰ[4],
pl.	3rd	ፈልገዋል	fḁ́lli̥ga͡uāl,
	2nd	ፈልጋችኋል	fḁlli̥gáč(č)i̥hwāl[5],
	1st	ፈልገናል	fḁ́lli̥gḁnāl.

Compound Imperfect (§ 32*a*)

sg.	3rd m.	ይፈልጋል	yi̥fḁ́lli̥gāl, he is seeking, seeks, will seek.
	3rd f.	ትፈልጋለች	ti̥fḁlli̥gálläč[6],
	2nd m.	ትፈልጋለህ	ti̥fḁlli̥gálläh,
	2nd f.	ትፈልግያለሽ	ti̥fḁlli̥gyálläš,
	1st	እፈልጋለሁ	i̥fḁlli̥gállḁ͡uʰ[7],
pl.	3rd	ይፈልጋሉ	yi̥fḁlli̥gállu,
	2nd	ትፈልጋላችሁ	ti̥fḁlli̥galláč(č)yuh[8],
	1st	እንፈልጋለን	i̥nn(i̥)fḁlli̥gállän.

---

[1] alternative form in G. (§ 32*c*) ፈለገናል fḁ́llḁgḁnnāl, conjugated like ለቀመናል (§ 34).

[2] -čč (§ 6).

[3] or -gäh-, ኻል -χāl (§ 7*d*).

[4] § 7*d*, also written -ለኍ.

[5] or -gāč(č)yuhāl (§ 7*d*).

[6] -čč (§ 6).

[7] § 7*d*, also written -ለኍ.

[8] § 7*d*.

Past Imperfect (§ 33*a*)

sg. 3rd m. ይፈልግ ፡ ነበረ yi̥fḁlli̥g nḁbbḁrḁ[1], } he was seeking,
or ይፈልግ ፡ ነበር yi̥fḁlli̥g nḁbbḁr[2], } used to seek.
etc.

Pluperfect (§ 33*b*)

sg. 3rd m. ፈልጎ ፡ ነበረ fḁlli̥gʷo nḁbbḁrḁ[1], } he had sought.
or ፈልጎ ፡ ነበር fḁlli̥gʷo nḁbbḁr[2], }
etc.

CONTINGENT (§ 26)

sg.	3rd m.	ይፈልግ	yi̥fḁlli̥g, (if, when, etc.) he seeks, sought, or will seek.
	3rd f.	ትፈልግ	ti̥fḁlli̥g,
	2nd m.	ትፈልግ	ti̥fḁlli̥g,
	2nd f.	ትፈልጊ	ti̥fḁlli̥gi,
	1st	እፈልግ	i̥fḁlli̥g,
pl.	3rd	ይፈልጉ	yi̥fḁlli̥gu,
	2nd	ትፈልጉ	ti̥fḁlli̥gu,
	1st	እንፈልግ	i̥nn(i̥)fḁlli̥g.

JUSSIVE (§ 27)

				IMPERATIVE (§ 28)
sg.	3rd m.	ይፈልግ	yi̥fḁlli̥g, let him seek.	
	3rd f.	ትፈልግ	ti̥fálli̥g,	
	2nd m.	[*ትፈልግ	ti̥fḁlli̥g,][3]	ፈልግ fḁlli̥g, seek.
	2nd f.	[*ትፈልጊ	ti̥fálli̥gi,][3]	ፈልጊ fḁlli̥gi,
	1st	[*እፈልግ	i̥fḁlli̥g,][4]	
pl.	3rd	ይፈልጉ	yi̥fḁlli̥gu	
	2nd	[*ትፈልጉ	ti̥fḁlli̥gu,][3]	ፈልጉ fḁlli̥gu.
	1st	እንፈልግ	i̥nn(i̥)fḁlli̥g.	

---

1 or -ärḁ. 2 or -är.

3 only used to form the neg. imperative (§ 38).

4 only occurs with ለ- l- prefixed: ልፈልግ li̥fḁlli̥g, let me seek.

GERUND (§ 29)

sg.	3rd m.	ፈልጎ	fḁ́lli̥g^{w}o, he seeking or having sought.
	3rd f.	ፈልጋ	fḁ́lli̥gã,
	2nd m.	ፈልገህ	fḁ́lli̥gḁh[1],
	2nd f.	ፈልገሽ	fḁ́lli̥gäš,
	1st	ፈልጌ	fḁ́lli̥gg^{y}e,
pl.	3rd	ፈልገው	fḁ́lli̥gḁ͡u,
	2nd	ፈልጋችሁ	fḁlli̥gáč(č)i̥hu[2],
	1st	ፈልገን	fḁ́lli̥gḁn[3].

INFINITIVE (§ 30)

መፈለግ mḁfḁ́llag̥, to seek, seeking.

PARTICIPLE (§ 31)

ፈላጊ fḁllági, one that seeks, seeker.

For the principal parts of triliterals with ቈ, ኰ, ጐ, (§ 4*a*) as 1st or 2nd rad., with 2nd and 3rd rad. the same, with 1st rad. አ, and other irregular triliterals see table of verbs in the appendix.

PARADIGM OF REGULAR QUADRILITERAL VERB.

§ 36 The conjugation of verbs with more or less than three radicals and of derived forms differs from that of triliterals in the formation of the stems of the principal parts, but not essentially in the inflexion of those stems (§ 34), nor in any way in the formation of

---

[1] or -äh, -ገኽ -gḁχ, -gäχ, (§ 7*d*).

[2] or -áč(č)yuh (§ 7*d*).

[3] or -än.

composite tenses (§ 24b). In this and the following paradigms the form of the tense given is the sg. 3rd m. unless otherwise stated.

መነዘረ mḁnḁ́zzḁrḁ[1], to change.

INDICATIVE.

Simp. perf. **መነዘረ** mḁnḁ́zzḁrḁ[1],

sg. 3rd f. **መነዘረች** mḁnḁ́zzḁräč[1,2] etc., like **ለቀመ** (§ 34).

Comp. perf.[3] (§ 32a) **መንዝሯል** mḁ́nzi̥ro͡āl,

sg. 3rd f. **መንዝራለች** mḁnzi̥rā́lläč[2], etc.

Comp. imperf. (§ 32a, b) **ይመነዝራል** yi̥mḁnḁ́zzi̥rāl,

sg. 3rd f. **ትመነዝራለች** ti̥mḁnḁzzi̥rā́lläč[2], etc.

CONT. (§ 26) **ይመነዝር** yi̥mḁnḁ́zzi̥r.

JUSS. (§ 27) **ይመንዝር** yi̥mḁ́nzi̥r.

IMP. (§ 28) **መንዝር** mḁ́nzi̥r.

GER. (§ 29) **መንዝሮ** mḁ́nzi̥rʷo.

INF. (§ 30) **መመንዘር** mḁmḁ́nzḁr[1].

PART. (§ 31) **መንዛሪ** mḁnzā́ri.

The principal parts of some verbs of more than four radicals will be found in the appendix.

NEGATIVE CONJUGATION.

Formation.

The negative verb is formed from the affirmative by the addition of the prefix **አል-** al- and the suffix **-ም** -m. § 37a

---

[1] or -zä- (§ 7d). [2] -čč (§ 6).

[3] G. also **መነዘረናል** mḁnḁ́zzḁrḁnnāl (-är-; § 32c).

For the assimilation of ል by a following consonant see § 7*c*; and for the doubling of m see § 6.

Both አል- and -ም are added to the

ind. simp. perf. (§ 25) to form the neg. ind. perf.,
cont. (§ 26) „ „ neg. ind. imperf.,
ger. (§ 29) „ „ neg. ger. (not much used).

For the formation of the neg. composite tenses see §§ 33*a*, *b*.

አል- [without -ም] is pref. to the juss. (§ 27) to form the neg. juss. and to the forms of the juss. 2nd (§§ 34, 35) to form the neg. imperative.

አለ- álḁ- or ያለ- yálḁ-[1] [without -ም] is pref. to the inf. (§ 30) to form the neg. inf.

The part. (§ 31) has no neg. form.

Nothing comes between አል- and the verb.

-ም comes after pronouns (§ 12*c*) or prepositions (§ 47*a*) which are suff. to the verb, but before other suff.:

e.g. አልፈለገውምወይ ። alfḁllḁgḁummwǝ̥i̥?[2] (§ 8), didn't he want it?

የተመኘው ፡ አልሆነለትምና ፡ ሞተ ። yätḁmḁññäu alhʷó-nḁllät̥imm̥inna mʷótḁ, his desire was not fulfilled and he died, (lit. what he longed for (it) did not happen[3] to him and ... for -ና see § 48*b*).

---

[1] G. gen. ያለ-, Š. gen. አለ-.

[2] or -ገውምይ ። -gḁummwí̥?, s.v. ወይ.

[3] ሆነ hʷónḁ, it happened.

Transference of -ም.

-ም may be transferred from the verb to an adjacent[1] word, the negative sense then applying specially to that word: (cp. § 62d): § 37b

e.g. ፈረሱን ፡ አልፈልግም ። fḁ́rḁsun alfḁ́lli̥gi̥m, I don't want the horse, (opposed to: I do want it);

ፈረሱንም ፡ አልፈልግ ፡ በቅሎውን ፡ እንጂ ። fḁ́rḁsuni̥mm alfḁ́lli̥g, yḁ́qlʷoun i̥njí, I don't want the horse but the mule.

ተከረጢት ፡ አይዶለም ። tḁkḁrḁtí̥t ḁidállām (§ 40), it is not in the bag, (opposed to: it is in);

ተከረጢትም ፡ አይዶል ። tḁkḁrḁtí̥ti̥mm ḁ́idäl, it is not in the bag, (but in something else).

Omission of -ም.

When the contingent (§§ 23b, 26, 37a) is used as such, i.e. in dependent clauses, in the neg. it takes አል- without -ም: § 37c

e.g. አይፈልግም ḁifḁ́lli̥gi̥m, he does not want (seek),

ባይፈልግ bḁifḁ́lli̥g (§ 48a), if he does not want,

የማይፈልግ yämmḁifḁ́lli̥g (§ 14), he who does not want;

አይፈልግ ḁifḁ́lli̥g, (juss. § 38), he is not to seek,

አይፈልግ ፡ እንደሆን ፡ ḁifḁ́lli̥g i̥ndahʷon[2], if he does not seek.

---

[1] gen. preceding, as the natural place of the verb in the clause is last (§ 73b).

[2] for የማይፈልግ ፡ እንደሆን ፡ yämmḁifḁ́lli̥g i̥ndḁhʷon; s.v. እንደሆን.

Similarly, when the simp. perf. or ger. are used in a dependent clause in the neg., -ም is dropped:

e.g. አልፈለገም alfḁ́llḁgḁm, he did not want,

ባልፈለገ balfḁ́llḁgḁ (§ 48*a*), if he did not want,

ያልፈለገ yalfḁ́llḁgḁ (§ 14), he who did not want,

አልፈለገ ፡ እንደሆን ፡ alfḁ́llḁgḁ́ndḁhʷon[1] (§ 8), if he did not want.

አልፈልጎም alfḁ́llḭgʷom, he not wanting, not having wanted,

አልፈልጎ ፡ እንደሆን ፡ alfḁ́llḭgʷóndḁhʷon (§ 8), if he had not wanted.

§ 37*d* -ም is dropped after an indef. pron. ending in -ም (§ 16):

e.g. ማንም ፡ አልመጣ ። mánnḭmm almḁ́ṭṭa, nobody came.

ምንም ፡ አልሰማ ። mí̥nḭmm alsḁ́mma, he heard nothing.

Substitution of Conjunction -ም for Negative -ም.

§ 37*e* The conj. -ም and, even, also, (§ 48*b*) may take the place of the neg. -ም which has been dropped (§ 37*c*, *d*):

e.g. ባይፈልግ ፡ አትስጠው ። ba͡i̥fḁ́llḭg, attí̥sṭḁ͡u, if he doesn't want it, don't give it to him,

ባይፈልግም ፡ ስጠው ። ba͡i̥fḁ́llḭgḭm sí̥ṭḁ͡u, even if he doesn't want it, give it to him.

ባልፈለገ ፡ ባልመጣ ። balfḁ́llḁgḁ balmḁ́ṭṭa, if he had not wanted to, he would not have come,

ባልፈለገም ፡ በመጣ ። balfḁ́llḁgḁm bḁmḁ́ṭṭa, even if he had not wanted to, he would have come.

---

[1] for ያልፈለገ ፡ እንደሆን ፡ yalfḁ́llḁgḁ́ndḁhʷon.

Optional omission of -ም.

-ም may be dropped without altering the sense in § 37*f*
የለም (§ 39) and አይደለም (§ 40), especially in questions:

e.g. የለችም ። yállăčči̥m, or የለች ። yálläč (§ 6), she is not present.

ይህ ፡ አይደለም ። yi̥he a͡i̥dállăm?, or ይህ ፡ አይደል ። yi̥he a͡i̥däl?, isn't it this?

ያለ ፡ አይደሎይ ። yállä[1] a͡i̥dällwi̥?[2], isn't he (it) here (there)?

PARADIGM OF NEGATIVE VERB.

INDICATIVE § 38

Perfect

sg. 3rd m. አልለቀመም allḁ́qqḁmḁm[3], he did not pick, has not picked.

3rd f. አልለቀመችም allḁ́qqḁmäčči̥m,

2nd m. አልለቀምህም allḁ́qqḁmhi̥m[4],

2nd f. አልለቀምሽም allḁ́qqḁmši̥m,

1st አልለቀምሁም allḁ́qqḁmhum[5],

pl. 3rd አልለቀሙም allḁ́qqḁmum,

2nd አልለቀማችሁም allḁqqḁmắč(č)i̥hum,

1st አልለቀምነም allḁ́qqḁmnḁm[6].

---

1 = የ- (§ 14) + አለ (§ 32*d*, § 7*a*).

2 § 6, § 8; s.v. ወይ.

3 here and throughout the conjug. -mm (§ 6).

4 or -ኽም -χi̥m, -ki̥m.

5 or -ኩም -kum.

6 or -ንም -ni̥m.

Imperfect

sg. 3rd m. አይለቅምም a͡i̥lḁ́qmi̥m, he is not picking, does (will) not pick.
3rd f. አትለቅምም ãtt(i̥)lḁ́qmi̥m,
2nd m. አትለቅምም ãtt(i̥)lḁ́qmi̥m,
2nd f. አትለቅሚም ãtt(i̥)lḁ́qmim,
1st አልለቅምም allḁ́qmi̥m[1],
pl. 3rd አይለቅሙም a͡i̥lḁ́qmum,
2nd አትለቅሙም ãtt(i̥)lḁ́qmum,
1st አንለቅምም ann(i̥)lḁ́qmi̥m.

Past Imperfect

አይለቅምም ፡ ነበረ a͡i̥lḁ́qmi̥m nḁ́bbḁrḁ[2], he was not picking, used not to pick.

Pluperfect

አልለቀመም ፡ ነበረ allḁ́qqḁmḁm nḁ́bbḁrḁ[2], he had not picked.

CONTINGENT

sg. 3rd m. አይለቅም a͡i̥lḁ́q(ĭ̥)m, (if, when, etc.) he does (did, will) not pick.
3rd f. አትለቅም ãtt(i̥)lḁ́q(ĭ̥)m,
2nd m. አትለቅም ãtt(i̥)lḁ́q(ĭ̥)m,
2nd f. አትለቅሚ ãtt(i̥)lḁ́qmi,
1st አልለቅም allḁ́q(ĭ̥)m[1],
pl. 3rd አይለቅሙ a͡i̥lḁ́qmu,
2nd አትለቅሙ ãtt(ĭ̥)lḁ́qmu,
1st አንለቅም ann(i̥)lḁ́q(ĭ̥)m.

---

[1] the እ- i̥- of the affirmative disappearing both in writing and pronunciation.

[2] or -är-; or ነበር, as in affirmative conjug. (§ 33*a*, *b*).

Jussive

sg. 3rd m. አይልቀም á͡i̥lqḁm, let him not pick.

3rd f. አትልቀም ãtti̥lqḁm,

1st አልልቀም ali̥lqḁm,

pl. 3rd አይልቀሙ á͡i̥lqḁmu,

1st አንልቀም anni̥lqḁm.

Imperative

sg. 2nd m. አትልቀም ãtti̥lqḁm, do not pick.

2nd f. አትልቀሚ ãtti̥lqḁmi,

pl. 2nd አትልቀሙ ãtti̥lqḁmu.

Gerund

sg. 3rd m. አልለቅሞም allḁqmʷõm, he not picking, not having picked.

3rd f. አልለቅማም allḁ́qmãm,

2nd m. አልለቅመህም allḁ́qmähi̥m[1],

2nd f. አልለቅመሽም allḁ́qmäši̥m,

1st አልለቅሚም allḁ́qi̥mmʸem,

pl. 3rd አልለቅመውም allḁ́qmḁ͡um,

2nd አልለቅማችሁም allḁqmá̌č(č)i̥hum,

1st አልለቅመንም allḁ́qmḁni̥m.

Infinitive

አለመልቀም ālḁmḁ́lqḁm[2], not to pick.

Participle

none[3].

---

[1] or -ኽም -χi̥m. [2] G. ያለመልቀም yālḁmḁ́lqḁm.

[3] expressed by rel. (§ 14): የማይለቅም yämma͡i̥lḁ́q(i̥)m, one that does not pick.

§ 39*a* The neg. of **አለ** állä (§ 32*a, d*) is

sg.	3rd m.	**የለም**	yä́lläm, he (it) is not present, there is not.
	3rd f.	**የለችም**	yä́lläčči̥m,
	2nd m.	**የለህም**	yä́llähi̥m,
	2nd f.	**የለሽም**	yä́lläši̥m,
	1st	**የለሁም**	yä́llḁhum,
pl.	3rd	**የሉም**	yä́llum,
	2nd	**የላችሁም**	yällä́č(č)i̥hum,
	1st	**የለንም**	yä́lläni̥m.

§ 39*b* When **የለም** loses its **-ም** in the cases mentioned in § 37*b, d, f*, i.e. in which it remains in the indicative, it becomes

sg. 3rd m. **የለ** yä́llä,
3rd f. **የለች** yä́lläč[1],
2nd m. **የለህ** yä́lläh, etc., conjug. like **አለ** (§ 32*a*):

e.g. **ትልቅም ፡ የለ ።** tı̥llı̥qı̥mm (§ 6) yä́llä, there is not a large one.

ምንም ፡ የለ ። mı̥nı̥mm yä́llä, there is nothing.

የሉ ። yä́llu ?, aren't they here (there)?

But in dependent clauses (§ 37*c*) it becomes

sg. 3rd m. **-ሌለ** -l^{y}ä́llä,
3rd f. **-ሌለች** -l^{y}ä́lläč[1],
2nd m. **-ሌለህ** -l^{y}ä́lläh, etc., conjug. like **አለ**, always with pref. (rel. **የ-** (§ 14) before **እንደሆን**):

---

[1] -čč (§ 6).

e.g. በሌለ bḁlʸällä or እንደሌለ (i̥)ndḁlʸällä, if he is not present, if there is not.

የሌለ ፡ እንደሆን ፡ yälʸälländḁhʷon (§ 8), if he were not present, if there were not.

The neg. conjug. of ነበረ (§ 33) is regular: § 39c

አልነበረም alnḁbbḁrḁm (-är-), etc. (§ 38).

A neg. conjug. is supplied for ነው (§ 13b) by § 40a

sg. 3rd m. አይደለም a͡i̥dḁ́lläm[1], he (it) is not[2],

3rd f. አይደለችም a͡i̥dḁ́lläčči̥m[1],

2nd m. አይደለህም a͡i̥dḁ́llähi̥m[1],

etc., conjug. like የለም (§ 39a):

e.g. እኔ ፡ አይደለሁም ። i̥nʸé a͡i̥dḁ́llḁhum, it is not I.

የኔ ፡ አይደለም ። yänʸé a͡i̥dḁ́lläm, it is not mine.

ራስ ፡ ደኅና ፡ አይደሉም ። rās dáhna a͡i̥dállum, the Ras is not well.

When አይደለም drops -ም (§ 37b, c, d, f), it becomes § 40b

sg. 3rd m. አይደል á͡i̥däl[3],

3rd f. አይደለች a͡i̥dḁ́lläč[1,4],

2nd m. አይደለህ a͡i̥dḁ́llāh,

etc., conjug. like አለ (§ 32a):

e.g.

(§ 37b) ትልቅም ፡ አይደል ። ti̥lli̥qi̥mm á͡i̥däl, it is not large.

(§ 37c) ያይደላችሁ ya͡i̥dḁllä́ččyuh, you (pl.) who are not.

(§ 37d) ምንም ፡ አይደል ። mi̥ni̥mm á͡i̥däl, it is nothing.

አይደል is not constr. with እንደሆን, but takes እንደ- (q.v.):

e.g. እንዳይደል ፡ (i̥)ndá͡i̥däl, if he (it) is not.

---

1 or ad-, -dä́- (§ 7d). 2 also used as neg. particle, no, not. 3 -ll (§ 6). 4 -čč (§ 6).

With በ- (§ 47*a*, § 48*a*) the -ል of አይደል becomes g̥͡i̥i̥z (§ 4*a*), and it has the meaning of a neg. of አለ (§ 32*d*):

e.g. በይደለ ፡ መንገድ ፡ ሔድን ። bḁ͡idállä mḁ́ṅgḁd hádnḁ, we went where there is no road, (= በሌለበት ፡ መንገድ ፡ bḁlʸällábbḁt mḁ́ṅgḁd, etc.)

Before the art. (§ 11) the -ል of አይደል becomes g̥͡i̥i̥z:

e.g. የርሱ ፡ የይደለው ፡ ፈረስ ፡ yärsú yḁ͡idállḁ͡u fḁ́rḁs, the horse which is not his.

CONJUGATION OF DERIVED FORMS OF VERB.

§ 41*a* See § 36, initial remarks.

Paradigm of Passive or Reflexive Form of Verb.

Type A. ተለቀመ tḁlḁ́qqḁmḁ, to be picked, (§ 22*a*, *a*).

Ind. Simp. perf. ተለቀመ tḁlḁ́qqḁmḁ,

sg. 3rd f. ተለቀመች tḁlḁ́qqḁmäč [1], etc., like ለቀመ (§ 34).

Comp. perf. (§ 32*a*) ተለቅሟል tḁlḁ́qmo͡āl [2],

sg. 3rd f. ተለቅማለች tḁlḁqmállač [1], etc.

Comp. imperf. (§ 32*a*, *b*) ይለቀማል yi̥llḁ́qqḁmāl [3],

sg. 3rd f. ትለቀማለች ti̥llḁqqḁmállač [1,3], etc.

---

[1] -čč (§ 6).

[2] G. also ተለቀመናል tḁlḁ́qqḁmḁnnāl (§ 32*c*).

[3] (§ 7*c*) the 1st rad. is doubled throughout the tense.

CONT. (§ 26) ይለቀግም yi̥llḁ́qqḁm [1].

JUSS. (§ 27) ይለቀግም yi̥llḁ́qḁm [1,2].

IMP. (§ 28) *ተለቀግም tḁlḁ́qḁm [2,3].

GER. (§ 29) ተለቅግም tḁlḁ́qmʷo.

INF. (§ 30) መለቀግም mḁllḁ́qḁm.

PART. (§ 31) ተለቃሚ tḁlḁqā́mi.

TYPE B. ተፈለገ tḁfḁ́llḁgḁ, to be sought, § 41b

differs from type A only in the formation of the stems of the

GER. (§ 29) ተፈልጎ tḁfḁ́lli̥gʷo, whence (§ 32a)

IND. Comp. perf. ተፈልጓል tḁfḁ́lli̥gŏāl,

and of the

PART. (§ 31) ተፈላጊ tḁfḁllā́gi.

For principal parts of passive form of verbs with § 41c 1st rad. አ, e.g. ታጠበ tā́ṭṭḁbḁ (-yḁ), to be washed, and other irregular verbs, e.g. ተነፈሰ tḁnḁ́ffḁsḁ, to breathe, and of verbs with more or less than three rad., see appendix.

---

[1] (§ 7c) the 1st rad. is doubled throughout the tense.

[2] 2nd rad. single throughout the tense.

[3] given as a paradigm; the meaning of this particular verb precludes its having a passive or reflexive imperative.

Paradigm of Causative Form of Verb.

§ 41*d* Causative in አ-:

አለቀመ alạ́qqạmạ, to take to pasture.

Ind. Simp. perf. (§ 25) አለቀመ alạ́qqạmạ.

Comp. perf. (§ 32*a*) አልቅሞኣል ā́lqịmo͡āl[1].

Comp. imperf. (§ 32*a*, *b*) ያለቅማል yālạ́qmāl[2],

sg. 1st አለቅማለሁ ālạqmā́llạ͡uh[3].

Cont. (§ 26) ያለቅም yālạ́q(ị̆)m[2],

sg. 3rd f. ታለቅም tālạ́q(ị̆)m[2].

Juss. (§ 27) ያልቅም yā́lqịm[2],

sg. 3rd f. ታልቅም tā́lqịm[2].

Imp. (§ 28) አልቅም ā́lqịm.

Ger. (§ 29) አልቅሞ ā́lqịmʷo.

Inf. (§ 30) ማልቀም mā́lqạm[2].

Part. (§ 31) አልቃሚ alqā́mi.

§ 41*e* Causative in አስ-:

አስለቀመ aslạ́qqạmạ, to cause to pick or be picked.

Ind. Simp. perf. (§ 25) አስለቀመ aslạ́qqạmạ.

Comp. perf. (32*a*) አስለቅሞኣል aslạ́qqịmo͡āl[4].

Comp. imperf. (32*a*, *b*) ያስለቅማል yāslạ́qqịmāl[2],

sg. 1st አስለቅማለሁ āslạqqịmā́llạ͡uh[3].

---

[1] G. also አለቀመናል alạ́qqạmạnnāl (§ 32*c*).

[2] § 7*a*. [3] § 26.

[4] G. also አስለቀመናል aslạ́qqạmạnnāl (§ 32*c*).

Cont. (§ 26) ያስለቅም yãsl̥áqqi̥m[1],
  sg. 3rd f. ታስለቅም tãsl̥áqqi̥m[1].

Juss. (§ 27) ያስለቅም yãsl̥áqqi̥m[1],
  sg. 3rd f. ታስለቅም tãsl̥áqqi̥m[1].

Imp. (§ 28) አስለቅም asl̥áqqi̥m.

Ger. (§ 29) አስለቅሞ asl̥áqqi̥mʷo.

Inf. (§ 30) ማስለቀም mãsl̥áqqḁm[1].

Part. (§ 31) አስለቃሚ asl̥aqqámi.

Some causatives in አ- are conjugated like a caus. § 41*f*
in አስ-, e.g. አበደረ ab̥áddḁrḁ (aẏ-, ắddä-), to lend. For this and other causatives, and the conjug. of other derived forms (§ 22*b*) see appendix.

CONJUGATION OF BILITERAL VERBS.

See § 36, initial remarks. § 42*a*

Biliteral verbs are in most cases triliteral roots which have lost a radical. When the lost rad. was the 3rd, the 2nd and now final rad. is (usually, but see § 42*b*) rãẏi̥, -ã (§ 4*a*), and a compensatory t appears in the ger. and inf.; -ã is retained as part of the stem of the cont., juss., imp. and inf. but disappears before a suff. -i or -u (§§ 25–28, §§ 30, 31):

---

[1] § 7*a*.

ሰማ sḁ́mmã, to hear, understand, (cp. Eth. **ሰምዐ**).

INDICATIVE

Simp. perf. (§ 25)

sg.	3rd m.	ሰማ	sḁ́mmã, he heard, etc.
	3rd f.	ሰማች	sḁ́mmãč[1],
	2nd m.	ሰማህ	sḁ́mmãh,
	2nd f.	ሰማሽ	sḁ́mmãš,
	1st	ሰማሁ	sḁ́mmãhu[2],
pl.	3rd	ሰሙ	sḁ́mmu,
	2nd	ሰማችሁ	sḁmmáč(č)i̥hu[3],
	1st	ሰማነ	sḁ́mmãnḁ[4].

Comp. perf. (32*a*) **ሰምቷል** sḁ́mt͡ŏal[5], he has heard.

sg. 3rd f. **ሰምታለች** sḁmtállăč[1], etc.

Comp. imperf. (§ 32*a*, *b*) **ይሰማል** yi̥sḁ́mãl, he is hearing, etc.

sg. 3rd f. **ትሰማለች** ti̥sḁmállăč[1], etc.

CONTINGENT (§ 26)

sg.	3rd m.	ይሰማ	yi̥sḁ́mă, (if, etc.) he hears, etc.
	3rd f.	ትሰማ	ti̥sḁ́mã,
	2nd m.	ትሰማ	ti̥sḁ́mã,
	2nd f.	ትሰሚ	ti̥sḁ́mi,
	1st	እሰማ	i̥sḁ́mã,
pl.	3rd	ይሰሙ	yi̥sḁ́mu,
	2nd	ትሰሙ	ti̥sḁ́mu,
	1st	እንሰማ	i̥nn(i̥)sḁ́mã.

---

[1] -čč (§ 6).

[2] or -mãhŭ, -m͡au[h] (§ 7*d*, under k͡ái̥y); also written **ሰማኍ**.

[3] or -áč(č)yuh (§ 7*d*). [4] or **ሰማን** sḁ́mmãn.

[5] G. also **ሰማናል** sḁ́mmãnnāl (§ 32*c*).

Jussive (§ 27)			Imperative (§ 28)
sg. 3rd m.	ይስማ	yi̥smã, let him hear.	
3rd f.	ትስማ	ti̥smã,	
2nd m.	[*ትስማ	ti̥smã,][1]	ስማ si̥mã, hear.
2nd f.	[*ትስሚ	ti̥smi,][1]	ስሚ si̥mi,
1st	[*እስማ	i̥smã,][2]	
pl. 3rd	ይስሙ	yi̥smu,	
2nd	[*ትስሙ	ti̥smu,][1]	ስሙ si̥mu.
1st	እንስማ	i̥nni̥smã.	

Ger. (§ 29) ሰምቶ sḁmt^{w}o, he hearing, etc.
 sg. 3rd f. ሰምታ sḁmtã,
 sg. 1st ሰምቼ sḁmi̥čč^{y}e[3], etc.
Inf. (§ 30) መስማት mḁsmãt[4].
Part. (§ 31) ሰሚ sḁmi[5].

ሰማ is analogous with type A (§ 34) in the formation of its stems. There are also biliterals inflected like ሰማ throughout their conjugation but forming stems analogous with type B (§ 35); see e.g. principal parts of ለካ lḁkkã, to measure, ቀማ qḁmmã, to rob, in appendix.

---

[1] only used to form neg. imp. (§ 37)
 sg. 2nd m. አትስማ ãtti̥smã, don't hear.
 2nd f. አትስሚ ãtti̥smi,
 pl. 2nd አትስሙ ãtti̥smu.

[2] only occurs with ል- (§ 48*a*) pref. ልስማ li̥smã, let me hear.

[3] § 7*b*. [4] § 8. [5] or sámi (§ 7*d*).

§ 42*b* See § 42*a*, initial remarks.

When the lost 3rd rad. was ወ, የ, in some verbs no trace of it remains in the ind. simp. perf. sg. 3rd m., but the 2nd and now final rad. retains ḁ in the rest of that tense except before the suff. -u of the pl. 3rd and in the inf. In the rest of the conjug. ḁ is lost. A compensatory t appears in the ger. and inf.:

ቀረ qḁ́rrḁ, to remain behind or over, (√*ቀረየ).

Ind. Simp. perf.

sg.	3rd m.	ቀረ	qḁ́rrḁ,
	3rd f.	ቀረች	qḁ́rräč[1],
	2nd m.	ቀረህ	qḁ́rrḁh[2],
	2nd f.	ቀረሽ	qḁ́rräš,
	1st	ቀረሁ	qḁ́rrḁu͡[h 3],
pl.	3rd	ቀሩ	qḁ́rru,
	2nd	ቀራችሁ	qḁrrā́č(č)i̥hu[4],
	1st	ቀረነ	qḁ́rrḁnḁ[5].

Comp. perf. (§ 32*a*) ቀርቷል qḁ́rtŏ͡āl[6].

Comp. imperf. (§ 32*a*, *b*) ይቀራል yi̥qḁ́rāl[7].

Cont. (§ 26) ይቀር yi̥qḁ́r[7],

sg. 3rd f. ትቀር ti̥qḁ́r[7], etc.

---

[1] -čč (§ 6). [2] or -äh.

[3] § 7*d* under kḁ́͡i̥y; also written ቀረኹ.

[4] or -ā́č(č)yuh (§ 7*d*).

[5] or ቀረን qḁ́rrḁn (-än).

[6] or qḁ́-. G. also ቀረናል qḁ́rrḁnnāl (§ 32*c*).

[7] or -qḁ́-.

			Imperative (§ 28)	
Juss. (§ 27)	ይቅር	yí̥qi̥r[1],		
sg. 3rd f.	ትቅር	tí̥qi̥r,		
2nd m.	[*ትቅር	tí̥qi̥r,][2]	ቅር	qi̥r,
2nd f.	[*ትቅሪ	tí̥qri,][2]	ቅሪ	qí̥ri,
1st	[*እቅር	í̥qi̥r,][3]		
pl. 3rd	ይቅሩ	yí̥qru,		
2nd	[*ትቅሩ	tí̥qru,][2]	ቅሩ	qí̥ru.
1st	እንቅር	i̥nní̥qi̥r[4].		

Ger. (§ 29)	ቀርቶ	qḁ́rt^{w}o[5],
sg. 3rd f.	ቀርታ	qḁ́rtã[5],
sg. 1st	ቀርቼ	qḁ́ri̥čč^{y}e[5,6] etc.
Inf. (§ 30)	መቅረት	mḁ́qrḁt[7].
Part. (§ 31)	ቀሪ	qḁ́ri[5].

ቀረ is analogous with type A (§ 34) in the formation of its stems; for verbs inflected like ቀረ but forming stems analogous with type B (§ 35), e.g. ባጀ bḁ́jjä (bắ-), to be good, ቈየ qwώyyä, to await, wait, see appendix.

---

[1] In some verbs the 1st rad. loses its vowel throughout the juss., e.g. ሰጠ sḁ́ṭṭḁ, to give,

juss. sg. 3rd m. ይስጥ yi̥sṭ,
3rd f. ትስጥ ti̥sṭ, etc.

[2] only used to form the neg. imp. (§ 37)

sg. 2nd m. አትቅር ãttí̥qi̥r,
2nd f. አትቅሪ ãttí̥qri,
pl. 2nd አትቅሩ ãttí̥qru;

ሰጠ makes sg. 2nd m. አትስጥ ắttí̥sṭ (§ 8).

[3] only in (§ 48*a*) ልቅር lí̥qi̥r, let me remain behind.

[4] or í̥nnqi̥r. [5] or qắ-. [6] § 7*b*. [7] or -ät.

§ 42*c* See § 42*a*, initial remarks.

When the lost rad. was the 2nd, the 1st rad. is (§ 4*a*) rā́yi̥ -ā, hā́mi̥s ʸẽ, or sā́yi̥ ʷõ, according as አ [ዐ, ሀ, ሐ, ኀ], የ or ወ respectively has disappeared:

ጣፈ ṭā́fḁ, to write, (cp. Eth. ጸሐፈ)
ጤሰ ṭʸẽ́sḁ, to smoke, to be enraged, (√ ጠየሰ)
ቆመ qʷṍmḁ, to stand, (√ ቀወመ)

Ind. Simp. perf. (§ 25)		
sg. 3rd m. ጣፈ ṭā́fḁ,	ጤሰ ṭʸẽ́sḁ	ቆመ qʷṍmḁ,
2nd m. ጣፍህ ṭā́f(ĭ̥)h[1].	ጤስህ ṭʸẽ́s(ĭ̥)h[2].	ቆምህ qʷṍm(ĭ̥)h[3].
Comp. perf. (§ 32*a*)		
ጥፏል ṭi̥fõ͡āl[4].	ጢሷል ṭísõ͡āl[5, 6].	ቁሟል qúmõ͡āl[7].
Comp. imperf. (§ 32*a*, *b*)		
ይጥፋል yi̥ṭí̥fāl.	ይጤሳል yi̥ṭʸẽ́sāl.	ይቆማል yi̥qʷṍmāl.
Cont. (§ 26) ይጥፍ yi̥ṭí̥f.	ይጤስ yi̥ṭʸẽ́s.	ይቆም yi̥qʷṍm.
Juss. (§ 27)		
ይጣፍ yí̥ṭāf[8].	ይጢስ yí̥ṭis[9].	ይቁም yí̥qum.
Imp. (§ 28) ጣፍ ṭāf.	ጢስ ṭis[5].	ቁም qum.
Ger. (§ 29) ጥፎ ṭí̥fʷo,	ጢሶ ṭísʷo[5, 10],	ቁሞ qúmʷo,
sg. 1st ጥፌ ṭi̥ffʸe.	ጢሼ ṭí̥ššʸe[11].	ቁሜ qúmmʸe.
Inf. (§ 30) መጣፍ mḁ́ṭāf[8].	መጤስ mḁ́ṭʸẽs[8].	መቆም mḁ́qʷṍm[8].
Part. (§ 31) ጣፊ ṭāfi.	ጢያሽ ṭyāś[12].	ቋሚ qwāmi.

1 or ṭāfχ, ṭāfk (§ 7*d*, under ሀ).
2 or ṭʸẽsχ, ṭʸẽsk. 3 or qʷõmχ, qʷõmk.
4 G. also ጣፈናል ṭā́fḁnnāl (§ 32*c*). 5 or ṭi̥- (§ 7*d*).
6 Š. ጤሷል ṭʸẽ́sõ͡āl, G. also ጤሰናል ṭẽ́sḁnnāl (§ 32*c*).
7 G. also ቆመናል qʷṍmḁnnāl (§ 32*c*).
8 § 8. 9 or -ṭi̥s. 10 Š. ጤሶ ṭʸẽ́sʷo.
11 § 7*b*. 12 or ṭāš; for *ጢያሺ (§ 7*b*).

For the principal parts of various anomalous and derived forms (§ 22) of biliterals see appendix. §42*d*

The Impersonal Verb.

Impersonal verbs are only used in the sg. 3rd m., expressing number, person and gender by means of the pers. suff. (§ 12*c*): §43*a*

e.g. ራበው rábau̯ (-áy̥-), to be or become hungry (§ 63*d*).

IND. Simp. perf.

sg. 3rd m.	ራበው	rábau̯[1], he (it) was or is		hungry.
3rd f.	ራበት	rábāt, she was or is		„
2nd m.	ራበህ	rábah̥[2], you (m.)	were or are	„
2nd f.	ራበሽ	rábäš, you (f.)	„ „	„
2nd pol.	ራበዎ	rábḁʷo[3], you (pol.)	„ „	„
1st	ራበኝ	rábḁñ[4], I was or am		„
pl. 3rd	ራባቸው	rābáč(č)ḁu,	they were or are	„
2nd	ራባችሁ	rābáč(č)yuh[5], you	„ „	„
1st	ራበን	rábḁn[6],	we „ „	„

Comp. perf. ርቦታል rɨ̥bʷṓtāl[7, 8], he (it) is hungry,

sg. 3rd f. ርቧታል rɨ̥bŏátāl[7], she is hungry, etc.

Comp. imperf. ይርበዋል yɨ̥́rbḁuāl[9], he will be hungry.

CONT. ይርበው yɨ̥́rbḁu[9], (if, when) he is hungry.

JUSS. ይራበው yɨ̥rábḁu[1], let him be hungry.

---

[1] or -āy̥- (§ 7*d*) throughout the tense.

[2] or -äh. [3] or ራበዎት rábḁʷot.

[4] or -bä-; -ññ (§ 6). [5] § 7*d*.

[6] or -bä-; -nn (§ 6); or ራበነ rábḁnnḁ.

[7] or -ɨ̥y̥-. [8] § 8. [9] or -ry̥-.

IMP. ይራብህ yirābih[1], be hungry.

GER. ርቦት ríbʷōt[2], he being hungry.

INF. መራብ márāb[1, 3], to be or become hungry.

PART. none.

Aux. verbs like ነበር (§ 33) do not take the pers. suff. when used impersonally.

§ 43*b* The contraction of adjacent vowels described in § 7*a* has been frequently exemplified in the preceding paragraphs.

The modification of consonants by a following i (y) or e described in § 7*b* occurs in the conjugation of verbs whose final radical is one of the letters there specified:

e.g. ከፈለ káffala (§ 34), to divide or pay, ሰጠ sáṭṭa, (like ቀረ § 42*b*), to give.

Ind. comp. perf.

sg. 1st. ከፍያለሁ kafiyyállauh[4], ሰጥቻለሁ saṭiččállauh[4].

Ind. comp. imperf.

sg. 2nd f. ትከፍያለሽ tikafyálläš[4], ትሰጭያለሽ tisačyálläš[4].

Cont.	sg. 2nd f.	ትከፍዪ tikáfī,	ትሰጪ tisáč[5].
Imp.	sg. 2nd f.	ክፈይ kífai,	ስጪ sič.
Neg. imp.	sg. 2nd f.	አትክፈይ āttíkfai,	አትስጪ āttísč[3].
Ger.	sg. 1st	ከፍዬ káfiyye,	ሰጥቼ sáṭiččʸe.
Part.		ከፋይ káfāi[3, 6],	ሰጪ sač[7].

---

[1] or -āy-, throughout the tense. [2] or -íy-.

[3] § 8. [4] § 7*a*. [5] or -sá-, -či.

[6] -áyy (§ 6). [7] or säč, ሰጪ. sáči (sá-; § 7*b*).

Common Anomalous Biliterals.

አለ álḁ, to say, (s.v. √በለ, cp. Eth. ብሀለ): §44a

Indicative

Simp. perf. (§ 25)

sg. 3rd m.	አለ	álḁ,	pl. 3rd	አሉ	álu,
3rd f.	አለች	áläč[1],	2nd	አላችሁ	ālā́č(č)i̥hu[5],
2nd m.	አልሀ	ā́lh[2],	1st	አልነ	ā́lnḁ[6].
2nd f.	አልሽ	ā́lš[3],			
1st	አልሁ	ā́lhu[4].			

Comp. perf. (§ 32a) ብሏል bí̥lŏ͡āl[7],
sg. 3rd f. ብላለች bi̥lā́lläč[1],
sg. 1st ብያለሁ biyyā́llḁu͡h[8], etc.

Comp. imperf. (§ 32a, b) ይላል yí̥lāl,
sg. 3rd f. ትላለች ti̥lā́lläč[1], etc.

Contingent (§ 26)

sg. 3rd m.	ይል	yi̥l,
3rd f.	ትል	ti̥l,
2nd m.	ትል	ti̥l,
2nd f.	ትይ	ti̥y[9],
1st	እል	i̥l,
pl. 3rd	ይሉ	yí̥lu,
2nd	ትሉ	tí̥lu,
1st	እንል	i̥nní̥l.

Jussive (§ 27)

ይበል yí̥bḁl[10, 11].
sg. 3rd f. ትበል tí̥bḁl[10, 11], etc.

Imperative (§ 28)

sg. 2nd m.	በል	bḁl[11],
2nd f.	በይ	bḁ͡i̥[12],
pl. 2nd	በሉ	bḁ́lu.

[1] -čč (§ 6). [2] or ‌áli̥h, አልኽ ā́lχ, አልክ ā́lk, (§ 7d).
[3] or ‌áli̥š.
[4] or -hŭ, áluh, አልኩ ā́lku (-kŭ); also አልኍ ā́lhw(ŭ), (§ 7d). [5] or -ā́č(č)yuh (§ 7d). [6] or አልን ā́ln, ā́li̥n.
[7] G. also አለናል álḁnnāl (§ 32c). [8] (§ 7d); or -ለኍ.
[9] or tī. [10] or -í̥y̥-. [11] or -äl. [12] § 7b.

Gerund (§ 29)	Infinitive (§ 30)
ብሎ bı̥l^{w}o,	ማለት mā́lḁt[2].
sg. 3rd f. ብላ bı̥lā,	Participle
1st ብዬ bíyye[1], etc.	none in use.

§ 44*b* አየ ā́yyä, to look, see, like ቀረ (§ 42*b*):

Indicative

Simp. perf. አየ ā́yyä,
sg. 3rd f. አየች ā́yyäč[3],
2nd m. አየህ ā́yyäh, etc.
Comp. perf. (§ 32*a*) አይቷል ā͡i̥tŏ͡āl[4],
sg. 3rd f. አይታለች a͡i̥tā́lläč[3],
sg. 1st አይቻለሁ a͡i̥ččā́llḁ͡uh[5], etc.
Comp. imperf. (§ 32*a*, *b*) ያያል yā͡i̥āl[6],
sg. 3rd f. ታያለች tā͡i̥ā́lläč[3,7],
sg. 1st አያለሁ ā͡i̥ā́llḁ͡uh[7,8], etc.

Contingent (§ 26)

sg. 3rd m.	ያይ	yā͡i̥,	pl. 3rd	ያዩ	yā͡i̥u[9],
3rd f.	ታይ	tā͡i̥,	2nd	ታዩ	tā͡i̥u[9],
2nd m.	ታይ	tā͡i̥,	1st	እናይ	i̥nnā͡i̥.
2nd f.	ታዪ	tā͡i,			
1st	አይ	ā͡i̥,			

---

[1] § 7*b*. [2] or -ät. [3] -čč (§ 6).
[4] G. also አየናል ā́yyännāl (§ 32*c*).
[5] or -ችያ- -ččyā́- (§ 7*a*); -ለኍ.
[6] or yā^{y}āl (§ 7*d*, under የ).
[7] or -ā^{y}ā́- (§ 7*d*, under የ). [8] § 26. [9] or -ā́^{y}u.

JUSSIVE (§ 27)

sg.	3rd m.	ይይ	yi̥y[1],
	3rd f.	ትይ	ti̥y[2],
	1st	[እይ	i̥y,][3]
pl.	3rd	ይዩ	yí̥yu[4],
	1st	እንይ	i̥nní̥y[5].

IMPERATIVE (§ 28)

sg.	2nd m.	እይ	i̥y[6],
	2nd f.	እዪ	í̥yi[7],
pl.	2nd	እዩ	í̥yu[8].

NEGATIVE IMPERATIVE (§ 38)

sg.	2nd m.	አትይ	ä̃́ttí̥y[9],
	2nd f.	አትዪ	ä̃ttí̥yi[10],
pl.	2nd	አትዩ	ä̃ttí̥yu[11].

GERUND (§ 29)

sg.	3rd m.	አይቶ	ä̃͡i̥tʷo,
	3rd f.	አይታ	ä̃͡i̥tä̃,
	1st	አይቼ	ä̃͡i̥ččʸe[12], etc.

INFINITIVE (§ 30)

ማየት mä̃͡i̥ät[13].

PARTICIPLE (§ 31)

†አዪ ä́yyi.

---

[1] or yī̥, yī. [2] or tī̥, tī.

[3] only with ለ- (§ 48*b*) ለይ li̥y, lī̥, lī.

[4] or yí̥u, yíu. [5] or -ní̥, -ní. [6] or ī̥, ī.

[7] or í̥i, íi. [8] or í̥u, íu. [9] (§ 8); or -tí̥, -tí.

[10] or -tí̥i, -tíi. [11] or -tí̥u, -tíu. [12] § 7*b*.

[13] or mä̃ʸät (§ 7*d*, under የ).

§ 44*c* ያዘ yá̄zḁ, to seize, take hold (of), like ጣፈ (§ 42*c*):

INDICATIVE

Simp. perf. (§ 25)

sg. 3rd m.	ያዘ	yá̄zḁ,	pl. 3rd	ያዙ	yá̄zu,
3rd f.	ያዘች	yá̄zäč[1],	2nd	ያዛችሁ	yāzá̄č(č)i̥hu[5],
2nd m.	ያዝህ	yā̃zh[2],	1st	ያዝነ	yá̄znḁ[6].
2nd f.	ያዝሽ	yā̃zš[3],			
1st	ያዝሁ	yā̃́zhu[4],			

Comp. perf. (§ 32*a*) ይዟል yí̥zŏ͡āl[7],
sg. 3rd f. ይዛለች yi̥zá̄lläč[1],
sg. 1st ይዥለሁ yi̥žá̄llḁ͡u[h][8].

Comp. imp. (§ 32*a*, *b*) ይይዛል yi̥(y)í̥zāl, or ይዛል yí̥zāl,
sg. 3rd f. ትይዛለች ti̥(y)i̥zá̄lläč[1], or ቲዛለች tī̥zá̄lläč[1], etc.

CONTINGENT (§ 26)

sg. 3rd m.	ይይዝ	yi̥(y)í̥z,	or	ይዝ	yī̥z,
3rd f.	ትይዝ	ti̥(y)í̥z,	„	ቲዝ	tī̥z,
2nd m.	ትይዝ	ti̥(y)í̥z,	„	ቲዝ	tī̥z,
2nd f.	ትይዥ	ti̥(y)í̥ž[9],	„	ቲዥ	tī̥ž[9],
1st	እይዝ	i̥(y)í̥z,	„	ኢዝ	ī̥z,
pl. 3rd	ይይዙ	yi̥(y)í̥zu,	„	ይዙ	yí̥zu,
2nd	ትይዙ	ti̥(y)í̥zu,	„	ቲዙ	tí̥zu,
1st	እንይዝ	i̥nni̥(y)í̥z[10],	„	እኒዝ	i̥nní̥z.

---

[1] čč (§ 6). [2] or yá̄zĭ̥h, yā̃sh, ያዝኽ yā̃zχ, yā̃sχ, ያዝክ yā̃zk (-sk), (§ 7*d*, under ዘ). [3] or yá̄zĭ̥š, yā̃šš (§ 7*d*).

[4] or -sh-, hŭ, yá̄zuh, ያዝኩ yā̃́zku (-sk-, -kŭ), ያዝኍ yā̃́zhw(ŭ), (-sh-), (§ 7*d*, under ká͡i̥y, ሀ, ዘ).

[5] or -á̄č(č)yuh (§ 7*d*). [6] or ያዝን yā̃zn, yá̄zĭ̥n.

[7] G. also ያዘናል yá̄zḁnnāl (-zä-; § 32*c*).

[8] (§ 7*d*); or -ለኍ. [9] or -žĭ (§ 7*b*). [10] or i̥nnyí̥z.

JUSSIVE (§ 27)

	ይያዝ	yi̥(y)ã́z[1],
sg. 3rd f.	ትያዝ	ti̥(y)ã́z[1], etc.

IMPERATIVE (§ 28)			NEG. IMP. (§ 38)	
sg. 2nd m.	ያዝ	yãz,	አትያዝ	ã́ttyã́z[1],
2nd f.	ያዥ	yãž[2],	አትያዥ	ã́ttyã́ž[1,3],
pl. 2nd	ያዙ	yázu.	አትያዙ	ãttyázu.

GERUND (§ 29)

	ይዞ	yí̥zʷo,
sg. 3rd f.	ይዛ	yí̥zã,
1st	ይዤ	yí̥žžʸe[4], etc.

INFINITIVE (§ 30) መያዝ mḁ́yã́z[1,5].

PARTICIPLE (§ 31) ያዥ yãž[6].

Prefixing of Conjunctions to Contingent. § 45

ለ-, ስ- ብ-, etc. (§ 48*a*), when pref. to the cont. (§ 26) modify its prefixes thus (§§ 5, 6, 7*a*):

sg. 3rd m.	ቢለቅም	bilḁ́q(i̥)m[7], if he picks,
3rd f.	ብትለቅም	bi̥tt(i̥)lḁ́q(i̥)m[8], if she picks, etc.
2nd m.	ብትለቅም	bi̥tt(i̥)lḁ́q(i̥)m[8],
2nd f.	ብትለቅሚ	bi̥tt(i̥)lḁ́qmi[8],
1st	ብለቅም	bi̥lḁ́q(i̥)m,
pl. 3rd	ቢለቅሙ	bilḁ́qmu[7],
2nd	ብትለቅሙ	bi̥tt(i̥)lḁ́qmu[8],
1st	ብንለቅም	bi̥nn(i̥)lḁ́q(i̥)m.

---

[1] § 8. [2] or -ži (§ 7*b*). [3] or ãttyã́ži. [4] § 7*b*.

[5] or mḁi̥ã́z, mḁ́ʸã́z (§ 7*d*, under የ).

[6] or ያዢ yáži (§ 7*b*). [7] or bi̥l- (§ 7*d*).

[8] or bi̥tl- (seldom in G.).

sg. 3rd m. ሲያጥብ syā̓ṭ(ı̥)y, when he washes.
3rd f. ስታጥብ si̥ttā̓ṭ(ı̥)y,
2nd m. ስታጥብ si̥ttā̓ṭ(ı̥)y,
2nd f. ስታጥቢ si̥ttā̓ṭyi,
1st ሳጥብ sā̓ṭ(ı̥)y,
pl. 3rd ሲያጥቡ syā̓ṭyu,
2nd ስታጥቡ si̥ttā̓ṭyu,
1st ስናጥብ si̥nnā̓ṭ(ı̥)y.

The Adverb.

§ 46 Adverbs have no special form:

ገና gḁ́nã, yet.
አሁን ā́hun (-ωn), now.
አወን ā́wω(n) (ā́u-), yes.

Substantives, alone or with a preposition, adjectives, pronouns with a preposition, and the gerund (§ 29) are used as adverbs:

e.g. ውስጥ wŭsṭ, s. interior,
ውስጥ, or በውስጥ bḁ́uŭ́sṭ (§ 8), adv. inside.
ፊት, ῑt[1], s. face,
ፊት or በፊት bḁ́fῑt[1,2], adv. in front, formerly.
መልካም mḁ́lkám[2], adj. beautiful, adv. well.
ከዚሁ kḁ́zzíh[2,3] (§ 47*a*, § 13*a*), at or from this (one); adv. here, hence.
እንደምን (i̥)ndḁ́mí̥n?[4,2], like what?; adv. how?

---

[1] or -i̥t. [2] § 8. [3] or hḁ́-, -ā́z-, -í̥h, § 7*d*.
[4] or -dā́-; § 8.

ደግሞ dḁ́gmʷo (dá́-), ger. he (it) repeating; adv. again.

Some adverbial particles are suffixes, s.v. -ን, -እ, -ወይ.

THE PREPOSITION.

Prepositions are of two kinds, simple and com- § 47*a*
posite.

The simple prepositions are prefixes:

e.g. ለ- lḁ-, for, to,

በ- bḁ-, by means of, with, at, in,

ተ- tḁ-, or ከ- kḁ-, at, in, from,

የ- yä-, of,

ስለ- si̥lḁ-[1], because of,

ያለ- yālḁ-[2], without

እንደ- (i̥)ndḁ-[3], like,

እስተ- i̥stḁ-, or እስከ- i̥skḁ-, as far as, up to.

When these are attached to a pers. pron. they take the disjunctive form (§ 12*a*).

E.g. ለፈረስ ፡ ነው ። lḁfḁrḁ́s[4] nḁu, it is for the horse.

ለኔ ፡ ነው ። lḁnʸé nḁu, it is for me.

በካራ ፡ ቍረጠው ፡ bḁkárra qwŭ́rḁtḁu, cut it with a knife.

ተቤት ፡ ነው ። tḁyʸét nḁu, he (it) is in the house.

ከቤት ፡ ወጣ ። kḁyʸét wǿṭṭa, he came out of the house.

ያንተ ፡ ነው ። yantá[5,4] nḁu, it is yours.

---

[1] or si̥lä-. [2] G. አለ- álḁ- (cp. § 37*a*).

[3] or (i̥)ndä-. [4] § 8. [5] § 7*a*.

ስለዝምብ ፡ ነው ። si̥lḁzí̥mbĭ̥ nḁu͡, it is because of the flies.

ያለገንዘብ ፡ ሔደ ። yālḁgḁ́nzḁy̥ hā̃dä, he went without money.

እንደፈረስ ፡ ነው ። ndḁfḁrḁ́s[1] nḁu͡, it is like a horse.

እስተቤት ፡ መጣ ። i̥stḁy̥ʸét mḁ́ṭṭa, he (it) came as far as the house.

ለ-, በ- are also attached with the pers. suff. (§ 12*c*) to a verb, or interposed between the verb and the aux. አለ (§ 32). In these positions their consonants are doubled (§ 5), and they become -ሊ- -lli̥-, -ቢ- -bbi̥- before -ኝ, -ህ [-ኽ], ሽ, -ነ [-ን]; with the sg. 3rd they make m. -ለት- -llḁt- (-ät-), f. -ላት- -llāt-, m. -በት- -bbḁt- (-ät-), f. -ባት- -bbāt-:

e.g. ላከ lā́kḁ, he sent:

ላከልኝ	lā́kḁlli̥ñ[2],	he sent to or for me.		
ላከልህ	lā́kḁlli̥h,	„	„	you.
ላከልሽ	lā́kḁlli̥š,	„	„	you (f.).
ላከለዎ	lā́kḁllḁ͡ʷo[3],	„	„	you (pol.).
ላከለት	lā́kḁllḁt[4],	„	„	him.
ላከላት	lā́kḁllāt,	„	„	her.
ላከልን	lā́kḁlli̥n[5],	„	„	us.
ላከላችሁ	lākḁllā́č(č)yuh[6],	„	„	you (pl.).
ላከላቸው	lākḁllā́č(č)ḁu͡,	„	„	them (him, pol.).

---

[1] § 8.

[2] -ññ (§ 6); this and the next six forms are also accented -kḁ́- (§ 8).

[3] or -ለዎት -llḁ͡ʷot.

[4] or -ät.

[5] or -ልነ -lli̥nnḁ.

[6] § 7*d*.

ይልካል yi̥lí̥kāl, he is sending, will send:

ይልክልኛል yi̥lí̥ki̥lli̥ññāl[1], he will send to or for me.				
ይልክልሃል yi̥lí̥ki̥lli̥hāl[2],	„	„	„	you.
ይልክልሻል yi̥lí̥ki̥lli̥šāl,	„	„	„	you (f.).
ይልክለዎአል yi̥lí̥ki̥llḁʷoāl[3],	„	„	„	you (pol.).
ይልክለታል yi̥lí̥ki̥llḁtāl,	„	„	„	him.
ይልክላታል yi̥lí̥ki̥llātāl,	„	„	„	her.
ይልክልናል yi̥lí̥ki̥lli̥nnāl,	„	„	„	us.
ይልክላችኋል yi̥li̥ki̥llá-č(č)i̥hwāl[4],	„	„	„	you (pl.).
ይልክላቸዋል yi̥li̥ki̥lláč(č)ḁuāl,	„	„	„	them (him, pol.).

ልኳል lí̥kŏāl, he has sent,

ልክልኛል lí̥kʷolli̥ññāl[5], he has sent to or for me.

Composite prepositions consist in a prefix and a word following the recipient of the prefix. This type of prp. is often a resolution into its component parts of an adv. composed of a prp. and a substantive (§ 46): § 47*b*

e.g. ከ- [ተ-] ... ፡ ጋር kḁ- (tḁ-) ... gār, with (accompanying),

በ- ... ፡ ውስጥ bḁ- ... wŭsṭ, inside,

በ- ... ፡ ፊት bḁ- ... fīt[6], in front of, before,

በ- ... ፡ ላይ bḁ- ... lái̥, on, upon, above;

---

[1] This and the next six forms often have the accent on -kí̥- (§ 8). [2] or -ኻል -χāl.

[3] or -ለዎታል -llḁʷotāl, -ልዎአል -llĭ̥ʷoāl, -ልዎታል -llĭ̥ʷotāl. [4] or -áč(č)yuhāl (§ 7*d*).

[5] or li̥kʷó- (§ 8); G. also ላክልኝናል lákalli̥ññi̥nnāl.

[6] or fi̥t.

or consists in a simp. prp. and an adv. of that type:

e.g. ከ- [ተ-] ... ፡ በውስጥ kḁ- (tḁ-) ... bḁu͡ŭst̥[1], inside.

ተኔ ፡ ጋር ፡ መጣ ። tḁnʸé[1] gār mḁt̥t̥a, he came with me.

በቤት ፡ ውስጥ ፡ bḁyʸét[1] wŭst̥, inside the house.

በቤት ፡ ፊት ፡ bḁyʸét[1] fit[2], in front of the house.

ከቤት ፡ በውስጥ ፡ ነው ። kḁyét yḁu͡ŭst̥i̥[3] nḁu, he (it) is inside the house.

The Conjunction.

§ 48*a* Conjunctions are of three kinds, prefixes, suffixes, and unattached.

Prefixed conjunctions, which[4] introduce dependent clauses, include several particles also used as prepositions (§ 47*a*);

e.g. pref. to simp. perf. (§ 25):

ብ- bḁ-, when, if,

ተ- tḁ-, or ከ- kḁ-, since, as, seeing that,

ስለ- silḁ- (-lä-), because,

እንደ- (i̥)ndḁ- (-dä-), as, in the same way that,

እስተ- i̥stḁ- or እስከ- i̥skḁ-, until;

pref. to cont. (§§ 26, 45):

ል- l(i̥)-, to, that; also pref. to juss. sg. 1st (§ 27),

ስ- s(i̥)-, when, while; with neg. cont. (§ 38) before,

ብ- b(i̥)-, if, when,

ክ- k(i̥)-, than that,

---

[1] § 8. [2] or fi̥t. [3] § 7*d*.

[4] except ል- with juss. (§ 27).

ስለም- si̥lḁmm- (i.e. ስለ- + rel. § 14), because,

እንድ-, (i̥)nd(i̥)-, in order that,

እስት- i̥st(i̥)-, or እስክ- i̥sk(i̥)-, until.

E.g. በሰማ፡ bḁsḁ́mma, if he had heard, when he heard,

ቢሰማ፡ bisḁ́ma[1], if he hears.

ከሰማ፡ kḁsḁ́mma, as (or, since) he heard,

ኪሰማ፡ kisḁ́ma[1], than that he should hear.

ስለሰማሁ፡ si̥lḁsḁ́mma͡u^{h}, because I heard,

ስለምሰማ፡ si̥lḁmmi̥sḁ́ma, because I shall hear.

እንደነበር፡ ndänḁ́bbär, as he (it) was,

እንዲሆን፡ ndih^{w}ón[2], in order that he (it) may be,

እንዳለ፡ ndállä[3], as he (it) is, if (whether) he (it) is present (§ 32*d*).

እስተሔደ፡ i̥stḁhắdä, until he went,

እስቲሔድ፡ i̥stihắd[2], until he goes.

ልመጣ፡ እፈልጋለሁ። li̥mḁ́ṭa i̥fḁlli̥gállḁ͡u^{h}, I want to come,

ልምጣ። li̥mṭa, let me come; or, li̥mṭa?, am I to come?

ስትመጣ፡ si̥tti̥mḁ́ṭa[4], when you come (or, came),

ሳትመጣ፡ satti̥mḁ́ṭa[5], before you come (or, came).

---

[1] or -i̥s-. [2] or -i̥h-. [3] § 7*a*.
[4] or si̥tm- (§ 45). [5] or sātm- (§ 45).

§ 48*b* *Suffixed Conjunctions.*

-ም -m (-mm § 6), and, even, also, too,

-ም . . . . -ም, both . . . . and,

-ና -nnã, and,

-ስ -ss, but.

These come after other suff., and -ም and -ስ are interposed between the verb and the aux. አለ (§ 32).

E.g. ፈረሲቱንም ፡ ያዙ ። fḁ́rḁsituni̥mm yázu, they caught the mare too.

ፈረሱንና ፡ በቅሎውን ፡ አምጣ ። fḁ́rḁsuni̥nna ỵḁ́ql^{w}o͡un ánṭa[1], bring the horse and the mule.

በልቶማል ፡ bḁ́lt^{w}ommāl, and he has eaten.

መጣስ ። mḁ́ṭṭass, but he has come.

ይመጣሳል ። yi̥mḁ́ṭassāl, but he will come.

ይህንንስ ፡ አላወቅሁም ። yi̥hánnäni̥ss alá͡uwωqhum, but I didn't know this.

§ 48*c* *Unattached Conjunctions.*

ግን ፡ gi̥n (q.v.) but ; gen. comes second in its clause ;

እንጂ (i̥)njí (q.v.), indeed, but ; ends its clause.

E.g. ሌላ ፡ ግን ፡ አውቃለሁ ። lēlá[2] gi̥n a͡uqállḁ͡u^{h}, but I know another.

ይህንን ፡ አልፈልግም ፡ ሌላውን ፡ እንጂ ። yi̥hánnän alfḁ́lli̥-gi̥m, lé͡laun i̥njí, I don't want this one, but the other.

---

[1] § 7*d*. [2] § 8.

The Interjection.

Interjections need no remark: § 49a

እሺ ịšši ![1], good !, all right !

ዝም zịmm !, hush !

አረግ ạrạg ![2], nonsense !

ቀስ qạss !, softly !, gently !

For the use of interj. with አላ álḁ (§ 44a), and § 49b
አሰኘ assá̈ññä, s.v. √በለ, √ሰኘ.

Formation of Nouns.

From a given root, existing or theoretical, various § 50
nouns both substantive and adjective are formed by means of prefixes, suffixes, and modification of vowels. In dictionaries words are grouped under such roots.

Taking the roots ለቀመ (type A § 34), ፈለገ (type B § 35), the following derivatives are formed:

*ለቂም láqqím[3] (-ịm[4]),

adj.

ከበደ kạ́bbạdạ, to be heavy,

ከቢድ kạ́bbíd[5], adj. heavy.

አደሰ áddạsạ, to renew,

አዲስ áddịs, adj. new.

*ለቃም lạ́qqám[3],

adj.

ጠበበ ṭạ́bbạbạ[6], to be narrow,

ጠባብ ṭạ́bbáb[7, 3], adj. narrow.

---

[1] or -šị (§ 7d). [2] § 7d; or ạrā̤ág ! [3] § 8.
[4] § 7d. [5] or -bịd. [6] or -yḁ. [7] or -ā́y.

*ልቁም lí̥qum,
*ፍሉግ fí̥llúg[1],
  adj. (passive), also used as s.

ከበረ kḁ́bbḁrḁ[2], to be rich,
ክቡር kí̥bur[3], adj. honoured, exalted.

√ቀደሰ
ቅዱስ qí̥ddús[1], adj. holy; s. saint.
*ልቅም lí̥q(i̥)m,
*ፍልግ fí̥lli̥g,
  s. and adj.

ደረቀ dḁ́rrḁqḁ, to be dry,
ድርቅ di̥rq, s. dryness; adj. dry.
ለበሰ lḁ́bbḁsḁ, to wear,
ልብስ li̥bs[4], s. dress; lí̥bbi̥s, adj. worn.
ቀቀለ qḁ́qqḁlḁ, to boil,
ቅቅል qí̥qqi̥l, boiled.

*ትልቃም tí̥lqám[1],
  s. abstract.
አዘዘ ázzḁzḁ, to command,
ትእዛዝ ፡ [ትዛዝ] tí̥záz[1], s. order.

*መልቀም mḁ́lqḁm, (inf. § 30),
  s. of place or instrument.
ነገደ nḁ̊ggḁ̊dḁ, to traffic,
መንገድ mḁ́ńgḁd, road.
ሰቀለ sḁ́qqḁlḁ, to suspend,
መስቀል mḁ́sqḁl, cross.

---

[1] § 8. [2] or -är-. [3] or -í̥y-. [4] or -ys.

*መልቀሚያ m̥alq̥ámyā,

*መፈለጊያ m̥af̥alľágyā,

adj. relative to or instrumental in effecting the action or state; commonly used as s.

ከደነ kḁ́ddan̥ḁ, to cover,

መክደኛ m̥akdḁ́ñā[1], lid.

ቈጠረ qwóṭṭḁrḁ[2], to count,

መቍጠሪያ m̥aqwŭṭḁ́ryā[2], s. instrument for counting.

ጀመረ jḁ́mmḁrḁ[2], v.t. to begin,

መጀመሪያ m̥ajḁmmḁ́ryā[2], adj. initial; s. beginning.

ቈፈረ qwóffḁrḁ[2], to dig,

መቈፈሪያ m̥aqwoffḁ́ryā[2], spade, hoe.

*ልቅማን lí̥q(i̥)mán[3],

s. abstract.

(√በረሀ) በራ bḁ́rrā, to shine,

ብርሃን bí̥rhán[3], s. light; adj. light.

ረገመ rḁ́ggḁmḁ, to curse,

ርግማን ri̥gí̥mán[4], s. curse.

Analogous formations are derived from roots of less or more than three letters and from derived verbal forms (§ 22):

e.g. ገባ gḁ́bbā, to enter,

መግቢያ mḁ́gbyā[5], s. entrance.

---

[1] for *መክደኒያ § 7*b*. [2] or -är-. [3] § 8.
[4] or እርግማን i̥rgí̥mán (§ 7*d*, § 8). [5] or -gy̆-.

caus. አገባ agḁ́bbā̃, to put in.

ማግቢያ mā́gbyā̃[1], instrument for putting in.

ገለበጠ gḁlḁ́bbḁtḁ, to invert,

ግልቢጥ gi̥lbi̥t[2], adj. inverted.

ጠመጠመ ṭḁmḁ́ṭṭḁmḁ, to wind, twine,

መጠምጠሚያ mḁṭḁmṭḁ́myā̃, s. turban.

ተቀመጠ tḁqḁ́mmḁṭḁ, to sit,

መቀመጫ mḁqqḁmḁ́čā̃[3], seat.

አበሰለ abḁ́ssḁlḁ[4], to cook,

ማብሰያ mābsḁ́yā̃[5], oven.

Suffixes:

-āም -ām,

adj. full of.

መልክ mḁlk, form, colour,

መልካም mḁ́lkām[6], beautiful, excellent.

-ማ -mmā̃, connected[7] by -i̥-,

adj. resembling.

አመድ ā́mḁd, ash,

አመድማ amḁdi̥mmā̃[8], ash-coloured, grey.

-ታ -tā̃, connected[7] by -i̥-,

s. abstract.

ዝግ zi̥gg!, interj. slowly!, gently!

ዝግታ zi̥ggi̥tā̃[6], patience, inexcitability.

---

[1] or -gy-. [2] or -ly-; also gi̥lí̥bbi̥ṭ.

[3] for *መተቀመጢያ (§ 7*b*, *c*). [4] or ay-.

[5] or -ys-, -ḁ́i̥ā̃; for *ማብሰሊያ (§ 7*b*). [6] § 8.

[7] with a final consonant. [8] or -äd-.

-ḁት -ḁt (-ät),
s. abstract.

ሙቅ muq, adj. hot,

ሙቀት múqḁt, s. heat.

-ነት -nnḁt (-nnät), connected[1] by -i̥-,
s. abstract.

ወታደር wωttáddḁr[2], soldier,

ወታደርነት wωttaddḁri̥nnḁt[2,3], being a soldier, military service.

-ኛ -ññã, connected[1] by -i̥- or -ḁ- (-ä-),
adj. relating to;
s. agent.

አማራ amắrã[4], Amhara,

አማርኛ amări̥ññã[4], adj. and s. Amharic.

ፈረስ fḁ́rḁs, s. horse,

ፈረሰኛ fḁrḁsḁ́ññã[5], adj. relating to horses; s. horseman.

---

[1] with a final consonant. [2] or -dä-. [3] or -ät.
[4] or -ምኃ- -mhắ-. [5] or -sắ-.

SYNTAX.

§ 51 *Note.* Various points of syntax have been treated in the Accidence, especially in that of the pronoun, verb and preposition, the accidence and syntax of which are often so intimately connected in this inflectional and synthetic language that they cannot be separated with either convenience or propriety.

Peculiarities of syntax which are not of wide application have usually been relegated to the vocabularies, where they are discussed under the particular words which exhibit or involve them.

Number.

Singular for Plural.

§ 52*a* The singular is frequently used with a plural force, especially

(*α*) after numerals (§ 20*a*).

(*β*) after ብዙ bı̥́zu, much, many; ስንት sı̥nt?, how many? (§ 15):

e.g. ብዙ ፡ ሰው ፡ ፈጀ ። bı̥́zu sḁu fǻjjä, he (it) destroyed many people.

ብዙ ፡ ሰው ፡ መጣ ። bı̥́zu sḁu mḁ́ṭṭa, many people came.

(*γ*) of parts of the body of which there are two or more:

e.g. ዓይን ấi̥n, etc., = eye or eyes, etc.

እጅህን ፡ እጠበው ። ı̥́jji̥hi̥n ı̥́ṭḁyḁu, wash your hands.

ጥርሴን ፡ እፍቃለሁ ። ṭ̥írsʸen i̥fi̥qállḁu͡ʰ, I brush my teeth.

(δ) of objects not usually occurring or used singly:

e.g. ምስጥ ፡ ይበላዋል ። mi̥sṭ yi̥v̥ḁ́lau͡āl, the white ants will destroy it.

ጫማ ፡ ሰጠኝ ። č̣ámma sḁ́ṭṭäñ, he gave me a pair of shoes.

ጉድብ gúdbã (-dv̥-), s., a ditch, channel formed by water: then, in pl. sense, broken ground, e.g. that along a river bank cut up by numerous channels draining into the river (كرب).

Plural for Singular.

In the 'polite' form, i.e. the mode of addressing or referring to superiors (§ 12*a*), the plural verb and pers. pron. (§ 12*a*, *b*, *c*) are used with a singular force: (the adj. remains in the sg. § 53*b*): § 52*b*

e.g. ያውቃሉ ፡ yau͡ŭqállu, you (sg. pol.) know, or, he (pol.) knows.

Concord in Number.

The concord in number between substantive, adjective, pronoun and verb is generally maintained except in the following cases: § 53*a*

A substantive in the pl. may be constr. with an adj. and occasionally (§§ 15, 16) with a pron. in the sg.:

e.g. ወታደሮች ፡ ደኅና ፡ ናቸው ። wωttáddar̥ʷōč dähná náččḁu͡[1], the troops are in good health.

---

[1] less commonly ው- ፡ ደኅኖች ፡ ናቸው ። wω- dähnʷṓč náččḁu͡; ደኅና (q.v., prob. for በደኅና) is one of certain adj. which generally remain in the sg.

ክፉ ፡ ልጆች ፡ ki̥fu li̥jʷōč, or

ክፎች ፡ ልጆች ፡ ki̥fʷōč li̥jʷōč, bad children.

ሰራተኞች ፡ ሁሉ ፡ sḁrrātáññōč húllu, or

ሰራተኞች ፡ ሁላቸው ፡ sḁrrātáññōč hulláččḁ͡u, all the labourers.

§ 53*b* The uses mentioned in § 52 may involve breaches of concord:

e.g. ብዙ ፡ ሰው ፡ መጡ ። bi̥zu sḁ͡u mḁ́ṭṭu, many people came.

እንፈጃጀዋለን ፡ እሊዚህን ፡ ቁንጫጭን ። i̥nni̥fḁjajjḁ͡uállän i̥lläzzi̥hi̥n qunč̣áč̣i̥n, we will thọroughly destroy these ants.

አፈ ፡ ንጉሥ ፡ ወፍራም ፡ ናቸው ። áfḁ ni̥gús wωfrám náččḁ͡u, the Chief Justice is stout.

ራስ ፡ አልመጡም ። rās almḁ́ṭṭum, the Ras has not come.

Gender.

Concord in Gender.

§ 54*a* The concord in gender between substantive, art. pron. and verb is generally maintained, but see § 54*d*.

Substantives denoting male objects are m., female objects f. Other substantives are usually m. but may be made f. (§ 9*a*):

e.g. ወንድሙ ፡ ነው ። wωndi̥mmu nḁ͡u, it is his brother.

ሴት ፡ ናት ። sʸēt nāt, it is a woman.

እናቱ ፡ ነበረች ። nnātu nḁbbäräč, it was his mother.

Determination of Gender.

The gender of words used for both sexes may be fixed § 54*b*

(*α*) when the object is determinate, by the art. (§ 11):

e.g. ፈረሱ ፡ fḁ́rḁsu, the horse,

ፈረሲቱ ፡ fḁ́rḁsi̥tu, the mare;

(*β*) when the object is indeterminate, by ወንድ wωnd, male, ሴት s^{y}ēt, female, of persons and[1] animals, and አውራ a͡urā́[2], male, እንስት i̥ní̥st[2], female, of animals:

e.g. ወንድ ፡ ልጅ ፡ wώndĭ̥[3] li̥j, a boy, son,

ሴት ፡ ልጅ ፡ s^{y}ḗtli̥j[2], a girl, daughter.

ወንድ ፡ ፈረስ ፡ wώnd(ĭ̥)[3] fḁ́rḁs, a stallion,

ሴት ፡ ፈረስ ፡ s^{y}ēt fḁ́rḁs, or

እንስት ፡ ፈረስ ፡ i̥ní̥st fḁ́rḁs, a mare.

ወንድ ፡ ዶሮ ፡ wώndĭ̥[3] d^{w}ór^{w}o, or

አውራ ፡ ዶሮ ፡ a͡urā́ d^{w}ór^{w}o, a cock,

ሴት ፡ ዶሮ ፡ s^{y}ēt d^{w}ór^{w}o, or

እንስት ፡ ዶሮ ፡ i̥ní̥stĭ̥[3] d^{w}ór^{w}o, a hen.

አውራ ፡ ዝሆን ፡ a͡urā́ zóh^{w}on, a bull elephant,

እንስት ፡ ዝሆን ፡ i̥ní̥stĭ̥[3] zóh^{w}on, a cow elephant.

(*γ*) The gender of a word of indeterminate gender may also be shown by the verb or its equivalent:

e.g. ክፉ ፡ ሰው ፡ ነበረች ። kí̥fu sḁ͡u nḁ́bbḁrăč, she was a bad lot.

ክፉ ፡ ሰው ፡ ናት ። kí̥fu sḁ́͡u[2] nāt, she is a bad lot.

---

[1] not gen. out of Š. [2] § 8. [3] § 7*d*.

§ 54c *Diminutive Use of Feminine.*

The feminine is used to denote smallness:

e.g. ትንሽ ፡ ትንሽ ፡ ናት ። tịnnịš tịnníš[1] nāt, it is very small.

አትታይም ። attịttáyyịm, it (is so small that it) is not seen.

Thus the f. art. (§ 11) or a f. dem. pron. (§ 13*a*) is added to a word to form a diminutive, the art. in this case often losing its determinative force:

e.g. ቀዳዳ qạdấdã, a hole,

ቀዳዳይቱ qạdấdaịtu[2], the (or, a) little hole.

ንዳድ nịdấd[1], fever,

ንዳዲቱ nịdấdịtu[3], a slight attack of fever.

ያች ፡ መጣፍ ፡ yač mạṭấf[1], that little book.

Similarly nouns expressing small objects, especially small animals and insects, are commonly feminine:

e.g. እንቍራሪት ፡ ትዘላለች ። ṅqwŭrārit tịzällálläč, the toad hops.

ሸረሪት ፡ ትሮጣለች ። šạrạrít tịr[w]oṭálläč, the spider runs.

§ 54d A diminutive formed by the f. art. (§ 54*c*) does not always have its verb in the feminine:

e.g. ንዳዲቱ ፡ አለችው ። nịdấdịtu álläččyu, and

ንዳዲቱ ፡ አለው ። nịdấdịtu állạu, he has a little fever.

---

[1] § 8. [2] Š. ቀዳዳዋ qạdấdauã.

[3] Š. ንዳዷ nịdấdwã.

Words of Variable Gender.

Several substantives, such as

ዛፍ zāf, tree,

ቀን qḁn, day,

ግዜ gi̥zʸe, time,

though usually m. are occasionally f. without the gender having a diminutive force[1].

Case.

Position of Nominative.

The usual position of the nom., which is used to indicate the subject, is at the beginning of a clause, the acc., indicating the object, coming between it and the verb: § 55*a*

e.g. ሰው፡ አንበሳ፡ ገደለ። sḁ́u ambḁ́ssa[2,3] gắddḁlḁ, a man has killed a lion.

አንበሳ፡ ሰው፡ ገደለ። ambḁ́ssa sḁ́u[4] gắddḁlḁ, a lion has killed a man.

Introductory Nominative.

A substantive, usually accompanied by a dem. pron. (§ 13*a*), may also stand in the nom. in an introductory manner at the head of a clause of which it is not the subject, and in which it may be referred to by § 55*b*

---

[1] Cp. the large number of diminutive forms in spoken Latin, esp. of the 'Animula vagula blandula' period, which have lost all diminutive force in the Romance languages.

[2] acc. (§ 56*a*).   [3] § 7*d*.   [4] § 8.

a pron. amounting to a possessive (genitive § 12*b*) or dative (§ 12*c*) case:

e.g. ይህ ፡ ሰው ፡ አባቱ ፡ ሞተ ። yi̥hé[1] sḁ͡u abbắtu mʷótḁ, this man's father is dead, (lit. this man his father is dead).

ይች ፡ ሴት ፡ ልጅ ፡ የላትም ። yí̥čči̥ sʸēt li̥j yällḁ́ti̥m, this woman has no child, (lit. this woman there is not a child to her).

A clause may contain more than one such nom.:

e.g. ይህ ፡ አገር ፡ እራብ ፡ መሆኑ ፡ ከፋ ። yí̥he ágär i̥rḁ́ɏ mḁhʷónu kḁ́ffa, this country has suffered from famine, (lit. this country famine the happening of it has been harmful).

The Accusative.

§ 56 The accusative is the case of the direct object. For its position in the clause see § 55*a*.

Indeterminate Accusative.

§ 56*a* When the acc. is indeterminate or indefinite the termination -ን (§ 9*c*) is usually dropped:

e.g. ቤት ፡ አየ ። bʸēt áyyä, he saw a house.

ትልቅ ፡ ቤት ፡ አየ ። ti̥llí̥q[1] ɏʸēt[2] áyyä, he saw a large house.

የሹም ፡ ቤት ፡ አየ ። yäšúm[1] bʸēt áyyä, he saw a chief's (§ 47*a*) house.

የወደቀ ፡ ቤት ፡ አየ ። yäwǿddḁqḁ́[1] ɏʸēt[2] áyyä, he saw a fallen house, (lit. which fell, § 14).

---

[1] § 8. [2] § 7*d*.

Amharic often uses the indeterminate form where English uses the determinate, i.e. the article (cp. § 59*a*):

e.g. He filled the skin with water: አቁማዳውን ፡ ውሃ ፡ መላው ። aqumăda͡un wŭ́ha mḁlla͡u, or አቁማዳ ፡ ውሃ ፡ መላ aqumắda wŭ́ha (-mādá͡uha) mḁlla, which last also = he filled a skin with water.

Determinate Accusative.

The acc. takes -ን when it is determinate or definite. When it is rendered so by the art., a pron., an epithet or its equivalent, it is these that take -ን and not the acc. which they determine: § 56*b*

e.g. ቤትን ፡ አየ ። b^{y}éti̥n áyyä, he saw the house.

ቤቱን ፡ አየ ። b^{y}étun áyyä, he saw the[1] house, or, his house.

ቤቴን ፡ አየ ። b^{y}ét^{y}en áyyä, he saw my house.

ይህን ፡ ቤት ፡ አየ ። yi̥hắn b^{y}ēt áyyä, he saw this house.

ትልቁን ፡ ቤት ፡ አየ ። ti̥lli̥qún[2] b^{y}ēt áyyä, he saw the large house.

የሹሙን ፡ ቤት ፡ አየ ። yäšumún[2] b^{y}ēt áyyä, he saw the chief's house.

የወደቀውን ፡ ቤት ፡ አየ ። yäwώddḁqḁ́͡un[2] b^{y}ēt áyyä, he saw the house which fell down.

---

[1] before-mentioned, this.

[2] § 8.

Adverbial or Specific Accusative.

§ 56c An acc. specifying or particularizing an action or state is found with verbs which are not transitive in the usual sense of the term, i.e. which do not admit a direct object. The action or state may be specified as cognate or germane to the sense of the verb, or particularized in regard to time, place, direction, manner or degree, or in regard to an object[1]:

e.g. **አለቀ** állḁqḁ, to come to an end,

ይህን ፡ ወር ፡ ያልቃል ። yi̥hán wωr yā́lqāl, it will come to an end this month.

ያን ፡ ግዜ ፡ ነበር ። yan gí̥zʸe nḁ́bbḁr, it was at that time.

ዞረ zʷórḁ, to go round, revolve,

ዙርያውን ፡ ዞረ ። zurya͡ún zʷórḁ, he went right round it, (lit. walked round as regards its circumference).

ገባ gḁ́bba, to go in,

ቤቱን ፡ ገባ ። bʸétun gḁ́bba, he went into his house, went home.

---

[1] When the action may be particularized in regard to a variety of objects one begins to feel that the verb may with some propriety be called transitive, (s.v. **ለበሰ**). There are grammarians who will distinguish between the accusatives in **በርኔታን ፡ ለበሰ ።** and **በርኔታን ፡ ሰረቀ ።** on the ground that **ለበሰ** is not a v.t., while admitting that the acc. of the direct object is, ultimately, an adv. acc. The inexpert compiler of a grammar may quote a remark the truth of which he has probably illustrated himself: *εἰ μὴ ἰατροὶ ἦσαν, οὐδὲν ἂν ἦν τῶν γραμματικῶν μωρότερον.*

ሔደ hădä, to go,

ጎንደር ፡ ሔደ ። gʷóndạr[1] hădä, he went to Gondar.

አከለ ákkạlạ (q.v.), to increase, amount to,

ያን ፡ ያህል ፡ ሰው ፡ ምን ፡ ሆነ ። yan yahl[2] sạu[3] mịn hʷónạ?, what has become of all those men?, (lit. the men[3] that amount to that number what have they become?).

ለበሰ lạ́bbạsạ, to dress oneself,

ባርኔታን ፡ ለበሰ ። barnētan lạ́bbạsạ, he put on the (§ 59*a*) hat.

ታጠበ táṭṭạvạ, to wash oneself,

እጄን ፡ እታጠባለሁ ። ịjjʸen[3,4] ịttāṭṭạvállạuʰ, I will wash my hands.

አመመው ámmạmạu (§ 43*a*, § 63*d*), to be ill, in pain,

ራሱን ፡ አመመው ። rásun ámmạmạu, he has a pain in his head[5].

This adv. acc. may occur with an adj. or adv.: § 56*d*

ራቁት ráqut, naked,

ራሱን ፡ ራቁት ፡ rásun ráqut, with his head bare.

ብቻ bịčča, alone,

ብቻዬን bịččāʸen, by myself.

---

[1] Here there may be an ellipse of ወደ- (q.v.).

[2] For የሚያህል, s.v. አከለ.

[3] § 52*a*.

[4] Cp. λούομαι τὰς χεῖρας.

[5] Cp. ἀλγεῖ τὴν κεφαλήν.

Determinate and Indeterminate Accusative together.

§ 56*e* A verb may take a determinate acc. and an indeterminate acc. at the same time[1]:

e.g. ገንዘቤን ፡ ሁሉ ፡ ሰረቀ ። gḁ́nzḁyʸen húllu sḁ́rrḁqḁ[2], he has stolen all my money.

Double Accusative.

§ 56*f* Two inco-ordinate accusatives may occur when a verb admits of two inco-ordinate objects (§ 68):

e.g. አሽከሩን ፡ ስራውን ፡ አስደረገ ። áškḁrun si̥ra͡un asdḁ́r-rḁgḁ, he made his servant do the work.

Or one acc. may be the direct object and the other a specific acc.:

e.g. ፊቱን ፡ ወዙን ፡ አበሰው ። fi̥tun wǿzun ábbḁsḁ͡u, he wiped the sweat off his face.

One of these acc. may remain when the verb is placed in the passive or reflexive:

e.g. ታበሰ ። tábbḁsḁ, he wiped himself.

ወዙን ፡ ታበሰ ። wǿzun tábbḁsḁ, he wiped the sweat off himself.

Other Accusatives.

§ 56*g* The acc. may be used without the word involving its use being expressed by the speaker:

e.g. ፈረስ ፡ ጫን ። fḁrḁ́s (§ 8) ç̣ān, saddle a horse.

የትኛውን ። yetí̥ñña͡un?, which one?

---

[1] Cp. § 83*b*. [2] ገንዘቤን ፡ ሁሉን ፡ ሰረቀ ። can hardly be distinguished from the above in Eng.; it approaches the meaning 'all the (that) money I had'; see § 16.

With the impersonal use of ነው n̥a͡u (q.v.), it is, § 56*h*
with the rel. (§ 14) the antecedent is sometimes placed in the acc. when logically it should be in the nom.:

e.g. የትኛውን ፡ ነው ፡ ያመጣው ፡፡ yet̥iññá͡un[1] n̥a͡u yam̥áṭṭa͡u?, which is it he has brought?

አመጣ here has three objects: የትኛውን, የ-[2] and -ው.

The Adjective.

Position of Adjective.

An adjective or its equivalent when used as an § 57*a*
epithet precedes, when used as a predicate follows the substantive it qualifies:

e.g. ትልቅ ፡ ቤት ፡ ነው ፡፡ t̥ill̥íq[1] ỵʸēt n̥a͡u, it is a large house.

ቤቱ ፡ ትልቅ ፡ ነው ፡፡ bʸétu t̥ill̥íq[1] n̥a͡u, the house is large.

የንጨት ፡ ወምበር ፡ ነው ፡፡ yắnc̣ăt[3] wωmbắr[1] n̥a͡u, it is a wooden chair.

ወምበር ፡ የንጨት ፡ ነው ፡፡ wώmbär yänc̣ắt[1] n̥a͡u, the (§ 59*a*) chair is (made) of wood.

Use of Substantive as Adjective.

Some substantives denoting abstract qualities are § 57*b*
used as adjectives:

e.g. ብርሃን ፡ b̥írhắn[1], s. light,

ብርሃን ፡ ስፍራ ፡ የለም ፡፡ b̥irhắn[4] s̥ífra yắlläm, there is not a light place.

For the use of adj. as substantives see § 50, § 59*c*.

---

[1] § 8. [2] in ያ- (§ 7*a*). [3] § 70*a*, § 7*a*; s.v. እንጨት.

[4] There is probably an ellipse of የ- in this usage.

Use of Adjective as Adverb.

§ 57*c* An adjective may be used as an adverb (§ 46) without any modification of form:

e.g. ግም ፡ ሰው ። gi̥m sḁ͡u, a bad man,

ግም ፡ አደረገ ። gi̥m adắrrḁgḁ, he behaved badly.

Degrees of Comparison.

§ 58*a* There are no forms of the adjective for comparative or superlative, which are expressed by the positive constr. with ከ- kḁ- or ተ- tḁ- (q.v.), the Am. preposition rendering the Eng. conjunction 'than'[1]:

e.g. ይህ ፡ ተዚህ ፡ ከባድ ፡ ነው ። yi̥he täzzi̥h kḁbbắd nḁ͡u, this is heavier than that.

ከሁሉ ፡ ከባድ ፡ ነው ። kḁhúllu kḁbbắd nḁ͡u, it is the heaviest of all.

§ 58*b* Similarly verbs expressing the possession of a quality may have the idea of degree imparted to the quality by being constr. with ከ- kḁ- or ተ- tḁ-:

e.g. ቀጠነ ፡ qắṭṭḁnḁ, to be thin:

ይህ ፡ ተዚህ ፡ ይቀጥናል ። yi̥he täzzi̥h yi̥qắṭnāl, this is thinner than that.

ነጣ nắṭṭa, to be white:

ከነዚህ ፡ ይህ ፡ ይነጣል ። kḁnnäzzi̥h yi̥he yi̥nắṭāl, of these this is the whitest.

§ 58*c* Another way of indicating degrees of comparison is by such words as (§ 64*a*):

---

[1] Cp. use of ablative in Latin and of genitive in Greek.

ይበልጥ yi̥bḁ́lṭ (-i̥y-, -ắl-), more, (s.v. በለጠ),

ይሻል yi̥ššāl, better, (s.v. √ሻለ),

e.g. ተትናንት ፡ ይበልጥ ፡ እንሔድ ። tḁti̥nánt yi̥vḁ́lṭ i̥nní̥hi̥d, we must march further than we did yesterday.

ይበልጥ ፡ ዝለል ። yi̥vḁ́lṭ zí̥lḁl, jump higher.

The Article.

Use of the Article.

The function of the article (§ 11) is to determine (§ 56*b*). It is generally only applied to objects that have been mentioned before, or are in the presence of the speaker, and even so is frequently omitted, especially in the pl., in Am. where Eng. requires it: § 59*a*

e.g. ቤት bʸēt, a house, or, the house.

ቤቱ bʸḗtu, the house in question.

He entered the house: ከቤት ፡ ገባ ። kḁyʸét gḁ́bba.

ከቤቱ ፡ ገባ ። kḁyʸḗtu gḁ́bba would usually mean: he entered his (§ 12*b*) house.

ስለዝናብ ፡ si̥läzí̥nắy[1], because of the rain.

በጠሐይ ፡ ነው ። bḁṭḁhâi̥[1] nḁ͡u, it is in the sun.

ተምድር ፡ tḁ́mdi̥r, on the ground.

ራስ ፡ አሉኝ ። rās ắluñ, the Ras told me.

ለፈረሶች ፡ ሰጠሁት ። lḁfḁ́rḁsʷōč sḁ́ṭṭḁhut, I gave it to the horses.

በቅሎች ፡ ሳጥኖችን ፡ ጣሉ ። bḁ́qlʷōč sāṭi̥nʷṓčči̥n ṭálu, the mules have thrown (threw) the boxes off.

---

[1] § 8.

Transference of the Article.

§ 59*b* When a substantive with the art. is qualified by an adj. or its equivalent the art. passes to the adj. or its equivalent, but still refers to the original substantive:

e.g. ቤቱ ፡ bʸétu, the house.

ትልቁ ፡ ቤት ፡ tilliqu yʸēt, the large house.

የሹሙ ፡ ቤት ፡ yäšúmu yʸēt, the chief's house.

የወደቀው ፡ ቤት ፡ yäwóddaqau[1] yʸēt, the house that fell down.

የምትመጣይቱ ፡ ሴት ፡ yämmittmatáitu[1,2] sʸēt, the woman who is coming.

§ 59*c* The art. may be attached to an epithet without its substantive being expressed:

e.g. ትልቁ ፡ ነው ፡ tilliqu[1] nau, it is the large one.

የወደቀው ፡ ነበር ። yäwóddaqau[3] nábbär, it was the one that fell down.

የምትመጣይቱ ፡ ናት ። yämmittmatáitu[1,3] nāt, it is the (female) one that is coming.

Generic Use of the Article.

§ 59*d* The article is occasionally used generically, i.e. to designate a class of object:

e.g. ልብሱን ፡ ያበላሻል ። líysun yabbalášsāl, it spoils the (= one's) clothes.

---

[1] § 8. [2] §§ 14, 45. [3] § 62*a*.

The Pronoun.

The Personal Pronoun.

The personal pronouns are inherent in the various persons of a verb, and need not be expressed except to avoid ambiguity: § 60*a*

e.g. አውቃለሁ ። a͡uŭqállḁ͡uʰ, I know.

እርሰዎ ፡ ያውቃሉ ። i̥rsḁ͡ʷo ya͡uŭqállu, you (pol.) know.

እርሳቸው ፡ ያውቃሉ ። i̥rsáččḁ͡u ya͡uŭqállu, they know, or, he (pol.) knows.

The 3rd pl. and 3rd sg. pol. cannot be distinguished by pronouns.

Use of the Disjunctive Personal Pronoun.

The disjunctive pers. pron. (§ 12*a*) is generally used to express emphasis or to distinguish between persons: § 60*b*

e.g. ስጠው ። si̥ṭḁ͡u, give it to him,

ስጠው ፡ ለርሱ ። si̥ṭḁ͡u lắrsu, give it to *him* (not to somebody else).

የኔይቱን ፡ ትታችሁ ፡ የናንተይቱን ፡ አምጡት ። yänʸé͡i̥tun ti̥tắččyuh[1,2] yännántä͡i̥tun ántwāt[1], leave (pl.) mine (f., e.g. cow) and bring yours.

Use of Personal Pronouns Conjunctive with Verbs. §61*a*

The pers. suff. conj. with verbs (§ 12*c*) render both the dative and the accusative:

e.g. ሰጠው ። sḁṭṭḁ͡u, (*α*) he gave to him,

(*β*) he gave him (it)—i.e. to somebody else.

---

[1] § 7*d*. [2] § 65*a*.

To avoid ambiguity ለ- (§ 47*a*) may be used to express the dative:

e.g. ሰጠለት ፡ sḁ́ṭṭḁllḁt, he gave it to him.

A verb cannot take more than one of these suff. at a time; of two cases, one being acc., Am. omits the acc.:

e.g. He gave it to me: ሰጠኝ ። sḁ́ṭṭḁñ.
I gave them to him: ሰጠሁት ። sḁ́ṭṭḁhut.

Thus ሰጠው above ordinarily means: he gave it (them) to him.

Kill him: ግደለው ። gi̥dḁlḁu.
Kill him with it: ግደልበት ። gi̥dḁli̥bbät.
Cp. ሰጠለት above.

§ 61*b* The suff. representing the acc. is commonly omitted, especially in the neg. conjug., when the omission does not injure the sense, which remains clear from what has been said before, the attendant circumstances, etc.:

e.g. ሒድ ፡ አምጣ ። hi̥d ánṭa, go and fetch him (her, it, them).
አላየሁም ። aláyyähum, I haven't seen him (her, it, them).

§ 61*c* As datives, these suff. are attached to intransitive verbs:

e.g. መሰለ mḁ́ssḁlḁ, to seem,
ይመስለኛል ፡ yi̥mḁ́släññäl, it seems to me, I think.
መጣ mḁ́ṭṭa, to come,
በረደ bḁ́rrḁdḁ, to be cold, (of the temperature),
ንፋስ ፡ ሲመታህ ፡ ይበርድሃል ። ni̥fás si̥mḁ́ṭāh, yi̥vḁ́rdä-hāl, when the wind strikes you, you will feel cold.

Redundant Personal Pronoun.

When the direct object is in the determinate acc. (§ 55*b*), the verb, unless it already has another pron. suff., often takes a redundant pron. suff. referring to the object: § 61*d*

e.g. ድንኳኑን ፡ ትከሉ ። dŭňkwánun tí̥kḁlu,

or

ድንኳኑን ፡ ትከሉት ። dŭňkwánun tí̥kḁlut, pitch (pl.) the tent;

but

ድንኳን ፡ ትከሉ ። dŭňkwán tí̥kḁlu, pitch (pl.) a tent;

ድንኳኑን ፡ ትከሉልኝ ። dŭňkwánun tí̥kḁlulli̥ñ, please[1] pitch the tent.

A redundant -ኝ (§ 12*c*) is sometimes added in the simp. perf. sg. 1st: § 61*e*

e.g. መጣሁኝ ። mḁ́ṭṭahuñ, = መጣሁ ። mḁ́ṭṭa͡u^{h}[2], I have come.

ተረታሁኝ ። tḁrḁ́ttahuñ, = ተረታሁ ። tḁrḁ́tta͡u^{h}[2], I have lost (the game, my case, etc.).

Use of the Relative Pronoun.

See § 14, initial remarks. § 62*a*

If an antecedent to the rel. is expressed, the rel. + verb, as an adjectival clause, amounts to an adj. qualifying that antecedent, and follows the analogy of an adj. (§ 57*a*) as regards position:

e.g. ወደቀ ፡ wǿddḁqḁ, he (it) fell,

የወደቀ ፡ yäwǿddḁqḁ, he who (that or one which) fell or has fallen,

---

[1] lit. for me (§ 47*a*). [2] § 7*d*, under kā͡i̥y.

የወደቀ ፡ ቤት ፡ ነው ። yäwǿddaqá[1] yʸēt nau, it is a house which has fallen, a fallen house.

ቤቱ ፡ የወደቀ ፡ ነው ። bʸétu yäwǿddaqá nau, the house is one which has fallen, a fallen one.

§ 62*b* If no antecedent is expressed, the rel. + verb amounts to a substantive:

e.g. የወደቀ ፡ ተሰብሯል ። yäwǿddaqa tasáyrōāl, what fell down is broken.

§ 62*c* The rel. + verb takes or drops the art. (§ 59*a*) and the -ን of the acc. (§ 56*a*, *b*) in the same way as a substantive or an adjective.

The rel. የ- and የ- and እ- of የም- and እም- (§ 14) are omitted (not transferred) in the same circumstances as the prp. የ- (§ 70*b*):

e.g. የተገደሉ ፡ ናቸው ። yätagáddalu náččau, they are some who have been killed.

የተገደሉቱ ፡ ናቸው ። yätagáddalutu náččau, they are those who were killed, the killed.

ያለን ፡ ስጠኝ ። yállän sitäñ, give me what there is.

የምትለኝን ፡ እሰራለሁ ። yämmittiláññin isarállauʰ, I will do what you tell me.

የተወለደበትን ፡ አላውቅም ። yätauálladabbatin[2] aláuŭqim, I don't know where he was born, (lit. that which he was born in it).

የተገደሉቱን ፡ አላውቅም ። yätagáddalutun aláuŭqim, I don't know who were killed.

---

[1] § 8. [2] § 47*a*.

ደብዳቤውን ፡ ያመጣውን ፡ ጥራ ። dḁỵdábbʸeun yāmḁ́ṭ-ṭaun ṭí̥ra, call the man who brought the letter.

የት ፡ አለ ፡ ፈረሱን ፡ የሸጠልኝ ፡ ሰው ። yēt állä fḁ́rḁsun yäšátällí̥ñ[1] sḁu ?, where is the man who sold me the horse to be found?

ጧት ፡ የወሰዱትን ፡ ሳጥን ፡ አምጥተዋል ። ṭwāt yäwώssḁ-duti̥n sā́ṭi̥n ánṭi̥tḁuāl[2], they have brought back the box which they took away early this morning.

ቢፈራኝ ፡ እወዳለሁ ፡ ከሚወደኝ ። bi̥fḁ́rañ i̥wωddállḁuʰ kḁmmi̥wώddäñ, I prefer his fearing me to his liking me.

አስታወስኩት ፡ ቡስጣ ፡ ተሔደ ፡ ወድያ ። astáuwωskut ỵústa tḁhádä wώdya, I remembered it after the post was gone, [(የ)ሔደ = adj. qualifying ጊዜ gí̥zʸe, time, not expressed].

በወረደው ፡ ይቀመጥ ። bḁuώrrḁdḁu yi̥qqḁ́mḁṭ, let it stay where it came down.

ተወደቀው ፡ ቤት ፡ ወጣ ። tḁuώddḁqḁ́u[1] ỵʸēt wώṭṭa, it came out of the fallen house.

የመጣበት ፡ ቀን ፡ ነበር ። yämḁ́ṭṭabbḁ́t[1] qḁn nḁ́bbär, it was the day on which he came.

እስከመጣበት ፡ ቀን ፡ ቈዩ ። i̥skḁmḁ́ṭṭabbḁ́t qḁn qwώyyu, they waited until the day on which he came.

The rel. + verb may receive the transferred -ም (§ 37*b*) of the neg.: § 62*d*

e.g. የሚያውቅም ፡ የለ ። yämmyáuŭqi̥mm yállä, there isn't anybody that knows.

---

[1] § 8. [2] § 7*d*.

Case of the Relative.

§ 62*e* Though the case of the rel. + verb can be determined (§ 62*c*), that of the rel. in itself, which is indecl. (§ 14), is ambiguous when it is prefixed to a transitive verb of which it may be either the subject or object:

e.g. የፈለገ yäfḁ́llḁgḁ, (*α*) he who sought,
(*β*) whom (or, what) he sought.

The presence of an antecedent may determine the case of the relative:

e.g. ገንዘቡን ፡ የፈለገው ፡ ሰው ፡ gḁ́nzḁỵun yäfḁ́llḁgḁ́͡u (§ 8) sḁ͡u, the man who looked for the money.

But when no antecedent is expressed the case of the rel. must be decided by the general sense; usually, however, it is that of the rel. + verb:

e.g. የፈለገው ፡ አገኘ ። yäfḁ́llḁgḁ͡u agḁ́ññä, he who sought, found.

የፈለገውን ፡ አገኘው ። yäfḁ́llḁgḁ͡un agḁ́ññä͡u, whom (what) he sought he found.

The Verb.

The Indicative: Forces of Tenses.

§ 63*a* The simple perfect expresses both our past indefinite and our present perfect: the compound perfect the latter only:

e.g. መጣ mḁ́ṭṭa, he came, or, he has come;

መጥቷል mḁ́ṭtŏ͡āl, G. መጣናል mḁ́ṭṭānāl, he has come.

§ 63*b* For variations in force of other tenses see § 24.

The circumstances in which the tense is used generally make its force clear, as they do the meaning of a verb:

e.g. ይታሰር ፡ ነበር ። yi̥ttássär nḁ́bbär, he (it) was being bound: (s.v. አሰረ).

ይህ ፡ እቃ ፡ ይታሰር ፡ ነበር ። yí̥he í̥qa yi̥ttássär nḁ́bbär, this baggage ought to have been tied up.

ያ ፡ ሰው ፡ ይታሰር ፡ ነበር ። yā sḁu͡ yi̥ttássär nḁ́bbär, that man ought to have been sent to prison.

The imperf. may have a potential force in some verbs: § 63c

e.g. ይጥፋል ። yi̥ṭí̥fāl, he is writing, writes, or, will write; also, he can write, knows how to write.

አይሰማም ። a͡i̥ssḁ́mmām, he (it) is not, or, cannot be heard.

In verbs expressing a state, process or a mental action the perf. is often used where Eng. uses the present: § 63d

e.g. አደፈ ። áddḁfḁ, or አድፏል ። ádfŏ͡āl, he (it) is dirty.

አወቅሁት ። áu͡wωqhut, or

አውቄዋለሁ ። au͡ŭqqʸewállḁu͡ʰ, I know (understand) him (it).

ሰማህ ። sḁ́mmāh?, do you hear?

ቈዩ ። qwώyyu, they are late.

ያን ፡ ሰው ፡ ታገር ፡ አወጣሁት ፡ ክፉ ፡ ስለሆነ ። yan sḁu͡ tágär au͡ώṭṭahut kí̥fu si̥lḁhʷónḁ, I expelled that man from the country because he is wicked.

Similarly, in such verbs, a plup. represents our imperf., and an imperf. our future: § 63e

e.g. አድፎ ፡ ነበር ። ádfʷo nḁ́bbär, he (it) was dirty,

ያድፋል ። yádfāl, he (it) will get dirty.

Use of the Contingent.

§ 64*a* The contingent does not stand alone (except in a few stereotyped forms which have lost the rel. pref. (§ 14) and which are practically adverbs, s.v. ላቀ, √ሻለ, በለጠ, አከለ, cp. § 58*c*) but is either used to form composite tenses (§ 24*b*) or the neg. imperf. (§ 37) or is introduced by a conj. (§ 48*a*) or the rel. (§ 14).

§ 64*b* The cont. is occasionally introduced by another verb expressing a state, instead of ነበረ (§ 33*a*) or ሆነ (§ 33*c*):

e.g. ይዘፍን ፡ ጀመረ ። yi̥zä́fi̥n jḁ̈mmḁ̈rḁ̈, he began to sing.

Use of the Gerund.

§ 65*a* The gerund denotes the attendant circumstances:

e.g. ዘፍኖ ፡ ሔደ ። zä́fnʷo hä́dä, he went off singing, he sang as he went.

ይሰክራሉ ፡ አይሔዱም ፡ ችለው ። yi̥sḁ̈krállu, a͡i̥hä́dum čí̥lḁ̈͡u, they get drunk and then can't walk.

Thus it is constantly used where we use co-ordinated principal clauses (§ 74*a*).

§ 65*b* The ger. is sometimes used as a past indicative:

e.g. ቈጥረሀውን ። qwǿṭrähḁ̈͡un[1]?, have you counted it?

ዋሽተን ። wä́štän[2], we were telling a lie.

በችኰላ ፡ ሁነን ። bḁ̈čǘkkola[3] húnän[2], we were in a hurry.

---

[1] -ን (q.v.) is here an interrogative particle (adv.).

[2] There is probably an ellipse of ነበር (§ 33*a*).

[3] § 7*d*, under kä͡i̥y.

Construction of the Gerund.

The construction of the ger. is the same as that of the indicative, e.g. the ger. of a transitive verb takes an object in the acc.: § 65*c*

e.g. ይህንን፡ ወስጄ፡ ልመለስ። yi̥hánnän wósi̥jjʸe li̥mmä́lḁs?, shall I come back when I have taken this away?

The subject of the ger. and that of the main verb are usually the same logically if not grammatically: § 65*d*

e.g. ተደጃፍ፡ ተቀምጬ፡ ጉንፋን፡ ያዘኝ። tḁdäjjáf tḁqḁ́mi̥ç̌ç̌ʸe gumfán yázäñ, I caught cold sitting on the verandah, (lit. a cold seized me).

Use of the Infinitive.

The infinitive is a verbal substantive (§ 30). It renders many of our abstract nouns, of which the active and passive senses may be distinguished in Amharic: § 66*a*

e.g. ፈተነ fḁ́ttḁnḁ[1], he tempted,

መፈተን mḁfḁ́ttḁn[1], to tempt, tempting, temptation;

ተፈተነ tḁfḁ́ttḁnḁ[1], he was tempted,

መፈተን mḁffḁ́tḁn[2], to be tempted, being tempted, temptation.

Construction of the Infinitive.

The constr. of the inf. is the same as that of the ind., e.g. the inf. of a transitive verb takes an obj. in the acc.: § 66*b*

e.g. መዝጊያውን፡ ከፈተ። mäzgyáun kḁ́ffḁtḁ, he opened the door,

---

[1] or -ä́ttä-. [2] or -ä́tä-.

መዝጊያውን ፡ መክፈት ፡ አያውቅም ። mäzgyáun mạ̊kfạ̊t a^{y}áuŭqi̥m, he doesn't know how to open the door.

ክራዩን ፡ አበለጠ ። ki̥rái̥un ay̥ḁ́llạ̥tạ̥, he raised the rent,

ክራዩን ፡ ማብለጥ ፡ አይቻለውም ። ki̥rái̥un máy̥lạ̥ṭ ai̥ččá-lḁum, he cannot raise the rent.

Use of the Participle.

§ 67*a* The participle is a verbal noun (§ 31), prop. an adj. but commonly used as a substantive:

e.g. ተቀመጠ tḁqḁ́mmạ̥ṭḁ, to ride,

ተቀማጭ ፡ ሰው ፡ ነው ። tḁqḁmmáč̣ sḁu nḁu, or

ተቀማጭ ፡ ነው ። he is a rider, a good horseman.

ሰፋ sḁ́ffa, to sow,

ሰፊ sáfi, a tailor.

ፈራ fḁ́rra, to fear,

ፈሪ fári, a coward.

Force of the Participle.

§ 67*b* The part. usually expresses an agent (§ 67*a*), but sometimes it has a sense of obligation or incumbency:

e.g. ተወሳጅ ፡ ነው ። tḁuωssáj nḁu, it ought to be removed, it is to be taken away.

ይህ ፡ ቀሪ ፡ ነው ። yi̥he qärí[1] nḁu?, is this to stay behind?

---

[1] § 8.

Construction of the Participle.

The constr. of the part. is that of a substantive: § 67c
e.g. የልብስ ፡ ሰፊ ፡ yäli̥ys sấfi, a sewer of clothes, tailor,
የስሜን ፡ ገዥ ፡ yäsi̥m^{y}én gḁž, ruler of Simyen.

The part. is also, in certain phrases, constr. with the Eth. acc. in -ḁ (§ 9*d*):
e.g. ልብሰ ፡ ሰፊ ፡ lí̥ysḁ sấfi, a sewer of clothes, tailor,
ሥጋ ፡ ሻጭ ፡ si̥gá[1] šāč̣, a seller of meat, butcher.

Rendering of the English Participle.

The Eng. part. may be rendered variously, according to its force: but hardly ever by the Am. part.: § 67d
e.g. I left him, thinking he was dead: የሞተ ፡ መስሎኝ ፡ ተውሁት ፡፡ yäm^{w}ótḁ mḁ́sl^{w}oñ tḁ́uhut.

They caught him going into the house: ተቤት ፡ ሲገባ ፡ ያዙት ፡፡ tḁy^{y}ét si̥gḁ́ya yázut.

You will spoil it using it like that: እንዲህ ፡ ብታደርግበት ፡ ታበላሻዋለህ ፡፡ ndí̥h yi̥ttadárgi̥bbḁt tabbḁlāššḁuállāh.

Use of Causative Form in አስ- (§ 22*a*). § 68

When the primitive verb is transitive, the causative in አስ- has two meanings[2]:

---

[1] § 7*a*, § 8.

[2] arising apparently thus: the causative merely expresses causation of the action: አስገደለ, he caused killing; an object, -ው him, is naturally (α) the object of -ገደለ, he caused (others) killing him: but is also

(α)[1] to cause or allow the object to suffer the action of the primitive verb:

(β) to cause or allow the object to perform that action:

e.g. ገደለ gắddạlạ, to kill,

አስገደለ asgắddạlạ, (α) to cause or allow to be killed, put to death, (β) to cause or allow to kill.

ያዘ yắzạ, to catch,

አስያዘ asyắzạ, (α) to cause or allow to be caught, (β) to cause or allow to catch.

When there is one object, it is the object of the action of the primitive verb:

e.g. አስገደለው ። asgắddạlạ͡u, he caused him to be killed, put him to death.

ልጁን ፡ አስያዘ ። lị́jun asyắzạ, he had the child caught.

When there are two objects the latter is the object of the action of the primitive verb:

e.g. ልጁን ፡ ድመቱን ፡ አስያዘ ። lị́jun dị́mmạtun asyắzạ, he made the child catch the cat.

In either case the verb may take a redundant -ው (§ 61*d*) without altering the sense:

e.g. ልጁን ፡ አስያዘው ። lị́jun asyắzạ͡u, he had the child caught.

---

taken as (β) the object of አስገደለ as a whole, he caused him killing (others).

[1] the usual meaning. Cp. faire tuer, far uccidere, töten lassen.

ልጁን ፡ ድመቱን ፡ አስያዘው ። lı̥́jun dı̥mmḁtun asyázḁu, he made the child catch the cat.

'He made the child catch it' would be: በልጁ ፡ እጅ ፡ አስያዘው ። bḁlı̥́ju ı̥jj asyázḁu.

The Preposition.

Construction of the Preposition.

Prepositions (§ 47) are constr. with the nominative: § 69*a*

e.g. ወደቤት ፡ ሔደ ። wωdḁv^{y}ét hádä, he went towards the house.

They may be constr. with an adverb:

የወዴት ፡ ነው ። yäwωd^{y}ét nḁu?, where is he (it) from?

Position of the Preposition.

When a substantive with which a prp. is con- § 69*b*
structed has an epithet, the prp., or that part of it which is a prefix, is pref. to the epithet:

e.g. እስከቤት ፡ ı̥skḁ́v^{y}ét (§ 8), as far as the house;

እስከትልቁ ፡ ቤት ፡ ı̥skḁtı̥llı̥́qu ṿ^{y}ēt, as far as the large house;

በቤት ፡ ላይ ፡ bḁyét lḁi, above the house,

በትልቁ ፡ ቤት ፡ ላይ ፡ bḁtı̥llı̥́qu ṿ^{y}ēt lḁi, above the large house.

The Preposition የ-.

The preposition የ- yä-, of, expresses our possessive § 70*a*
case, or with the substantive to which it is attached may amount to an adj.:

ሹም šum, a chief,

የሹም yášúm[1], of a chief, a chief's.

እንጨት ńč̣ät, wood,

የንጨት yáńč̣ät[2], of wood, wooden.

ብረት bı̥́rḁt, iron,

የብረት ፡ ሳጥን ፡ yäṿı̥́rḁt sắṭı̥n, an iron box.

§ 70*b* የ- with its substantive occupies the same position as epithet or predicate as an adj. (§ 57*a*), and receives -ን (§ 56*a*, *b*) and the art. (§ 59*a*) in the same way as an adj.

If another prp. is prefixed, የ- disappears[3]; or if የ- is prefixed to a word already bearing የ-, one የ- disappears:

e.g. የሹም ፡ ቤት ፡ ነው ፡፡ yäšúm bʸēt nḁ͡u, it is a chief's house.

ቤቱ ፡ የሹም ፡ ነው ፡፡ bʸḗtu yäšúm nḁ͡u, the house is a chief's.

የሹሙን ፡ ቤት ፡ ያውቃል ፡፡ yäšumún bʸēt yá͡uŭqāl, he knows the chief's house.

ተሹሙ ፡ ቤት ፡ ወጣ ፡፡ tḁšúmu ṿʸēt wώṭṭa, he came out of the chief's house.

ተብረት ፡ ሳጥን ፡ tḁṿı̥́rḁt sắṭı̥n, in an iron box.

ወደሹም ፡ ቤት ፡ ሔደ ፡፡ wωdḁšúm bʸēt hádä, he went towards the chief's house.

---

[1] § 8. [2] § 7*a*.

[3] In most composite prps. (§ 47*b*) there is this ellipse of የ-: በቤት ፡ ውስጥ ፡ standing for *በየቤት ፡ ውስጥ ፡, etc.

If the substantive to which የ- is pref. is qualified by an adj. or its equivalent as an epithet, የ- is transferred from the qualified to the qualifying word. If the qualifying word is itself a word with የ- pref., the second የ- disappears: § 70*c*

e.g. የትልቅ ፡ ሹም ፡ ቤት ፡ ነው ። yäti̥llí̥q šum b^{y}ēt nḁ͡u, it is the house of an old chief.

ትልቅ ፡ የሹም ፡ ቤት ፡ ነው ። ti̥lli̥q yäšúm b^{y}ēt nḁ͡u[1], it is a large chief's house.

የልጁ ፡ ቤት ፡ ነው ። yälí̥ju ỵ^{y}ēt nḁ͡u, it is his son's house.

የሹሙ ፡ ልጅ ፡ ቤት ፡ ነው ። yäšúmu li̥j ỵ^{y}ēt nḁ͡u, it is the chief's son's house.

የትልቁ ፡ ሹም ፡ ልጅ ፡ ቤት ፡ ነው ። yäti̥llí̥qu šum li̥j ỵ^{y}ēt nḁ͡u, it is the old chief's son's house.

ወደሹሙ ፡ ልጅ ፡ ቤት ፡ ሔደ ። wωdḁšúmu li̥j ỵ^{y}ēt hắdä, he went to the chief's son's house.

ወደትልቁ ፡ ሹም ፡ ልጅ ፡ ቤት ፡ ሔደ ። wωdḁti̥llí̥qu šum li̥j ỵ^{y}ēt hắdä, he went to the old chief's son's house.

ወደሹሙ ፡ ልጅ ፡ ትልቁ ፡ ቤት ፡ ሔደ ። wωdḁšúmu li̥j ti̥llí̥qu ỵ^{y}ēt hắdä, he went to the chief's son's large house.

The Prepositions ለ- *and* በ-.

ለ- and በ- (q.v.), esp. when attached with the pers. suff. to a verb (§ 47*a*), often mean § 71

---

[1] or የሹም ፡ ትልቅ ፡ ቤት ፡, which emphasizes የሹም ፡ (§ 83*c*).

ለ- to the advantage of,

በ- to the disadvantage of[1]:

e.g. ያንበሳ ፡ ቍርበት ፡ ሰጠልኝ ። yambḁ́ssa qʷóry̥ḁt sḁ́t̥ḁllịñ, he gave him (them) a lion-skin for me.

ግም ፡ ብር ፡ ሰጠብኝ ። gi̥m bi̥rr sḁ́t̥t̥ḁbbi̥ñ, he gave him (them) a bad dollar for me.

But they are also commonly used merely to denote direction or position:

e.g. ምን ፡ አለበት ። mi̥n állăbbḁt ?, what is there in it ?

The Conjunction.

Use of -ም and -ና.

§ 72*a* -ም and -ና (§ 48*b*) join substantives, -ና being attached to the former of two, -ም to both:

e.g. ውሃም ፡ ዳቦም ፡ አለ ። wŭ́ham dábbʷomm (§ 6) állä,

or ውሃና ፡ ዳቦ ፡ አለ ። wŭ́hanna dábbʷo állä, there is water and bread.

§ 72*b* They may join sentences, especially if there is a logical change of subject, though asyndeton (§ 74*c*) is commoner; otherwise the gerund (§ 74*a*, *b*) and relative (§ 62) constructions are much commoner:

e.g. ፈረስ ፡ ገዛ ፡ ፈረሱም ፡ ሞተ ። fḁ́rḁs gḁ́zza, fḁ́rḁsum mʷótḁ, he bought a horse and the horse died.

---

[1] A good illustration is given in Guidi, Grammatica § 52:

መሰከረለት mḁsḁ́kkḁrḁllḁt, he gave evidence for him, was a witness for him, (شهد له).

መሰከረበት mḁsḁ́kkḁrḁbbḁt, he gave evidence against him, (شهد عليه).

ፈረስ ፡ ገዝቶ ፡ ሞተ ፡፡ fáras gáztʷo mʷóta, would mean he bought a horse and died;—he bought a horse and it died: የገዛ ፡ ፈረስ ፡ ሞተ ፡፡ yägázza fáras mʷóta.

-ና occasionally joins verbs without there being a change of subject: § 72c

ውሰደውና ፡ ተመለስ ፡፡ wúsadaunna tamálas, take it away and come back; more idiomatically ወስደህ ፡ ተመለስ ፡፡ wósdäh tamálas.

The Sentence.

The Simple Sentence.

The simple sentence consists in a verb, which includes a pronominal subject, may in itself express a predicate (i.e. an adjectival predicate), or may have a pron. object attached to it: § 73a

e.g. በልቷል ፡፡ báltōāl, he has eaten, he has had a meal.

ይነጣል ፡፡ yinátāl, it becomes white.

በልቶታል ፡፡ báltʷotāl, he has eaten it.

እሰጠኻለኍ ፡፡ isatahállau[h] (§ 61a), I will give it (them) to you.

Order of Words in the Simple Sentence.

When the subject, predicate, or object are expressed separately, the usual order is: § 73b

(1) Subject, (2) predicate (§ 73a) or object, (3) verb;

(ነው (§ 13b), though not etymologically a verb, is used as one):

e.g. ፈረስ ፡ ውድ ፡ ነው ፡፡ fáras wúddi nau, the horse is dear.

ፈረስ ፡ ውሃ ፡ ይፈልጋል ። fḁ́rḁs wŭha yi̥fḁ́lli̥gāl, the horse wants water.

ለጓሚ ፡ ለፈረስ ፡ ማሽላ ፡ ይስጥ ። lωggwā́mi lḁfḁ́rḁs mā-ši̥llá (§ 8) yi̥sṭ[1], let the groom give the horse some millet.

§ 73*c* Epithets (§ 57*a*), adverbs, adverbial expressions and other determinatives are placed before the verb, which comes last:

e.g. ይህ ፡ ፈረስ ፡ ተዚያ ፡ በብዙ ፡ ይሻላል ። yi̥he fḁ́rḁs tḁzzyā́ ṿḁṿí̥zu yi̥ššálāl, this horse is much better than that one.

§ 73*d* Adverbs, however, and adverbial expressions and even an object may be placed after the verb, being thrown in more or less as after-thoughts, to amplify or explain:

e.g. አሉ ፡ ከዚህ ። állu kắzzi̥h, there are some, here.

አምጣው ፡ ፈረሱን ። ánṭa͡u (§ 7*d*) fḁ́rḁsun, bring it, the horse (I mean).

ስጠው[2] ፡ ለወታደር ። sí̥ṭḁ͡u lḁwωttáddär, give it to the soldier,

ይህ ፡ ይሻላል ፡ ተዚያ ። yi̥he yi̥ššálāl tḁ́zzya, this is better than that.

---

[1] or the direct object may precede the indirect: ለጓሚ ፡ ማሽላ ፡ ለፈረስ ፡ ይስጥ ። lωggwā́mi māši̥lla lḁfḁrḁ́s (§ 8) yi̥sṭ, let the groom give some millet to the horse. The word immediately preceding the verb is in the more prominent position.

[2] -ው = to him (§ 61*a*).

Co-ordinated Principal Clauses.

When in English two or more verbs of which the subject is the same are co-ordinated, in Amharic they are all placed in the gerund except the last; in other words, where Eng. co-ordinates, Am. subordinates: § 74*a*

e.g. ሒዶ ፡ መጣ ። hí̥dʷo mḁ́ṭṭa, he went and has come back.

ሒጄ ፡ ጠይቄ ፡ ደርሼ ፡ መጣኹ ። hí̥jjʸe ṭḁ́yyi̥qqʸe dḁ́ri̥-ššʸe mḁ́ṭṭau͡ʰ, I went and asked and I have got back here, (lit. I going, asking, arriving, have come).

The gerund assumes the imperative or jussive force of a final verb in those moods: § 74*b*

e.g. ይህነን ፡ ይዘህ ፡ ሒድ ። yi̥hánnän yi̥záh[1] hi̥d, take this and go.

ለወታደር ፡ ሰጥቼው ፡ ልምጣ ። lḁ͡uωttáddär sḁ́ṭi̥ččʸe͡u lí̥mṭa?, shall I go and give it to the soldier?, (lit. giving it...am I to come?).

When there is a change of subject Eng. co-ordinated clauses may be co-ordinated in Am., but are usually without connectives: § 74*c*

e.g. ይህ ፡ መጣ ፡ ያ ፡ ሔደ ። yí̥he mḁ́ṭṭa yā hádä, this one has come and that other has gone away.

Such clauses are less commonly joined by -ም and -ና (§ 72*b*, *c*), or rendered by the ger. constr. (§ 65*c*).

---

[1] § 8.

Clauses are also co-ordinated in this way without there being a change of subject:

e.g. እንሔዳለን ፡ እናያለን ። i̥nnhädállän, i̥nnai̥állän, we will go and see; (but ሒደን ፡ እናያለን ። hí̥dän i̥n-nai̥állän, is more idiomatic).

The Adversative Proposition.

§ 75 An adversative proposition is indicated by እንጂ or ግን (q.v.):

e.g. አያምጣው ፡ ይውሰደው ፡ እንጂ ። aʸánṭau[1], yúsḁdḁu nji, he is not to bring it, he is to take it away.

ይህ ፡ ያምራል ፤ ይህ ፡ ግን ፡ አያምርም ። yí̥he yā́mrāl, yi̥hé[2] gi̥n aʸā́mri̥m, this is pleasant, that isn't.

QUESTIONS.

The Direct Question.

§ 76*a* Direct questions are introduced by a determinative interrogative adverb or pronoun:

e.g. የት ፡ ናቸው ። yēt náččḁu?, where are they?

ምን ፡ ይፈልጋል ። mi̥n yi̥fḁ́lli̥gāl?, what does he want?

ለምን ፡ መጣ ። lḁmí̥n mḁ́ṭṭa?, why has he come?

§ 76*b* Or they are expressed by an indeterminative inter. particle (adv.) s.v. -ወይ (§ 6), -ኦ (§ 6), -ን:

e.g. መጣወይ ። mḁ́ṭṭawwí̥?, has he come?

ይመጣሉይ ። yi̥mḁ́ṭāllwí̥?, is he coming?

---

[1] § 7*d*. [2] § 8.

If no interrogative word is used a question is indicated by the tone of the voice, which is modulated as in English: § 76c

e.g. መጣ ። mḁ́ṭṭa ?, has he come?

ይመጣል ። yi̥mḁ́ṭāl ?, is he coming?

A question may be asked not to elicit a reply but to express emphasis or surprise (s.v. **እኮስ**): § 77

e.g. ብናየው ፡ አናመጣውም ፡ ይዘን ። bi̥nná͡i̥ḁ͡u, annamḁ́-ṭa͡umm yí̥zän ?, if we see him (it) shall we not catch and bring him (it) ?, i.e. we certainly will, etc.

ይህ ፡ ሰው ፡ ንግግሩ ፡ ምንድር ፡ ነው ። yi̥hé[1] sḁ͡u[2] ni̥gíggi̥ru mi̥ndír[1] nḁ͡u ?, what is this man's pronunciation ?, i.e. how odd it is!

The Indirect Question.

An indirect question may be left in its direct form if it is introduced by a determinative inter. adv. or pron.: § 78a

e.g. ጠይቀው ፡ ዬት ፡ ናቸው ፡ tḁ́yyi̥qḁ͡u yēt náččḁ͡u, ask him where they are.

ጠይቀው ፡ ምን ፡ ይፈልጋል ። tḁ́yyi̥qḁ͡u mi̥n yi̥fálli̥gāl, ask him what he wants.

አላውቅም ፡ ለምን ፡ መጣ ። alá͡uŭqi̥m lḁmín mḁ́ṭṭa, I don't know why he has come.

Or, esp. when the principal verb is in the neg., it may be rendered by a substantival or adjectival clause introduced by the rel. (§ 62): § 78b

---

[1] § 8. [2] § 55b.

e.g. I don't know where they are: ያሉበትን ፡ አላውቅም ። yállubbäti̥n alá͡uŭqi̥m.

They didn't tell me what they want: የሚፈልጉትን ፡ አላሉኝም ። yämmi̥fḁ́lli̥guti̥n aláluññi̥m.

I don't know what day I shall go: የምሔድበትን ፡ ቀን ፡ አላውቅም ። yämmi̥hắdi̥bbätí̥n qḁn alá͡uŭqi̥m.

§ 78*c* Or by the inf. (§ 66):

e.g. It remains to be seen whether he will go: ገና ፡ መሔዱ ፡ አልታየም ። gḁ́na mḁhắdu altắyyäm, (lit. his going has not yet been seen, is not yet apparent; s.v. አየ).

§ 79*a* When no determinative interrogative adverb or pronoun introduces the direct question (§ 76*b*, *c*) its indirect form is introduced by እንደሆን (í̥)ndḁhʷon (-dä-; § 8) q.v., constructed with the gerund or contingent:

e.g. ጠይቀው ፡ መጥቶ ፡ እንደሆን ። ṭḁ́yyi̥qḁ͡u mḁṭṭʷóndа̥hʷon, ask him whether he (it) has come.

ጠይቀው ፡ ይመጣ ፡ እንደሆን ። ṭḁ́yyi̥qḁ͡u yi̥mḁṭándа̥hʷon, ask him whether he (it) is coming.

§ 79*b* For types of indirect question, s.v. how, what, when, where, whether, who, why; እንደ-, እንድ-, እንደሆን.

Indirect Narration.

§ 80 Indirect narration retains the same form as direct narration (s.v. √በለ):

e.g. ሔዱ ፡ ይላል ። hắdu yí̥lāl, he says that they have gone.

ተጎንደር ፡ ተነሥተው ፡ መተማ ፡ ገቡ ፡ የሚል ፡ ወሬ ፡ መጣ ። tḁg^{w}óndḁr tḁnḁ́stḁ͡u mätámma gḁ́bbu yḁ́mmi̥l wǿr^{y}e mḁ́ṭṭa, news has come that they have arrived at Gallabat from Gondar.

ስመጣ ፡ አሳየሃለኍ ፡ አለ ። si̥mḁ́ṭa asayyähállḁ͡u^{h} álḁ, he said that when he came he would show me.

አያውቅም ፡ ይምላል ። a^{y}á͡uqi̥m yi̥mi̥lāl, he swears he (another) doesn't know.

The Conditional Sentence.

The following are the principal types[1]: §81*a*

I. Possibility:

Protasis ብ- + cont. (§ 45), or ger.
Apodosis comp. imperf., juss. or imp.

(α) ቢወድ ፡ ይመጣል ። bi̥wǿdd, yi̥mḁ́ṭāl, if he wishes, he comes.

(β) ወዶ ፡ ይሔዳል ። wǿdd^{w}o yi̥hádāl, if he wishes, he goes.

(γ) ቢወድ ፡ ይምጣ ። bi̥wǿdd, yí̥mṭa, if he wishes, let him come.

(δ) ወዶ ፡ ይሒድ ። wǿdd^{w}o yí̥hi̥d, if he wishes, let him go.

(ε) ብትወድ ፡ ና ። bi̥ttwǿdd, na, if you wish, come.

(ζ) ወደህ ፡ ሒድ ። wǿddäh hi̥d, if you wish, go.

---

[1] taking Farrar's classification of conditional sentences.

§ 81*b* II. Probability:

as in I.

(*α*) ብትመጡ ፡ ታያላችሁ ። bi̥ttmḁ́ṭu, ta͡i̥allắččyuh, if you come, you will see.

(*β*) ከዚያ ፡ ተቀምጠህ ፡ ይበርድሃል ። käzzyá̄ tḁqḁ́mṭäh yi̥ṿắrdḁhāl, if you sit there you will catch cold.

(*γ*) ብታውቅ ፡ ንገረኝ ። bi̥ttá͡uŭq, ní̥gäräñ, if you know, tell me.

(*ε*) ባያውቅ ፡ ዝም ፡ ይበል ። ba͡i̥á͡uŭq, zi̥mm yí̥ṿḁl, if he doesn't know, let him be quiet.

The protasis may also be expressed by

(*η*) ብ- + cont. followed by እንዳለ (i̥)ndállä, which may be used personally or impersonally[1].

(*θ*) cont. followed by እንደሆን (í̥)ndḁhʷon[2,3] or እንደሆነ (i̥)ndḁhʷónḁ[3], which may be used pers. or impers.[1]

(*ι*) rel. + cont. followed by እንደሆን [-ሆነ etc.].

(*κ*) rel. + cont. followed by ቢሆን bíhʷón[2,4].

Thus ብትመጡ in (*α*) may be replaced, without changing the sense, by

(*η*) ብትመጡ ፡ እንዳለ ፡ bi̥ttmḁ́ṭu ndállä,

or ብትመጡ ፡ እንዳላችሁ ፡ bi̥ttmḁ́ṭu ndallắččyuh.

(*θ*) ትመጡ ፡ እንደሆን ፡ ti̥mḁṭúndḁhʷon,

ትመጡ ፡ እንደሆነ ፡ ti̥mḁ́ṭu ndḁhʷónḁ,

or ትመጡ ፡ እንደሆናችሁ ፡ ti̥mḁ́ṭu ndḁhʷonắččyuh.

---

[1] cp. ነበረ (§ 33*a*). [2] § 8. [3] or -dä-. [4] or bí̥.

(ι) የምትመጡ ፡ እንደሆን ፡ yämmi̥ttmḁṭúndḁhʷon, etc., as in (θ).

(κ) የምትመጡ ፡ ቢሆን ፡ yämmi̥ttmḁ́ṭu ẏí̥hʷon.

III. Uncertainty: § 81*c*

(λ) Protasis, -ቢ- + cont.
Apodosis, past imperf.

(λ) ቢመጣ ፡ እከፍለው ፡ ነበር ። bi̥mḁ́ṭa, i̥kḁ́flḁu nḁ́bbär, if he were to come, I should pay him.

The protasis may also be expressed by

(μ) ger. followed by ቢሆን or እንደሆን [-ሆነ, etc.].

(ν) rel.[1] + cont. followed by ቢሆን or እንደሆን.

(ξ) rel.[1] + simp. perf. followed by ቢሆን or እንደሆን.

Thus ቢመጣ in (λ) may be replaced, without altering the sense, by

(μ) መጥቶ ፡ ቢሆን ፡ mḁ́ṭtʷo ẏí̥hʷon,
መጥቶ ፡ እንደሆን ፡ mḁṭtʷóndḁhʷon,
or መጥቶ ፡ እንደሆነ ፡ mḁṭtʷó ndḁḥʷónḁ;

(ν) የሚመጣ ፡ ቢሆን ፡ yämmi̥mḁ́ṭa ẏí̥hʷon,
የሚመጣ ፡ እንደሆን ፡ yämmi̥mḁṭándḁhʷon,
or የሚመጣ ፡ እንደሆነ ፡ yämmi̥mḁ́ṭa ndḁhʷónḁ;

(ξ) የመጣ ፡ ቢሆን ፡ yämḁ́ṭṭa ẏí̥hʷon,
የመጣ[2] ፡ እንደሆን ፡ yämḁṭṭándḁhʷon,
or የመጣ[2] ፡ እንደሆነ ፡ yämḁ́ṭṭa ndḁhʷónḁ.

---

[1] the rel. is sometimes dropped before እንደሆን.

[2] sometimes መጣ.

(*o*) Protasis, ቢ- + cont.
Apodosis, በ- + simp. perf.

(*o*) ቢወድ : በሔደ :: bi̥wǿdd, bḁhắdä, if he wished, he would go.

§ 81*d* IV. Impossibility:

as in III (*μ*), (*ξ*), (*o*), which also mean:

'if he had come, I should be paying him', or, 'should have paid him';

'if he had wished, he would have gone.'

(*π*) Protasis, ger. followed by ቢሆን.
Apodosis, በ- + simp. perf.

(*π*) ሰምቼ : ቢሆን : በመጣሁ :: sḁmi̥čč^{y}e ẏi̥h^{w}on, bḁmắṭṭau^{h}, if I had heard, I should have come.

The apodosis of (*π*) may be expressed by

(*ρ*) the plup. (§ 33*b*, *α*).

(*σ*) በ- + plup. (§ 33*b*, *β*).

Thus በመጣሁ in (*π*) may be replaced, without changing the sense, by

(*ρ*) መጥቼ : ነበር :: mḁṭi̥čč^{y}e nḁbbär.

(*σ*) በመጣሁ : ነበር :: bḁmḁṭṭau^{h} nḁbbär.

Finally

(*τ*) both protasis and apodosis may be expressed by በ- + simp. perf.

(*τ*) በሰማሁ : በመጣሁ :: bḁsḁmmau^{h}, bḁmḁṭṭau^{h}, if I had heard, I should have come.

The Compound Sentence.

Substantival, adjectival and adverbial clauses take, in the compound sentence, the places of substantives, adjectives and adverbs, respectively, in the simple sentence (§ 73): § 82

e.g. ትናንት ፡ ወደጎንደር ፡ ልሔድ ፡ ነኝ ፡ ብሎ ፡ የተነሣ ፡ ወንድሜ ፡ ክፉ ፡ አስቦ ፡ በባቴ ፡ ሳጥን ፡ ያለበትን ፡ ገንዘብ ፡ ተቤት ፡ ገብቶ ፡ ሰርቆ ፡ ሔደ ። t̥inánt wωdḁg^{w}óndär li̥hád

yesterday "to Gondar to go

näñ y̥íl^{w}o yätа̥nḁ́ssa wώndi̥mm^{y}e kí̥fu ássi̥y^{w}o

I am" saying who started my brother evilly thinking

yabbát^{y}e sát̥i̥n yallábbäti̥n gḁ́nzḁy tḁy^{y}ét

in my father's box which there is in it money into the house

gḁ́yt^{w}o sárq^{w}o hádä, my brother who started

entering stealing went

yesterday for Gondar, led by evil thoughts, entered the house, stole the money from my father's box, and went off.

Emphasis.

A word may be emphasized by being repeated: § 83*a*

e.g. ፈልጌ ፡ ፈልጌ ፡ አገኘኹ ። fḁ́lli̥gg^{y}e fḁ́lli̥gg^{y}e agḁ́ññäu^{h}, I searched and searched till I found him (her, it, them, § 61*b*).

እጅግ ፡ እጅግ ፡ እሩቅ ፡ ነው ። í̥jji̥g í̥jji̥g i̥rúq nḁu, it is a very long way off.

But words, especially numerals, may be repeated not for emphasis but in a distributive sense:

e.g. በቅሎች ፡ ስምንት ፡ ስምንት ፡ ነጥር ፡ ይበላሉ ። bḁ́ql^{w}ōč sí̥mmi̥nt sí̥mmi̥nt nát̥i̥r yi̥y̥ḁlállu, the mules eat 8 lbs. each.

ባመት ፡ ባመት ፡ ይሔዳል ። bámḁt ẏámḁt yi̥hádāl, he goes every year.

§ 83*b* When the repeated word has the article or the -ን of the acc. (§ 55*a*), it may drop them the first time it is said:

e.g. ደኅና ፡ ደኅናውን ፡ መርጬ ፡ ነው ፡ ያመጣሁት ። dähná dähnáun mári̥ç̌ç̌^{y}é nḁu yāmḁ́ṭṭahut, I selected the very best and brought it (them, § 52*a*).

§ 83*c* A word or expression may be emphasized by being placed at the beginning of the sentence:

e.g. ይች ፡ ምንጭ ፡ በታች ፡ ፈይ ፡ ናት ። yí̥čči̥ mi̥nç̌ ẏḁtáč fḁ́i̥ nāt, this spring is boiling down below;

ፈይ ፡ ናት ፡ ይች ፡ ምንጭ ፡ በታች ። emphasizes 'boiling'.

ይህ ፡ ጩኸት ፡ ዝም ፡ ይበል ። yi̥he ç̌úhät zi̥mm yí̥ẏḁl, that noise must stop;

ዝም ፡ ይበል ፡ ይህ ፡ ጩኸት ። emphasizes 'stop'.

Concrete for Abstract.

§ 84 Though Amharic is not lacking in abstract terms (§§ 50, 66*a*) yet it frequently uses the concrete where English uses the abstract:

e.g. A trade route: የነጋዴ ፡ መንገድ ፡ yänḁggád^{y}e mḁ́n-gḁd.

He suppressed brigandage: ወንበዴ ፡ አቆመ ። wωm-bḁ́d^{y}e aq^{w}ómḁ, (lit. he caused brigands (§ 52*a*, δ) to stop).

He (pol.) employed military force against him: ወታደር ፡ ሰደዱበት ። wωttáddär (§ 52*a*, δ) sḁ́ddḁ-dubbḁt.

Similarly an English abstract noun is often best rendered by a verb in Amharic:

e.g. During my absence: እኔ ፡ ባልኖር ፡ i̥n^{y}é ỵāln^{w}ór.

Note.

Certain words commonly omitted in English must be rendered in Amharic, such as § 85

that, because,

e.g. I'm glad they're coming: ደስ ፡ ይሎኛል ፡ ስለሚመጡ ።
däss ỵi̥l^{w}oññāl si̥lḁmmi̥mḁ́ṭu;

or the relative,

e.g. Where is the man they sent? የላኩ ፡ ሰው ፡ የት ፡ ነው ። yäláku sḁ͡u yēt nḁ͡u?

APPENDIX.

PRINCIPAL PARTS OF VERBS OCCURRING IN PARTS I—III.

Simp. perf. (§ 25)	—	Comp. perf. (§ 32)	Contingent (§ 26)	Comp. imperf. (§ 32)
ሆነ h^{w}ŏ́nḁ	be, i.	ሁኗል húnŏ͡āl ሆኗል Š. h^{w}ŏ́nŏ͡āl	ይሆን yi̥h^{w}ŏ́n	ይሆናል yi̥h^{w}ŏ́nāl
ኀተመ háttḁmḁ	seal, t.	ኀትሟል hátti̥mŏ͡āl	ይኀትም yi̥háttim	ይኀትማል yi̥hátti̥māl
ሔደ hä̈́dä (h^{y}ḗ-, hḁ́-, -dḁ)	go, i.	ሒዷል hí̥dŏ͡āl ሔዷል Š. hä̈́dŏ͡āl (hḁ́-)	ይሔድ yi̥hä́d (-h^{y}ḗ-)	ይሔዳል yi̥hä́dāl (-h^{y}ḗ-)
ላላ lállã	be loose, i.	ላልቷል láltŏ͡āl	ይላላ yi̥lállã	ይላላል yi̥lállāl
ለመለመ lḁmḁ́llḁmḁ	be verdant, i.	ለምልሟል lḁ́mli̥mŏ͡āl	ይለመልም yi̥lḁmḁ́lli̥m	ይለመልማል yi̥lḁmḁ́lli̥- māl
ለመነ lḁ́mmḁnḁ	beg, t.	ለምኗል lḁ́mmi̥nŏ͡āl	ይለምን yi̥lḁ́mmi̥n	ይለምናል yi̥lḁ́mmi̥nāl
ለመደ lḁ́mmḁdḁ	learn, t.	ለምዷል lḁ́mdŏ͡āl	ይለምድ yi̥lḁ́md	ይለምዳል yi̥lḁ́mdāl
ለመጠ lḁ́mmḁṭ̥	strop, t.	ለምጧል lḁ́mmi̥ṭŏ͡āl	ይለምጥ yi̥lḁ́mmi̥ṭ	ይለምጣል yi̥lḁ́mmi̥ṭāl
ላሰ lásḁ	lick, t.	ልሷል lí̥sŏ͡āl	ይልስ yi̥lí̥s	ይልሳል yi̥lí̥sāl
ለሰለሰ lḁsḁ́llḁsḁ	be soft, i.	ለስልሷል lḁ́sli̥sŏ͡āl	ይለሰልስ yi̥lḁsḁ́lli̥s	ይለሰልሳል yi̥lḁsḁ́lli̥sāl

Jussive (§ 27)	Imperative (§ 28)	Gerund (§ 29)	Infinitive (§ 30)	Participle (§ 31)
ይሁን yí̥hun	ሁን hun	ሁኖ húnʷo ሆኖ Š. hʷṓnʷo	መሆን mḁ́hʷṓn (§ 8)	†ኋኝ hwāñ (-ññ § 6)
ይኅትም yi̥háttti̥m	ኅትም hátti̥m	ኅትሞ hátti̥mʷo	መኅተም mḁhátttḁm	ኅታሚ hattā́mi
ይሒድ yí̥hi̥d	ሒድ hi̥d f. ሒጅ hi̥j (-jj § 6)	ሒዶ hí̥dʷo ሔዶ Š. hḗdʷo (hḁ́-)	መሔድ mḁ́hḗd (§ 8; -hʸḗ-)	ሐያጅ hḁ́ā́j (§ 8; hāj, -ጂ -ji)
ይላላ yi̥lálā̃		ላልቶ lā́ltʷo	መላላት mḁlā́lát (§ 8)	
ይለምልም yi̥lḁ́mli̥m		ለምልሞ lḁ́mli̥mʷo	መለምለም mḁlḁ́mlḁm	ለምላሚ lḁmlā́mi
ይለምን yi̥lḁ́mmi̥n	ለምን lḁ́mmi̥n	ለምኖ lḁ́mmi̥nʷo	መለመን mḁlḁ́mmḁn	ለማኝ lḁ́mmā́ñ (-ññ § 6; § 8)
ይልመድ yí̥lmḁd	ልመድ lí̥mḁd	ለምዶ lḁ́mdʷo	መልመድ mḁ́lmḁd	ለማጅ lḁ́mā́j (§ 8)
ይለምጥ yi̥lḁ́mmi̥ṭ	ለምጥ lḁ́mmi̥ṭ	ለምጦ lḁ́mmi̥ṭʷo	መለመጥ mḁlḁ́mmḁṭ	ለማጭ lḁ́mmā́č̣ (§ 8)
ይላስ yí̥lā́s (§ 8)	ላስ lās	ልሶ lí̥sʷo	መላስ mḁ́lā́s (§ 8)	ላሽ lāš (-ሺ -ši)
ይለስልስ yi̥lḁ́sli̥s	ለስልስ lḁ́sli̥s	ለስልሶ lḁ́sli̥sʷo	መለስለስ mḁlḁ́slḁs	

Simp. perf. (§ 25)		Comp. perf. (§ 32)	Contingent (§ 26)	Comp. imperf. (§ 32)
ላቀ lắqḁ	be more, i.	ልቋል lí̥qŏ͡āl	ይልቅ yi̥lí̥q	ይልቃል yi̥lí̥qāl
ለቀመ lḁ́qqḁmḁ	pick, t.	ለቅሟል lḁ́qmŏ͡āl	ይለቅም yi̥lḁ́q(ĭ̥)m	ይለቅማል yi̥lḁ́qmāl
ለቀቀ lḁ́qqḁqḁ	give up, t.	ለቋል lḁ́qqŏ͡āl	ይለቅ yi̥lḁ́qq	ይለቃል yi̥lḁ́qqāl
ለቃቀመ lḁqắqqḁmḁ	pick a little, t.	ለቃቅሟል lḁqáq(ĭ̥)-mŏ͡āl	ይለቃቅም yi̥lḁqắqqi̥m	ይለቃቅማል yi̥lḁqắqqi̥-māl
ለበሰ lḁ́bbḁsḁ	dress one-self, i.	ለብሷል lḁ́bsŏ͡āl (-ṿs-)	ይለብስ yi̥lḁ́bs (-ṿs)	ይለብሳል yi̥lḁ́bsāl (-ṿs-)
ለበበ lḁ́bbḁbḁ (-ṿḁ)	put a halter on, t.	ለብቧል lḁ́bbi̥bŏ͡āl (-i̥ṿ-)	ይለብብ yi̥lḁ́bbi̥b (-i̥ṿ)	ይለብባል yi̥lḁ́bbi̥bāl (-i̥ṿ-)
ለካ lḁ́kkã	measure, t.	ለክቷል lḁ́kki̥tŏ͡āl (lắ-)	ይለካ yi̥lḁ́kkã	ይለካል yi̥lḁ́kkāl
ላከ lắkḁ	send, t.	ልኳል lí̥kŏ͡āl	ይልክ yi̥lí̥k	ይልካል yi̥lí̥kāl
ለወጠ lḁ́͡uwḁṭḁ	alter, t.	ለውጧል lḁ́͡uwŭṭŏ͡āl	ይለውጥ yi̥lḁ́͡uwŭṭ	ይለውጣል yi̥lḁ́͡uwŭṭāl
ለየ lḁ́yyä 2nd ለየህ lḁ́yyäh, etc.	distinguish, t.	ለይቷል lḁ́yyi̥tŏ͡āl	ይለይ yi̥lḁ́yy	ይለያል yi̥lḁ́yyāl

Jussive (§ 27)	Imperative (§ 28)	Gerund (§ 29)	Infinitive (§ 30)	Participle (§ 31)
ይላቅ yí̥lā́q (§ 8)		ሊቆ lí̥qʷo	መላቅ mḁ́lā́q (§ 8)	
ይልቀም yí̥lqḁm	ልቀም lí̥qḁm	ለቅሞ lḁ́qmʷo	መልቀም mḁ́lqḁm	ለቃሚ lḁqā́mi
ይልቀቅ yí̥lqḁq	ልቀቅ lí̥qḁq	ለቆ lḁ́qqʷo	መልቀቅ mḁ́lqḁq	ለቃቂ lḁqā́qi
ይለቃቅም yi̥lḁqā́qi̥m	ለቃቅም lḁqā́qi̥m	ለቃቅሞ lḁqā́- q(ĭ̥)mʷo	መለቃቀም mḁlḁqā́- qḁm	ለቃቃሚ lḁqāqā́mi
ይልበስ yí̥lbḁs (-lẏ-)	ልበስ lí̥bḁs (-í̥ẏ-)	ለብሶ lḁ́bsʷo (-ẏs-)	መልበስ mḁ́lbḁs (-lẏ-)	ለባሽ lḁ́bā́š (-ḁ́ẏ-; § 8)
ይለብብ yi̥lḁ́bbi̥b (-i̥ẏ)	ለብብ lḁ́bbi̥b (-i̥ẏ)	ለብቦ lḁ́bbi̥bʷo (-i̥ẏ-)	መለበብ mḁlḁ́bbḁb (-ḁẏ)	†ለባቢ lḁbbā́bi (-ẏi)
ይለካ yi̥lḁ́kkā̃	ለካ lḁ́kkā̃	ለክቶ lḁ́kki̥tʷo (lā́-)	መለካት mḁlḁ́kkā́t (§ 8)	†ለኪ lḁ́kki (lā́-)
ይላክ yí̥lā́k (§ 8)	ላክ lāk	ሊኮ lí̥kʷo	መላክ mḁ́lā́k (§ 8)	ላኪ lā́ki
ይለውጥ yi̥lḁ́͡uwŭṭ	ለውጥ lḁ́͡uwŭṭ	ለውጦ lḁ́͡uwŭṭʷo	መለወጥ mḁlḁ́͡uwḁṭ	ለዋጭ lḁ́͡uwā́č̣ (§ 8)
ይለይ yí̥lḁ́yy (§ 8)	ለይ lḁ́yyĭ̥	ለይቶ lḁ́yyi̥tʷo	መለየት mḁlḁ́yyät	ለዪ lḁ́yyi

Simp. perf. (§ 25)		Comp. perf. (§ 32)	Contingent (§ 26)	Comp. imperf. (§ 32)
ለጐመ lḁ́ggwωmḁ	put a bridle on, t.	ለጕሟል lḁ́ggwŭ-mŏ͡āl	ይለጕም yi̥lḁ́ggwŭm	ይለጕማል yi̥lḁ́ggwŭ-māl
ላጨ láčča̤ 2nd ላጨህ láččäh, etc.	shave, t.	ላጭቷል láč(i̥)tŏ͡āl	ይላጭ yi̥láčč	ይላጫል yi̥láččāl
ለፋ lḁ́ffã	tire oneself, i.	ለፍቷል lḁ́ftŏ͡āl	ይለፋ yi̥lḁ́fã	ይለፋል yi̥lḁ́fāl
መላ mḁ́llã	fill, i. & t.	መልቷል mḁ́ltŏ͡āl	ይመላ yi̥mḁ́lã	ይመላል yi̥mḁ́lāl
ማለ málḁ	swear, i.	ምሏል mí̥lŏ͡āl	ይምል yi̥mí̥l	ይምላል yi̥mí̥lāl
ሞላ mʷóllã	fill, i. & t.	ሞልቷል mʷóltŏ͡āl	ይሞላ yi̥mʷólã	ይሞላል yi̥mʷólāl
መለሰ mḁ́llḁsḁ (mắ-)	return, t.	መልሷል mḁ́lli̥sŏ͡āl (mắ-)	ይመልስ yi̥mḁ́lli̥s (-mắ-)	ይመልሳል yi̥mḁ́lli̥sāl (-mắ-)
ማለደ mállа̥dḁ	rise early, i.	ማልዷል máldŏ͡āl	ይማልድ yi̥mállі̥d	ይማልዳል yi̥mállі̥dāl
መራ mḁ́rrã	guide, t.	መርቷል mḁ́rtŏ͡āl (mắ-)	ይመራ yi̥mḁ́rã (-mắ-)	ይመራል yi̥mḁ́rāl (-mắ-)
ማረ márḁ	forgive, t.	ምሯል mí̥rŏ͡āl	ይምር yi̥mí̥r	ይምራል yi̥mí̥rāl

Jussive (§ 27)	Imperative (§ 28)	Gerund (§ 29)	Infinitive (§ 30)	Participle (§ 31)
ይለጕም yi̥lḁ́ggwŭm	ለጕም lḁ́ggwŭm	ለጕሞ lḁ́ggwŭmʷo	መለጐም mḁlḁ́g-gwωm	ለጓሚ lωggwấmi (§ 7*d*)
ይላጭ yi̥lấc̣ (-č̣č̣; § 8)	ላጭ lāč̣ (-č̣č̣)	ላጭቶ lấč̣(i̥)tʷo	መላጨት mḁlấč̣(č̣)ät	ላጪ lấč̣(č̣)i
ይልፋ yi̥lfã	ልፋ lí̥fã	ለፍቶ lḁ́ftʷo	መልፋት mḁ́lfất (§ 8)	ለፊ lḁ́fi
ይምላ yí̥mlã	ምላ mí̥lã	መልቶ mḁ́ltʷo	መምላት mḁ́mlất (§ 8)	†መይ mḁ́i̥ (mḁyy § 6)
ይማል yí̥mấl (§ 8)	ማል māl	ምሎ mí̥lʷo	መማል mḁ́mấl (§ 8)	ማይ mấi̥ (māyy § 6)
ይሙላ yí̥mŭlã	ሙላ mŭ́lã	ሞልቶ mʷóltʷo	መሙላት mḁ́mŭlất (§ 8)	†ሞይ mʷói̥ (mʷoyy § 6)
ይመልስ yi̥mḁ́lli̥s (-mấ-)	መልስ mḁ́lli̥s (mấ-)	መልሶ mḁ́lli̥sʷo (mấ-)	መመለስ mḁmḁ́llḁs (-mấl-)	መላሽ mḁ́llấš (mấ-; § 8)
ይማልድ yí̥mấld (§ 8)	ማልድ māld	ማልዶ mấldʷo	መማለድ mḁmấlḁd	ማላጅ mấlấj (§ 8)
ይምራ yí̥mrã	ምራ mí̥rã	መርቶ mḁ́rtʷo (mấ-)	መምራት mḁ́mrất (§ 8)	መሪ mḁ́ri (mấ-)
ይማር yí̥mấr (§ 8)	ማር mār	ምሮ mí̥rʷo	መማር mḁ́mấr (§ 8)	ማሪ mấri

Simp. perf. (§ 25)		Comp. perf. (§ 32)	Contingent (§ 26)	Comp. imperf. (§ 32)
መረመረ mḁrḁ́m-mḁrḁ (-ärḁ́mmä-)	examine, t.	መርምሯል mḁ́rmi̥rŏ͡āl (mä́-)	ይመረምር yi̥mḁrḁ́m-mi̥r (-i̥mä-)	ይመረምራል yi̥mḁrḁ́m-mi̥rāl (-i̥mä-)
መረቀ mḁ́rrḁqḁ	bless, t.	መርቋል mḁ́rri̥qŏ͡āl (mä́-)	ይመርቅ yi̥mḁ́rri̥q (-mä́-)	ይመርቃል yi̥mḁ́rri̥qāl (-mä́-)
ማረከ mā́rrḁkḁ	capture, t.	ማርኳል mā́rkŏ͡āl	ይማርክ yi̥mā́rri̥k	ይማርካል yi̥mā́rri̥kāl
ሞረደ mʷórrḁdḁ	file, t.	ሞርዷል mʷórri̥dŏ͡āl	ይሞርድ yi̥mʷórri̥d	ይሞርዳል yi̥mʷórri̥dāl
መረጠ mḁ́rrḁṭḁ	choose, t.	መርጧል mḁ́rṭŏ͡āl (mä́-)	ይመርጥ yi̥mḁ́rṭ (-mä́-)	ይመርጣል yi̥mḁ́rṭāl (-mä́-)
መሰለ mḁ́ssḁlḁ	seem, i. resemble, t.	መስሏል mḁ́s(ĭ̥)lŏ͡āl	ይመስል yi̥mḁ́s(ĭ̥)l	ይመስላል yi̥mḁ́s(ĭ̥)lāl
መሰለ mḁ́ssḁlḁ	fashion, t.	መስሏል mḁ́ssi̥lŏ͡āl	ይመስል yi̥mḁ́ssi̥l	ይመስላል yi̥mḁ́ssi̥lāl
መሰከረ mḁsḁ́kkḁrḁ (-kä-)	testify, t.	መስክሯል mḁ́ski̥rŏ͡āl	ይመሰክር yi̥mḁsḁ́kki̥r	ይመሰክራል yi̥mḁsḁ́k-ki̥rāl
መሸ mḁ́ššä (mä́-)	become evening, i.	መሽቷል mḁ́štŏ͡āl (mä́-)	ይመሽ yi̥mḁ́š (-mä́-)	ይመሻል yi̥mḁ́šāl (-mä́-)

Jussive (§ 27)	Imperative (§ 28)	Gerund (§ 29)	Infinitive (§ 30)	Participle (§ 31)
ይመርምር yi̥mḁ́rmi̥r (-mä́-)	**መርምር** mḁ́rmi̥r (mä́-)	**መርምሮ** mḁ́rmi̥r^{w}o (mä́-)	**መመርመር** mḁmḁ́rmḁr (-ä́rmä-)	**መርማሪ** mḁrmä́ri (mä-)
ይመርቅ yi̥mḁ́rri̥q (-mä́-)	**መርቅ** mḁ́rri̥q (mä́-)	**መርቆ** mḁ́rri̥q^{w}o (mä́-)	**መመረቅ** mḁmḁ́rrḁq	**መራቂ** mḁrrä́qi
ይማርክ yí̥mä́rk (§ 8)	**ማርክ** mārk	**ማርኮ** mä́rk^{w}o	**መማረክ** mḁmä́rḁk	**ማራኪ** mārä́ki
ይሞርድ yi̥m^{w}órri̥d	**ሞርድ** m^{w}órri̥d	**ሞርዶ** m^{w}órri̥d^{w}o	**መሞረድ** mḁm^{w}ór- rḁd	**ሞራጅ** m^{w}órrä́j (§ 8)
ይምረጥ yí̥mrḁṭ	**ምረጥ** mí̥rḁṭ	**መርጦ** mḁ́rṭ^{w}o (mä́-)	**መምረጥ** mḁ́mrḁṭ	**መራጭ** mḁ́rä́č̣ (§ 8)
ይምሰል yí̥msḁl (-äl)	**ምሰል** mí̥sḁl (-äl)	**መስሎ** mḁ́s(ĭ̥)l^{w}o	**መምሰል** mḁ́msḁl (-äl)	**መሳይ** mḁ́sä́i̥ (-ä́yy § 6; § 8)
ይመስል yi̥mḁ́ssi̥l	**መስል** mḁ́ssi̥l	**መስሎ** mḁ́ssi̥l^{w}o	**መመሰል** mḁmḁ́ssḁl (-äl)	**መሳይ** mḁ́ssä́i̥ (-ä́yy § 6; § 8)
ይመስክር yi̥mḁ́ski̥r	**መስክር** mḁ́ski̥r	**መስክሮ** mḁ́ski̥r^{w}o	**መመስከር** mḁmḁ́skḁr (-kä-)	**መስካሪ** mḁskä́ri
		መሽቶ mḁ́št^{w}o (mä́-)	**መምሸት** mḁ́mšḁt (-šä-)	

Simp. perf. (§ 25)		Comp. perf. (§ 32)	Contingent (§ 26)	Comp. imperf. (§ 32)
ሞሸረ m^{w}óššḁrḁ (-šä-)	celebrate a marriage, i.	ሞሽሯል m^{w}óšši̥rŏ͡āl	ይሞሽር yi̥m^{w}óšši̥r	ይሞሽራል yi̥m^{w}óšši̥rāl
ሞቀ m^{w}óqḁ	be warm, i.	ሙቋል múqŏ͡āl ሞቋል Š. m^{w}óqŏ͡āl	ይሞቅ yi̥m^{w}óq	ይሞቃል yi̥m^{w}óqāl
መታ mḁ́ttã	strike, t.	መትቷል mḁ́ttŏ͡āl	ይመታ yi̥mḁ́tã	ይመታል yi̥mḁ́tāl
ሞተ m^{w}ŏ́tḁ	die, i.	ሙቷል mútŏ͡āl ሞ- m^{w}ŏ́- Š.	ይሞት yi̥m^{w}ŏ́t	ይሞታል yi̥m^{w}ŏ́tāl
መነነ mḁ́nnḁnḁ	retire from the world, i.	መንኗል mḁ́nni̥nŏ͡āl	ይመንን yi̥mḁ́nni̥n	ይመንናል yi̥mḁ́nni̥nāl
መነዘረ mḁnḁ́zzḁrḁ (-zä-)	change, t. (money).	መንዝሯል mḁ́nzi̥rŏ͡āl	ይመነዝር yi̥mḁnḁ́zzi̥r	ይመነዝራል yi̥mḁnḁ́zzi̥- rāl
መከረ mḁ́kkḁrḁ (-kä-)	advise, t. reflect, i.	መክሯል mḁ́krŏ͡āl	ይመክር yi̥mḁ́k(ĭ̥)r	ይመክራል yi̥mḁ́k(ĭ̥)rāl
ሞከረ m^{w}ókkḁrḁ (-kä-)	try, t.	ሞክሯል m^{w}ókki̥rŏ͡āl	ይሞክር yi̥m^{w}ókki̥r	ይሞክራል yi̥m^{w}ókki̥- rāl
መዘነ mḁ́zzḁnḁ	weigh, t.	መዝኗል mḁ́zzi̥nŏ͡āl	ይመዝን yi̥mḁ́zzi̥n	ይመዝናል yi̥mḁ́zzi̥nāl

Jussive (§ 27)	Imperative (§ 28)	Gerund (§ 29)	Infinitive (§ 30)	Participle (§ 31)
ይሟሽር yi̥mʷóšši̥r	ሟሽር mʷóšši̥r	ሟሽሮ mʷóšši̥rʷo	መሟሽር mḁmʷóššḁr (-šä-)	ሟሻሪ mʷoššā́ri
ይሙቅ yí̥muq		ሙቆ múqʷo ሞቆ Š. mʷóqʷo	መሞቅ mḁ́mʷóq (§ 8)	†ሟቂ mwā́qi
ይምታ yí̥mtã	ምታ mí̥tã	መትቶ mḁ́ttʷo	መምታት mḁ́mtā́t (§ 8)	መች mḁč (mä-, -ቺ -či)
ይሙት yí̥mut	ሙት mut	ሙቶ mútʷo ሞ- mʷṓ- Š.	መሞት mḁ́mʷṓt (§ 8)	ሟች mwāč (-ቺ -či)
ይመንን yi̥mḁ́nni̥n	መንን mḁ́nni̥n	መንኖ mḁ́nni̥nʷo	መመነን mḁmḁ́nnḁn	መናኝ mḁ́nnā́ñ (-ññ § 6; § 8)
ይመንዝር yi̥mḁ́nzi̥r	መንዝር mḁ́nzi̥r	መንዝሮ mḁ́nzi̥rʷo	መመንዝር mḁmḁ́nzḁr (-zä-)	መንዛሪ mḁnzā́ri
ይምክር yí̥mkḁr (-kä-)	ምክር mí̥kḁr (-kä-)	መክሮ mḁ́krʷo	መምክር mḁ́mkḁr (-kä-)	መካሪ mḁkā́ri
ይሟክር yi̥mʷókki̥r	ሟክር mʷókki̥r	ሟክሮ mʷókki̥rʷo	መሟክር mḁmʷók- kḁr (-kä-)	ሟካሪ mʷokkā́ri
ይመዝን yi̥mḁ́zzi̥n	መዝን mḁ́zzi̥n	መዝኖ mḁ́zzi̥nʷo	መመዘን mḁmḁ́zzḁn	መዛኝ mḁ́zzā́ñ (-ññ § 6; § 8)

Simp. perf. (§ 25)		Comp. perf. (§ 32)	Contingent (§ 26)	Comp. imperf. (§ 32)
መገበ mḁ́ggḁbḁ (-ỵḁ)	feed, t.	መግቦል mḁ́ggi̥bŏ͡āl (-i̥ỵ-)	ይመግብ yi̥mḁ́ggi̥b (-i̥ỵ)	ይመግባል yi̥mḁ́ggi̥bāl (-i̥ỵ-)
መጣ mḁ́ṭṭã	come, i.	መጥቷል mḁ́ṭtŏ͡āl	ይመጣ yi̥mḁ́ṭã	ይመጣል yi̥mḁ́ṭāl
መጠነ mḁ́ṭṭḁnḁ	measure out, t.	መጥኗል mḁ́ṭṭi̥nŏ͡āl	ይመጥን yi̥mḁ́ṭṭi̥n	ይመጥናል yi̥mḁ́ṭṭi̥nāl
ሟጨረ mŏ͡ā́č̣č̣ärḁ	scratch, t.	ሟጭሯል mŏ͡ā́č̣č̣i̥rŏ͡āl	ይሟጭር yi̥mŏ͡ā́č̣č̣i̥r	ይሟጭራል yi̥mŏ͡ā́č̣č̣i̥rāl
መጻ G. mḁ́ṣṣã	come, i. (= መጣ)	መጽቷል mḁ́ṣtŏ͡āl	ይመጻ yi̥mḁ́ṣã	ይመጻል yi̥mḁ́ṣāl
[እ]ረሳ (ĭ̥)rḁ́ssã	forget, t.	[እ]ረስቷል (ĭ̥)rḁ́stŏ͡āl	ይረሳ yi̥rḁ́sã	ይረሳል yi̥rḁ́sāl
[እ]ራሰ (ĭ̥)rā́sḁ	be wet, i.	[እ]ርሷል rí̥sŏ͡āl (í̥rs-)	ይርስ yi̥rí̥s	ይርሳል yi̥rí̥sāl
[እ]ራቀ (ĭ̥)rā́qḁ	be distant, i.	[እ]ርቋል rí̥qŏ͡āl (í̥rq-)	ይርቅ yi̥rí̥q	ይርቃል yi̥rí̥qāl
[እ]ረባ (ĭ̥)rḁ́bbã	be useful, i.	[እ]ረብቷል (ĭ̥)rḁ́btŏ͡āl (-ỵt-)	ይረባ yi̥rḁ́bã (-ỵã)	ይረባል yi̥rḁ́bāl (-ỵā-)

Jussive (§ 27)	Imperative (§ 28)	Gerund (§ 29)	Infinitive (§ 30)	Participle (§ 31)
ይመግብ yi̥mḁ́ggi̥b (-i̥y̥)	መግብ mḁ́ggi̥b (-i̥y̥)	መግቦ mḁ́ggi̥bʷo (-i̥y̥-)	መመገብ mḁmḁ́ggḁb (-ḁy̥)	መጋቢ mḁggā́bi (-y̥i)
ይምጣ yí̥mṭā	use ና፡ነይ፡ኑ nā, f. nḁ͡i, pl. nū neg. አትምጣ āttí̥mṭā	መጥቶ mḁ́ṭṭʷo	መምጣት mḁ́mṭā́t (§ 8)	መጪ mḁč̣ (mä-,-ጪ.-č̣i)
ይመጥን yi̥mḁ́ṭṭi̥n	መጥን mḁ́ṭṭi̥n	መጥኖ mḁ́ṭṭi̥nʷo	መመጠን mḁmḁ́ṭṭḁn	መጣኝ mḁ́ṭṭā́ñ (-ññ § 6; § 8)
ይሟጭር yi̥mŏ͡ā̆č̣č̣i̥r	ሟጭር mŏ͡ā̆č̣č̣i̥r	ሟጭሮ mŏ͡ā̆č̣č̣i̥rʷo	መሟጨር mḁmŏ͡ā̆č̣č̣är	ሟጫሪ mŏ͡ā̆č̣č̣ā́ri
ይምጻ yí̥mṣā	ና nā, etc.	መጽቶ mḁ́ṣṭʷo	መምጻት mḁ́mṣā́t (§ 8)	መጪ mḁč̣ (mä-,-ጪ.-č̣i)
ይርሳ yí̥rsā	[እ]ርሳ rí̥sā (í̥rs-)	[እ]ረስቶ (i̥)rḁ́stʷo	መርሳት mḁ́rsā́t (mä́- § 8)	[እ]ረሽ (i̥)rḁ́š (-ā́š, -ሺ. -ši)
ይራስ yí̥rā́s (§ 8)		[እ]ርሶ rí̥sʷo (í̥rsʷo)	መራስ mḁ́rā́s (mä́-; § 8)	[እ]ራሽ (i̥)rā́š (-ሺ. -ši)
ይራቅ yí̥rā́q (§ 8)	[እ]ራቅ (i̥)rā́q	[እ]ርቆ rí̥qʷo (í̥rq-)	መራቅ mḁ́rā́q (mä́-; § 8)	[እ]ራቂ (i̥)rā́qi
ይርባ yí̥rbā (-y̥ā)	[እ]ርባ rí̥bā (í̥rb-, -y̥ā)	[እ]ረብቶ (i̥)rḁ́btʷo (-y̥t-)	መርባት mḁ́rbā́t (mä́-,-ry̥-; § 8)	[እ]ረቢ (i̥)rḁ́bi (-y̥i)

Simp. perf. (§ 25)		Comp. perf. (§ 32)	Contingent (§ 26)	Comp. imperf. (§ 32)
[እ]ራበው (ĭ̥)rábḁ͡u (-y̥ḁ͡u ; § 43*a*)	be hungry, i.	[እ]ርቦታል rı̥́bʷṓtāl (ı̥́rb-, -y̥ʷṓ-; § 8)	ይርበው yı̥́rbḁ͡u (-ry̥-)	ይርበዋል yı̥́rbḁuāl (-ry̥-)
[እ]ረታ (ĭ̥)rḁ́ttã	overcome, t.	[እ]ረትቷል (ĭ̥)rḁ́ttŏ͡āl	ይረታ yı̥rḁ́tã	ይረታል yı̥rḁ́tāl
ረዘመ rḁ́zzḁmḁ	be long, i.	ረዝሟል rḁ́zmŏ͡āl	ይረዝም yı̥rḁ́z(ĭ̥)m	ይረዝማል yı̥rḁ́z(ĭ̥)māl
[እ]ረዳ (ĭ̥)rḁ́ddã	help, t.	[እ]ረድቷል (ĭ̥)rḁ́dtŏ͡āl (-rḁ́rt-, -rắrt- § 7*d*)	ይረዳ yı̥rḁ́dã	ይረዳል yı̥rḁ́dāl
[እ]ረጋ (ĭ̥)rḁ́ggã	coagulate, i.	[እ]ረግቷል (ĭ̥)rḁ́gtŏ͡āl	ይረጋ yı̥rḁ́gã	ይረጋል yı̥rḁ́gāl
ረገመ rḁ́ggḁmḁ	curse, t.	ረግሟል rḁ́gmŏ͡āl	ይረግም yı̥rḁ́g(ĭ̥)m	ይረግማል yı̥rḁ́g(ĭ̥)māl
[እ]ሮጠ (ĭ̥)rʷṓṭḁ	run, i.	[እ]ሩጧል (ĭ̥)rúṭŏ͡āl -ሮ- -rʷṓ- Š.	ይሮጥ yı̥rʷṓṭ	ይሮጣል yı̥rʷṓṭāl
ረጠበ rḁ́ṭṭḁbḁ (-y̥ḁ)	be wet, i. assist, t.	ረጥቧል rḁ́ṭ(ĭ̥)bŏ͡āl (-y̥ŏ-)	ይረጥብ yı̥rḁ́ṭ(ĭ̥)b [-(ĭ̥)y̥]	ይረጥባል yı̥rḁ́ṭ(ĭ̥)bāl [-(ĭ̥)y̥-]
ረፈደ rḁ́ffḁdḁ	be forenoon, i.	ረፍዷል rḁ́fdŏ͡āl	ይረፍድ yı̥rḁ́fd	ይረፍዳል yı̥rḁ́fdāl

Jussive (§ 27)	Imperative (§ 28)	Gerund (§ 29)	Infinitive (§ 30)	Participle (§ 31)
ይራበው yi̥rábḁu͡ (-y̥ḁu͡)	**ይራብህ** yi̥rábi̥h (-y̥i̥-)	**[እ]ርቦት** rí̥bʷṓt (í̥rb-, -y̥ʷṓ-; § 8)	**መራብ** mḁ́ráb (mấ-,-ấy̥; § 8)	
ይርታ yí̥rtã	**[እ]ርታ** rí̥tã (í̥rt-)	**[እ]ረትቶ** (ĭ̥)rḁ́ttʷo	**መርታት** mḁ́rtất (mấ- ; § 8)	**[እ]ረች** (ĭ̥)rḁ́č (-ấč, -ቺ -či)
ይርዘም yí̥rzḁm		**ረዝሞ** rḁ́zmʷo	**መርዘም** mḁ́rzḁm (mấ-)	**†ረዛሚ** rḁzấmi
ይርዳ yí̥rdã	**[እ]ርዳ** rí̥dã (í̥rd-)	**[እ]ረድቶ** (ĭ̥)rḁ́dtʷo (-rḁ́rt-,-rấrt- § 7*d*)	**መርዳት** mḁ́rdất (mấ-; § 8)	**[እ]ረጅ** (ĭ̥)rḁ́j (-ấj, -ጂ -ji)
ይርጋ yí̥rgã	**[እ]ርጋ** rí̥gã (í̥rg-)	**[እ]ረግቶ** (ĭ̥)rḁ́gtʷo	**መርጋት** mḁ́rgất (mấ-; § 8)	**[እ]ረጊ** (ĭ̥)rḁ́gi
ይርገም yí̥rgḁm	**[እ]ርገም** rí̥gḁm (í̥rg-)	**ረግሞ** rḁ́gmʷo	**መርገም** mḁ́rgḁm (mấ-)	**†ረጋሚ** rḁgấmi
ይሩጥ yí̥ruṭ	**[እ]ሩጥ** (í̥)ruṭ	**[እ]ሩጦ** (ĭ̥)rúṭʷo -ሮ- -rʷṓ- Š.	**መሮጥ** mḁ́rʷṓṭ (mấ-; § 8)	**[እ]ሯጭ** (ĭ̥)rwấč̣ (-ጪ -č̣i)
ይርጠብ yí̥rṭḁb (-ḁy̥)	**[እ]ርጠብ** rí̥ṭḁb (í̥rṭ-, -ḁy̥)	**ረጥቦ** rḁ́ṭ(ĭ̥)bʷo (-y̥ʷo)	**መርጠብ** mḁ́rṭḁb (mấ-, -ḁy̥)	**†ረጣቢ** rḁṭấbi (-y̥i)
		ረፍዶ rḁ́fdʷo	**መርፈድ** mḁ́rfḁd (mấ-)	

14—2

Simp. perf. (§ 25)		Comp. perf. (§ 32)	Contingent (§ 26)	Comp. imperf. (§ 32)
ሳለ sā́lḁ	cough, i.	ስሏል sí̥lŏ͡āl	ይስል yi̥sí̥l	ይስላል yi̥sí̥lāl
ሰለለ sḁ́llḁlḁ (sǟ́-)	be paralysed, i.	ሰሏል sḁ́llŏ͡āl (sǟ́-)		
ሰለለ sḁ́llḁlḁ (sǟ́-)	spy on, t.	ሰልሏል sḁ́lli̥lŏ͡āl (sǟ́-)	ይሰልል yi̥sḁ́lli̥l (-sǟ́-)	ይሰልላል yi̥sḁ́lli̥lāl (-sǟ́-)
ሰማ sḁ́mmā̃	hear, t.	ሰምቷል sḁ́mtŏ͡āl	ይሰማ yi̥sḁ́mā̃	ይሰማል yi̥sḁ́māl
ሳመ sā́mḁ	kiss, t.	ስሟል sí̥mŏ͡āl	ይስም yi̥sí̥m	ይስማል yi̥sí̥māl
ሰራ sḁ́rrā̃ (sǟ́-)	work, build, } t. decree, t.	ሰርቷል sḁ́rtŏ͡āl (sǟ́-)	ይሰራ yi̥sḁ́rā̃ (-sǟ́-)	ይሰራል yi̥sḁ́rāl (-sǟ́-)
ሰረሰረ sḁrḁ́ssḁrḁ (sä-, -ärḁ)	bore through, t.	ሰርስሯል sḁ́rsi̥rŏ͡āl (sǟ́-)	ይሰረስር yi̥sḁrḁ́ssi̥r (-i̥sä-)	ይሰረስራል yi̥sḁrḁ́ssi̥rāl (-i̥sä-)
ሰረቀ sḁ́rrḁqḁ (sǟ́-)	steal, t.	ሰርቋል sḁ́rqŏ͡āl (sǟ́-)	ይሰርቅ yi̥sḁ́rq (-sǟ́-)	ይሰርቃል yi̥sḁ́rqāl (-sǟ́-)
ሣሣ sā́ssā̃	be thin, i.	ሣሥቷል sā́s(i̥)tŏ͡āl	ይሣሣ yi̥sā́ssā̃	ይሣሣል yi̥sā́ssāl

Jussive (§ 27)	Imperative (§ 28)	Gerund (§ 29)	Infinitive (§ 30)	Participle (§ 31)
ይሳል yí̥sḁ̄l (§ 8)	ሳል sāl	ስሎ sí̥lʷo	መሳል mḁ́sā́l (§ 8)	ሳይ sā́i̥ (säyy § 6)
		ሰሎ sḁ́llʷo (sä́-)	መስለል mḁ́slḁl (-äl)	
ይሰልል yi̥sḁ́lli̥l (-sä́-)	ሰልል sḁ́lli̥l (sä́-)	ሰልሎ sḁ́lli̥lʷo (sä́-)	መሰለል mḁsḁ́llḁl (-sä́-, -äl)	ሰላይ sḁ́llā́i̥ (sä́-; -ā́yy § 6; § 8)
ይስማ yí̥smā̃	ስማ sí̥mā̃	ሰምቶ sḁ́mtʷo	መስማት mḁ́smā́t (§ 8)	ሰሚ sḁ́mi (sä́-)
ይሳም yí̥sā́m (§ 8)	ሳም sām	ስሞ sí̥mʷo	መሳም mḁ́sā́m (§ 8)	ሳሚ sā́mi
ይስራ yí̥srā̃	ስራ sí̥rā̃	ሰርቶ sḁ́rtʷo (sä́-)	መስራት mḁ́srā́t (§ 8)	ሰሪ sḁ́ri (sä́-)
ይሰርስር yi̥sḁ́rsi̥r (-i̥sä́-)	ሰርስር sḁ́rsi̥r (sä́-)	ሰርስሮ sḁ́rsi̥rʷo (sä́-)	መሰርሰር mḁsḁ́rsḁr (-ä́rsä-)	ሰርሳሪ sḁrsā́ri (sä-)
ይስረቅ yí̥srḁq	ስረቅ sí̥rḁq	ሰርቆ sḁ́rqʷo (sä́-)	መስረቅ mḁ́srḁq	ሰራቂ sḁrā́qi (sä-)
ይሣሣ yi̥sā́sā̃		ሣሥቶ sā́s(i̥)tʷo	መሣሣት mḁsā́sā́t (§ 8)	†ሣሽ sāš

Simp. perf. (§ 25)		Comp. perf. (§ 32)	Contingent (§ 26)	Comp. imperf. (§ 32)
ሣቀ sā́qḁ	laugh, i.	ሥቋል sí̥qŏ͡āl	ይሥቅ yi̥sí̥q	ይሥቃል yi̥sí̥qāl
ሰቀለ sḁ́qqḁlḁ	suspend, t.	ሰቅሏል sḁ́qlŏ͡āl	ይሰቅል yi̥sḁ́q(ĭ̥)l	ይሰቅላል yi̥sḁ́q(ĭ̥)lāl
ሳበ sā́bḁ (-ỵḁ)	draw, t.	ስቧል sí̥bŏ͡āl (-í̥ỵ-)	ይስብ yi̥sí̥b (-í̥ỵ)	ይስባል yi̥sí̥bāl (-í̥ỵ-)
ሰበረ sḁ́bbḁrḁ (-bä-)	break, t.	ሰብሯል sḁ́brŏ͡āl (-ỵr-)	ይሰብር yi̥sḁ́b(ĭ̥)r (-ḁ́ỵ-)	ይሰብራል yi̥sḁ́b(ĭ̥)rāl (-ḁ́ỵ-)
ሰበሰበ sḁbḁ́ssḁbḁ (-ỵḁ́ssḁỵ-)	collect, t.	ሰብስቧል sḁ́bsi̥bŏ͡āl (-ỵsi̥ỵ-)	ይሰበስብ yi̥sḁbḁ́ssi̥b (-ỵḁ́ssi̥ỵ)	ይሰበስባል yi̥sḁbḁ́ssi̥bāl (-ỵḁ́ssi̥ỵ-)
ሰባበረ sḁbábbḁrḁ (-ỵá-, -är-)	shatter, t.	ሰባብሯል sḁbā́brŏ͡āl (-ỵā́ỵ-)	ይሰባብር yi̥sḁbábbi̥r (-ỵá-)	ይሰባብራል yi̥sḁbábbi̥rāl (-ỵá-)
ሳተ sā́tḁ	miss, t.	ስቷል sí̥tŏ͡āl	ይስት yi̥sí̥t	ይስታል yi̥sí̥tāl
ሰነበተ sḁnḁ́bbḁtḁ (-bä-)	remain, i.	ሰንብቷል sḁ́nbi̥tŏ͡āl (sắ-, -nỵ-)	ይሰነብት yi̥sḁnḁ́bbi̥t	ይሰነብታል yi̥sḁnḁ́bbi̥tāl
ሰነጠቀ sḁnḁ́ṭṭḁqḁ	split, t.	ሰንጥቋል sḁ́nṭi̥qŏ͡āl (sắ-)	ይሰነጥቅ yi̥sḁnḁ́ṭṭi̥q	ይሰነጥቃል yi̥sḁnḁ́ṭṭi̥qāl

Jussive (§ 27)	Imperative (§ 28)	Gerund (§ 29)	Infinitive (§ 30)	Participle (§ 31)
ይሣቅ yí̥sā́q (§ 8)	**ሣቅ** sāq	**ሥቆ** sí̥qʷo	**መሣቅ** mḁ́sā́q (§ 8)	† **ሣቂ** sā́qi
ይስቀል yí̥sqḁl	**ስቀል** sí̥qḁl	**ሰቅሎ** sḁ́qlʷo	**መስቀል** mḁ́sqḁl	**ሰቃይ** sḁ́qā́i̥ (-ā́yy § 6 ; § 8)
ይሳብ yí̥sā́b (-ā́ỵ ; § 8)	**ሳብ** sāb (-āỵ)	**ስቦ** sí̥bʷo (-í̥ỵ-)	**መሳብ** mḁ́sā́b (-ā́ỵ ; § 8)	**ሳቢ** sā́bi (-ỵi)
ይስበር yí̥sbḁr (-sỵ-, -är)	**ስበር** sí̥bḁr (-í̥ỵ-, -är)	**ሰብሮ** sḁ́brʷo (-ỵr-)	**መስበር** mḁ́sbḁr (-sỵ-, -är)	**ሰባሪ** sḁbā́ri (-ḁỵ-)
ይሰብስብ yi̥sḁ́bsi̥b (-ỵsi̥ỵ)	**ሰብስብ** sḁ́bsi̥b (-ỵsi̥ỵ)	**ሰብስቦ** sḁ́bsi̥bʷo (-ỵsi̥ỵ-)	**መሰብሰብ** mḁsḁ́bsḁb (-ỵsḁỵ)	**ሰብሳቢ** sḁbsā́bi (-ỵsā́ỵ-)
ይሰባብር yi̥sḁbā́bi̥r (-ỵā́ỵ-)	**ሰባብር** sḁbā́bi̥r (-ỵā́ỵ-)	**ሰባብሮ** sḁbā́brʷo (-ỵā́ỵ-)	**መሰባበር** mḁsḁbā́bḁr (-ỵā́ỵ-, -är)	**ሰባባሪ** sḁbābā́ri (-ỵāỵ-)
ይሳት yí̥sā́t (§ 8)	**ሳት** sāt	**ስቶ** sí̥tʷo	**መሳት** mḁ́sā́t (§ 8)	**ሳች** sāč (-ቺ -či)
ይሰንብት yi̥sḁ́nbi̥t (-sä́-, -nỵ-)	**ሰንብት** sḁ́nbi̥t (sä́-, -nỵ-)	**ሰንብቶ** sḁ́nbi̥tʷo (sä́-, -nỵ-)	**መሰንበት** mḁsḁ́nbḁt (-sä́-, -nỵ-, -ät)	**ሰንባች** sḁ́nbā́č (sä́-, -nỵ- ; § 8)
ይሰንጥቅ yi̥sḁ́nṭi̥q (-sä́-)	**ሰንጥቅ** sḁ́nṭi̥q (sä́-)	**ሰንጥቆ** sḁ́nṭi̥qʷo (sä́-)	**መሰንጠቅ** mḁsḁ́nṭḁq (-sä́-)	**ሰንጣቂ** sḁnṭā́qi (sä-)

Simp. perf. (§ 25)		Comp. perf. (§ 32)	Contingent (§ 26)	Comp. imperf. (§ 32)
ሰከረ sḁ́kkḁrḁ (-kä-)	be intoxicated, i.	**ሰክሯል** sḁkrŏ͡āl	**ይሰክር** yi̥sḁ́k(ĭ̥)r	**ይሰክራል** yi̥sḁ́k(ĭ̥)rāl
ሰወረ sḁ́͡uwḁrḁ	hide, t.	**ሰውሯል** sḁ͡uwŭrŏ͡āl	**ይሰውር** yi̥sḁ́͡uwŭr	**ይሰውራል** yi̥sḁ́͡uwŭrāl
ሰደበ sḁ́ddḁbḁ (-ṿḁ)	abuse, t.	**ሰድቧል** sḁ́d(ĭ̥)bŏ͡āl (-ṿŏ-)	**ይሰድብ** yi̥sḁ́d(ĭ̥)b (-ṿ)	**ይሰድባል** yi̥sḁ́d(ĭ̥)bāl (-ṿā-)
ሰደደ sḁ́ddḁdḁ	send, t.	**ሰዷል** sḁ́ddŏ͡āl	**ይሰድ** yi̥sḁ́dd	**ይሰዳል** yi̥sḁ́ddāl
ሰጋ sḁ́ggã (sắ-)	be afraid, i.	**ሰግቷል** sḁ́gtŏ͡āl (sắ-)	**ይሰጋ** yi̥sḁ́gã (-sắ-)	**ይሰጋል** yi̥sḁ́gāl (-sắ-)
ሠገረ sḁ́ggḁrḁ (-gä-)	amble, i.	**ሠግሯል** sḁ́grŏ͡āl	**ይሠግር** yi̥sḁ́g(ĭ̥)r	**ይሠግራል** yi̥sḁ́g(ĭ̥)rāl
ሰገደ sḁ́ggḁdḁ (-ắggä-)	adore, t.	**ሰግዷል** sḁ́gdŏ͡āl (sắ-)	**ይሰግድ** yi̥sḁ́gd (-sắ-)	**ይሰግዳል** yi̥sḁ́gdāl (-sắ-)
ሰጠ sḁ́ṭṭḁ 2nd **ሰጠህ** sḁ́ṭṭḁh (-äh), etc.	give, t.	**ሰጥቷል** sḁ́ṭ(ĭ̥)tŏ͡āl	**ይሰጥ** yi̥sḁ́ṭ	**ይሰጣል** yi̥sḁ́ṭāl
ሰፋ sḁ́ffã	(*a*) sew, t. (*b*) be broad, i.	**ሰፍቷል** sḁ́ftŏ͡āl	**ይሰፋ** yi̥sḁ́fã	**ይሰፋል** yi̥sḁ́fāl

Jussive (§ 27)	Imperative (§ 28)	Gerund (§ 29)	Infinitive (§ 30)	Participle (§ 31)
ይስከር yí̥skḁr (-kä-)	ስከር sí̥kḁr (-kä-)	ሰክሮ sḁ́kr^{w}o	መስከር mḁ́skḁr (-kä-)	ሰካሪ sḁkā́ri
ይሰውር yi̥sḁ́͡uwŭr	ሰውር sḁ́͡uwŭr	ሰውሮ sḁ́͡uwŭr^{w}o	መሰወር mḁsḁ́͡uwḁr	ሰዋሪ sḁ͡uwā́ri
ይስደብ yí̥sdḁb (-ḁẏ)	ስደብ sí̥dḁb (-ḁẏ)	ሰድቦ sḁ́d(ĭ̥)b^{w}o (-ẏ^{w}o)	መስደብ mḁ́sdḁb (-ḁẏ)	†ሰዳቢ sḁdā́bi (-ẏi)
ይስደድ yí̥sdḁd	ስደድ sí̥dḁd	ሰዶ sḁ́dd^{w}o	መስደድ mḁ́sdḁd	ሰዳጅ sḁ́dā́j (§ 8)
ይስጋ yí̥sgã	ስጋ sí̥gã	ሰግቶ sḁ́gt^{w}o (sā́-)	መስጋት mḁ́sgā́t (§ 8)	†ሰጊ sḁ́gi (sā́-)
ይሥገር yí̥sgḁr (-gä-)		ሥግሮ sḁ́gr^{w}o	መሥገር mḁ́sgḁr (-gä-)	ሠጋሪ sḁgā́ri
ይስገድ yí̥sgḁd (-gä-)	ስገድ sí̥gḁd (-gä-)	ሰግዶ sḁ́gd^{w}o (sā́-)	መስገድ mḁ́sgḁd (-gä-)	ሰጋጅ sḁ́gā́j (sā́-; § 8)
ይስጥ yi̥sṭ	ስጥ si̥ṭ	ሰጥቶ sḁ́ṭ(ĭ̥)t^{w}o	መስጠት mḁ́sṭḁt (-ät)	ሰጭ sḁč̣ (sä-, -ጪ -č̣i)
ይስፋ yí̥sfã	ስፋ sí̥fã	ሰፍቶ sḁ́ft^{w}o	መስፋት mḁ́sfā́t (§ 8)	ሰፊ (*a*) sḁ́fi (sā́-) (*b*) sḁ́ffi

Simp. perf. (§ 25)		Comp. perf. (§ 32)	Contingent (§ 26)	Comp. imperf. (§ 32)
ሰፈረ sḁ́ffḁrḁ (-fä-)	measure, t. encamp, i.	ሰፍሯል sḁ́frŏ͡āl	ይሰፍር yi̥sḁ́f(i̥)r	ይሰፍራል yi̥sḁ́f(i̥)rāl
[እ]ሻ (i̥)šā̃ (í̥šā̃ § 8)	need, seek, t.	[እ]ሽቷል (i̥)ší̥tŏ͡āl	ይሻ yí̥šā̃	ይሻል yí̥šāl
ሾመ šʷṓmḁ	set in authority, t.	ሹሟል šúmŏ͡āl ሾ- šʷṓ- Š.	ይሾም yi̥šʷṓm	ይሾማል yi̥šʷṓmāl
ሸሸ šḁ́ššä (šá-) 2nd -ሸህ -ššäh, etc.	flee from, t.	ሸሽቷል šḁ́štŏ͡āl (šá-)	ይሸሽ yi̥šḁ́š (-áš)	ይሸሻል yi̥šḁ́šāl (-šá-)
ሸሸገ šḁ́ššḁgḁ (-áššä-)	hide, t.	ሸሽጓል šḁ́šši̥gŏ͡āl (šá-)	ይሸሽግ yi̥šḁ́šši̥g (-šá-)	ይሸሽጋል yi̥šḁ́šši̥gāl (-šá-)
ሸበሸበ šḁbḁ́ššḁbḁ (-ṿḁ́ššḁṿ-)	plait, t.	ሸብሽቧል šḁ́bši̥bŏ͡āl (-ṿši̥ṿ-)	ይሸበሽብ yi̥šḁbḁ́šši̥b (-ṿḁ́šši̥ṿ)	ይሸበሽባል yi̥šḁbḁ́šši̥bāl (-ṿḁ́šši̥ṿ-)
ሸተተ šḁ́ttḁtḁ (šá-)	smell, i.	ሸቷል šḁ́ttŏ͡āl (šá-)	ይሸት yi̥šḁ́tt (-šá-)	ይሸታል yi̥šḁ́ttāl (-šá-)
ሸና šḁ́nnḁ 2nd ሸነህ šḁ́nnḁh (-äh), etc.	make water, i.	ሸንቷል šḁ́ntŏ͡āl	ይሸን yi̥šḁ́n	ይሸናል yi̥šḁ́nāl

Jussive (§ 27)	Imperative (§ 28)	Gerund (§ 29)	Infinitive (§ 30)	Participle (§ 31)
ይስፈር yí̥sfḁr (-fä-)	**ስፈር** sí̥fḁr (-fä-)	**ሰፍሮ** sḁ́frʷo	**መስፈር** mḁ́sfḁr (-fä-)	**ሰፋሪ** sḁfári
ይሻ yí̥šā̃	[**እ**]**ሻ** (ĭ̥)šā̃́ (í̥šā̃ § 8)	[**እ**]**ሽቶ** (ĭ̥)ší̥tʷo	**መሻት** mḁ́šā́t (§ 8)	
ይሹም yí̥šum	**ሹም** šum	**ሹሞ** šúmʷo **ሾ**- šʷṓ- Š.	**መሾም** mḁ́šʷṓm (§ 8)	**ሿሚ** šwā́mi
ይሽሽ yí̥ši̥š	**ሽሽ** ši̥š	**ሸሽቶ** šḁ́štʷo (šắ-)	**መሸሽ** mḁ́šḁ́š (-ắšắ-; § 8)	†**ሸሺ** šḁ́ši (šắ-)
ይሸሽግ yi̥šḁ́šši̥g (-šắ-)	**ሸሽግ** šḁ́šši̥g (šắ-)	**ሸሽጎ** šḁ́šši̥gʷo (šắ-)	**መሸሸግ** mḁšḁ́ššḁg (-ắššä-)	**ሸሻጊ** šḁššā́gi (šä-)
ይሸብሽብ yi̥šḁ́bši̥b (-ṿši̥ṿ)	**ሸብሽብ** šḁ́bši̥b (-ṿši̥ṿ)	**ሸብሽቦ** šḁ́bši̥bʷo (-ṿši̥ṿ-)	**መሸብሸብ** mḁšḁ́bšḁb (-ṿšḁṿ)	†**ሸብሻቢ** šḁbšā́bi (-ṿšā́ṿ-)
ይሽተት yí̥štḁt (-ät)	**ሽተት** ší̥tḁt (-ät)	**ሸቶ** šḁ́ttʷo (šắ-)	**መሽተት** mḁ́štḁt (-ät)	**ሸታች** šḁ́tā́č (šắ-; § 8)
ይሽን yí̥ši̥n	**ሽን** ši̥n	**ሸንቶ** šḁ́ntʷo	**መሽነት** mḁ́šnḁt (-ät) **መሸን** mḁ́šḁ́n (§ 8)	

Simp. perf. (§ 25)		Comp. perf. (§ 32)	Contingent (§ 26)	Comp. imperf. (§ 32)
ሸኘ šḁ́ññä (šä́-) 2nd -ኘህ -ññäh, etc.	escort, t.	ሸኝቷል šḁ́ññi̥tŏ͡āl (šä́-)	ይሸኝ yi̥šḁ́ññ (-šä́-)	ይሸኛል yi̥šḁ́ññāl (-šä́-)
ሻገተ šã́ggḁtḁ	be mouldy, i.	ሻግቷል šã́gtŏ͡āl	ይሻግት yi̥šã́ggi̥t	ይሻግታል yi̥šã́ggi̥tāl
ሸጠ šḁ́ṭḁ (šä́-)	sell, t.	ሺጧል ší̥ṭŏ͡āl ሺ- šä́- Š.	ይሸጥ yi̥šḁ́ṭ (-šä́-)	ይሸጣል yi̥šḁ́ṭāl (-šä́-)
ሸፈነ šḁ́ffḁnḁ (šä́-)	wrap, t.	ሸፍኗል šḁ́ffi̥nŏ͡āl (šä́-)	ይሸፍን yi̥šḁ́ffi̥n (-šä́-)	ይሸፍናል yi̥šḁ́ffi̥nāl (-šä́-)
ቀላ qḁ́llã	be red, i.	ቀልቷል qḁ́ltŏ͡āl	ይቀላ yi̥qḁ́lã	ይቀላል yi̥qḁ́lāl
ቀለመ qḁ́llḁmḁ	stain, t.	ቀልሟል qḁ́lmŏ͡āl qḁ́lli̥mŏ͡āl	ይቀልም yi̥qḁ́lm yi̥qḁ́lli̥m	ይቀልማል yi̥qḁ́lmāl yi̥qḁ́lli̥māl
†ቀለቀለ qḁlḁ́qqḁlḁ	mix, t.	ቀልቅሏል qḁ́lqi̥lŏ͡āl	†ይቀለቅል yi̥qḁlḁ́qqi̥l	†ይቀለቅላል yi̥qḁlḁ́qqi̥lāl
ቀላቀለ qḁlã́qqḁlḁ	mix, t.	ቀላቅሏል qḁlã́q(i̥)lŏ͡āl	ይቀላቅል yi̥qḁ́lã́qqi̥l	ይቀላቅላል yi̥qḁlã́qqi̥lāl
ቀለጠ qḁ́llḁṭḁ	melt, i.	ቀልጧል qḁ́lṭŏ͡āl	ይቀልጥ yi̥qḁ́lṭ	ይቀልጣል yi̥qḁ́lṭāl

Jussive (§ 27)	Imperative (§ 28)	Gerund (§ 29)	Infinitive (§ 30)	Participle (§ 31)
ይሸኝ yí̥šḁ́ññ (-šä́-; § 8)	ሸኝ šḁññ (šä-)	ሸኝቶ šḁ́ññi̥tʷo (šắ-)	መሸኘት mḁšḁ́ññät (-šắ-)	ሸኚ šḁ́ññi (šắ-)
ይሻግት yi̥šắgt		ሻግቶ šắgtʷo	መሻገት mḁšắgḁt (-ät)	ሻጋች šắgắč (§ 8)
ይሺጥ yí̥ší̥ṭ (§ 8)	ሺጥ ši̥ṭ	ሺጦ ší̥ṭʷo ሼ- šắ- Š.	መሸጥ mḁ́šḁ́ṭ (-šắ-; § 8)	ሻጭ šāč̣ (-ጪ. -č̣i)
ይሸፍን yi̥šḁ́ffi̥n (-šắ-)	ሸፍን šḁ́ffi̥n (šắ-)	ሸፍኖ šḁ́ffi̥nʷo (šắ-)	መሸፈን mḁšḁ́ffḁn (-šắ-)	ሸፋኝ šḁ́ffắñ (šắ-, -ắññ § 6; § 8)
ይቅላ yí̥qlā̃		ቀልቶ qḁ́ltʷo	መቅላት mḁ́qlắt (§ 8)	ቀይ qḁ́i̥ (qḁyy § 6)
ይቅለም yí̥qlḁm ይቀልም yi̥qḁ́lli̥m	ቅለም qí̥lḁm ቀልም qḁ́lli̥m	ቀልሞ qḁ́lmʷo qḁ́lli̥mʷo	መቅለም mḁ́qlḁm መቀለም mḁqḁ́llḁm	ቀላሚ qḁl(l)ắmi
ይቀልቅል yi̥qḁ́lqi̥l	ቀልቅል qḁ́lqi̥l	ቀልቅሎ qḁ́lqi̥lʷo	መቀልቀል mḁqḁ́lqḁl	ቀልቃይ qḁ́lqắi̥ (-ắyy § 6; § 8)
ይቀላቅል yi̥qḁlắqi̥l	ቀላቅል qḁlắqi̥l	ቀላቅሎ qḁlắq(ĭ̥)lʷo	መቀላቀል mḁqḁlắqḁl	ቀላቃይ qḁlắqắi̥ (-ắyy § 6; § 8)
ይቅለጥ yí̥qlḁṭ		ቀልጦ qḁ́lṭʷo	መቅለጥ mḁ́qlḁṭ	ቀላጭ qḁ́lắč̣ (§ 8)

Simp. perf. (§ 25)		Comp. perf. (§ 32)	Contingent (§ 26)	Comp. imperf. (§ 32)
ቈለፈ qwώllḁfḁ	lock, t.	ቈልፏል qwώlli̥fŏ͡āl	ይቈልፍ yi̥qwώlli̥f	ይቈልፋል yi̥qwώlli̥fāl
ቀማ qḁ́mmã	rob, t.	ቀምቷል qḁ́mmi̥tŏ͡āl	ይቀማ yi̥qḁ́mmã	ይቀማል yi̥qḁ́mmāl
ቆመ qʷő́mḁ	stand, i.	ቊሟል qúmŏ͡āl ቆ- qʷő́- Š.	ይቆም yi̥qʷő́m	ይቆማል yi̥qʷő́māl
ቀመሰ qḁ́mmḁsḁ	taste, t.	ቀምሷል qḁ́msŏ͡āl	ይቀምስ yi̥qḁ́ms	ይቀምሳል yi̥qḁ́msāl
ቀረ qḁ́rrḁ 2nd ቀረህ qḁ́rrḁh (-äh), etc.	remain behind, i.	ቀርቷል qḁ́rtŏ͡āl (qä́-)	ይቀር yi̥qḁ́r (-qä́-)	ይቀራል yi̥qḁ́rāl (-qä́-)
ቀረበ qḁ́rrḁbḁ (-ṿḁ)	approach, i.	ቀርቧል qḁ́rbŏ͡āl (qä́-, -rṿ-)	ይቀርብ yi̥qḁ́rb (-qä́-, -rṿ)	ይቀርባል yi̥qḁ́rbāl (-qä́-, -rṿ-)
ቀረጠ qḁ́rrḁṭḁ	charge dues, i.	ቀርጧል qḁ́rṭŏ͡āl (qä́-)	ይቀርጥ yi̥qḁ́rṭ (-qä́-)	ይቀርጣል yi̥qḁ́rṭāl (-qä́-)
ቈረጠ qwώrrḁṭḁ	cut, t.	ቈርጧል qwώrṭŏ͡āl	ይቈርጥ yi̥qwώrṭ	ይቈርጣል yi̥qwώrṭāl
ቈሰለ qwώssḁlḁ	be wounded, p.	ቈስሏል qwώs(i̥)lŏ͡āl	ይቈስል yi̥qwώs(i̥)l	ይቈስላል yi̥qwώs(i̥)lāl

Jussive (§ 27)	Imperative (§ 28)	Gerund (§ 29)	Infinitive (§ 30)	Participle (§ 31)
ይቈልፍ yi̥qwώlli̥f	ቈልፍ qwώlli̥f	ቈልፎ qwώlli̥f^{w}o	መቈለፍ mḁqwώllḁf	ቈላፊ qwωllā́fi
ይቀማ yi̥qḁ́mmã	ቀማ qḁ́mmã	ቀምቶ qḁ́mmi̥t^{w}o	መቀማት mḁqḁ́mmā́t (§ 8)	ቀሚ qḁ́mmi
ይቊም yí̥qum	ቊም qum	ቊሞ qúm^{w}o ቆ- q^{w}ǒ́- Š.	መቆም mḁ́q^{w}ǒ́m (§ 8)	ቋሚ qwā́mi
ይቅመስ yí̥qmḁs	ቅመስ qí̥mḁs	ቀምሶ qḁ́ms^{w}o	መቅመስ mḁ́qmḁs	ቀማሽ qḁ́mā́š (§ 8)
ይቅር yí̥qi̥r	ቅር qi̥r	ቀርቶ qḁ́rt^{w}o (qä́-)	መቅረት mḁ́qrḁt (-ät)	ቀሪ qḁ́ri (qä́-)
ይቅረብ yí̥qrḁb (-ḁy̥)	ቅረብ qí̥rḁb (-ḁy̥)	ቀርቦ qḁ́rb^{w}o (qä-, -ry̥-)	መቅረብ mḁ́qrḁb (-ḁy̥)	ቀራቢ qḁrā́bi (-y̥i)
ይቅረጥ yí̥qrḁṭ	ቅረጥ qí̥rḁṭ	ቀርጦ qḁ́rṭ^{w}o (qä́-)	መቅረጥ mḁ́qrḁṭ	ቀራጭ qḁ́rā́č̣ (§ 8)
ይቍረጥ yí̥qwŭrḁṭ	ቍረጥ qwŭ́rḁṭ	ቈርጦ qwώrṭ^{w}o	መቍረጥ mḁ́qwŭrḁṭ	ቈራጭ qwώrā́č̣ (§ 8)
ይቍሰል yí̥qwŭsḁl (-äl)	ቍሰል qwŭ́sḁl (-äl)	ቈስሎ qwώs(ĭ̥)l^{w}o	መቍሰል mḁ́qwŭsḁl (-äl)	ቈሳይ qwώsā́i̥ (-ā́yy §6; §8)

Simp. perf. (§ 25)		Comp. perf. (§ 32)	Contingent (§ 26)	Comp. imperf. (§ 32)
ቀሰቀሰ qḁsḁ́qqḁsḁ	rouse, t.	ቀስቅሷል qḁ́sqi̥sŏ͡āl	ይቀሰቅስ yi̥qḁsḁ́qqi̥s	ይቀሰቅሳል yi̥qḁsḁ́qqi̥sāl
ቀቀለ qḁ́qqḁlḁ	boil, t.	ቀቅሏል qḁ́qqi̥lŏ͡āl	ይቀቅል yi̥qḁ́qqi̥l	ይቀቅላል yi̥qḁ́qqi̥lāl
ቀባ qḁ́bbã	anoint, t.	ቀብቷል qḁ́btŏ͡āl (-ỵt-)	ይቀባ yi̥qḁ́bã (-ḁ́ỵ-)	ይቀባል yi̥qḁ́bāl (-ḁ́ỵ-)
ቀበረ qḁ́bbḁrḁ (-bä-)	bury, t.	ቀብሯል qḁ́brŏ͡āl (-ỵr-)	ይቀብር yi̥qḁ́b(ĭ̥)r (-ḁ́ỵ-)	ይቀብራል yi̥qḁ́b(ĭ̥)rāl (-ḁ́ỵ-)
ቀበጠ qḁ́bbḁṭḁ	play the fool, i.	ቀብጧል qḁ́bṭŏ͡āl (-ỵṭ-)	ይቀብጥ yi̥qḁ́bṭ (-ỵṭ)	ይቀብጣል yi̥qḁ́bṭāl (-ỵṭ-)
ቀና qḁ́nnã	be straight, i. be jealous, i.	ቀንቷል qḁ́ntŏ͡āl	ይቀና yi̥qḁ́nã	ይቀናል yi̥qḁ́nāl
ቀነተ qḁ́nnḁtḁ	put girths on, t.	ቀንቷል qḁ́nni̥tŏ͡āl	ይቀንት yi̥qḁ́nni̥t	ይቀንታል yi̥qḁ́nni̥tāl
ቈነጠጠ qʷωnḁ́ṭṭḁṭḁ	pinch, t.	ቈንጥጧል qʷώnṭi̥ṭŏ͡āl	ይቈነጥጥ yi̥qʷωnḁ́ṭṭi̥ṭ	ይቈነጥጣል yi̥qʷωnḁ́ṭṭi̥ṭāl
ቀዘቀዘ qḁzḁ́qqḁzḁ	be cold, i.	ቀዝቅዟል qḁ́zqi̥zŏ͡āl	ይቀዘቅዝ yi̥qḁzḁ́qqi̥z	ይቀዘቅዛል yi̥qḁzḁ́qqi̥zāl

Jussive (§ 27)	Imperative (§ 28)	Gerund (§ 29)	Infinitive (§ 30)	Participle (§ 31)
ይቀስቅስ yi̥qḁ́sqi̥s	ቀስቅስ qḁ́sqi̥s	ቀስቅሶ qḁ́sqi̥s^{w}o	መቀስቀስ mḁqḁ́sqḁs	ቀስቃሽ qḁ́sqā́š (§ 8)
ይቀቅል yi̥qḁ́qqi̥l	ቀቅል qḁ́qqi̥l	ቀቅሎ qḁ́qqi̥l^{w}o	መቀቀል mḁqḁ́qqḁl	ቀቃይ qḁ́qqā́i̥ (-ā́yy § 6 ; § 8)
ይቅባ yí̥qbā̃ (-qỵ-)	ቅባ qí̥bā̃ (-í̥ỵ-)	ቀብቶ qḁ́bt^{w}o (-ỵt-)	መቅባት mḁ́qbā́t (-qỵ- ; § 8)	ቀቢ qḁ́bi (-ḁ́ỵ-)
ይቅበር yí̥qbḁr (-qỵ-, -är)	ቅበር qí̥bḁr (-í̥ỵ-, -är)	ቀብሮ qḁ́br^{w}o (-ỵr-)	መቅበር mḁ́qbḁr (-qỵ-, -är)	ቀባሪ qḁbā́ri (-ỵā́-)
ይቅበጥ yí̥qbḁṭ (-qỵ-)	ቅበጥ qí̥bḁṭ (-í̥ỵ-)	ቀብጦ qḁ́bṭ^{w}o (-ỵṭ-)	መቅበጥ mḁ́qbḁṭ (-qỵ-)	ቀባጭ qḁ́bā́č̣ (-ḁ́ỵ- ; § 8)
ይቅና yí̥qnā̃	ቅና qí̥nā̃	ቀንቶ qḁ́nt^{w}o	መቅናት mḁ́qnā́t (§ 8)	ቀኝ qḁñ (-ññ § 6; -ኚ -ññi)
ይቀንት yi̥qḁ́nni̥t	ቀንት qḁ́nni̥t	ቀንቶ qḁ́nni̥t^{w}o	መቀነት mḁqḁ́nnḁt (-ät)	ቀናች qḁ́nnā́č (§ 8)
ይቈንጥጥ yi̥qwώnṭi̥ṭ	ቈንጥጥ qwώnṭi̥ṭ	ቈንጥጦ qwώnṭi̥ṭ^{w}o	መቈንጠጥ mḁqwώnṭḁṭ	ቈንጣጭ qwώnṭā́č̣ (§ 8)
ይቀዝቅዝ yi̥qḁ́zqi̥z		ቀዝቅዞ qḁ́zqi̥z^{w}o	መቀዝቀዝ mḁqḁ́zqḁz	ቀዝቃዥ qḁ́zqā́ž (§ 8)

Simp. perf. (§ 25)		Comp. perf. (§ 32)	Contingent (§ 26)	Comp. imperf. (§ 32)
ቀዘነ qḁ́zzḁnḁ	have diarrhœa, i.	ቀዝኗል qḁ́z(ĭ̥)nŏ͡āl	ይቀዝን yi̥qḁ́z(ĭ̥)n	ይቀዝናል yi̥qḁ́z(ĭ̥)nāl
ቈየ qwώyyä 2nd ቈየህ qwώyyäh, etc.	await, t.	ቈይቷል qwώyyi̥tŏ͡āl	ይቈይ yi̥qwώ͡i̥ (-ώyy § 6)	ይቈያል yi̥qwώyyāl
ቀዳ qḁ́ddā̃	draw (liquids), t.	ቀድቷል qḁ́d(ĭ̥)tŏ͡āl (qä-,-rt-§7*d*)	ይቀዳ yi̥qḁ́dā̃	ይቀዳል yi̥qḁ́dāl
ቀደመ qḁ́ddḁmḁ	precede, t.	ቀድሟል qḁ́dmŏ͡āl (qǟ́-, -rm-§ 7*d*)	ይቀድም yi̥qḁ́d(ĭ̥)m	ይቀድማል yi̥qḁ́d(ĭ̥)māl (-qǟ́-, -rm-§ 7*d*)
ቀደደ qḁ́ddḁdḁ	tear, t.	ቀዷል qḁ́ddŏ͡āl	ይቀድ yi̥qḁ́dd	ይቀዳል yi̥qḁ́ddāl
ቀጣ qḁ́ṭṭā̃	punish, t.	ቀጥቷል qḁ́ṭtŏ͡āl	ይቀጣ yi̥qḁ́ṭā̃	ይቀጣል yi̥qḁ́ṭāl
ቀጠለ qḁ́ṭṭḁlḁ	join, t.	ቀጥሏል qḁ́ṭṭi̥lŏ͡āl	ይቀጥል yi̥qḁ́ṭṭi̥l	ይቀጥላል yi̥qḁ́ṭṭi̥lāl
ቀጠረ qḁ́ṭṭḁrḁ (-ṭä-)	engage, t.	ቀጥሯል qḁ́ṭrŏ͡āl	ይቀጥር yi̥qḁ́ṭ(ĭ̥)r	ይቀጥራል yi̥qḁ́ṭ(ĭ̥)rāl
ቈጠረ qwώṭṭḁrḁ (-ṭä-)	count, t.	ቈጥሯል qwώṭrŏ͡āl	ይቈጥር yi̥qwώṭ(ĭ̥)r	ይቈጥራል yi̥qwώṭ(ĭ̥)rāl

Jussive (§ 27)	Imperative (§ 28)	Gerund (§ 29)	Infinitive (§ 30)	Participle (§ 31)
		ቀዝኖ qḁ́z(ĭ̥)nʷo	መቅዘን mḁ́qzḁn	ቀዛኝ qḁ́zā́ñ (-ññ § 6; § 8)
ይቈይ yḭ̊qwώ͡i̥ (-ώyy § 6; § 8)	ቈይ qwώ͡i̥ (-ωyy § 6) pl. ቈዩ qwώyyu	ቈይቶ qwώyyi̥tʷo	መቈየት mḁqwώyyät	
ይቅዳ yí̥qdā̃	ቅዳ qí̥dā̃	ቀድቶ qḁ́d(ĭ̥)tʷo (qā́-, -rt- § 7*d*)	መቅዳት mḁ́qdā́t (§ 8)	ቀጅ qḁj (qä-, -ጂ -ji)
ይቅደም yí̥qdḁm	ቅደም qí̥dḁm	ቀድሞ qḁ́dmʷo (qā́-, -rm- § 7*d*)	መቅደም mḁ́qdḁm	ቀዳሚ qḁdā́mi
ይቅደድ yí̥qdḁd	ቅደድ qí̥dḁd	ቀዶ qḁ́ddʷo	መቅደድ mḁ́qdḁd	ቀዳጅ qḁ́dā́j (§ 8)
ይቅጣ yí̥qṭā̃	ቅጣ qí̥ṭā̃	ቀጥቶ qḁ́ṭtʷo	መቅጣት mḁ́qṭā́t (§ 8)	ቀጭ qḁč̣ (qä-, -ጪ -č̣i)
ይቀጥል yi̥qḁ́ṭṭi̥l	ቀጥል qḁ́ṭṭi̥l	ቀጥሎ qḁ́ṭṭi̥lʷo	መቀጠል mḁqḁ́ṭṭḁl	ቀጣይ qḁ́ṭṭā͡i̥ (-ā́yy § 6; § 8)
ይቅጠር yí̥qṭḁr (-ṭä-)	ቅጠር qí̥ṭḁr (-ṭä-)	ቀጥሮ qḁ́ṭrʷo	መቅጠር mḁ́qṭḁr (-ṭä-)	ቀጣሪ qḁṭā́ri
ይቍጠር yí̥qwŭṭḁr (-ṭä-)	ቍጠር qwŭ́ṭḁr (-ṭä-)	ቈጥሮ qwώṭrʷo	መቍጠር mḁ́qwŭṭḁr (-ṭä-)	ቈጣሪ qwωṭā́ri

Simp. perf. (§ 25)		Comp. perf. (§ 32)	Contingent (§ 26)	Comp. imperf. (§ 32)
ቋጠረ qwắṭṭḁrḁ (-ṭä-)	knot, t.	ቋጥሯል qwắṭrŏ͡āl	ይቋጥር yi̥qwắṭṭi̥r	ይቋጥራል yi̥qwắṭṭi̥rāl
ቀጠቀጠ qḁṭḁ́qqḁṭḁ	strike repeatedly, t.	ቀጥቅጧል qḁ́ṭqi̥ṭŏ͡āl	ይቀጠቅጥ yi̥qḁṭḁ́qqi̥ṭ	ይቀጠቅጣል yi̥qḁṭḁ́qqi̥ṭāl
ቈጠበ qwώṭṭḁbḁ (-ḁy-)	save, (money etc.) t.	ቈጥቧል qwώṭṭi̥bŏ͡āl (-i̥y-)	ይቈጥብ yi̥qwώṭṭi̥b (-i̥y)	ይቈጥባል yi̥qwώṭṭi̥bāl (-i̥y-)
ቀጠነ qḁ́ṭṭḁnḁ	be thin, i.	ቀጥኗል qḁ́ṭnŏ͡āl	ይቀጥን yi̥qḁ́ṭ(i̥)n	ይቀጥናል yi̥qḁ́ṭ(i̥)nāl
ቀጠፈ qḁ́ṭṭḁfḁ	cheat, t.	ቀጥፏል qḁ́ṭfŏ͡āl	ይቀጥፍ yi̥qḁ́ṭ(i̥)f	ይቀጥፋል yi̥qḁ́ṭ(i̥)fāl
ቈፈረ qwώffḁrḁ (-fä-)	dig, t.	ቈፍሯል qwώffi̥rŏ͡āl	ይቈፍር yi̥qwώffi̥r	ይቈፍራል yi̥qwώffi̥rāl
በላ bḁ́llã	eat, t.	በልቷል bḁ́ltŏ͡āl (bắ-)	ይበላ yi̥bḁ́lã (-yḁ́-)	ይበላል yi̥bḁ́lāl (-yḁ́-)
በለጠ bḁ́llḁṭḁ	be more, i.	በልጧል bḁ́lṭŏ͡āl (bắ-)	ይበልጥ yi̥bḁ́lṭ (-i̥y-, -ắl-)	ይበልጣል yi̥bḁ́lṭāl (-i̥y-, -ắl-)
በራ bḁ́rrã	shine, i.	በርቷል bḁ́rtŏ͡āl (bắ-)	ይበራ yi̥bḁ́rã (-i̥y-, -ắr-)	ይበራል yi̥bḁ́rāl (-i̥y-, -ắr-)

Jussive (§ 27)	Imperative (§ 28)	Gerund (§ 29)	Infinitive (§ 30)	Participle (§ 31)
ይቋጥር yi̥qwā́ṭi̥r	ቋጥር qwā́ṭi̥r	ቋጥሮ qwā́ṭrʷo	መቋጠር mḁqwā́ṭḁr (-ṭä-)	ቋጣሪ qwāṭā́ri
ይቀጥቅጥ yi̥qḁ́ṭqi̥ṭ	ቀጥቅጥ qḁ́ṭqi̥ṭ	ቀጥቅጦ qḁ́ṭqi̥ṭʷo	መቀጥቀጥ mḁqḁ́ṭqḁṭ	ቀጥቃጭ qḁ́ṭqā́č̣ (§ 8)
ይቈጥብ yi̥qwώṭṭi̥b (-i̥ṿ)	ቈጥብ qwώṭṭi̥b (-i̥ṿ)	ቈጥቦ qwώṭṭi̥bʷo (-i̥ṿ-)	መቈጠብ mḁqwώṭṭḁb (-ḁṿ)	ቈጣቢ qwωṭṭā́bi (-ṿi)
ይቅጠን yí̥qṭḁn		ቀጥኖ qḁ́ṭnʷo	መቅጠን mḁ́qṭḁn	ቀጣኝ qḁ́ṭā́ñ (-ññ § 6; § 8)
ይቅጠፍ yí̥qṭḁf	ቅጠፍ qí̥ṭḁf	ቀጥፎ qḁ́ṭfʷo.	መቅጠፍ mḁ́qṭḁf	ቀጣፊ qḁṭā́fi
ይቈፍር yi̥qwώffi̥r	ቈፍር qwώffi̥r	ቈፍሮ qwώffi̥rʷo	መቈፈር mḁqwώffḁr (-fä-)	ቈፋሪ qwωffā́ri
ይብላ yí̥blā̃ (-ṿl-)	ብላ bí̥lā̃	በልቶ bḁ́ltʷo (bā́-)	መብላት mḁ́blā́t (-ṿl-; § 8)	በይ bḁ́͡i̥ (bḁyy § 6)
ይብለጥ yí̥blḁṭ (-ṿl-)		በልጦ bḁ́lṭʷo (bā́-)	መብለጥ mḁ́blḁṭ (-ṿl-)	†በላጭ bḁ́lā́č̣ (§ 8)
ይብራ yí̥brā̃ (-ṿr-)		በርቶ bḁ́rtʷo (bā́-)	መብራት mḁ́brā́t (-ṿr-; § 8)	†በሪ bḁ́ri (bā́-)

Simp. perf. (§ 25)		Comp. perf. (§ 32)	Contingent (§ 26)	Comp. imperf. (§ 32)
በረረ bḁ́rrḁrḁ (-rär-)	fly, i.	በሯል bḁ́rrŏāl	ይበር yi̥bḁ́rr (-ỵḁ́-)	ይበራል yi̥bḁ́rrāl (-ỵḁ́-)
በረታ bḁrḁ́ttã (bä-)	be strong, i.	በርትቷል bḁ́rti̥tŏāl (bắ-)	ይበረታ yi̥bḁrḁ́ttã (-i̥ỵ-, -är-)	ይበረታል yi̥bḁrḁ́ttāl (-i̥ỵ-, -är-)
በረደ bḁ́rrḁdḁ (bắ-)	be cold, i.	በርዷል bḁ́rdŏāl (bắ-)	ይበርድ yi̥bḁ́rd (-i̥ỵ-, -ắr-)	ይበርዳል yi̥bḁ́rdāl (-i̥ỵ-, -ắr-)
በሰለ bḁ́ssḁlḁ	ripen, i.	በስሏል bḁ́slŏāl	ይበስል yi̥bḁ́s(i̥)l (-i̥ỵ-)	ይበስላል yi̥bḁ́s(i̥)lāl (-i̥ỵ-)
በሰበሰ bḁsḁ́bbḁsḁ	be drenched, i.	በስብሷል bḁ́sbi̥sŏāl (-sỵ-)	ይበሰብስ yi̥bḁsḁ́bbi̥s (-i̥ỵ-)	ይበሰብሳል yi̥bḁsḁ́bbi̥sāl (-i̥ỵ-)
በቃ bḁ́qqã (bắ-)	suffice, i.	በቅቷል bḁ́qtŏāl (bắ-)	ይበቃ yi̥bḁ́qã (-i̥ỵ-, -ắq-)	ይበቃል yi̥bḁ́qāl (-i̥ỵ-, -ắq-)
በቀለ bḁ́qqḁlḁ (bắ-)	sprout, i.	በቅሏል bḁ́qlŏāl (bắ-)	ይበቅል yi̥bḁ́q(i̥)l (-i̥ỵ-, -ắq-)	ይበቅላል yi̥bḁ́q(i̥)lāl (-i̥ỵ-, -ắq-)
በተነ bḁ́ttḁnḁ (-ắttä-)	scatter, t.	በትኗል bḁ́tti̥nŏāl (bắ-)	ይበትን yi̥bḁ́tti̥n (-i̥ỵ-, -ắt-)	ይበትናል yi̥bḁ́tti̥nāl (-i̥ỵ-, -ắt-)
በዛ bḁ́zzã (bắ-)	be much, i.	በዝቷል bḁ́ztŏāl (bắ-)	ይበዛ yi̥bḁ́zã (-i̥ỵ-, -ắz-)	ይበዛል yi̥bḁ́zāl (-i̥ỵ-, -ắz-)

Jussive (§ 27)	Imperative (§ 28)	Gerund (§ 29)	Infinitive (§ 30)	Participle (§ 31)
ይብረር yí̥brar̥ (-ỵr-, -är)	ብረር bí̥rar̥ (-är)	በሮ bḁ́rr^{w}o	መብረር mḁ́brar̥ (-ỵr-, -är)	በራሪ bḁrári (bä-)
ይበርታ yi̥bḁ́rtã (-i̥ỵ-, -ắr-)	በርታ bḁ́rtã (bắ-)	በርትቶ bḁ́rtĭ̥t^{w}o (bắ-)	መበርታት mḁbḁ́rtắt (-ḁỵ-,-ăr-; § 8)	በርች bḁrč (bä-, -ቺ -či)
ይብረድ yí̥brad̥ (-ỵr-)		በርዶ bḁ́rd^{w}o (bắ-)	መብረድ mḁ́brad̥ (-ỵr-)	
ይብሰል yí̥bsal̥ (-ỵs-, -äl)	ብሰል bí̥sal̥ (-äl)	በስሎ bḁ́sl^{w}o	መብሰል mḁ́bsal̥ (-ỵs-, -äl)	በሳይ bḁ́sắi̥ (-ắyy § 6; § 8)
ይበስብስ yi̥bḁ́sbi̥s (-ỵḁ́sỵ-)	በስብስ bḁ́sbi̥s (-sỵ-)	በስብሶ bḁ́sbi̥s^{w}o (-sỵ-)	መበስበስ mḁbḁ́sbḁs (-ỵḁ́sỵ-)	በስባሽ bḁ́sbắš (-sỵ-; § 8)
ይብቃ yí̥bqã (-ỵq-)		በቅቶ bḁ́qt^{w}o (bắ-)	መብቃት mḁ́bqắt (-ỵq-; § 8)	†በቂ bḁ́qi (bắ-)
ይብቀል yí̥bqal̥ (-ỵq-)		በቅሎ bḁ́ql^{w}o (bắ-)	መብቀል mḁ́bqal̥ (-ỵq-)	በቃይ bḁ́qắi̥ (bắ-; -ắyy § 6; § 8)
ይበትን yi̥bḁ́tti̥n (-i̥ỵ-, -ắt-)	በትን bḁ́tti̥n (bắ-)	በትኖ bḁ́tti̥n^{w}o (bắ-)	መበተን mḁbḁ́ttḁn (-ḁỵ-, -ắttä-)	በታኝ bḁ́ttắñ (bắ-; -ắññ § 6; § 8)
ይብዛ yí̥bzã (-ỵz-)	ብዛ bí̥zã	በዝቶ bḁ́zt^{w}o (bắ-)	መብዛት mḁ́bzắt (-ỵz-; § 8)	በዥ bḁž (bä-, -ዢ -ži)

Simp. perf. (§ 25)		Comp. perf. (§ 32)	Contingent (§ 26)	Comp. imperf. (§ 32)
በደለ bḁ́ddḁlḁ (bắ-)	ill-treat, t.	በድሏል bḁ́ddi̥lŏ͡āl (bắ-)	ይበድል yi̥bḁ́ddi̥l (-i̥y-, -ắd-)	ይበድላል yi̥bḁ́ddi̥lāl (-i̥y-, -ắd-)
በደነ bḁ́ddḁnḁ (bắ-)	be paralysed, i.	በድኗል bḁ́dnŏ͡āl (bắ-)	ይበድን yi̥bḁ́d(ĭ̥)n (-i̥y-, -ắd-)	ይበድናል yi̥bḁ́d(ĭ̥)nāl (-i̥y-, -ắd-)
በጀ bḁ́jjä (bắ-) 2nd -ጀህ -jjäh, etc.	be good, i.	በጅቷል bḁ́jji̥tŏ͡āl (bắ-)	ይበጅ yi̥bḁ́jj (-i̥y-, -ắj-)	ይበጃል yi̥bḁ́jjāl (-i̥y-, -ắj-)
ተለላከ G. tḁlḁlắkḁ	be sent to and fro, p.	ተለልኳል tḁlḁ́l(ĭ̥)kŏ͡āl (-lắl-)	ይለላክ yi̥llḁlắk	ይለላካል yi̥llḁlắkāl
ተላላከ Š. tḁlālắkḁ	be sent to and fro, p.	ተላልኳል tḁlắl(ĭ̥)kŏ͡āl	ይላላክ yi̥llālắk	ይላላካል yi̥llālắkāl
ተለመደ tḁlḁ́mmḁdḁ	be used, p.	ተለምዷል tḁlḁ́mdŏ͡āl	ይለመድ yi̥llḁ́mmḁd	ይለመዳል yi̥llḁ́mmḁ- dāl
ተላሰ tḁlắsḁ	be licked, p.	ተልሷል tḁ́li̥sŏ͡āl (tắ-)	ይላስ yi̥llắs	ይላሳል yi̥llắsāl
ተለቀመ tḁlḁ́qqḁmḁ	be picked, p.	ተለቅሟል tḁlḁ́qmŏ͡āl	ይለቀም yi̥llḁ́qqḁm	ይለቀማል yi̥llḁ́qqḁmāl
ተላቀሰ tḁlắqqḁsḁ	mourn publicly, i.	ተላቅሷል tḁlắqsŏ͡āl	ይላቀስ yi̥llắqqḁs	ይላቀሳል yi̥llắqqḁsāl

Jussive (§ 27)	Imperative (§ 28)	Gerund (§ 29)	Infinitive (§ 30)	Participle (§ 31)
ይበድል yi̥bḁ́ddi̥l (-i̥y-, -ā́d-)	በድል bḁ́ddi̥l (bā́-)	በድሎ bḁ́ddi̥lʷo (bā́-)	መበደል mḁbḁ́ddḁl (-ḁy-, -ā́ddä-)	†በዳይ bḁ́ddā́i̥ (bā́-; -ā́yy § 6; § 8)
		በድኖ bḁ́dnʷo (bā́-)	መብደን mḁ́bdḁn (-y̥d-, -än)	
ይበጅ yí̥bḁ́jj (-í̥y-, -ā́j-; § 8)		በጅቶ bḁ́jji̥tʷo (bā́-)	መበጀት mḁbḁ́jjät (-ḁy-, -ā́j-)	
ይለላክ yi̥llḁ́lák (§ 8)	ተለላክ tḁlḁ́lák (§ 8)	ተለልኮ tḁlḁ́l(i̥)kʷo (-lā́l-)	መለላክ mḁllḁ́lák (§ 8)	ተለላኪ tḁlḁlā́ki
ይላላክ yi̥llálák (§ 8)	ተላላክ tḁlálák (§ 8)	ተላልኮ tḁlál(i̥)kʷo	መላላክ mḁllálák (§ 8)	ተላላኪ tḁlāláki
ይለመድ yi̥llḁ́mḁd	ተለመድ tḁlḁ́mḁd	ተለምዶ tḁlḁ́mdʷo	መለመድ mḁllḁ́mḁd	ተለማጅ tḁlḁ́mmā́j (§ 8)
ይላስ yí̥llā́s (§ 8)	ተላስ tḁ́lā́s (§ 8)	ተልሶ tḁ́li̥sʷo (tā́-)	መላስ mḁ́llā́s (§ 8)	ተላሽ tḁ́lā́š (§ 8; -ሺ -ši)
ይለቀም yi̥llḁ́qḁm		ተለቅሞ tḁlḁ́qmʷo	መለቀም mḁllḁ́qḁm	ተለቃሚ tḁlḁqā́mi
ይላቀስ yi̥llā́qḁs	ተላቀስ tḁlā́qḁs	ተላቅሶ tḁlā́qsʷo	መላቀስ mḁllā́qḁs	ተላቃሽ tḁlā́qā́š (§ 8)

Simp. perf. (§ 25)		Comp. perf. (§ 32)	Contingent (§ 26)	Comp. imperf. (§ 32)
ተለቀቀ tḁlḁ́qqḁqḁ	be given up, p.	ተለቋል tḁlḁ́qqŏ͡āl	ይለቀቅ yi̥llḁ́qqḁq	ይለቀቃል yi̥llḁ́qqḁqāl
ተለቃቀመ tḁlḁqā́qqḁ-mḁ	be picked out, p.	ተለቃቅሟል tḁlḁqā́q-mŏ͡āl	ይለቃቀም yi̥llḁqā́q-qḁm	ይለቃቀማል yi̥llḁqā́qqḁ-māl
ተለበበ tḁlḁ́bbḁbḁ (-ỵḁ)	have a halter put on, p.	ተለብቧል tḁlḁ́bbi̥bŏ͡āl (-i̥ỵ-)	ይለበብ yi̥llḁ́bbḁb (-ḁỵ)	ይለበባል yi̥llḁ́bbḁbāl (-ỵā-)
ታለበች tā́llḁbäč (-ḁỵä-; -äčč § 6)	be milked, p.	ታልባለች tālbálläč (-lỵá-; -äčč § 6)	ቲታለብ ti̥ttā́llḁb (-ḁỵ)	ቲታለባለች ti̥ttā́llḁbálläč (-ỵá-; -äčč § 6)
ተለካ tḁlḁ́kkã	be measured, p.	ተለክቷል tḁlḁ́kki̥tŏ͡āl (-lḁ́-)	ይለካ yi̥llḁ́kkã	ይለካል yi̥llḁ́kkāl
ተላከ tḁlā́kḁ	be sent, p.	ተልኳል tḁ́li̥kŏ͡āl (tā́-)	ይላክ yi̥llā́k	ይላካል yi̥llā́kāl
ተለወጠ tḁlḁ͡uwḁṭḁ	be changed, p.	ተለውጧል tḁlḁ͡uwŭ-ṭŏ͡āl	ይለወጥ yi̥llḁ͡uwḁṭ	ይለወጣል yi̥llḁ͡uwḁṭāl
ተለየ tḁlḁ́yyä 2nd ተለየሁ tḁlḁ́yyäh, etc.	be distinguished, p.	ተለይቷል tḁlḁ́yyi̥tŏ͡āl	ይለይ yi̥llḁ́yy	ይለያል yi̥llḁ́yyāl

Jussive (§ 27)	Imperative (§ 28)	Gerund (§ 29)	Infinitive (§ 30)	Participle (§ 31)
ይለቀቅ yi̥llḁ́qḁq	**ተለቀቅ** tḁlḁ́qḁq	**ተለቆ** tḁlḁ́qqʷo	**መለቀቅ** mḁllḁ́qḁq	**ተለቃቂ** tḁlḁqqā́qi
ይለቃቀም yi̥llḁqā́qḁm		**ተለቃቅሞ** tḁlḁqā́qmʷo	**መለቃቀም** mḁllḁqā́-qḁm	**ተለቃቃሚ** tḁlḁqāqā́mi
ይለበብ yi̥llḁ́bḁb (-v̥ḁv̥)		**ተለብቦ** tḁlḁ́bbi̥bʷo (-i̥v̥-)	**መለበብ** mḁllḁ́bḁb (-v̥ḁv̥)	**ተለባቢ** tḁlḁbbábi (-v̥i)
ትታለብ ti̥ttā́lḁb (-ḁv̥)	**ታለቢ** tā́lḁbi (-v̥i)	**ታልባ** tā́lbā (-lv̥-)	**መታለብ** mḁttā́lḁb (-ḁv̥)	**ታላቢ** tālā́bi (-v̥i)
ይለካ yi̥llḁ́kā̃	**ተለካ** tḁlḁ́kā̃	**ተለኪቶ** tḁlḁ́kki̥tʷo (-lā́-)	**መለካት** mḁllḁ́kā́t (§ 8)	†**ተለኪ** tḁlḁ́kki (-lā́-)
ይላኽ yí̥llā́k (§ 8)	**ተላኽ** tḁ́lā́k (§ 8)	**ተሊኾ** tḁ́li̥kʷo (tā́-)	**መላኽ** mḁ́llā́k (§ 8)	**ተላኺ** tḁlā́ki
ይለወጥ yi̥llḁ́͡uḁṭ	**ተለወጥ** tḁlḁ́͡uḁṭ	**ተለውጦ** tḁlḁ́͡uwŭ̈ṭʷo	**መለወጥ** mḁllḁ́͡uḁṭ	**ተለዋጪ** tḁlḁ́͡uwā́č̣ (§ 8)
ይለይ yí̥llḁ́͡i̥ (-ḁ́yy § 6; § 8) pl. **ይለዩ** yi̥llḁ́yyu		**ተለይቶ** tḁlḁ́yyi̥tʷo	**መለየት** mḁllḁ́yät (-lḁ́͡i̥ät)	†**ተለዪ** tḁlḁ́yyi

Simp. perf. (§ 25)		Comp. perf. (§ 32)	Contingent (§ 26)	Comp. imperf. (§ 32)
ተለጐመ tḁlḁ́ggwω-mḁ	have a bridle put on, p.	ተለጕሟል tḁlḁ́ggwŭ-mŏ͡āl	ይለጐም yi̥llḁ́ggwωm	ይለጐማል yi̥llḁ́ggwω-māl
ተላጨ tḁlā́č̣č̣ä 2nd ተላጨህ tḁlā́č̣č̣äh, etc.	be shaved, p. shave one-self, r.	ተላጭቷል tḁlā́č̣(ĭ̥)tŏ͡āl	ይላጭ yi̥llā́č̣č̣	ይላጫል yi̥llḁ̄́č̣č̣āl
ተመላለሰ tḁmḁlā́llḁsḁ	come and go, i.	ተመላልሷል tḁmḁlā́l(ĭ̥)-sŏ͡āl	ይመላለስ yi̥mmḁlā́l-lḁs	ይመላለሳል yi̥mmḁlā́l-lḁsāl
ተመለሰ tḁmḁ́llḁsḁ (-mǟ́-)	return, i.	ተመልሷል tḁmḁ́lli̥sŏ͡āl (-mǟ́-)	ይመለስ yi̥mmḁ́llḁs (-mǟ́-)	ይመለሳል yi̥mmḁ́llḁ-sāl (-mǟ́-)
ተመለከተ tḁmḁlḁ́k-kḁtḁ	watch, t.	ተመልክቷል tḁmḁ́lki̥tŏ͡āl (-mǟ́-)	ይመለከት yi̥mmḁlḁ́k-kḁt (-ät)	ይመለከታል yi̥mmḁlḁ́k-kḁtāl
ታመመ tā́mmḁmḁ	be ill, i.	ታሟል tā́mmŏ͡āl	ይታመም yi̥ttā́mmḁm	ይታመማል yi̥ttā́mmḁ-māl
ተመራ tḁmḁ́rrā̃	be guided, p.	ተመርቷል tḁmḁ́rtŏ͡āl (-mǟ́-)	ይመራ yi̥mmḁ́rrā̃	ይመራል yi̥mmḁ́rrāl
ተማረ tḁmā́rḁ	(*a*) learn, i. (*b*) be for-given, p.	ተምሯል tḁ́m(ĭ̥)rŏ͡āl	ይማር yi̥mmā́r	ይማራል yi̥mmā́rāl
ተመረመረ tḁmḁrḁ́m-mḁrḁ (-ärḁ́mmä-)	be ex-amined, p.	ተመርምሯል tḁmḁ́rmi̥-rŏ͡āl (-mǟ́-)	ይመረመር yi̥mmḁrḁ́m-mḁr (-ärḁ́mmä-)	ይመረመራል yi̥mmḁrḁ́m-mḁrāl (-ärḁ́mmä-)

Jussive (§ 27)	Imperative (§ 28)	Gerund (§ 29)	Infinitive (§ 30)	Participle (§ 31)
ይለጉም yi̥llḁ́gwωm		ተለጉሞ tḁlḁ́ggwŭ-mʷo	መለጉም mḁllḁ́gwωm	
ይላጭ yílláč̣ (§ 8)	ተላጭ tḁ́láč̣ (§ 8)	ተላጭቶ tḁláč̣(ı̥)tʷo	መላጨት mḁlláč̣ät	ተላጪ tḁláč̣(č̣)i
ይመላለስ yi̥mmḁlálḁs	ተመላለስ tḁmḁlálḁs	ተመላልሶ tḁmḁ-lál(ı̥)sʷo	መመላለስ mḁmmḁ-lálḁs	ተመላላሽ tḁmḁláláś (§ 8)
ይመለስ yi̥mmḁ́lḁs (-mä́-)	ተመለስ tḁmḁ́lḁs (-mä́-)	ተመልሶ tḁmḁ́llı̥sʷo (-mä́-)	መመለስ mḁmmḁ́lḁs (-mä́-)	ተመላሽ tḁmḁ́lláś (-mä́-; § 8)
ይመልከት yi̥mmḁ́lkḁt (-mä́-, -ät)	ተመልከት tḁmḁ́lkḁt (-mä́-, -ät)	ተመልክቶ tḁmḁ́lki̥tʷo (-mä́-)	መመልከት mḁmmḁ́lkḁt (-mä́-, -ät)	ተመልካች tḁmḁ́lkáč (-mä́-; § 8)
ይታመም yi̥ttámḁm		ታሞ tã́mmʷo	መታመም mḁttámḁm	ታማሚ tãmámi
ይመራ yi̥mmḁ́rã (-mä́-)	ተመራ tḁmḁ́rã (-mä́-)	ተመርቶ tḁmḁ́rtʷo (-mä́-)	መመራት mḁmmḁ́rát (-ä́r-; § 8)	ተመሪ tḁmḁ́ri (-mä-)
ይማር yí̥mmár (§ 8)	ተማር tḁ́már (§ 8)	ተምሮ tḁ́m(ı̥)rʷo	መማር mḁ́mmár (§ 8)	(*a*) ተማሪ tḁmári
ይመርመር yi̥mmḁ́rmḁr (-ármä-)		ተመርምሮ tḁmḁ́rmi̥rʷo (-mä́-)	መመርመር mḁmmḁ́r-mḁr (-ármä-)	†ተመርማሪ tḁmḁrmári (-ḁmä-)

Simp. perf. (§ 25)		Comp. perf. (§ 32)	Contingent (§ 26)	Comp. imperf. (§ 32)
ተመረረ tḁmárrḁrḁ (-rär-)	be annoyed, i.	ተመሯል tḁmárrŏ͡āl	ይመረር yi̥mmárrḁr (-rär)	ይመረራል yi̥mmárrḁrāl (-rär-)
ተማረከ tḁmā́rrḁkḁ	be captured, p.	ተማርኳል tḁmā́rkŏ͡āl	ይማረክ yi̥mmā́rrḁk	ይማረካል yi̥mmā́rrḁkāl
ተመረጠ tḁmárrḁṭḁ	be chosen, p.	ተመርጧል tḁmárṭŏ͡āl (-mä́-)	ይመረጥ yi̥mmárrḁṭ	ይመረጣል yi̥mmárrḁṭāl
ተመሰገነ tḁmḁsággḁnḁ	be praised, p.	ተመስግኗል tḁmásgi̥nŏ͡āl	ይመሰገን yi̥mmḁsággḁn	ይመሰገናል yi̥mmḁsággḁnāl
ተምበረከከ tḁmbḁrákkḁkḁ (-bä-)	kneel, i.	ተምበርክኳል tḁmbárki̥kŏ͡āl (-bä́-)	ይምበረከክ yi̥mbḁrákkḁk (-bä-; § 7*c*)	ይምበረከካል yi̥mbḁrákkḁkāl (-bä-; § 7*c*)
ተመታ tḁmáttā	be struck,	ተመትቷል tḁmáttŏ͡āl	ይመታ yi̥mmáttā	ይመታል yi̥mmáttāl
ተማታ tḁmā́ttā	come to blows, i.	ተማትቷል tḁmā́ttŏ͡āl	ይማታ yi̥mmā́ttā	ይማታል yi̥mmā́ttāl
ተመቸ tḁmáččä (-mä́-)	be suitable, i.	ተመችቷል tḁmáč(č)i̥tŏ͡āl (-mä́-)	ይመች yi̥mmáčč (-mä́-)	ይመቻል yi̥mmáččāl (-mä́-)

Jussive (§ 27)	Imperative (§ 28)	Gerund (§ 29)	Infinitive (§ 30)	Participle (§ 31)
neg. አይመረር a͡i̥mmḁ́rḁr (-ä́rär)	neg. አትመረር ãtti̥mmḁ́rḁr (-ä́rär)	ተመሮ tḁmḁ́rr^{w}o	መመረር mḁmmḁ́rḁr (-ä́rär)	ተመራሪ tḁmḁrā́ri (-mä-)
ይማረክ yi̥mmā́rḁk	ተማረክ tḁmā́rḁk	ተማርኮ tḁmā́rk^{w}o	መማረክ mḁmmā́rḁk	ተማራኪ tḁmārā́ki
ይመረጥ yi̥mmḁ́rḁṭ (-mä́-)	ተመረጥ tḁmḁ́raṭ (-mä́-)	ተመርጦ tḁmḁ́rṭ^{w}o (-mä́-)	መመረጥ mḁmmḁ́rḁṭ (-mä́-)	ተመራጭ tḁmḁ́r(r)ā́č̣ (§ 8)
ይመስገን yi̥mmḁ́sgḁn	ተመስገን tḁmḁ́sgḁn	ተመስግኖ tḁmḁ́sgi̥n^{w}o	መመስገን mḁmmḁ́s-gḁn	ተመስጋኝ tḁmḁ́sgā́ñ (-ññ § 6; § 8)
ይምበርከክ yi̥mbḁ́rkḁk (-bä́-; § 7*c*)	ተምበርከክ tḁmbḁ́rkḁk (-bä́-)	ተምበርክኮ tḁmbḁ́r-ki̥k^{w}o (-bä́-)	መምበርከክ mḁmbḁ́r-kḁk (-bä́-; § 7*c*)	†ተምበርካኪ tḁmbḁrkā́ki (-bä-)
ይመታ yi̥mmḁ́tã	ተመታ tḁmḁ́tã	ተመትቶ tḁmḁ́tt^{w}o	መመታት mḁmmḁ́tā́t (§ 8)	ተመች tḁ́mḁ́č (-ā́č; § 8; -ቺ -či)
ይማታ yi̥mmā́tã	ተማታ tḁmā́tã	ተማትቶ tḁmā́tt^{w}o	መማታት mḁmmā́tā́t (§ 8)	ተማች tḁ́mā́č (§ 8; -ቺ -či)
ይመች yí̥mmḁ́č (-mä́-; § 8)		ተመችቶ tḁmḁ́č(č)i̥t^{w}o (-mä́-)	መመቸት mḁmmḁ́čät (-mä́-)	ተመች tḁ́mḁ́č (-mä́-; § 8; -ቺ -či)

Simp. perf. (§ 25)		Comp. perf. (§ 32)	Contingent (§ 26)	Comp. imperf. (§ 32)
ታመነ tā́mmḁnḁ	be believed, p. believe. t.	ታምኗል (p.) tā́mnŏ͡āl (t.) tā́mmi̥-nŏ͡āl	ይታመን yi̥ttā́mmḁn	ይታመናል yi̥ttā́mmḁ-nāl
ተመነዘረ tḁmḁnḁ́z-zḁrḁ (-zä-)	be changed, p.	ተመንዝሯል tḁmḁ́nzi̥-rŏ͡āl	ይመነዘር yi̥mmḁnḁ́z-zḁr (-zä-)	ይመነዘራል yi̥mmḁnḁ́z-zḁrāl (-zä-)
ተመኘ tḁmḁ́ññä (-mā́-) 2nd -ኘህ -ññäh, etc.	long for, t.	ተመኝቷል tḁmḁ́ññi̥-tŏ͡āl (-mā́-)	ይመኝ yi̥mmḁ́ññ (-mā́-)	ይመኛል yi̥mmḁ́ññāl (-mā́-)
ተማከረ tḁmā́kkḁrḁ (-kä-)	deliberate, i.	ተማክሯል tḁmā́krŏ͡āl	ይማከር yi̥mmā́kkḁr (-kä-)	ይማከራል yi̥mmā́kkḁ-rāl (-kä-)
ተሞከረ tḁmʷók-kḁrḁ (-kä-)	be tried, p.	ተሞክሯል tḁmʷókki̥-rŏ͡āl	ይሞከር yi̥mmʷók-kḁr (-kä-)	ይሞከራል yi̥mmʷók-kḁrāl (-kä-)
ተመዘነ tḁmḁ́zzḁnḁ	weigh, i. be weighed, p.	ተመዝኗል tḁmḁ́zzi̥-nŏ͡āl	ይመዘን yi̥mmḁ́zzḁn	ይመዘናል yi̥mmḁ́zzḁ-nāl
ተመገበ tḁmḁ́ggḁbḁ (-ỵḁ)	be fed, p.	ተመግቧል tḁmḁ́ggi̥-bŏ͡āl (-i̥ỵ-)	ይመገብ yi̥mmḁ́ggḁb (-ḁỵ)	ይመገባል yi̥mmḁ́ggḁ-bāl (-ḁỵ-)
ታረመ tā́rrḁmḁ	be weeded, p.	ታርሟል tā́rri̥mŏ͡āl	ይታረም yi̥ttā́rrḁm	ይታረማል yi̥ttā́rrḁmāl

Jussive (§ 27)	Imperative (§ 28)	Gerund (§ 29)	Infinitive (§ 30)	Participle (§ 31)
ይታመን yi̥ttā́mḁn	ታመን tā́mḁn	ታምኖ (p.) tā́mn^{w}o (t.) tā́m- mi̥n^{w}o	መታመን mḁttā́mḁn	ታማኝ (p.) tā́mā́ñ (-ññ § 6; § 8) (t.) tā́mmā́ñ (-ññ § 6; § 8)
ይመንዘር yi̥mmḁ́nzḁr (-zä-)		ተመንዝሮ tḁmḁ́nzi̥r^{w}o	መመንዘር mḁmmḁ́n- zḁr (-zä-)	†ተመንዛሪ tḁmḁnzā́ri
ይመኝ yí̥mmḁ́ñ (-mā́-; -ññ § 6; § 8)	ተመኝ tḁ́mḁ́ñ (-mā́-; -ññ § 6; § 8)	ተመኝቶ tḁmḁ́ññi̥t^{w}o (-mā́-)	መመኘት mḁmmḁ́ñät (-mā́-)	ተመኝ tḁ́mḁ́ññ (-mā́- ; § 8)
ይማከር yi̥mmā́kḁr (-kä-)	ተማከር tḁmā́kḁr (-kä-)	ተማክሮ tḁmā́kr^{w}o	መማከር mḁmmā́kḁr (-kä-)	ተማካሪ tḁmākā́ri
ይሞከር yi̥mm^{w}ókḁr (-kä-)		ተሞክሮ tḁm^{w}ók- ki̥r^{w}o	መሞከር mḁmm^{w}ó- kḁr (-kä-)	†ተሞካሪ tḁm^{w}ok- kā́ri
ይመዘን yi̥mmḁ́zḁn	ተመዘን tḁmḁ́zḁn	ተመዝኖ tḁmḁ́zzi̥n^{w}o	መመዘን mḁmmḁ́zḁn	†ተመዛኝ tḁmḁ́zzā́ñ (-ññ § 6; § 8)
ይመገብ yi̥mmḁ́gḁb (-ḁv̥)	ተመገብ tḁmḁ́gḁb (-ḁv̥)	ተመግቦ tḁmḁ́ggi̥b^{w}o (-i̥v̥-)	መመገብ mḁmmḁ́gḁb (-ḁv̥)	ተመጋቢ tḁmḁggā́bi (-v̥i)
ይታረም yi̥ttā́rḁm		ታርሞ tā́rri̥m^{w}o	መታረም mḁttā́rḁm	

Simp. perf. (§ 25)		Comp. perf. (§ 32)	Contingent (§ 26)	Comp. imperf. (§ 32)
ተረራቁ G. tḁrḁráqu (tärä-)	be separated, p.	ተረርቀዋል tḁrḁ́r(ǐ̥)- qḁ͡uāl (tärá-)	ይረራቁ yi̥rrḁráqu (-ärá-)	ይረራቃሉ yi̥rrḁrāqállu (-ärá-)
ተራረቀ tḁrā́rrḁqḁ (tä-)	make peace, i.	ተራርቋል tḁrár(ǐ̥)qŏ͡āl (tä-)	ይተራረቅ yi̥ttḁrā́rrḁq (-tä-)	ይተራረቃል yi̥ttḁrā́rrḁ- qāl (-tä-)
ተራራቁ Š. tḁrārā́qu (tä-)	be separated, p.	ተራርቀዋል tḁrár(ǐ̥)- qḁ͡uāl (tä-)	ይራራቁ yi̥rrārā́qu	ይራራቃሉ yi̥rrārāqállu
ተረሳ tḁrḁ́ssã (tä-)	be forgotten, p.	ተረስቷል tḁrḁ́stŏ͡āl (-ärá-)	ይረሳ yi̥rrḁ́ssã	ይረሳል yi̥rrḁ́ssāl
ተረበ tḁ́rrḁbḁ (tá-, -ỵḁ)	play, i.	ተርቧል tḁ́rri̥bŏ͡āl (tá-, -i̥ỵ-)	ይተርብ yi̥tḁ́rri̥b (-tá-, -i̥ỵ)	ይተርባል yi̥tḁ́rri̥bāl (-tá-, -i̥ỵ-)
ተራበ tḁrā́bḁ (tä-, -ỵḁ)	be hungry, i.	ተርቧል tḁ́ri̥bŏ͡āl (tá-, -i̥ỵ-)	ይራብ yi̥rrā́b (-ā́ỵ)	ይራባል yi̥rrā́bāl (-ā́ỵ-)
ተረታ tḁrḁ́ttã (tä-)	be overcome, p.	ተረትቷል tḁrḁ́ttŏ͡āl (tä-)	ይረታ yi̥rrḁ́ttã	ይረታል yi̥rrḁ́ttāl
ተረተረ tḁrḁ́ttḁrḁ (-ärḁ́ttä-)	crack, t.	ተርትሯል tḁ́rti̥rŏ͡āl (tá-)	ይተረትር yi̥tḁrḁ́tti̥r (-i̥tä-)	ይተረትራል yi̥tḁrḁ́tti̥rāl (-i̥tä-)

Jussive (§ 27)	Imperative (§ 28)	Gerund (§ 29)	Infinitive (§ 30)	Participle (§ 31)
ይረራቁ yi̥rrḁrā́qu (-ärā́-)	ተረራቁ tḁrḁrā́qu (tärä-)	ተረርቀው tḁrḁ́r(i̥)qḁu (tärā́-)	መረራቅ mḁrrḁ́rā́q (-ärrā́-; § 8)	ተረራቆች tḁrḁrā́qʷōč (tärä-; -čč § 6)
ይተራረቅ yi̥ttḁrā́rḁq (-tä-)	ተራረቅ tḁrā́rḁq (tä-)	ተራርቆ tḁrā́r(i̥)qʷo (tä-)	መተራረቅ mḁttḁrā́rḁq (-tä-)	ተራራቂ tḁrārā́qi (tä-)
ይራራቁ yi̥rrārā́qu	ተራራቁ tḁrārā́qu (tä-)	ተራርቀው tḁrā́r(i̥)qḁu (tä-)	መራራቅ mḁrrā́rā́q (§ 8)	ተራራቆች tḁrārā́qʷōč (tä-; -čč § 6)
ይረሳ yi̥rrḁ́sā̃		ተረስቶ tḁrḁ́stʷo (-ärā́-)	መረሳት mḁrrḁ́sā́t (§ 8)	ተረሽ tḁ́rḁ́š (-ā́rā́-; § 8; ሺ- -ši)
ይተርብ yi̥tḁ́rri̥b (-tā́-, -i̥y̥)	ተርብ tḁ́rri̥b (tā́-, -i̥y̥)	ተርቦ tḁ́rri̥bʷo (tā́-, -i̥y̥-)	መተረብ mḁtḁ́rrḁb (-tā́-, -ḁy̥)	ተራቢ tḁrrābi (tā́-, -y̥i)
ይራብ yí̥rrāb (-ā́y̥; § 8)	ተራብ tḁ́rāb (tā́-, -ā́y̥; § 8)	ተርቦ tḁ́ri̥bʷo (tā́-, -i̥y̥-)	መራብ mḁ́rrāb (-ā́y̥; § 8)	ተራቢ tḁrābi (tä-, -y̥i)
ይረታ yi̥rrḁ́tā̃	ተረታ tḁrḁ́tā̃ (tä-)	ተረትቶ tḁrḁ́ttʷo (tä-)	መረታት mḁrrḁ́tā́t (§ 8)	ተረች tḁ́rḁ́č (-ā́rā́-; § 8; -ቺ -či)
ይተርትር yi̥tḁ́rti̥r (-i̥tā́-)	ተርትር tḁ́rti̥r (tā́-)	ተርትሮ tḁ́rti̥rʷo (tā́-)	መተርተር mḁtḁ́rtḁr (-ārtä-)	ተርታሪ tḁrtā́ri (tä-)

Simp. perf. (§ 25)		Comp. perf. (§ 32)	Contingent (§ 26)	Comp. imperf. (§ 32)
ተረከ tḁ́rrḁkḁ (tắ-)	narrate, t.	**ተርኳል** tḁ́rkŏ͡āl (tḁ́rri̥k-, tắ-)	**ይተርክ** yi̥tḁ́rk (-tḁ́rri̥k, -tắ-)	**ይተርካል** yi̥tḁ́rkāl (-tḁ́rri̥k-, -tắ-)
ተረጐመ tḁrḁ́ggwω- mḁ (tä-)	interpret, t.	**ተርጕሟል** tḁ́rgwŭ- mŏ͡āl (tắ-)	**ይተረጕም** yi̥tḁrḁ́g- gwŭm (-tä-)	**ይተረጕማል** yi̥tḁrḁ́ggwŭ- māl (-tä-)
ተርገበገበ tḁrgḁbḁ́g- gḁbḁ (tä-, -ỵḁ́ggḁỵ-)	wave, i.	**ተርገብግቧል** tḁrgḁ́bgi̥- bŏ͡āl (tä-, -ỵgi̥ỵ-)	**ይርገበገብ** yi̥r(r)gḁbḁ́g- gḁb (§ 7*c*; -ỵḁ́ggḁỵ)	**ይርገበገባል** yi̥r(r)gḁbḁ́g- gḁbāl (§ 7*c*; -ỵḁ́ggḁỵ-)
ተረፈ tḁ́rrḁfḁ (tắ-)	remain over, i.	**ተርፏል** tḁ́rfŏ͡āl (tắ-)	**ይተርፍ** yi̥tḁ́rf (-tắ-)	**ይተርፋል** yi̥tḁ́rfāl (-tắ-)
ተሰለፈ tḁsḁ́llḁfḁ (-äsắ-)	be paraded, p.	**ተሰልፏል** tḁsḁ́lli̥fŏ͡āl (-äsắ-)	**ይሰለፍ** yi̥ssḁ́llḁf (-sắ-)	**ይሰለፋል** yi̥ssḁ́llḁfāl (-sắ-)
ተሰማ tḁsḁ́mmā̃ (tä-)	be heard, p.	**ተሰምቷል** tḁsḁ́mtŏ͡āl (tä-)	**ይሰማ** yi̥ssḁ́mmā̃	**ይሰማል** yi̥ssḁ́mmāl
ተሰማማ tḁsḁmắm- mā̃ (-äsä-) [**ተስማማ**] (tḁsmắm- mā̃, tä-)	make peace, i.	**ተሰማምቷል** tḁsḁmắm- tŏ͡āl (-äsä-) [**ተስማ-**] (tḁsmắ-, tä-)	**ይሰማማ** yi̥ssḁmắm- mā̃ [**ይስማ-**] (yi̥s(s)mắ-; § 7*c*)	**ይሰማማል** yi̥ssḁmắm- māl [**ይስማ-**] (yi̥s(s)mắ-; § 7*c*)

Jussive (§ 27)	Imperative (§ 28)	Gerund (§ 29)	Infinitive (§ 30)	Participle (§ 31)
ይትረክ yí̥trḁk **ይተርክ** yi̥tḁ́rri̥k (-tā́-)	**ትረክ** tí̥rḁk **ተርክ** tḁ́rri̥k (tā́-)	**ተርኮ** tḁ́rkʷo (tḁ́rri̥k-, tā́-)	**መትረክ** mḁ́trḁk **መተረክ** mḁtḁ́rrḁk (-tā́-)	**ተራኪ** tḁr(r)ā́ki (tä-)
ይተርጕም yi̥tḁ́rgwŭm (-tā́-)	**ተርጕም** tḁ́rgwŭm (tā́-)	**ተርጕሞ** tḁ́rgwŭmʷo (tā́-)	**መተርጐም** mḁtḁ́r- gwωm (-tā́-)	**ተርጓሚ** tḁrgwā́mi (tä-)
ይርገበገብ yi̥r(r)gḁ́b- gḁb (§ 7*c*; -ɣ̣gḁɣ̣)	**ተርገበገብ** tḁrgḁ́bgḁb (tä-, -ɣ̣gḁɣ̣)	**ተርገብግቦ** tḁrgḁ́b- gi̥bʷo (tä-, -ɣ̣gi̥ɣ̣-)	**መርገበገብ** mḁr(r)gḁ́b- gḁb (§ 7*c*; mä-, -ɣ̣gḁɣ̣)	**ተርገብጋቢ** tḁrgḁbgā́bi (tä-, -ɣ̣gā́ɣ̣-)
ይትረፍ yí̥trḁf		**ተርፎ** tḁ́rfʷo (tā́-)	**መትረፍ** mḁ́trḁf	†**ተራፊ** tḁrā́fi (tä-)
ይሰለፍ yi̥ssḁ́lḁf (-sā́-)	**ተሰለፍ** tḁsḁ́lḁf (-äsā́-)	**ተሰልፎ** tḁsḁ́lli̥fʷo (-äsā́-)	**መሰለፍ** mḁssḁ́lḁf (-sā́-)	**ተሰላፊ** tḁsḁllā́fi (-äsä-)
ይሰማ yi̥ssḁ́mã	**ተሰማ** tḁsḁ́mã (tä-)	**ተሰምቶ** tḁsḁ́mtʷo (tä-)	**መሰማት** mḁssḁ́mā́t (§ 8)	**ተሰሚ** tḁsḁ́mi (tä-)
ይሰማማ yi̥ssḁmā́mã [**ይስማ-**] (yi̥s(s)mā́-; § 7*c*)	**ተሰማማ** tḁsḁmā́mã (-äsä-) [**ተስማ-**] (tḁsmā́-, tä-)	**ተሰማምቶ** tḁsḁmā́mtʷo (-äsä-) [**ተስማ-**] (tḁsmā́-, tä-)	**መሰማማት** mḁssḁmā́- mā́t (§ 8) [**መስማ-**] (mḁs(s)mā́-; § 7*c*)	**ተሰማሚ** tḁsḁmā́mi (-äsä-) [**ተስማ-**] (tḁsmā́-, tä-)

Simp. perf. (§ 25)		Comp. perf. (§ 32)	Contingent (§ 26)	Comp. imperf. (§ 32)
ተሰመረ Š. tḁsḁmḁ́rrḁ (-äsä-) 2nd -ረሀ -rrḁh (-äh), etc.	graze, i.	ተሰመርቷል tḁsḁmḁ́rtŏ͡āl (-äsämắ-)	ይሰመር yi̥ssḁmḁ́rr	ይሰመራል yi̥ssḁmḁ́rrāl
ተሰማራ G. tḁsḁmā́rrā̃ (-äsä-)	graze, i.	ተሰማርቷል tḁsḁmā́rtŏ͡āl (-äsä-)	ይሰማራ yi̥ssḁmā́rrā̃	ይሰማራል yi̥ssḁmā́rrāl
ተሰራ tḁsḁ́rrā̃ (-äsắ-)	be built, p. be decreed, p.	ተሰርቷል tḁsḁ́rtŏ͡āl (-äsắ-)	ይሰራ yi̥ssḁ́rrā̃ (-sắ-)	ይሰራል yi̥ssḁ́rrāl (-sắ-)
ታሰረ tā́ssḁrḁ (-sä-)	be tied, p.	ታስሯል tā́srŏ͡āl	ይታሰር yi̥ttā́ssḁr (-sä-)	ይታሰራል yi̥ttā́ssḁrāl (-sä-)
ተሰረሰረ tḁsḁrḁ́ssḁrḁ (-ärḁ́ssä-)	be bored, p.	ተሰርስሯል tḁsḁ́rsi̥rŏ͡āl (-äsắ-)	ይሰረሰር yi̥ssḁrḁ́ssḁr (-ärḁ́ssä-)	ይሰረሰራል yi̥ssḁrḁ́ssḁ-rāl(-ärḁ́ssä-)
ተሰረቀ tḁsḁ́rrḁqḁ (-äsắ-)	be stolen, p.	ተሰርቋል tḁsḁ́rqŏ͡āl (-äsắ-)	ይሰረቅ yi̥ssḁ́rrḁq (-sắ-)	ይሰረቃል yi̥ssḁ́rrḁqāl (-sắ-)
ተሰሳተ G. tḁsḁsā́tḁ (-äsä-)	be confused, i.	ተሰስቷል tḁsḁ́s(ĭ̥)tŏ͡āl (-äsắ-)	ይሰሳት yi̥ssḁsā́t (-säs-)	ይሰሳታል yi̥ssḁsā́tāl (-säs-)
ተሳሳተ Š. tḁsāsā́tḁ (tä-)	be confused, i.	ተሳስቷል tḁsā́s(ĭ̥)tŏ͡āl (tä-)	ይሳሳት yi̥ssāsā́t	ይሳሳታል yi̥ssāsā́tāl

Jussive (§ 27)	Imperative (§ 28)	Gerund (§ 29)	Infinitive (§ 30)	Participle (§ 31)
ይሰመር yi̥ssḁ́mḁr (-är)		**ተሰመርቶ** tḁsḁmḁ́rt^{w}o (-äsämā́-)	**መሰመረት** mḁssḁmḁ́- rḁt (-ā́rä-)	**ተሰማሪ** tḁsḁmā́ri (-äsä-)
ይሰማሩ yi̥ssḁmā́rã		**ተሰማርቶ** tḁsḁmā́rt^{w}o (-äsä-)	**መሰማሩት** mḁssḁmā́- rā́t (§ 8)	**ተሰማሪ** tḁsḁmā́ri (-äsä-)
ይሰሩ yi̥ssḁ́rã (-sā́-)		**ተሰርቶ** tḁsḁ́rt^{w}o (-äsā́-)	**መሰሩት** mḁssḁ́rā́t (-sā́-; § 8)	**ተሰሪ** tḁsḁ́ri (-äsā́-)
ይታሰር yi̥ttā́sḁr (-sä-)	**ታሰር** tā́sḁr (-sä-)	**ታስሮ** tā́sr^{w}o	**መታሰር** mḁttā́sḁr (-sä-)	**ታሳሪ** tāsā́ri
ይሰርሰር yi̥ssḁ́rsḁr (-ā́rsä-)		**ተሰርስሮ** tḁsḁ́rsi̥r^{w}o (-äsā́-)	**መሰርሰር** mḁssḁ́rsḁr (-ā́rsä-)	†**ተሰርሳሪ** tḁsḁrsā́ri (-äsä-)
ይሰረቅ yi̥ssḁ́rḁq (-sā́-)		**ተሰርቆ** tḁsḁ́rq^{w}o (-äsā́-)	**መሰረቅ** mḁssḁ́rḁq (-sā́-)	† **ተሰራቂ** tḁsḁrā́qi (-äsä-)
ይሰሳት yi̥ssḁ́sā́t (-sā́s-; § 8)	**ተሰሳት** tḁsḁ́sā́t (-äsā́-; § 8)	**ተሰስቶ** tḁsḁ́s(i̥)t^{w}o (-äsā́-)	**መሰሳት** mḁssḁ́sā́t (-sā́s-; § 8)	**ተሰሳች** tḁsḁ́sā́č (-äsā́-; § 8)
ይሳሳት yi̥ssā́sā́t (§ 8)	**ተሳሳት** tḁsā́sā́t (tä-; § 8)	**ተሳስቶ** tḁsā́s(i̥)t^{w}o (tä-)	**መሳሳት** mḁssā́sā́t (§ 8)	**ተሳሳች** tḁsā́sā́č (tä-; § 8)

Simp. perf. (§ 25)		Comp. perf. (§ 32)	Contingent (§ 26)	Comp. imperf. (§ 32)
ተሰቀለ tḁsḁ́qqḁlḁ (tä-)	be suspended, p. ride, i.	ተሰቅሏል tḁsḁ́qlŏ͡āl (tä-)	ይሰቀል yi̥ssḁ́qqḁl	ይሰቀላል yi̥ssḁ́qqḁlāl
ተሳበ tḁsā́bḁ (tä-, -ỵḁ)	be drawn, p.	ተስቧል tḁ́si̥bŏ͡āl (tä́-, -i̥ỵ-)	ይሳብ yi̥ssā́b (-ā́ỵ)	ይሳባል yi̥ssā́bāl (-ā́ỵ-)
ተሰበረ tḁsḁ́bbḁrḁ (tä-, -bä-)	be broken, p.	ተሰብሯል tḁsḁ́brŏ͡āl (tä-, -ỵr-)	ይሰበር yi̥ssḁ́bbḁr (-bä-)	ይሰበራል yi̥ssḁ́bbḁrāl (-bä-)
ተሰበሰበ tḁsḁbḁ́ssḁbḁ (tä-, -ỵḁ́ssḁỵ-)	be gathered, p.	ተሰብስቧል tḁsḁ́bsi̥bŏ͡āl (tä-, -ỵsi̥ỵ-)	ይሰበሰብ yi̥ssḁbḁ́ssḁb (-ỵḁ́ssḁỵ)	ይሰበሰባል yi̥ssḁbḁ́ssḁbāl (-ỵḁ́ssḁỵ-)
ተሰባበረ tḁsḁbā́bbḁrḁ (-äsä-, -ỵā́-, -är-)	be shattered, p.	ተሰባብሯል tḁsḁbā́brŏ͡āl (-äsä-, -ỵā́ỵ-)	ይሰባበር yi̥ssḁbā́bbḁr (-ỵā́-, -är)	ይሰባበራል yi̥ssḁbā́bbḁrāl (-ỵā́-, -är-)
ተሳተ tḁsā́tḁ (tä-)	be missed, p.	ተስቷል tḁ́si̥tŏ͡āl (tä́-)	ይሳት yi̥ssā́t	ይሳታል yi̥ssā́tāl
ተሰናበተ tḁsḁnā́bbḁtḁ (-äsä-, -bä-)	be dismissed, p.	ተሰናብቷል tḁsḁnā́btŏ͡āl (-äsä-, -ỵt-)	ይሰናበት yi̥ssḁnā́bbḁt (-sä-, -bä-)	ይሰናበታል yi̥ssḁnā́bbḁtāl (-sä-, -bä-)
ተሰናዳ tḁsḁnā́ddā̃ (-äsä-)	be prepared, p.	ተሰናድቷል tḁsḁnā́d(i̥)tŏ͡āl (-äsä-, -ā́rt- § 7*d*)	ይሰናዳ yi̥ssḁnā́ddā̃	ይሰናዳል yi̥ssḁnā́ddāl

Jussive (§ 27)	Imperative (§ 28)	Gerund (§ 29)	Infinitive (§ 30)	Participle (§ 31)
ይሰቀል yi̥ssḁ́qḁl	ተሰቀል tḁsḁ́qḁl (tä-)	ተሰቅሎ tḁsḁ́qlʷo (tä-)	መሰቀል mḁssḁ́qḁl	ተሰቃይ tḁsḁ́qā́i̥ (tä-; -ā́yy § 6; § 8)
ይሳብ yí̥ssáb (-ā́ỵ; § 8)	ተሳብ tḁ́sáb (tā́-, -ā́ỵ; § 8)	ተስቦ tḁ́si̥bʷo (tā́-, -i̥ỵ-)	መሳብ mḁ́ssáb (-ā́ỵ; § 8)	ተሳቢ tḁsábi (tä-, -ỵi)
ይሰበር yi̥ssḁ́bḁr (-ḁ́ỵ-, -är)	ተሰበር tḁsḁ́bḁr (tä-, -ḁ́ỵ-, -är)	ተሰብሮ tḁsḁ́brʷo (tä-, -ỵr-)	መሰበር mḁssḁ́bḁr (-ḁ́ỵ-, -är)	ተሰባሪ tḁsḁbā́ri (tä-, -ỵā́-)
ይሰብሰብ yi̥ssḁ́bsḁb (-ỵsḁỵ)	ተሰብሰብ tḁsḁ́bsḁb (tä-, ỵsḁỵ)	ተሰብስቦ tḁsḁ́bsi̥bʷo (tä-, -ỵsi̥ỵ-)	መሰብሰብ mḁssḁ́bsḁb (-ỵsḁỵ)	ተሰብሳቢ tḁsḁbsā́bi (tä-, -ỵsā́ỵ-)
ይሰባበር yi̥ssḁbā́bḁr (-ỵā́ỵ-, -är)	ተሰባበር tḁsḁbā́bḁr (-äsä-, -ỵā́ỵ-, -är)	ተሰባብሮ tḁsḁbā́brʷo (-äsä-, -ỵā́ỵ-)	መሰባበር mḁssḁbā́-bḁr (-ỵā́ỵ-, -är)	ተሰባባሪ tḁsḁbābā́ri (-äsä-, -ỵāỵ-)
ይሳት yí̥ssát (§ 8)		ተስቶ tḁ́si̥tʷo (tā́-)	መሳት mḁ́ssát (§ 8)	
ይሰናበት yi̥ssḁnā́bḁt (-sä-, -ā́ỵ-, -ät)	ተሰናበት tḁsḁnā́bḁt (-äsä-, -ā́ỵ-, -ät)	ተሰናብቶ tḁsḁnā́btʷo (-äsä-, -ỵt-)	መሰናበት mḁssḁnā́bḁt (-sä-, -ā́ỵ-, -ät)	†ተሰናባች tḁsḁnā́bā́č (-äsä-, -ā́ỵ-; § 8)
ይሰናዳ yi̥ssḁnā́dā̃	ተሰናዳ tḁsḁnā́dā̃ (-äsä-)	ተሰናድቶ tḁsḁnā́d(i̥)-tʷo (-äsä-, -ā́rt- § 7*d*)	መሰናዳት mḁssḁnā́dā́t (§ 8)	ተሰናጅ tḁsḁ́nāj (-äsā́-; § 8)

Simp. perf. (§ 25)		Comp. perf. (§ 32)	Contingent (§ 26)	Comp. imperf. (§ 32)
ተሰነጠቀ tḁsḁnḁ́ṭṭḁqḁ (-äsä-)	be split, p.	**ተሰንጥቋል** tḁsḁ́nṭi̥qŏ͡āl (tä-)	**ይሰነጠቅ** yi̥ssḁnḁ́ṭṭḁq	**ይሰነጠቃል** yi̥ssḁnḁ́ṭṭḁ- qāl
ተሰወረ tḁsḁ́͡uwḁrḁ (tä-)	be hidden, p.	**ተሰውሯል** tḁsḁ́͡uwŭrŏ͡āl (tä-)	**ይሰወር** yi̥ssḁ́͡uwḁr	**ይሰወራል** yi̥ssḁ́͡uwḁrāl
ተሰደበ tḁsḁ́ddḁbḁ (tä-, -ẏḁ)	be abused, p.	**ተሰድቧል** tḁsḁ́d(ĭ̥)bŏ͡āl (tä-, -ẏŏ-)	**ይሰደብ** yi̥ssḁ́ddḁb (-ḁẏ)	**ይሰደባል** yi̥ssḁ́ddḁbāl (-ẏāl)
ተሳደደ tḁsā̃́ddḁdḁ (tä-)	migrate, i.	**ተሳዷል** tḁsā̃́ddŏ͡āl (tä-)	**ይሳደድ** yi̥ssā̃́ddḁd	**ይሳደዳል** yi̥ssā̃́ddḁ- dāl
ተሰዳደቡ tḁsḁdā̃́d- dḁbu (-äsä-, -ẏu)	quarrel, i.	**ተሰዳድበዋል** tḁsḁdā̃́d(ĭ̥)- bḁ͡uāl (-äsä-, -ẏḁ͡u-)	**ይሰዳደቡ** yi̥ssḁdā̃́d- dḁbu (-ẏu)	**ይሰዳደባሉ** yi̥ssḁdā̃d- dḁbállu (-ẏál-)
ተሰጠ tḁsḁ́ṭṭḁ (-äsā̃́-) 2nd -**ጠህ** -ṭṭḁh (-äh), etc.	be given, p.	**ተሰጥቷል** tḁsḁ́ṭ(ĭ̥)tŏ͡āl (-äsā̃́-)	**ይሰጥ** yi̥ssḁ́ṭṭ	**ይሰጣል** yi̥ssḁ́ṭṭāl
ተሰፋ tḁsḁ́ffā̃ (tä-)	be sewn, p.	**ተሰፍቷል** tḁsḁ́ftŏ͡āl (tä-)	**ይሰፋ** yi̥ssḁ́ffā̃	**ይሰፋል** yi̥ssḁ́ffāl

Jussive (§ 27)	Imperative (§ 28)	Gerund (§ 29)	Infinitive (§ 30)	Participle (§ 31)
ይሰንጠቅ yi̥ssḁ́nṭḁq		**ተሰንጥቆ** tḁsḁ́nṭi̥qʷo (tä-)	**መሰንጠቅ** mḁssḁ́nṭḁq	**ተሰንጣቂ** tḁsḁnṭā́qi (tä-)
ይሰወር yi̥ssḁ́͡uḁr	**ተሰወር** tḁsḁ́͡uḁr (tä-)	**ተሰውሮ** tḁsḁ́͡uwŭrʷo (tä-)	**መሰወር** mḁssḁ́͡uḁr	**ተሰዋሪ** tḁsḁ͡uwā́ri (tä-)
ይሰደብ yi̥ssḁ́dḁb (-ḁỵ)		**ተሰድቦ** tḁsḁ́d(ĭ̥)bʷo (tä-, -ỵʷo)	**መሰደብ** mḁssḁ́dḁb (-ḁỵ)	**ተሰዳቢ** tḁsḁddā́bi (tä-, -ỵi)
ይሳደድ yi̥ssā́dḁd	**ተሳደድ** tḁsā́dḁd (tä-)	**ተሳዶ** tḁsā́ddʷo (tä-)	**መሳደድ** mḁssā́dḁd	**ተሳዳጅ** tḁsā́dā́j (tä- ; § 8)
ይሰዳደቡ yi̥ssḁdā́- dḁbu (-ỵu)	**ተሰዳደቡ** tḁsḁdā́dḁbu (-äsä-, -ỵu)	**ተሰዳድበው** tḁsḁdā́d(ĭ̥)- bḁ͡u (-äsä-, -ỵḁ͡u)	**መሰዳደብ** mḁssḁdā́- dḁb (-ḁỵ)	**ተሰዳዳቦች** tḁsḁdādā́- bʷōč (-äsä-, -ā́ỵ- ; -čč § 6)
ይሰጥ yí̥ssḁ́ṭ (§ 8)		**ተሰጥቶ** tḁsḁ́ṭ(ĭ̥)tʷo (-äsā́-)	**መሰጠት** mḁssḁ́ṭḁt (-ät)	†**ተሰጭ** tḁ́sḁ́č̣ (-ā́sä-; § 8 ; -**ጪ** -č̣i)
ይሰፋ yi̥ssḁ́fã		**ተሰፍቶ** tḁsḁ́ftʷo (tä-)	**መሰፋት** mḁssḁ́fā́t (§ 8)	†**ተሰፊ** tḁsḁ́fi (tä-, -sā́-)

Simp. perf. (§ 25)		Comp. perf. (§ 32)	Contingent (§ 26)	Comp. impert. (§ 32)
ታሸ tā́ššä 2nd ታሸህ tā́ššäh, etc.	be rubbed, p.	ታሽቷል tā́št͡ŏāl	ይታሽ yi̥ttā́šš	ይታሻል yi̥ttā́ššāl
ተሻለ tḁšā́lḁ (tä-)	be better, i.	ተሽሏል tḁ́ši̥l͡ŏāl (tä́-)	ይሻል yi̥ššā́l	ይሻላል yi̥ššā́lāl
ተሻማ tḁšā̃́mmā̃ (tä-)	scramble for, t.	ተሻምቷል tḁšā́mt͡ŏāl (tä-)	ይሻማ yi̥ššā̃́mmā̃	ይሻማል yi̥ššā̃́mmāl
ተሾመ tḁšʷṓmḁ (tä-)	be set in authority, p.	ተሹሟል tḁšúm͡ŏāl (tä-) -ሾ- -šʷṓ- Š.	ይሾም yi̥ššʷṓm	ይሾማል yi̥ššʷṓmāl
ተሸሸገ tḁšḁ́ššḁgḁ (-äšā́ššä-)	be hidden, p.	ተሸሽጓል tḁšḁ́šši̥g͡ŏāl (täšā́-)	ይሸሸግ yi̥ššḁ́ššḁg (-ā́ššä-)	ይሸሸጋል yi̥ššḁ́ššḁgāl (-ā́ššä-)
ተሸኘ tḁšḁ́ññä (-äšā́-) 2nd -ኘህ -ññäh, etc.	be escorted, p.	ተሸኝቷል tḁšḁ́ññi̥t͡ŏāl (-äšā́-)	ይሸኝ yi̥ššḁ́ññ (-šā́-)	ይሸኛል yi̥ššḁ́ññāl (-šā́-)
ተሸከመ tḁšḁ́kkḁmḁ (-äšā́-)	be laden, p.	ተሸክሟል tḁšḁ́kki̥m͡ŏāl (-äšā́-)	ይሸከም yi̥ššḁ́kkḁm (-šā́-)	ይሸከማል yi̥ššḁ́kkḁ- māl (-šā́-)
ተሻገረ tḁšā́ggḁrḁ (tä-, -gä-)	cross, t.	ተሻግሯል tḁšā́gr͡ŏāl (tä-)	ይሻገር yi̥ššā́ggḁr (-är)	ይሻገራል yi̥ššā́ggḁrāl (-gä-)

Jussive (§ 27)	Imperative (§ 28)	Gerund (§ 29)	Infinitive (§ 30)	Participle (§ 31)
ይታሽ yi̥ttä́š (§ 8)		ታሽቶ tä́štʷo	መታሸት mḁttä́šät	
		ተሽሎ tḁ́ši̥lʷo (tä́-)	መሻል mḁ́ššä́l (§ 8)	
ይሻማ yi̥ššä́mã	ተሻማ tḁšä́mã (tä-)	ተሻምቶ tḁšä́mtʷo (tä-)	መሻማት mḁššä́mä́t (§ 8)	ተሻሚ tḁšä́mi (tä-)
ይሾም yí̥ššʷő́m (§ 8)	ተሾም tḁ́šʷő́m (tä́-; § 8)	ተሹሞ tḁšúmʷo (tä-) -ሾ- -šʷő́- Š.	መሾም mḁ́ššʷő́m (§ 8)	ተሿሚ tḁšwä́mi (tä-)
ይሸሸግ yi̥ššḁ́šḁg (-šä́šä-)	ተሸሸግ tḁšḁ́šḁg (-äšä́šä-)	ተሸሽጎ tḁšḁ́šši̥gʷo (täšä́-)	መሸሸግ mḁššḁ́šḁg (-äššä́šä-)	ተሸሻጊ tḁšḁššä́gi (täšä-)
ይሸኝ yí̥ššḁñ (-šä́-; § 8)	ተሸኝ tḁ́šḁñ (-ä́šä́-; § 8)	ተሸኝቶ tḁšḁ́ññi̥tʷo (-äšä́-)	መሸኘት mḁššḁ́ñ(ñ)ät (-šä́-)	†ተሸኚ tḁšḁ́ññi (-äšä́-)
ይሸከም yi̥ššḁ́kḁm (-šä́-)	ተሸከም tḁšḁ́kḁm (-äšä́-)	ተሸክሞ tḁšḁ́kki̥mʷo (-äšä́-)	መሸከም mḁššḁ́kḁm (-šä́-)	ተሸካሚ tḁšḁkkä́mi (-äšä-)
ይሻገር yi̥ššä́gḁr (-är)	ተሻገር tḁšä́gḁr (tä-, -är)	ተሻግሮ tḁšä́grʷo (tä-)	መሻገር mḁššä́gḁr (-är)	ተሻጋሪ tḁšāgā́ri (tä-)

Simp. perf. (§ 25)		Comp. perf. (§ 32)	Contingent (§ 26)	Comp. imperf. (§ 32)
ተሸጠ tḁšḁ́ṭḁ (-äšá-)	be sold, p.	ተሺጧል tḁ́ši̥ṭŏ͡āl (tá-) -ሺ- -šá- Š.	ይሸጥ yi̥ššḁ́ṭ (-šá-)	ይሸጣል yi̥ššḁ́ṭāl (-šá-)
ተሸፈነ tḁšḁ́ffḁnḁ (-äšá-)	be wrapped, p.	ተሸፍኗል tḁšḁ́ffi̥nŏ͡āl (-äšá-)	ይሸፈን yi̥ššḁ́ffḁn (-šá-)	ይሸፈናል yi̥ššḁ́ffḁnāl (-šá-)
ተቀለመ tḁqḁ́llḁmḁ	be stained, p.	ተቀልሟል tḁqḁ́lmŏ͡āl (-ḁ́lli̥m-)	ይቀለም yi̥qqḁ́llḁm	ይቀለማል yi̥qqḁ́llḁmāl
†ተቀለቀለ tḁqḁlḁ́q- qḁlḁ	be mixed, p.	†ተቀልቅሏል tḁqḁ́lqi̥lŏ͡āl	†ይቀለቀል yi̥qqḁlḁ́q- qḁl	†ይቀለቀላል yi̥qqḁlḁ́q- qḁlāl
ተቀላቀለ tḁqḁlā́q- qḁlḁ	be mixed, p.	ተቀላቅሏል tḁqḁlā́q(ĭ̥)- lŏ͡āl	ይቀላቀል yi̥qqḁlā́q- qḁl	ይቀላቀላል yi̥qqḁlā́q- qḁlāl
ተቈለፈ tḁqwώllḁfḁ	be locked, p.	ተቈልፏል tḁqwώlli̥fŏ͡āl	ይቈለፍ yi̥qqwώllḁf	ይቈለፋል yi̥qqwώllḁfāl
ተቀማ tḁqḁ́mmã	be robbed, p.	ተቀምቷል tḁqḁ́mmi̥- tŏ͡āl	ይቀማ yi̥qqḁ́mmã	ይቀማል yi̥qqḁ́mmāl
ተቀመሰ tḁqḁ́mmḁsḁ	be tasted, p.	ተቀምሷል tḁqḁ́msŏ͡āl	ይቀመስ yi̥qqḁ́mmḁs	ይቀመሳል yi̥qqḁ́mmḁ- sāl
ተቀመጠ tḁqḁ́mmḁṭḁ	sit, ride, i.	ተቀምጧል tḁqḁ́m(mi̥)- ṭŏ͡āl	ይቀመጥ yi̥qqḁ́mmḁṭ	ይቀመጣል yi̥qqḁ́mmḁ- ṭāl

Jussive (§ 27)	Imperative (§ 28)	Gerund (§ 29)	Infinitive (§ 30)	Participle (§ 31)
ይሸጥ yi̥ššḁ́ṭ (-šä́-; § 8)		**ተሺጦ** tḁ́ši̥ṭʷo (tä́-) -ሺ- -šä́- Š.	**መሸጥ** mḁ́ššḁ́ṭ (-šä́-; § 8)	**ተሻጭ** tḁ́šä́č̣ (tä́-; § 8)
ይሸፈን yi̥ššḁ́fḁn (-šä́-)	**ተሸፈን** tḁšḁ́fḁn (-äšä́-)	**ተሸፍኖ** tḁšḁ́ffi̥nʷo (-äšä́-)	**መሸፈን** mḁššḁ́fḁn (-šä́-)	**ተሸፋኝ** tḁšḁ́ffä́ñ (-äšä́-; -ññ § 6; § 8)
ይቀለም yi̥qqḁ́lḁm		**ተቀልሞ** tḁqḁ́lmʷo (-ḁ́lli̥m-)	**መቀለም** mḁqqḁ́lḁm	**ተቀላሚ** tḁqḁl(l)ä́mi
†**ይቀልቀል** yi̥qqḁ́lqḁl		†**ተቀልቅሎ** tḁqḁ́lqi̥lʷo	†**መቀልቀል** mḁqqḁ́lqḁl	†**ተቀልቃይ** tḁqḁ́lqä́i̥ (-ä́yy § 6; § 8)
ይቀላቀል yi̥qqḁlä́qḁl		**ተቀላቅሎ** tḁqḁlä́- q(i̥)lʷo	**መቀላቀል** mḁqqḁlä́- qḁl	†**ተቀላቃይ** tḁqḁlä́qä́i̥ (-ä́yy § 6; § 8)
ይቈለፍ yi̥qqwώlḁf		**ተቈልፎ** tḁqwώlli̥fʷo	**መቈለፍ** mḁqqwώlḁf	†**ተቈላፊ** tḁqwωllä́fi
ይቀማ yi̥qqḁ́mã	**ተቀማ** tḁqḁ́mã	**ተቀምቶ** tḁqḁ́m- mi̥tʷo	**መቀማት** mḁqqḁ́mä́t (§ 8)	**ተቀሚ** tḁqḁ́mi
ይቀመስ yi̥qqḁ́mḁs		**ተቀምሶ** tḁqḁ́msʷo	**መቀመስ** mḁqqḁ́mḁs	**ተቀማሽ** tḁqḁ́mä́š (§ 8)
ይቀመጥ yi̥qqḁ́maṭ	**ተቀመጥ** tḁqḁ́mḁṭ	**ተቀምጦ** tḁqḁ́m(mi̥)- ṭʷo	**መቀመጥ** mḁqqḁ́mḁṭ	**ተቀማጭ** tḁqḁ́mmä́č̣ (§ 8)

Simp. perf. (§ 25)		Comp. perf. (§ 32)	Contingent (§ 26)	Comp. imperf. (§ 32)
ተቀራረቡ tḁqḁrā̆r- rḁbu (-ỵu)	be close together, i.	ተቀራርበዋል tḁqḁrā́r(ĭ̥) bḁ͡uāl (-ỵḁ͡u-)	ይቀራረቡ yi̥qqḁrā̆r- rḁbu (-ỵu)	ይቀራረባሉ yi̥qqḁrā̃rrḁ- bállu (-ỵá-)
ተቀረጠ tḁqḁ́rrḁṭḁ	pay dues, i.	ተቀርጧል tḁqḁ́rṭ͡ŏāl (-qā́-)	ይቀረጥ yi̥qqḁ́rrḁṭ	ይቀረጣል yi̥qqḁ́rrḁṭāl
ተቈረጠ tḁqwώrrḁṭḁ	be cut, p.	ተቈርጧል tḁqwώrṭ͡ŏāl	ይቈረጥ yi̥qqwώrrḁṭ	ይቈረጣል yi̥qqwώrrḁ- ṭāl
ተቀሰቀሰ tḁqḁsḁ́q- qḁsḁ	be roused, p.	ተቀስቅሷል tḁqḁ́sqi̥s͡ŏāl	ይቀሰቀስ yi̥qqḁsḁ́q- qḁs	ይቀሰቀሳል yi̥qqḁsáq- qḁsāl
ተቀቀለ tḁqḁ́qqḁlḁ	be boiled, p.	ተቀቅሏል tḁqḁ́qqi̥l͡ŏāl	ይቀቀል yi̥qqḁ́qqḁl	ይቀቀላል yi̥qqḁ́qqḁlāl
ተቀባ tḁqḁ́bbā̃	be anointed, p.	ተቀብቷል tḁqḁ́btŏāl (-ỵt-)	ይቀባ yi̥qqḁ́bbā̃	ይቀባል yi̥qqḁ́bbāl
ተቀበለ tḁqḁ́bbḁlḁ	accept, t.	ተቀብሏል tḁqḁ́bbi̥l͡ŏāl	ይቀበል yi̥qqḁ́bbḁl (-äl)	ይቀበላል yi̥qqḁ́bbḁlāl
ተቀበረ tḁqḁ́bbḁrḁ (-bä-)	be buried, p.	ተቀብሯል tḁqḁ́br͡ŏāl (-ỵr-)	ይቀበር yi̥qqḁ́bbḁr (-bä-)	ይቀበራል yi̥qqḁ́bbḁ- rāl (-bä-)
ተቀዳ tḁqḁ́ddā̃	be drawn, p.	ተቀድቷል tḁqḁ́dĭ̥t͡ŏāl (-ä́rt- § 7*d*)	ይቀዳ yi̥qqḁ́ddā̃	ይቀዳል yi̥qqḁ́ddāl

Jussive (§ 27)	Imperative (§ 28)	Gerund (§ 29)	Infinitive (§ 30)	Participle (§ 31)
ይቀራረቡ yi̥qqḁrā́rḁbu (-ỵu)	**ተቀራረቡ** tḁqḁrā́rḁbu (-ỵu)	**ተቀራርበው** tḁqḁrā́r(ĭ̥)bḁu (-ỵḁu)	**መቀራረብ** mḁqqḁrā́rḁb (-ḁỵ)	**ተቀራራቢዎች** tḁqḁrārā́bʷōč (-ā́ỵ-; -ʷōčč § 6)
ይቀረጥ yi̥qqḁ́rḁṭ	**ተቀረጥ** tḁqḁ́rḁṭ	**ተቀርጦ** tḁqḁ́rṭʷo (-qā́-)	**መቀረጥ** mḁqqḁ́rḁṭ	**ተቀራጭ** tḁqḁ́rā́č̣ (§ 8)
ይቈረጥ yi̥qqwώrḁṭ	**ተቈረጥ** tḁqwώrḁṭ	**ተቈርጦ** tḁqwώrṭʷo	**መቈረጥ** mḁqqwώrḁṭ	**ተቈራጭ** tḁqwώrā́č̣ (§ 8)
ይቀስቀስ yi̥qqḁ́sqḁs	**ተቀስቀስ** tḁqḁ́sqḁs	**ተቀስቅሶ** tḁqḁ́sqi̥sʷo	**መቀስቀስ** mḁqqḁ́sqḁs	**ተቀስቃሽ** tḁqḁ́sqā́š (§ 8)
ይቀቀል yi̥qqḁ́qḁl		**ተቀቅሎ** tḁqḁ́qqi̥lʷo	**መቀቀል** mḁqqḁ́qḁl	**ተቀቃይ** tḁqḁ́qqā́i̥ (-ā́yy § 6; § 8)
ይቀባ yi̥qqḁ́bā̃ (-ḁ́ỵ-)	**ተቀባ** tḁqḁ́bā̃ (-ḁ́ỵ-)	**ተቀብቶ** tḁqḁ́btʷo (-ỵt-)	**መቀባት** mḁqqḁ́bā́t (-ḁ́ỵ-; § 8)	**ተቀቢ** tḁqḁ́bi (-ḁ́ỵ-)
ይቀበል yi̥qqḁ́bḁl (-ḁ́ỵ-, -äl)	**ተቀበል** tḁqḁ́bḁl (-ḁ́ỵ-, -äl)	**ተቀብሎ** tḁqḁ́bbi̥lʷo	**መቀበል** mḁqqḁ́bḁl (-ḁ́ỵ-, -äl)	**ተቀባይ** tḁqḁ́bbā́i̥ (-ā́yy § 6; § 8)
ይቀበር yi̥qqḁ́bḁr (-ḁ́ỵ-, -är)		**ተቀብሮ** tḁqḁ́brʷo (-ỵr-)	**መቀበር** mḁqqḁ́bḁr (-ḁ́ỵ-, -är)	†**ተቀባሪ** tḁqḁbā́ri (-ỵā́-)
ይቀዳ yi̥qqḁ́dā̃		**ተቀድቶ** tḁqḁ́dĭ̥tʷo (-ärt- § 7*d*)	**መቀዳት** mḁqqḁ́dā́t (§ 8)	**ተቀጅ** tḁ́qḁ́j (-qā́-; § 8; -**ጂ** -ji)

Simp. perf. (§ 25)		Comp. perf. (§ 32)	Contingent (§ 26)	Comp. imperf. (§ 32)
ተቀደመ tḁqḁ́ddḁmḁ	go in front, i.	ተቀድሟል tḁqḁ́dmŏ͡āl (-qā́-, -rm- § 7*d*)	ይቀደም yi̥qqḁ́ddḁm	ይቀደማል yi̥qqḁ́ddḁ-māl
ተቀደደ tḁqḁ́ddḁdḁ	be pierced, p.	ተቀዷል tḁqḁ́ddŏ͡āl	ይቀደድ yi̥qqḁ́ddḁd	ይቀደዳል yi̥qqḁ́ddḁ-dāl
ተቀጣ tḁqḁ́ṭṭã	be punished, p.	ተቀጥቷል tḁqḁ́ṭtŏ͡āl	ይቀጣ yi̥qqḁ́ṭṭã	ይቀጣል yi̥qqḁ́ṭṭāl
ተቈጣ tḁqwώṭṭã	be angry, i.	ተቈጥቷል tḁqwώṭ(i̥)-tŏ͡āl	ይቈጣ yi̥qqwώṭṭã	ይቈጣል yi̥qqwώṭṭāl
ተቀጠለ tḁqḁ́ṭṭḁlḁ	be joined, p.	ተቀጥሏል tḁqḁ́ṭṭi̥lŏ͡āl	ይቀጠል yi̥qqḁ́ṭṭḁl (-äl)	ይቀጠላል yi̥qqḁ́ṭṭḁlāl
ተቃጠለ tḁqā́ṭṭḁlḁ	be burnt, p.	ተቃጥሏል tḁqā́ṭ(i̥)lŏ͡āl	ይቃጠል yi̥qqā́ṭṭḁl (-äl)	ይቃጠላል yi̥qqā́ṭṭḁlāl
ተቀጠረ tḁqḁ́ṭṭḁrḁ (-ṭä-)	be engaged, p.	ተቀጥሯል tḁqḁ́ṭrŏ͡āl	ይቀጠር yi̥qqḁ́ṭṭḁr (-ṭä-)	ይቀጠራል yi̥qqḁ́ṭṭḁrāl (-ṭä-)
ተቈጠረ tḁqwώṭṭḁrḁ (-ṭä-)	be counted, p.	ተቈጥሯል tḁqwώṭrŏ͡āl	ይቈጠር yi̥qqwώṭṭḁr (-ṭä-)	ይቈጠራል yi̥qqwώṭṭḁ-rāl (-ṭä-)
ተቈጠበ tḁqwώṭṭḁbḁ (-ḁỵ-)	be saved, p.	ተቈጥቧል tḁqwώṭṭi̥-bŏ͡āl (-i̥ỵ-)	ይቈጠብ yi̥qqwώṭṭḁb (-ḁỵ)	ይቈጠባል yi̥qqwώṭṭḁ-bāl (-ḁỵ-)

Jussive (§ 27)	Imperative (§ 28)	Gerund (§ 29)	Infinitive (§ 30)	Participle (§ 31)
ይቀደም yi̥qqḁ́dḁm	ተቀደም tḁqḁ́dḁm	ተቀድሞ tḁqḁ́dmʷo (-qā́-, -rm- § 7*d*)	መቀደም mḁqqḁ́dḁm	†ተቀዳሚ tḁqḁdā́mi
ይቀደድ yi̥qqḁ́dḁd		ተቀዶ tḁqḁ́ddʷo	መቀደድ mḁqqḁ́dḁd	ተቀዳጅ tḁqḁ́d(d)ā́j (§ 8)
ይቀጣ yi̥qqḁ́ṭã	ተቀጣ tḁqḁ́ṭã	ተቀጥቶ tḁqḁ́ṭtʷo	መቀጣት mḁqqḁ́ṭā́t (§ 8)	†ተቀጭ tḁ́qḁ́č̣ (-qā́-; § 8 ; -ጪ -č̣i)
ይቈጣ yi̥qqwώṭã	ተቈጣ tḁqwώṭã	ተቈጥቶ tḁqwώṭ(i̥)tʷo	መቈጣት mḁqqwώṭā́t (§ 8)	ተቈጭ tḁqwώč̣ (-ጪ -č̣i)
ይቀጠል yi̥qqḁ́ṭḁl (-äl)	ተቀጠል tḁqḁ́ṭḁl (-äl)	ተቀጥሎ tḁqḁ́ṭṭi̥lʷo	መቀጠል mḁqqḁ́ṭḁl (-äl)	ተቀጣይ tḁqḁ́ṭṭā́i̥ (-ā́yy § 6; § 8)
ይቃጠል yi̥qqā́ṭḁl (-äl)	ተቃጠል tḁqā́ṭḁl (-äl)	ተቃጥሎ tḁqā́ṭ(i̥)lʷo	መቃጠል mḁqqā́ṭḁl (-äl)	ተቃጣይ tḁqā́ṭā́i̥ (-ā́yy § 6; § 8)
ይቀጠር yi̥qqḁ́ṭḁr (-ṭä-)	ተቀጠር tḁqḁ́ṭḁr (-ṭä-)	ተቀጥሮ tḁqḁ́ṭrʷo	መቀጠር mḁqqḁ́ṭḁr (-ṭä-)	ተቀጣሪ tḁqḁṭṭā́ri
ይቈጠር yi̥qqwώṭḁr (-ṭä-)	ተቈጠር tḁqwώṭḁr (-ṭä-)	ተቈጥሮ tḁqwώṭrʷo	መቈጠር mḁqqwώṭḁr (-ṭä-)	†ተቈጣሪ tḁqwωṭā́ri
ይቈጠብ yi̥qqwώṭḁb (-ḁy̱)		ተቈጥቦ tḁqwώṭṭi̥bʷo (-i̥y̱-)	መቈጠብ mḁqqwώṭḁb (-ḁy̱)	†ተቈጣቢ tḁqwωṭṭā́bi (-y̱i)

Simp. perf. (§ 25)		Comp. perf. (§ 32)	Contingent (§ 26)	Comp. imperf. (§ 32)
ተቀጠፈ tḁqḁ́ṭṭḁfḁ	be cheated, p.	ተቀጥፏል tḁqḁ́ṭfŏ͡āl	ይቀጠፍ yi̥qqḁ́ṭṭḁf	ይቀጠፋል yi̥qqḁ́ṭṭḁfāl
ተቈፈረ tḁqwώffḁrḁ (-fä-)	be dug, p.	ተቈፍሯል tḁqwώffi̥- rŏ͡āl	ይቈፈር yi̥qqwώffḁṛ (-fä-)	ይቈፈራል yi̥qqwώffḁ- rāl (-fä-)
ተበላ tḁbḁ́llã (-ḁẏ-)	be eaten, p.	ተበልቷል tḁbḁ́ltŏ͡āl (-ḁẏ-, -ā́l-)	ይበላ yi̥bbḁ́llã	ይበላል yi̥bbḁ́llāl
ተባለ tḁbā́lḁ (-ḁẏ-)	be said, p.	ተብሏል tḁ́b(ĭ̥)lŏ͡āl (tā́-, -ẏ(ĭ̥)-)	ይባል yi̥bbā́l	ይባላል yi̥bbā́lāl
ተበላሸ tḁbḁlā́ššä (-ḁẏ-) 2nd -ሸህ -ššäh, etc.	be spoiled, p.	ተበላሽቷል tḁbḁlā́štŏ͡āl (-ḁẏ-)	ይበላሽ yi̥bbḁlā́šš	ይበላሻል yi̥bbḁlā́ššāl
ተበራ tḁbḁ́rrã (-ḁẏ-)	be lit, p.	ተበርቷል tḁbḁ́rtŏ͡āl (-ḁẏ-, -ā́r-)	ይበራ yi̥bbḁ́rrã	ይበራል yi̥bbḁ́rrāl
ተባረከ tḁbā́rrḁkḁ (-ḁẏ-)	be blessed, i.	ተባርኳል tḁbā́rkŏ͡āl (-ḁẏ-)	ይባረክ yi̥bbā́rrḁk	ይባረካል yi̥bbā́rrḁkāl
ታበሰ tā́bbḁsḁ	be wiped, p.	ታብሷል tā́bbi̥sŏ͡āl	ይታበስ yi̥ttā́bbḁs	ይታበሳል yi̥ttā́bbḁsāl

Jussive (§ 27)	Imperative (§ 28)	Gerund (§ 29)	Infinitive (§ 30)	Participle (§ 31)
ይቀጠፍ yi̥qqḁ́ṭḁf		**ተቀጥፎ** tḁqḁ́ṭfʷo	**መቀጠፍ** mḁqqḁ́ṭḁf	†**ተቀጣፊ** tḁqḁṭā́fi
ይቈፈር yi̥qqwώfḁr (-fä-)		**ተቈፍሮ** tḁqwώffi̥rʷo	**መቈፈር** mḁqqwώfḁr (-fä-)	**ተቈፋሪ** tḁqwωffā́ri
ይበላ yi̥bbḁ́lã	**ተበላ** tḁbḁ́lã (-ḁẏ-)	**ተበልቶ** tḁbḁ́ltʷo (-ḁẏ-, -ā́l-)	**መበላት** mḁbbḁ́lā́t (§ 8)	**ተበይ** tḁ́bḁ͡i̥ (-ḁ́ẏ-; -ḁ́yy § 6; § 8)
ይባል yí̥bbā́l (§ 8)		**ተበሎ** tḁ́b(ĭ̥)lʷo (tā́-, -ẏ(ĭ̥)-)	**መባል** mḁ́bbā́l (§ 8)	**ተባይ** tḁ́bā́͡i̥ (-ḁ́ẏ-; -ā́yy § 6; § 8)
ይበላሽ yi̥bbḁ́lā́š (§ 8)		**ተበላሽቶ** tḁbḁlā́štʷo (-ḁẏ-)	**መበላሸት** mḁbbḁlā́šät	
ይበራ yi̥bbḁ́rã (-ā́r-)		**ተበርቶ** tḁbḁ́rtʷo (-ḁẏ-, -ā́r-)	**መበራት** mḁbbḁ́rā́t (-ā́r-; § 8)	†**ተበሪ** tḁbḁ́ri (-ḁẏ-, -ā́r-)
ይባረክ yi̥bbā́rḁk	**ተባረክ** tḁbā́rḁk (-ḁẏ-)	**ተባርኮ** tḁbā́rkʷo (-ḁẏ-)	**መባረክ** mḁbbā́rḁk	**ተባራኪ** tḁbārā́ki (-ḁẏ-)
ይታበስ yi̥ttā́bḁs (-ā́ẏ-)		**ታበሶ** tā́bbi̥sʷo	**መታበስ** mḁttā́bḁs (-ā́ẏ-)	**ታባሽ** tā́bbā́š (§ 8)

Simp. perf. (§ 25)		Comp. perf. (§ 32)	Contingent (§ 26)	Comp. imperf. (§ 32)
ተበተነ tḁbḁ́ttḁnḁ (-ḁy-, -ắttä-)	be scattered, p.	ተበትኗል tḁbḁ́tti̥nŏ͡āl (-ḁy-, -ắtt-)	ይበተን yi̥bbḁ́ttḁn (-ắttä-)	ይበተናል yi̥bbḁ́ttḁnāl (-ắttä-)
ተበደለ tḁbḁ́ddḁlḁ (-ḁy-, -ắd-)	be ill-treated, p.	ተበድሏል tḁbḁ́ddi̥lŏ͡āl (-ḁy-, -ắd-)	ይበደል yi̥bbḁ́ddḁl (-ắddä-)	ይበደላል yi̥bbḁ́ddḁlāl (-ắd-)
ተበደረ tḁbḁ́ddḁrḁ (-ḁy-,-ắddä-)	borrow, t.	ተበድሯል tḁbḁ́ddi̥rŏ͡āl (-ḁy-, -ắd-)	ይበደር yi̥bbḁ́ddḁr (-ắddä-)	ይበደራል yi̥bbḁ́ddḁ-rāl (-ắddä-)
ተበጀ tḁbḁ́jjä (-ḁy-, -ắj-) 2nd -ጀህ -jjäh, etc.	be made, p.	ተበጅቷል tḁbḁ́jji̥tŏ͡āl (-ḁy-, -ắj-)	ይበጅ yi̥bbḁ́jj (-ắj-)	ይበጃል yi̥bbḁ́jjāl (-ắj-)
ተታለለ tḁtállа̥lḁ	be deceived, p.	ተታሏል tḁtállŏ͡āl	ይታለል yi̥ttállḁl (-äl)	ይታለላል yi̥ttállḁlāl
ታተመ táttа̥mḁ	be sealed, p.	ታትሟል tátti̥mŏ͡āl	ይታተም yi̥ttáttа̥m	ይታተማል yi̥ttáttа̥māl
ተተረተረ tḁtḁrḁ́ttḁrḁ (-ärḁ́ttä-)	be cracked, p.	ተተርትሯል tḁtḁ́rti̥rŏ͡āl (-tḁ́-)	ይተረተር yi̥ttḁrḁ́ttḁr (-ärḁ́ttä-)	ይተረተራል yi̥ttḁrḁ́ttḁrāl (-ärḁ́ttä-)
ተተረጐመ tḁtḁrḁ́ggwω-mḁ (-är-)	be interpreted, p.	ተተርጕሟል tḁtḁ́rgwŭ-mŏ͡āl (-ắr-)	ይተረጐም yi̥ttḁrḁ́g-gwωm (-är-)	ይተረጐማል yi̥ttḁrḁ́ggwω-māl (-är-)

Jussive (§ 27)	Imperative (§ 28)	Gerund (§ 29)	Infinitive (§ 30)	Participle (§ 31)
ይበተን yi̥bbḁ́tḁn (-ā́tä-)	pl. ተበተኑ tḁbḁ́t(t)ḁnu (-ḁy̥-,-ā́t(t)ä-)	ተበትኖ tḁbḁ́tti̥nʷo (-ḁy̥-, -ā́tt-)	መበተን mḁbbḁ́tḁn (-ā́tä-)	ተበታኝ tḁbḁ́ttā́ñ (-ḁy̥-, -ā́tt-; ññ § 6; § 8)
ይበደል yi̥bbḁ́dḁl (-ā́dä-)	ተበደል tḁbḁ́dḁl (-ḁy̥-, -ā́dä-)	ተበድሎ tḁbḁ́ddi̥lʷo (-ḁy̥-, -ā́d-)	መበደል mḁbbḁ́dḁl (-ā́dä-)	ተበዳይ tḁbḁ́ddā́i̥ (-ḁy̥-, -ā́d-; -ā́yy § 6; § 8)
ይበደር yi̥bbḁ́dḁr (-ā́dä-)	ተበደር tḁbḁ́dḁr (-ḁy̥-, -ā́dä-)	ተበድሮ tḁbḁ́ddi̥rʷo (-ḁy̥-, -ā́d-)	መበደር mḁbbḁ́dḁr (-ā́dä-)	ተበዳሪ tḁbḁddā́ri (-ḁy̥-, -äd-)
ይበጅ yi̥bbḁ́j (-ā́j ; § 8)		ተበጅቶ tḁbḁ́jji̥tʷo (-ḁy̥-, -ā́j-)	መበጀት mḁbbḁ́jät (-ā́j-)	
ይታለል yi̥ttā́lḁl (-äl)		ተታሎ tḁtā́llʷo	መታለል mḁttā́lḁl (-äl)	ተታላይ tḁtā́lā́i̥ (-ā́yy §6; §8)
ይታተም yi̥ttā́tḁm		ታትሞ tā́tti̥mʷo	መታተም mḁttā́tḁm	ታታሚ tāttā́mi
ይተርተር yi̥ttḁ́rtḁr (-ā́rtä-)	ተተርተር tḁtḁ́rtḁr (-ā́rtä-)	ተተርትሮ tḁtḁ́rti̥rʷo (-tā́-)	መተርተር mḁttḁ́rtḁr (-ā́rtä-)	ተተርታሪ tḁtḁrtā́ri (-ḁtä-)
ይተርጐም yi̥ttḁ́rgwωm (-ā́r-)		ተተርጕሞ tḁtḁ́rgwŭ́mʷo (-ā́r-)	መተርጐም mḁttḁ́rgwωm (-ā́r-)	ተተርጓሚ tḁtḁrgwā́mi (-är-)

Simp. perf. (§ 25)		Comp. perf. (§ 32)	Contingent (§ 26)	Comp. imperf. (§ 32)
ተተከለ tḁtḁ́kkḁlḁ	be planted, p.	ተተክሏል tḁtḁ́k(ĭ̥)lŏ͡āl (-tá̄-)	ይተከል yi̥ttḁ́kkḁl	ይተከላል yi̥ttḁ́kkḁlāl
ተተኰሰ tḁtḁ́kkwωsḁ (-ώkko-)	be scorched, p.	ተተኵሷል tḁtḁ́kkwŭ-sŏ͡āl (-ώk-)	ይተኰስ yi̥ttḁ́kkwωs (-ώkko-)	ይተኰሳል yi̥ttḁ́kkwω-sāl (-ώkko-)
ተተወ tḁtḁ́wḁ (-ḁ́͡uḁ)	be left, p.	ተትቷል tḁ́ti̥tŏ͡āl (tá̄-)	ይተው yi̥ttḁ́͡u	ይተዋል yi̥ttḁ́wāl (-tḁ́͡uā-)
ተቻለ tḁčá̄lḁ	be possible, i.	ተችሏል tḁ́či̥lŏ͡āl (tá̄-)	ይቻል yi̥ččá̄l	ይቻላል yi̥ččá̄lāl
ተነሣ tḁnḁ́ssā̃	rise, i.	ተነሥቷል tḁnḁ́stŏ͡āl	ይነሣ yi̥nnḁ́ssā̃	ይነሣል yi̥nnḁ́ssāl
ተንሸተተ tḁnšá̄ttḁtḁ (-ätḁ)	slide, i.	ተንሸቷል tḁnšá̄ttŏ͡āl	ይንሸተት yi̥nšá̄ttḁt (§ 7*c*; -ät)	ይንሸተታል yi̥nšá̄ttḁtāl (§ 7*c*; -ätāl)
ተንቀሳቀሰ tḁṅqḁsá̄-qqḁsḁ (§ 7*d*)	be moved, p.	ተንቀሳቅሷል tḁṅqḁsá̄q(ĭ̥)-sŏ͡āl	ይንቀሳቀስ yi̥nqḁsá̄-qqḁs (§ 7*c*; -i̥ṅq-)	ይንቀሳቀሳል yi̥nqḁsá̄-qqḁsāl (§ 7*c*; -i̥ṅq-)
ተነቀነቀ tḁnḁqḁ́-nnḁqḁ	be shaken, p.	ተነቅንቋል tḁnḁ́qni̥-qŏ͡āl	ይነቀነቅ yi̥nnḁqḁ́-nnḁq	ይነቀነቃል yi̥nnḁqḁ́-nnḁqāl
ተነቃነቀ tḁnḁqá-nnḁqḁ	be shaken, p.	ተነቃንቋል tḁnḁqá̄ṅ-qŏ͡āl	ይነቃነቅ yi̥nnḁqá-nnḁq	ይነቃነቃል yi̥nnḁqá-nnḁqāl

Jussive (§ 27)	Imperative (§ 28)	Gerund (§ 29)	Infinitive (§ 30)	Participle (§ 31)
ይተከል yi̥ttḁkḁl		ተተክሎ tḁtḁk(i̥)l^{w}o (-tắ-)	መተከል mḁttḁkḁl	ተተካይ tḁtḁkâi̥ (-ấyy § 6; § 8)
ይተኰስ yi̥ttḁkwωs (-ώko-)		ተተኰሶ tḁtḁkkwŭ-s^{w}o (-ώk-)	መተኰስ mḁttḁkwωs (-ώko-)	ተተኳሽ tḁtḁkkwấš (-ώk-; § 8)
ይተው yíttḁ͡u (§ 8)		ተትቶ tḁti̥t^{w}o (tắ-)	መተወት mḁttḁwḁt (-tḁ͡uḁ-)	
ይቻል yíččấl (§ 8)		ተችሎ tḁči̥l^{w}o (tắ-)	መቻል mḁ́ččấl (§ 8)	
ይነሣ yi̥nnḁ́sã	ተነሣ tḁnḁ́sã	ተነሥቶ tḁnḁ́st^{w}o	መነሣት mḁnnḁ́sất (§ 8)	ተነሽ tḁ́nḁ́š (-nắ-; § 8; -ሺ -ši)
ይንሻተት yi̥nšà̈tḁt (§ 7*c*; -ät)	ተንሻተት tḁnšấtḁt (-ät)	ተንሻቶ tḁnšấtt^{w}o	መንሻተት mḁnšấtḁt (§ 7*c*; -ät)	†ተንሻታች tḁnšấtấč (§ 8)
ይንቀሳቀስ yi̥nqḁsấqḁs (§ 7*c*; -i̥ṅq-)	ተንቀሳቀስ tḁṅqḁsấqḁs	ተንቀሳቅሶ tḁṅqḁsấ-q(i̥)s^{w}o	መንቀሳቀስ mḁnqḁsấ-qḁs (§ 7*c*; -ḁṅq-)	ተንቀሳቃሽ tḁṅqḁsấqấš (§ 8)
ይነቅነቅ yi̥nnḁ́qnḁq	ተነቅነቅ tḁnḁ́qnḁq	ተነቅንቆ tḁnḁ́qni̥q^{w}o	መነቅነቅ mḁnnḁ́q-nḁq	ተነቅናቂ tḁnḁqnấqi
ይነቃነቅ yi̥nnḁqấnḁq		ተነቃንቆ tḁnḁqấṅq^{w}o	መነቃነቅ mḁnnḁqấ-nḁq	

Simp. perf. (§ 25)		Comp. perf. (§ 32)	Contingent (§ 26)	Comp. imperf. (§ 32)
ተንቀጠቀጠ tḁṅqḁṭḁ́- qqḁṭḁ (§ 7*d*)	tremble, i.	ተንቀጥቅጧል tḁṅqḁ́ṭqi̥- ṭŏ͡āl	ይንቀጠቀጥ yi̥nqḁṭḁ́- qqḁṭ (§ 7*c*; -i̥ṅq-)	ይንቀጠቀጣል yi̥nqḁṭḁ́qqḁ- ṭāl (§ 7*c*; -i̥ṅq-)
ተነካ tḁnḁ́kkã	be touched, p.	ተነክቷል tḁnḁ́ktŏ͡āl (-nä́-)	ይነካ yi̥nnḁ́kkã	ይነካል yi̥nnḁ́kkāl
ተነከረ tḁnḁ́kkḁrḁ (-ä́kkä-)	be wetted, p.	ተነክሯል tḁnḁ́krŏ͡āl (-ä́k-)	ይነክር yi̥nnḁ́kkḁr (-ä́kkä-)	ይነከራል yi̥nnḁ́kkḁrāl (-ä́kkä-)
ተነከሰ tḁnḁ́kkḁsḁ	be bitten, p.	ተነክሷል tḁnḁ́ksŏ͡āl	ይነክስ yi̥nnḁ́kkḁs	ይነከሳል yi̥nnḁ́kkḁsāl
ተናከሰ tḁnā́kkḁsḁ	bite, i.	ተናክሷል tḁnā́ksŏ͡āl	ይናክስ yi̥nnā́kkḁs	ይናከሳል yi̥nnā́kkḁsāl
ተንኰሻኰሸ tḁṅkwωšá- kkwωšḁ (§ 7*d*)	rustle, i.	ተንኰሻኵሿል tḁṅkwωšā́- kwŭšŏ͡āl	ይንኰሻኰሽ yi̥nkwωšá- kkwωš (§ 7*c*; -i̥ṅk-)	ይንኰሻኰሻል yi̥nkwωšá- kkwωšāl (§ 7*c*; -i̥ṅk-)
ተንከባለለ tḁṅkḁbá- llḁlḁ (§ 7*d*; -ṿá-)	be rolled, p.	ተንከባሏል tḁṅkḁbá- llŏ͡āl (-ṿá-)	ይንከባለል yi̥nkḁbállḁl (§ 7*c*; -i̥ṅk-, -ṿá-, -äl)	ይንከባለላል yi̥nkḁbállḁ- lāl (§ 7*c*; -i̥ṅk-, -ṿá-)
ተንኳኳ tḁṅkwā́- kkwã (§ 7*d*)	creak, i.	ተንኳኵቷል tḁṅkwā́kwŭ- tŏ͡āl (-ä́kt-)	ይንኳኳ yi̥nkwā́- kkwã (§ 7*c*; -i̥ṅk-)	ይንኳኳል yi̥nkwā́- kkwāl (§ 7*c*; -i̥ṅk-)

Jussive (§ 27)	Imperative (§ 28)	Gerund (§ 29)	Infinitive (§ 30)	Participle (§ 31)
ይንቀጥቀጥ yi̥nqḁ́ṭqḁṭ (§ 7*c*; -i̥ṅq-)	ተንቀጥቀጥ tḁṅqḁ́ṭqḁṭ	ተንቀጥቅጦ tḁṅqḁ́ṭ-qi̥ṭʷo	መንቀጥቀጥ mḁnqḁ́ṭqḁṭ (§ 7*c*; -ḁṅq-)	ተንቀጥቃጭ tḁṅqḁ́ṭqā́č̣ (§ 8)
ይነካ yi̥nnḁ́kā̃ (-nā́-)		ተነክቶ tḁnḁ́ktʷo (-nā́-)	መነካት mḁnnḁ́kā́t (-nā́-; § 8)	ተነኪ tḁnḁ́ki (-nā́-)
ይነክር yi̥nnḁ́kḁr (-ā́kä-)	ተነክር tḁnḁ́kḁr (-ā́kä-)	ተነክሮ tḁnḁ́krʷo (-ā́k-)	መነክር mḁnnḁ́kḁr (-ā́kä-)	ተነካሪ tḁnḁkā́ri (-äk-)
ይነክስ yi̥nnḁ́kḁs		ተነክሶ tḁnḁ́ksʷo	መነክስ mḁnnḁ́kḁs	ተነካሽ tḁnḁ́kā́š (§ 8)
ይናክስ yi̥nnā́kḁs	ተናክስ tḁnā́kḁs	ተናክሶ tḁnā́ksʷo	መናክስ mḁnnā́kḁs	ተናካሽ tḁnā́kā́ś (§ 8)
ይንኰሻኰሽ yi̥nkwωšā́-kwωš (§ 7*c*; -i̥ṅk-)	ተንኰሻኰሽ tḁṅkwωšā́-kwωš	ተንኰሻኵሾ tḁṅkwωšā́-kwŭšʷo	መንኰሻኰሽ mḁnkwωšā́-kwωš (§ 7*c*; -ḁṅk-)	ተንኰሻኳሽ tḁṅkwωšā́-kwā́š (§ 8)
ይንከባለል yi̥nkḁbā́lḁl (§ 7*c*; -i̥ṅk-, -ỵā́-, -äl)	ተንከባለል tḁṅkḁbā́lḁl (-ỵā́-, -äl)	ተንከባሎ tḁṅkḁ-ḅállʷo (-ỵá-)	መንከባለል mḁnkḁbā́-lḁl (§ 7*c*; -ḁṅk-, -ỵā́-, -äl)	ተንከባላይ tḁṅkḁbā́lā́i̥ (-ỵā́-; -ā́yy § 6; § 8)
ይንኳኳ yi̥nkwā́kwā̃ (§ 7*c*; -i̥ṅk-)		ተንኳኵቶ tḁṅkwā́-kwŭtʷo (-ā́kt-)	መንኳኳት mḁnkwā́-kwā́t (§ 7*c*; -ḁṅk-; § 8)	

Simp. perf. (§ 25)		Comp. perf. (§ 32)	Contingent (§ 26)	Comp. imperf. (§ 32)
ተናወጠ tḁnā̃uwḁṭḁ (-wω-)	be disturbed, p.	ተናውጧል tḁnā̃uŭṭŏāl	ይናወጥ yi̥nnā̃uwḁṭ (-wω-)	ይናወጣል yi̥nnā̃uwḁ-ṭāl (-wω-)
ተነዳ tḁnḁddã	be driven, p.	ተነድቷል tḁnḁdi̥tŏāl (-nḁ́rt-, -nā̃rt- § 7*d*)	ይነዳ yi̥nnḁddã	ይነዳል yi̥nnḁddāl
ተናደደ tḁnā̃ddḁdḁ	be annoyed, i.	ተናዷል tḁnā́ddŏāl	ይናደድ yi̥nnā̃ddḁd	ይናደዳል yi̥nnā̃ddḁ-dāl
ተነደፈ tḁnḁddḁfḁ	be stung, p.	ተነድፏል tḁnḁdfŏāl	ይነደፍ yi̥nnḁddḁf	ይነደፋል yi̥nnḁddḁ-fāl
ተናደፈ tḁnáddḁfḁ	sting, i.	ተናድፏል tḁnā́dfŏāl	ይናደፍ yi̥nnáddḁf	ይናደፋል yi̥nnáddḁ-fāl
ተናገረ tḁnā̃ggḁrḁ (-är-)	speak, i.	ተናግሯል tḁnā́grŏāl	ይናገር yi̥nnā̃ggḁr (-är)	ይናገራል yi̥nnā̃ggḁ-rāl (-är-)
ተነጋገረ tḁnḁgā̃ggḁ-rḁ (-är-)	converse, i.	ተነጋግሯል tḁnḁgā́-grŏāl	ይነጋገር yi̥nnḁgā́-ggḁr (-är)	ይነጋገራል yi̥nnḁgā́ggḁ-rāl (-är-)
ተንጠለጠለ tḁnṭḁlḁ́ṭṭḁlḁ	be hung, p.	ተንጠልጥሏል tḁnṭḁ́lṭi̥lŏāl (-ṭḁ́-)	ይንጠለጠል yi̥nṭḁlḁ́ṭṭḁl (§ 7*c*; -äl)	ይንጠለጠላል yi̥nṭḁlḁ́ṭṭḁ-lāl (§ 7*c*)

Jussive (§ 27)	Imperative (§ 28)	Gerund (§ 29)	Infinitive (§ 30)	Participle (§ 31)
ይናወጥ yi̥nnā́͡uḁṭ (-ωṭ)		ተናውጦ tḁnā́͡uŭṭʷo	መናወጥ mḁnnā́͡uḁṭ (-ωṭ)	ተናዋጭ tḁnā́͡uā́č̣ (§ 8)
ይነዳ yi̥nnḁdã	ተነዳ tḁnḁdã	ተነድቶ tḁnḁdi̥tʷo (-nḁrt-, -nā́rt- § 7*d*)	መነዳት mḁnnḁdā́t (§ 8)	ተነጅ tánḁj (-nā́-; § 8; -ጂ -ji)
ይናደድ yi̥nnā́dḁd	ተናደድ tḁnā́dḁd	ተናዶ tḁnā́ddʷo	መናደድ mḁnnā́dḁd	ተናዳጅ tḁnā́dā́j (§ 8)
ይነደፍ yi̥nnḁdḁf	ተነደፍ tḁnḁdḁf	ተነድፎ tḁnḁdfʷo	መነደፍ mḁnnḁdḁf	ተነዳፊ tḁnḁdā́fi
ይናደፍ yi̥nnā́dḁf		ተናድፎ tḁnā́dfʷo	መናደፍ mḁnnā́dḁf	ተናዳፊ tḁnādā́fi
ይናገር yi̥nnā́gḁr (-är)	ተናገር tḁnā́gḁr (-är)	ተናግሮ tḁnā́grʷo	መናገር mḁnnā́gḁr (-är)	ተናጋሪ tḁnāgā́ri
ይነጋገር yi̥nnḁgā́gḁr (-är)	ተነጋገር tḁnḁgā́gḁr (-är)	ተነጋግሮ tḁnḁgā́grʷo	መነጋገር mḁnnḁgā́- gḁr (-är)	ተነጋጋሪ tḁnḁgāgā́ri
ይንጠልጠል yi̥nṭḁlṭḁl (§ 7*c*; -ā́lṭä-)	ተንጠልጠል tḁnṭḁlṭḁl (-ā́ltä-)	ተንጠልጥሎ tḁnṭḁlṭi̥lʷo (-ṭā́-)	መንጠልጠል mḁnṭḁlṭḁl (§ 7*c*; -ā́lṭä-)	ተንጠልጣይ tḁnṭḁlṭā́͡i̥ (-ṭā́-; -ā́yy § 6; § 8)

Simp. perf. (§ 25)		Comp. perf. (§ 32)	Contingent (§ 26)	Comp. imperf. (§ 32)
ተነጨ tḁnä́ç̣ç̣ä 2nd ተነጨህ tḁnä́ç̣ç̣äh, etc.	be plucked out, p.	ተነጭቷል tḁnä́ç̣tŏ͡āl	ይነጭ yi̥nnä́ç̣ç̣	ይነጫል yi̥nnä́ç̣ç̣āl
ተነፋ tḁnḁ́ffã	be inflated, p.	ተነፍቷል tḁnḁ́ftŏ͡āl (-nä́-)	ይነፋ yi̥nnḁ́ffã	ይነፋል yi̥nnḁ́ffāl
ተነፈሰ tḁnḁ́ffḁsḁ	breathe, i.	ተንፍሷል tḁ́nfi̥sŏ͡āl (tä́-, -mf-)	ይተነፍስ yi̥tḁnḁ́ffi̥s	ይተነፍሳል yi̥tḁnḁ́ffi̥sāl
ተናፈሰ tḁnä́ffḁsḁ	get fresh air, i.	ተናፍሷል tḁnä́fsŏ͡āl	ይናፈስ yi̥nnä́ffḁs	ይናፈሳል yi̥nnä́ffḁsāl
ተኛ tḁ́ññã (tä́-, -ñä)	recline, i.	ተኝቷል tḁ́ññi̥tŏ͡āl (tä́-)	ይተኛ yi̥tḁ́ññã (-tä́-, -ñä)	ይተኛል yi̥tḁ́ññāl (-tä́-)
ተከለ tḁ́kkḁlḁ	plant, t.	ተክሏል tḁ́k(ĭ̥)lŏ͡āl (tä́-)	ይተክል yi̥tḁ́k(ĭ̥)l (-tä́-)	ይተክላል yi̥tḁ́k(ĭ̥)lāl (-tä́-)
ተከለከለ tḁkḁlḁ́kkḁ- lḁ	be hindered, p.	ተከልክሏል tḁkḁ́lki̥lŏ͡āl	ይከለከል yi̥kkḁlḁ́kkḁl	ይከለከላል yi̥kkḁlḁ́kkḁ- lāl
ተከመረ tḁkḁ́mmḁrḁ (-mä-)	be piled, p.	ተከምሯል tḁkḁ́mmi̥- rŏ͡āl	ይከመር yi̥kkḁ́mmḁr (-mä-)	ይከመራል yi̥kkḁ́mmḁ- rāl (-mä-)

Jussive (§ 27)	Imperative (§ 28)	Gerund (§ 29)	Infinitive (§ 30)	Participle (§ 31)
ይነጭ yí̥nnắč̣ (§ 8)		ተነጭቶ tḁnắč̣tʷo	መነጨት mḁnnắč̣ät	ተነጭ tḁ́nắč̣ (§ 8; -ጪ -č̣i)
ይነፋ yi̥nnḁfã (-nắ-)	ተነፋ tḁnḁfã (-nắ-)	ተነፍቶ tḁnḁftʷo (-nắ-)	መነፋት mḁnnḁfắt (-nắ-; § 8)	ተነፊ tḁnḁfi (-nắ-)
ይተንፍስ yi̥tḁnfi̥s (-tắ-, -mf-)	ተንፍስ tḁ́nfi̥s (tắ-, -mf-)	ተንፍሶ tḁ́nfi̥sʷo (tắ-, -mf-)	መተንፈስ mḁtḁ́nfḁs (-tắ-, -mf-)	ተነፋሽ tḁnḁffắš (§ 8)
ይናፈስ yi̥nnắfḁs	ተናፈስ tḁnắfḁs	ተናፍሶ tḁnắfsʷo	መናፈስ mḁnnắfḁs	ተናፋሽ tḁnắfắš (§ 8)
ይተኛ yi̥tḁ́ññã (-tắ-, -ñä)	ተኛ tḁ́ññã (tắ-, -ñä)	ተኝቶ tḁ́ññi̥tʷo (tắ-)	መተኛት mḁtḁ́ññắt (-tắ-; § 8)	
ይትከል yí̥tkḁl	ትከል tí̥kḁl	ተክሎ tḁ́k(ĭ̥)lʷo (tắ-)	መትከል mḁ́tkḁl	ተካይ tḁ́kắi̯ (-ắyy § 6; § 8)
ይከልከል yi̥kkḁ́lkḁl	ተከልከል tḁkḁ́lkḁl	ተከልክሎ tḁkḁ́lki̥lʷo	መከልከል mḁkkḁ́lkḁl	ተከልካይ tḁkḁ́lkắi̯ (-ắyy § 6; § 8)
ይከመር yi̥kkḁ́mḁr (-mä-)	ተከመር tḁkḁ́mḁr (-mä-)	ተከምሮ tḁkḁ́mmi̥rʷo	መከመር mḁkkḁ́mḁr (-mä-)	ተከማሪ tḁkḁmmắri

Simp. perf. (§ 25)		Comp. perf. (§ 32)	Contingent (§ 26)	Comp. imperf. (§ 32)
ተከራከረ tḁkḁrā́kkḁrḁ (-ärā́kkä-)	dispute, i.	ተከራክሯል tḁkḁrā́kro͡āl (-ärā́-)	ይከራከር yi̥kkḁrā́kkḁr (-ärā́kkä-)	ይከራከራል yi̥kkḁrā́kkḁrāl (-ärā́kkä-)
ተከራየ tḁkḁrā́yyä (-kä-) 2nd -ራየህ -rā́yyäh, etc.	take on hire, t.	ተከራይቷል tḁkḁráyi̥to͡āl (-kä-, -á͡i̥t-)	ይከራይ yi̥kkḁrā́yy (-kä-)	ይከራያል yi̥kkḁrā́yyāl (-kä-)
ተኰሰ tḁ́kkwωsḁ (tώkkosḁ)	scorch, t.	ተኵሷል tḁ́kkwŭso͡āl (tώ-)	ይተኵስ yi̥tḁ́kkwŭs (-tώ-)	ይተኵሳል yi̥tḁ́kkwŭsāl (-tώ-)
ተከሰሰ tḁkḁ́ssḁsḁ	be accused, p.	ተከሷል tḁkḁ́sso͡āl	ይከሰስ yi̥kkḁ́ssḁs	ይከሰሳል yi̥kkḁ́ssḁsāl
ተከበረ tḁkḁ́bbḁrḁ (-bä-)	be honoured, p.	ተከብሯል tḁkḁ́bro͡āl (-ḁ́y̥-)	ይከበር yi̥kkḁ́bbḁr (-bä-)	ይከበራል yi̥kkḁ́bbḁrāl (-bä-)
ተከተለ tḁkḁ́ttḁlḁ	follow, t.	ተከትሏል tḁkḁ́tti̥lo͡āl	ይከተል yi̥kkḁ́ttḁl (-äl)	ይከተላል yi̥kkḁ́ttḁlāl
ታከከ tā́kkḁkḁ	be scratched, p.	ታኳል tā́kko͡āl	ይታከክ yi̥ttā́kkḁk	ይታከካል yi̥ttā́kkḁkāl

Jussive (§ 27)	Imperative (§ 28)	Gerund (§ 29)	Infinitive (§ 30)	Participle (§ 31)
ይከራከር y̥ikkḁrắkḁr (-ärắkä-)	**ተከራከር** tḁkḁrắkḁr (-ärắkä-)	**ተከራክሮ** tḁkḁrắkrʷo (-ärắ-)	**መከራከር** mḁkkḁrắ-kḁr (-ärắkä-)	**ተከራካሪ** tḁkḁrākắri (-ärā-)
ይከራይ y̥ikkḁráį̥ (-kä-)	**ተከራይ** tḁkḁráį̥ (-kä-)	**ተከራይቶ** tḁkḁráyi̥tʷo (-kä-, -áį̥t-)	**መከራየት** mḁkkḁrá-yät (-kä-, -áį̥ät)	
ይተኰስ y̥itḁ́kkwŭs (-tώ-)	**ተኰስ** tḁ́kkwŭs (tώ-)	**ተኵሶ** tḁ́kkwŭsʷo (tώ-)	**መተኰስ** mḁtḁ́kkwωs (-tώkkos)	**ተኳሽ** tḁ́kkwắš (tώ-; § 8)
ይከሰስ y̥ikkḁ́sḁs	**ተከሰስ** tḁkḁ́sḁs	**ተከሶ** tḁkḁ́ssʷo	**መከሰስ** mḁkkḁ́sḁs	**ተከሳሽ** tḁkḁ́sắš (§ 8)
ይከበር y̥ikkḁ́bḁr (-ḁ́ɣ-, -är)		**ተከብሮ** tḁkḁ́brʷo (-ɣr-)	**መከበር** mḁkkḁ́bḁr (-ḁ́ɣ-, -är)	**ተከባሪ** tḁkḁbắri (-ɣắ-), honoured; tḁkḁbbắri, conceited
ይከተል y̥ikkḁ́tḁl (-äl)	**ተከተል** tḁkḁ́t(t)ḁl (-äl)	**ተከትሎ** tḁkḁ́tti̥lʷo	**መከተል** mḁkkḁ́tḁl (-äl)	**ተከታይ** tḁkḁ́ttắį̥ (-ắyy § 6; § 8)
ይታከክ y̥ittắkḁk		**ታኮ** tắkkʷo	**መታከክ** mḁttắkḁk	**ታካኪ** tākắki

Simp. perf. (§ 25)		Comp. perf. (§ 32)	Contingent (§ 26)	Comp. imperf. (§ 32)
ተካከለ tḁkắkkḁlḁ	be equal, i.	ተካክሏል tḁkáklŏ͡āl	ይተካከል yi̥ttḁkắkkḁl	ይተካከላል yi̥ttḁkắkkḁ-lāl
ተከፈለ tḁkḁ́ffḁlḁ	be divided, p.	ተከፍሏል tḁkḁ́flŏ͡āl (-kắ-)	ይከፈል yi̥kkḁ́ffḁl (-äl)	ይከፈላል yi̥kkḁ́ffḁlāl
ተካፈለ tḁkáffḁlḁ	share, t.	ተካፍሏል tḁkắflŏ͡āl	ይካፈል yi̥kkáffḁl (-äl)	ይካፈላል yi̥kkáffḁlāl
ተከፈተ tḁkḁ́ffḁtḁ	be opened, p.	ተከፍቷል tḁkḁ́ftŏ͡āl	ይከፈት yi̥kkḁ́ffḁt (-ät)	ይከፈታል yi̥kkḁ́ffḁtāl
ተወ tḁ́wḁ (tḁ́͡uḁ)	leave, t.	ትቷል tí̥tŏ͡āl	ይተው yi̥tḁ́͡u	ይተዋል yi̥tḁ́wāl (-tḁ́͡uā-)
ተወለወለ tḁwḁlḁ́͡u-wḁlḁ (tḁ͡uḁ-)	be wiped, p.	ተወልውሏል tḁwḁ́lwi̥lŏ͡āl (tḁ͡uḁ́-, -lwŭl-)	ይወለወል yi̥wwḁlḁ́͡u-wḁl (yuwḁ-)	ይወለወላል yi̥wwḁlḁ́͡u-wḁlāl (yuwḁ-)
ተወለደ tḁwḁ́llḁdḁ (tḁ͡uḁ́-, -ắl-, -ώl-)	be born, i.	ተወልዷል tḁwḁ́ldŏ͡āl (tḁ͡uḁ́-, -ώl-)	ይወለድ yi̥wwḁ́llḁd (yuwḁ́-, -ắl- -ώl-)	ይወለዳል yi̥wwḁ́llḁdāl (yuwḁ́-, -ắl- -ώl-)
ተወራረደ tḁwḁrắr-rḁdḁ (tḁ͡uḁ-, -ωrắ-)	bet, i.	ተወራርዷል tḁwḁrắr-dŏ͡āl (tḁ͡uḁ-, -ωrắ-)	ይወራረድ yi̥wwḁrắr-rḁd (yuwḁ-, -ωrắ-)	ይወራረዳል yi̥wwḁrắr-rḁdāl (yuwḁ-, -ωrắ-)

Jussive (§ 27)	Imperative (§ 28)	Gerund (§ 29)	Infinitive (§ 30)	Participle (§ 31)
ይተከከል yi̥ttḁkā́kḁl	ተከከል tḁkā́kḁl	ተከክሎ tḁkā́klʷo	መተከከል mḁttḁkā́kḁl	ተከካይ tḁkā́ká͡i̥ (-ā́yy §6; §8)
ይከፈል yi̥kkḁ́fḁl (-äl)	ተከፈል tḁkḁ́fḁl (-äl)	ተከፍሎ tḁkḁ́flʷo (-kā́-)	መከፈል mḁkkḁ́fḁl (-äl)	ተከፋይ tḁkḁ́fá͡i̥ (-ā́yy § 6; §8)
ይከፈል yi̥kkā́fḁl (-äl)	ተከፈል tḁkā́fḁl (-äl)	ተከፍሎ tḁkā́flʷo	መከፈል mḁkkā́fḁl (-äl)	ተከፋይ tḁkā́fá͡i̥ (-ā́yy §6; §8)
ይከፈት yi̥kkḁ́fḁt (-ät)		ተከፍቶ tḁkḁ́ftʷo	መከፈት mḁkkḁ́fḁt (-ät)	ተከፋች tḁkḁ́ffā́č (§ 8)
ይተው yí̥tḁ́͡u (§ 8)	ተው tḁ́͡u f. ተይ tḁ́͡i̥	ትቶ tí̥tʷo	መተው mḁ́tḁ́͡u (§ 8)	ተዪ tḁ́͡i
ይወልወል yi̥wwḁ́lwḁl (yuwḁ́-)		ተወልውሎ tḁwḁ́lwi̥lʷo (tḁ͡uḁ́-, -lwŭl-)	መወልወል mḁwwḁ́lwḁl (mḁ͡uwḁ́-)	
		ተወልዶ tḁwḁ́ldʷo (tḁ͡uḁ́-, -ώl-)	መወለድ mḁwwḁ́lḁd (mḁ͡uwḁ́-, -ā́l-, -ώl-)	ተወላጅ tḁwḁ́lā́j (tḁ͡uḁ́-, -ā́l-, -ώl-; § 8)
ይወራረድ yi̥wwḁrā́rḁd (yuwḁ-, -ωrā́-)	ተወራረድ tḁwḁrā́rḁd (tḁ͡uḁ-, -ωrā́-)	ተወራርዶ tḁwḁrā́rdʷo (tḁ͡uḁ-, -ωrā́-)	መወራረድ mḁwwḁrā́rḁd (mḁ͡uwḁ-, -ωrā́-)	ተወራራጅ tḁwḁrā́rā́j (tḁ͡uḁ-, -ωrā́-; § 8)

Simp. perf. (§ 25)		Comp. perf. (§ 32)	Contingent (§ 26)	Comp. imperf. (§ 32)
ተወረወረ tḁwḁrḁ́u-wḁrḁ (tḁuḁ-)	be thrown, p.	ተወርውሯል tḁwḁ́rwŭ-rŏāl (tḁuḁ́-)	ይወረወር yi̥wwḁrḁ́u-wḁr (yuwḁ-)	ይወረወራል yi̥wwḁrḁ́u-wḁrāl (yuwḁ-)
ተዋሰ tḁwā́sḁ (tḁuā́-)	be guarantor, i.	ተውሷል tḁ́wŭsŏāl (tḁ́uŭs-)	ይዋስ yi̥wwā́s (yuwā́s)	ይዋሳል yi̥wwā́sāl (yuwā́s-)
ተወሰደ tḁwḁ́ssḁdḁ (tḁuḁ́-, -ώs-)	be removed, p.	ተወስዷል tḁwḁ́s(i̥)-dŏāl (tḁuḁ́-, -ώs-)	ይወሰድ yi̥wwḁ́ssḁd (yuwḁ́-, -ώs-)	ይወሰዳል yi̥wwḁ́ssḁ-dāl (yuwḁ́-, -ώs-)
ታወቀ táuwḁqḁ (-wω-)	be known, p.	ታውቋል táu(ŭ)qŏāl	ይታወቅ yi̥ttáuwḁq (-ωq)	ይታወቃል yi̥ttáu-wḁqāl (-wω-)
ተወቀጠ tḁwώqqḁṭḁ (tḁuώ-)	be crushed, p.	ተወቅጧል tḁwώqṭŏāl (tḁuώ-)	ይወቀጥ yi̥wwώqqḁṭ (yuwώ-)	ይወቀጣል yi̥wwώqqḁ-ṭāl (yuwώ-)
ተወዘወዘ tḁwḁzḁ́u-wḁzḁ (tḁuḁ-, -ωzḁ́uwω-)	be shaken, p.	ተወዝውዟል tḁwḁ́zwŭ-zŏāl (tḁuḁ́-, -ώz-)	ይወዘወዝ yi̥wwḁzḁ́u-wḁz (yuwḁ-, -ωzḁ́uwω-)	ይወዘወዛል yi̥wwḁzḁ́u-wḁzāl (yuwḁ-, -ωzḁ́uwω-)
ተወደደ tḁwώddḁdḁ (tḁuώ-)	be loved, p.	ተወዷል tḁwώddŏāl (tḁuώ-)	ይወደድ yi̥wwώddḁd (yuwώ-)	ይወደዳል yi̥wwώddḁ-dāl (yuwώ-)

Jussive (§ 27)	Imperative (§ 28)	Gerund (§ 29)	Infinitive (§ 30)	Participle (§ 31)
ይወርወር yi̥wwḁ́rwḁr (yuwḁ́-)		ተወርውሮ tḁwḁ́r-wŭrʷo (tḁ͡uḁ́-)	መወርወር mḁwwḁ́r-wḁr (mḁ͡uwḁ́-)	ተወርዋሪ tḁwḁrwā́ri (tḁ͡uḁ-)
ይዋስ yí̥wwā́s (yúwā́s; § 8)	ተዋስ tḁ́wā́s (tḁ́͡uā́s; § 8)	ተውሶ tḁ́wŭsʷo (tḁ́͡uŭsʷo)	መዋስ mḁ́wwā́s (mḁ́͡uwā́s; § 8)	ተዋሽ tḁ́wā́š (tḁ́͡uā́š; § 8; -ሺ -ši)
ይወሰድ yi̥wwḁ́sḁd (yuwḁ́-, -ώs-)		ተወስዶ tḁwḁ́s(i̥)dʷo (tḁ͡uḁ́-, -ώs-)	መወሰድ mḁwwḁ́sḁd (mḁ͡uwḁ́-, -ώs-)	ተወሳጅ tḁwḁ́ssā́j (tḁ͡uḁ́-, -ώs-; § 8)
ይታወቅ yi̥ttá͡uḁq (-ωq)		ታውቆ tá͡u(ŭ)qʷo	መታወቅ mḁttá͡uḁq (-ωq)	ታዋቂ tawā́qi (ta͡uā́-)
ይወቀጥ yi̥wwώqḁṭ (yuwώ-)		ተወቅጦ tḁwώqṭʷo (tḁ͡uώ-)	መወቀጥ mḁwwώqḁṭ (mḁ͡uwώ-)	ተወቃጭ tḁwώqā́č̣ (tḁ͡uώ-; § 8)
ይወዘወዝ yi̥wwḁ́zwḁz (yuwḁ́-, -ώzwω-)	ተወዘወዝ tḁwḁ́zwḁz (tḁ͡uḁ́-, -ώzwω-)	ተወዘውዞ tḁwḁ́z-wŭzʷo (tḁ͡uḁ́-, -ώz-)	መወዘወዝ mḁwwḁ́z-wḁz (mḁ͡uwḁ́-, -ώzwω-)	ተወዘዋዥ tḁwḁ́zwā́ž (tḁ͡uḁ́-, -ώz-; § 8)
ይወደድ yi̥wwώdḁd (yuwώ-)	ተወደድ tḁwώdḁd (tḁ͡uώ-)	ተወዶ tḁwώddʷo (tḁ͡uώ-)	መወደድ mḁwwώdḁd (mḁ͡uwώ-)	ተወዳጅ tḁwώd(d)ā́j (tḁ͡uώ-; § 8)

Simp. perf. (§ 25)		Comp. perf. (§ 32)	Contingent (§ 26)	Comp. imperf. (§ 32)
ተዋደዱ tḁwáddḁdu (tḁ͡uá-)	agree, i.	ተዋደዋል tḁwáddḁ͡uāl (tḁ͡uá-)	ይዋደዱ yi̥wwáddḁ-du (yuwá-)	ይዋደዳሉ yi̥wwaddḁ-dállu (yuwa-)
ተወጋ tḁwώggã (tḁ͡uώ-)	be pricked, p.	ተወግቷል tḁwώgt͡ŏāl (tḁ͡uώ-)	ይወጋ yi̥wwώggã (yuwώ-)	ይወጋል yi̥wwώggāl (yuwώ-)
ተዋጋ tḁwã́ggã (tḁ͡uã́-)	fight; butt, i.	ተዋግቷል tḁwã́gt͡ŏāl (tḁ͡uã́-)	ይዋጋ yi̥wwã́ggã (yuwã́-)	ይዋጋል yi̥wwã́ggāl (yuwã́-)
ተዘራ tḁzḁ́rrã (-äzã́-)	be sown, p.	ተዘርቷል tḁzḁ́rt͡ŏāl (-äzã́-)	ይዘራ yi̥zzḁ́rrã (-zã́-)	ይዘራል yi̥zzḁ́rrāl (-zã́-)
ተዘረፈ tḁzḁ́rrḁfḁ (-äzã́-)	be looted, p.	ተዘርፏል tḁzḁ́rf͡ŏāl (-äzã́-)	ይዘረፍ yi̥zzḁ́rrḁf (-zã́-)	ይዘረፋል yi̥zzḁ́rrḁfāl (-zã́-)
ተዘቀዘቀ tḁzḁqḁ́zzḁ-qḁ	beinclined, p.	ተዘቅዝቋል tḁzḁ́qzi̥q͡ŏāl	ይዘቀዘቅ yi̥zzḁqḁ́z-zḁq	ይዘቀዘቃል yi̥zzḁqḁ́zzḁ-qāl
ተዘወረ tḁzḁ́͡uwḁrḁ	be turned, p.	ተዘውሯል tḁzḁ́͡uŭr͡ŏāl	ይዘወር yi̥zzḁ́͡uwḁr	ይዘወራል yi̥zzḁ́͡uwḁrāl
ታዘዘ tã́zzḁzḁ	obey, t.	ታዟል tã́zz͡ŏāl	ይታዘዝ yi̥ttã́zzḁz	ይታዘዛል yi̥ttã́zzḁzāl

Jussive (§ 27)	Imperative (§ 28)	Gerund (§ 29)	Infinitive (§ 30)	Participle (§ 31)
ይዋደዱ yi̥wwā́dḁdu (yuwā́-)	**ተዋደዱ** tḁwā́dḁdu (tḁ͡uā́-)	**ተዋደው** tḁwáddа̥͡u (tḁ͡uá-)	**መዋደድ** mḁwwā́dḁd (mḁ͡uwā́-)	**ተዋዳጆች** tḁwādā́jʷōč (tḁ͡uā-; -ʷōčč § 6)
ይወጋ yi̥wwώgã (yuwώ-)		**ተወግቶ** tḁwώgtʷo (tḁ͡uώ-)	**መወጋት** mḁwwώgā́t (mḁ͡uwώ-; § 8)	**ተወጊ** tḁwḁ́gi (tḁ͡uḁ́-, -ώg-)
ይዋጋ yi̥wwā́gã (yuwā́-)	**ተዋጋ** tḁwā́gã (tḁ͡uā́-)	**ተዋግቶ** tḁwā́gtʷo (tḁ͡uā́-)	**መዋጋት** mḁwwā́gā́t (mḁ͡uwā́-; § 8)	**ተዋጊ** tḁwā́gi (tḁ͡uā́-)
ይዘራ yi̥zzḁ́rã (-zā́-)		**ተዘርቶ** tḁzḁ́rtʷo (-äzā́-)	**መዘራት** mḁzzḁ́rā́t (-zā́-; § 8)	
ይዘረፍ yi̥zzḁ́rḁf (-zā́-)		**ተዘርፎ** tḁzḁ́rfʷo (-äzā́-)	**መዘረፍ** mḁzzḁ́rḁf (-zā́-)	**ተዘራፊ** tḁzḁrā́fi (-äzä-)
ይዘቅዘቅ yi̥zzḁ́qzḁq	**ተዘቅዘቅ** tḁzḁ́qzḁq	**ተዘቅዝቆ** tḁzḁ́qzi̥qʷo	**መዘቅዘቅ** mḁzzḁ́qzḁq	**†ተዘቅዛቂ** tḁzḁqzā́qi
ይዘወር yi̥zzḁ́͡uḁr		**ተዘውሮ** tḁzḁ́͡uŭrʷo	**መዘወር** mḁzzḁ́͡uḁr	**†ተዘዋሪ** tḁzḁuwā́ri
ይታዘዝ yi̥ttā́zḁz	**ታዘዝ** tā́zḁz	**ታዞ** tā́zzʷo	**መታዘዝ** mḁttā́zḁz	**ታዛዥ** tā́zā́ž (§ 8)

Simp. perf. (§ 25)		Comp. perf. (§ 32)	Contingent (§ 26)	Comp. imperf. (§ 32)
ተዘጋ tḁzḁ́ggã	be shut, p.	ተዘግቷል tḁzḁ́gtŏ͡āl	ይዘጋ yi̥zzḁ́ggã	ይዘጋል yi̥zzḁ́ggāl
ታየ tā́yyä 2nd ታየህ tā́yyäh, etc.	be seen, p.	ታይቷል tā́͡i̥tŏ͡āl	ይታይ yi̥ttā́yy	ይታያል yi̥ttā́yyāl
ተያዘ tḁyā́zḁ (tḁ͡i̥ā́-)	be seized, p.	ተይዟል tḁ́yi̥zŏ͡āl (tḁ́͡i̥z-)	ይያዝ yi̥yyā́z	ይያዛል yi̥yyā́zāl
ተዳመጠ tḁdámmḁṭḁ	be ginned, p.	ተዳምጧል tḁdā́mṭŏ͡āl	ይዳመጥ yi̥ddámmḁṭ	ይዳመጣል yi̥ddámmḁ- ṭāl
ተደረገ tḁdḁ́rrḁgḁ	be done, p.	ተደርጓል tḁdḁ́rgŏ͡āl (-dā́-)	ይደረግ yi̥ddḁ́rrḁg	ይደረጋል yi̥ddḁ́rrḁ- gāl
ተደበለቀ tḁdḁbḁ́llḁqḁ (-ỵḁ́-)	be mixed, p. interfere, i.	ተደብልቋል tḁdḁ́bli̥qŏ͡āl (-dā́-, -ỵl-)	ይደበለቅ yi̥ddḁbḁ́l- lḁq (-dä-, -ḁỵḁ́-, -ā́ll-)	ይደበለቃል yi̥ddḁbḁ́llḁ- qāl (-dä-, -ḁỵḁ́-, -ā́ll-)
ተደባለቀ Š. tḁdḁbállḁqḁ (-ỵá-)	be mixed, p. interfere, i.	ተደባልቋል tḁdḁbā́l- qŏ͡āl (-ỵā́-)	ይደባለቅ yi̥ddḁbál- lḁq (-ỵá-)	ይደባለቃል yi̥ddḁbállḁ- qāl (-ỵá-)
ተደገፈ tḁdḁ́ggḁfḁ	lean, i. (= ተገደፈ)	ተደግፏል tḁdḁ́ggi̥fŏ͡āl (-dā́-)	ይደገፍ yi̥ddḁ́ggḁf	ይደገፋል yi̥ddḁ́ggḁ- fāl

Jussive (§ 27)	Imperative (§ 28)	Gerund (§ 29)	Infinitive (§ 30)	Participle (§ 31)
ይዘጋ yi̥zzḁ́gã		ተዘግቶ tḁzḁ́gtʷo	መዘጋት mḁzzḁ́gā̃t (§ 8)	ተዘጊ tḁzḁ́gi (-zắ-)
ይታይ yíttā̃i̥ (-ā̃yy §6; §8)	ታይ tā̃i̥ (tãyy § 6)	ታይቶ tā̃i̥tʷo	መታየት mḁttā̃i̥ät (-ā̃ʸät)	
ይያዝ yíyyā̃z (§ 8)	ተያዝ tḁ́yā̃z (tḁ́i̥ā̃z ; § 8)	ተይዞ tḁ́yi̥zʷo (tḁ́i̥zʷo)	መያዝ mḁ́yyā̃z (§ 8)	ተያዥ tḁ́yā̃ž (tḁ́ʸā̃ž ; § 8)
ይዳመጥ yi̥ddámḁṭ		ተዳምጦ tḁdámṭʷo	መዳመጥ mḁddámḁṭ	ተዳማጭ tḁdámā̃č̣ (§ 8)
ይደረግ yi̥ddḁ́rḁg (-dắ-)		ተደርጎ tḁdḁ́rgʷo (-dắ-)	መደረግ mḁddḁ́rḁg (-dắ-)	†ተደራጊ tḁdḁr(r)ā̃gi (-dä-)
ይደብለቅ yi̥ddḁ́blḁq (-dắ-, -ỵl-)	ተደብለቅ tḁdḁ́blḁq (-dắ-, -ỵl-)	ተደብልቆ tḁdḁ́bli̥qʷo (-dắ-, -ỵl-)	መደብለቅ mḁddḁ́blḁq (-dắ-, -ỵl-)	ተደብላቂ tḁdḁblā̃qi (-dä-, -ỵl-)
ይደባለቅ yi̥ddḁbálḁq (-ỵắ-)	ተደባለቅ tḁdḁbálḁq (-ỵắ-)	ተደባልቆ tḁdḁbálqʷo (-ỵắ-)	መደባለቅ mḁddḁbắ-lḁq (-ỵắ-)	ተደባላቂ tḁdḁbālā̃qi (-ḁỵā-)
ይደገፍ yi̥ddḁ́gḁf	ተደገፍ tḁdḁ́gḁf	ተደግፎ tḁdḁ́ggi̥fʷo (-dắ-)	መደገፍ mḁddḁ́gḁf	ተደጋፊ tḁdḁggā̃fi

Simp. perf. (§ 25)		Comp. perf. (§ 32)	Contingent (§ 26)	Comp. imperf. (§ 32)
ተጀመለ tḁjḁ́mmḁlḁ	be added, p.	ተጀምኋል tḁjḁ́mmi̥- lŏ͡āl	ይጀመል yi̥jjḁ́mmḁl (-äl)	ይጀመላል yi̥jjḁ́mmḁ- lāl
ተጀመረ tḁjḁ́mmḁrḁ (-mä-)	be begun, p.	ተጀምሯል tḁjḁ́mmi̥- rŏ͡āl	ይጀመር yi̥jjḁ́mmḁr (-mä-)	ይጀመራል yi̥jjḁ́mmḁ- rāl (-mä-)
ተጋ tḁ́ggā̃	persevere, p.	ተግቷል tḁ́gtŏ͡āl	ይተጋ yi̥tḁ́gā̃	ይተጋል yi̥tḁ́gāl
ታገለ tā́ggḁlḁ	struggle, i.	ታግሏል tā́glŏ͡āl	ይታገል yi̥ttā́ggḁl	ይታገላል yi̥ttā́ggḁlāl
ተገለባበጠ tḁgḁlḁbā́b- bḁṭḁ (-ỵā̃-)	be completely inverted, p.	ተገለባብጧል tḁgḁlḁbā́b- ṭŏ͡āl (-ỵā́ỵ-)	ይገለባበጥ yi̥ggḁlḁbā́b- bḁṭ (-gä-, -ỵā́-)	ይገለባበጣል yi̥ggḁlḁbā́b- bḁṭāl (-gä-, -ỵā́-)
ተገለበጠ tḁgḁlḁ́bbḁṭḁ	be inverted, p.	ተገልብጧል tḁgálbi̥ṭŏ͡āl (-lỵ-)	ይገለበጥ yi̥ggḁlḁ́bbḁṭ (-gä-)	ይገለበጣል yi̥ggḁlḁ́bbḁ- ṭāl (-gä-)
ተገራ tḁgḁ́rrā̃	be tamed, p.	ተገርቷል tḁgḁ́rtŏ͡āl (-gā́-)	ይገራ yi̥ggḁ́rrā̃	ይገራል yi̥ggḁ́rrāl
ተገረመ tḁgḁ́rrḁmḁ	be surprised, i.	ተገርሟል tḁgḁ́rmŏ͡āl (-gā́-)	ይገረም yi̥ggḁ́rrḁm	ይገረማል yi̥ggḁ́rrḁ- māl

Jussive (§ 27)	Imperative (§ 28)	Gerund (§ 29)	Infinitive (§ 30)	Participle (§ 31)
ይጀመል yi̥jjḁ́mḁl (-äl)		ተጀምሎ tḁjḁ́mmi̥l^{w}o	መጀመል mḁjjḁ́mḁl (-äl)	
ይጀመር yi̥jjḁ́mḁr (-mä-)		ተጀምሮ tḁjḁ́m- mi̥r^{w}o	መጀመር mḁjjḁ́mḁr (-är)	ተጀማሪ tḁjḁmmā́ri
ይትጋ yí̥tgã	ትጋ tí̥gã	ተግቶ tḁ́gt^{w}o	መትጋት mḁ́tgā́t (§ 8)	ተጊ tḁ́gi (tä́-)
ይታገል yi̥ttā́gḁl	ታገል tā́gḁl	ታግሎ tā́gl^{w}o	መታገል mḁttā́gḁl	ታጋይ tā́gā́i̥ (-ā́yy §6; §8)
ይገለባበጥ yi̥ggḁlḁbā́- bḁṭ (-gä-, -ỵā́ỵ-)	ተገለባበጥ tḁgḁlḁbā́bḁṭ (-ỵā́ỵ-)	ተገለባብጦ tḁgḁlḁ- bā́bṭ^{w}o (-ỵā́ỵ-)	መገለባበጥ mḁggḁlḁ- bā́bḁṭ (-ỵā́ỵ-)	ተገለባባጭ tḁgḁlḁbā́- bā́č̣ (-ỵā́ỵ-; § 8)
ይገልበጥ yi̥ggā́lbḁṭ (-lỵ-, -äṭ)		ተገልብጦ tḁgā́lbi̥ṭ^{w}o (-lỵ-)	መገልበጥ mḁggā́lbḁṭ (-lỵ-, -äṭ)	ተገልባጭ tḁgā́lbā́č̣ (-lỵ-; § 8)
ይገሩ yi̥ggḁ́rã (-gä́-)		ተገርቶ tḁgḁ́rt^{w}o (-gä́-)	መገሩት mḁggḁ́rā́t (-gä́-; § 8)	†ተገሪ tḁgḁ́ri (-gä́-)
ይገረም yi̥ggḁ́rḁm (-gä́-)		ተገርሞ tḁgḁ́rm^{w}o (-gä́-)	መገረም mḁggḁ́rḁm (-gä́-)	ተገራሚ tḁgḁrrā́mi

Simp. perf. (§ 25)		Comp. perf. (§ 32)	Contingent (§ 26)	Comp. imperf. (§ 32)
ተገረፈ tḁgḁ́rrḁfḁ (-gá̈-)	be beaten, p.	ተገርፏል tḁgḁ́rtŏ͡āl (-gá̈-)	ይገረፍ yi̥ggḁ́rrḁf (-gá̈-)	ይገረፋል yi̥ggḁ́rrḁfāl (-gá̈-)
ታገሠ tá̃ggḁsḁ	be patient, i.	ታግሿል tá̃ggi̥sŏ͡āl	ይታገሥ yi̥ttá̃ggḁs	ይታገሣል yi̥ttá̃ggḁsāl
ተገባ tḁgḁ́bbā̃	be proper, i.	ተገብቷል tḁgḁ́btŏ͡āl (-ỵt-)	ይገባ yi̥ggḁ́bbā̃	ይገባል yi̥ggḁ́bbāl
ተጋባ tḁgá̃bbā̃	be married, p.	ተጋብቷል tḁgábtŏ͡āl (-ỵt-)	ይጋባ yi̥ggá̃bbā̃	ይጋባል yi̥ggá̃bbāl
ተጐነበሰ tḁgwωnḁ́b- bḁsḁ	be bent, p.	ተጐንብሷል tḁgwώm- bi̥sŏ͡āl	ይጐነበስ yi̥ggwωnḁ́b- bḁs	ይጐነበሳል yi̥ggwωnḁ́b- bḁsāl
ተገናኘ tḁgḁná̃ññä 2nd -ኘህ -ññäh, etc.	meet, t.	ተገናኝቷል tḁgḁnáñ- tŏ͡āl	ይገናኝ yi̥ggḁná̃ññ (-ã́ñ § 6)	ይገናኛል yi̥ggḁná̃ñ- ñāl
ተገኘ tḁgḁ́ññä (-gá̈-) 2nd -ኘህ -ññäh, etc.	be found, p.	ተገኝቷል tḁgḁ́ñtŏ͡āl (-gá̈-)	ይገኝ yi̥ggḁ́ññ (-gä-; -ḁ́ñ § 6)	ይገኛል yi̥ggḁ́ññāl (-gá̈-)
ተገዛ tḁgḁ́zzā̃	be bought, p.	ተገዝቷል tḁgḁ́ztŏ͡āl	ይገዛ yi̥ggḁ́zzā̃	ይገዛል yi̥ggḁ́zzāl

Jussive (§ 27)	Imperative (§ 28)	Gerund (§ 29)	Infinitive (§ 30)	Participle (§ 31)
ይገረፍ yi̥ggḁ́rḁf (-gä́-)	ተገረፍ tḁgḁ́rḁf (-gä́-)	ተገርፎ tḁgḁ́rf^{w}o (-gä́-)	መገረፍ mḁggḁ́rḁf (-gä́-)	ተገራፊ tḁgḁrä́fi (-gä-)
ይታገሥ yi̥ttä́gḁs	ታገሥ tágḁs	ታግሦ tä́ggi̥s^{w}o	መታገሥ mḁttä́gḁs	ታጋሽ tä́ggä́š (§ 8)
		ተገብቶ tḁgḁ́bt^{w}o (-ṿt-)	መገባት mḁggḁ́bä́t (-ḁ́ṿ- ; § 8)	
ይጋባ yi̥ggábã (-ṿã)	ተጋባ tḁgábã (-ṿã)	ተጋብቶ tḁgábt^{w}o (-ṿt-)	መጋባት mḁggábä́t (-ṿä́t ; § 8)	ተጋቢ tḁgábi (-ṿi)
ይጐንበስ yi̥ggwώm- bḁs	ተጐንበስ tḁgwώmbḁs	ተጐንብሶ tḁgwώm- bi̥s^{w}o	መጐንበስ mḁggwώm- bḁs	ተጐንባሽ tḁgwώmbä́š (§ 8)
ይገናኝ yi̥ggḁ́nä́ñ (§ 8)	ተገናኝ tḁgḁ́nä́ñ (§ 8)	ተገናኝቶ tḁgḁnä́ñt^{w}o	መገናኘት mḁggḁnä́ñ- (ñ)ät	ተገናኝ tḁgḁ́nä́ñ (-ññ § 6; § 8)
ይገኝ yí̥ggḁ́ñ (-gä́- ; § 8)	ተገኝ tḁ́gḁ́ñ (-gä́- ; § 8)	ተገኝቶ tḁgḁ́ñt^{w}o (-gä́-)	መገኘት mḁggḁ́ñ(ñ)ät (-gä́-) መገኝ mḁ́ggḁ́ñ (-gä́-; -ññ § 6; § 8)	
ይገዛ yi̥ggḁ́zã	ተገዛ tḁgḁ́zã	ተገዝቶ tḁgḁ́zt^{w}o	መገዛት mḁggḁ́zä́t (§ 8)	ተገዥ tḁ́gḁ́ž (-ä́ž; § 8; -ገዢ -ži)

Simp. perf. (§ 25)		Comp. perf. (§ 32)	Contingent (§ 26)	Comp. imperf. (§ 32)
ተጓዘ tḁgwā́zḁ	set out, i.	ተጕዟል tḁ́gwŭzŏ͡āl	ይጓዝ yi̥ggwā́z	ይጓዛል yi̥ggwā́zāl
ተጎዳ tḁgwώddã	be injured, p.	ተጎድቷል tḁgwώd(i̥)-tŏ͡āl (-ώrt- § 7*d*)	ይጎዳ yi̥ggwώddã	ይጎዳል yi̥ggwώddāl
ተጋደለ tḁgā́ddḁlḁ	fight, i.	ተጋድሏል tḁgā́dlŏ͡āl	ይጋደል yi̥ggā́ddḁl	ይጋደላል yi̥ggā́ddḁ-lāl
ተገደፈ tḁgḁ́ddḁfḁ	lean, i.	ተገድፏል tḁgḁ́ddi̥fŏ͡āl (-gā́-)	ይገደፍ yi̥ggḁ́ddḁf	ይገደፋል yi̥ggḁ́ddḁ-fāl
ተጋጨ tḁgā́č̣č̣ä 2nd -ጨህ -č̣č̣äh, etc.	be knocked, p.	ተጋጭቷል tḁgā́č̣tŏ͡āl	ይጋጭ yi̥ggā́č̣č̣	ይጋጫል yi̥ggā́č̣č̣āl
ተገፋ tḁgḁ́ffã	be pushed, p.	ተገፍቷል tḁgḁ́ftŏ͡āl	ይገፋ yi̥ggḁ́ffã	ይገፋል yi̥ggḁ́ffāl
ታጣ tā́ṭṭã	be lacking, i.	ታጥቷል tā́ṭtŏ͡āl	ይታጣ yi̥ttā́ṭṭã	ይታጣል yi̥ttā́ṭṭāl
ተጣለ tḁṭā́lḁ	be thrown, p.	ተጥሏል tḁ́ṭi̥lŏ͡āl (tā́-)	ይጣል yi̥ṭṭā́l	ይጣላል yi̥ṭṭā́lāl

Jussive (§ 27)	Imperative (§ 28)	Gerund (§ 29)	Infinitive (§ 30)	Participle (§ 31)
ይጓዝ yi̥ggwā́z (§ 8)	ትጓዝ tḁ́gwā́z (§ 8)	ትጒዞ tḁ́gwŭz^{w}o	መጓዝ mḁ́ggwā́z (§ 8)	ትጓዥ tḁ́gwā́ž (§ 8; -ዢ -ži)
ይጐዳ yi̥ggwṓdã		ትጐድቶ tḁgwṓd(ĭ̥)- t^{w}o (-ṓrt- § 7*d*)	መጐዳት mḁggwṓ- dā́t (§ 8)	ትጐጅ tḁ́gwṓj (§ 8; -ጂ -ji)
ይጋደል yi̥ggā́dḁl	ትጋደል tḁgā́dḁl	ትጋድሎ tḁgā́dl^{w}o	መጋደል mḁggā́dḁl	ትጋዳይ tḁgā́dā́i̥ (-ā́yy § 6; § 8)
ይገደፍ yi̥ggḁ́dḁf	ትገደፍ tḁgḁ́dḁf	ትገድፎ tḁgḁ́ddi̥f^{w}o (-gā́-)	መገደፍ mḁggḁ́dḁf	ትገዳፊ tḁgḁddā́fi
ይጋጭ yi̥ggā́č̣ (§ 8)	ትጋጭ tḁ́gā́č̣ (§ 8)	ትጋጭቶ tḁgā́č̣t^{w}o	መጋጨት mḁggā́č̣ät	ትጋጭ tḁ́gā́č̣ (§ 8) [ትጋጪ] (tḁgā́č̣i)
ይገፋ yi̥ggḁ́fã	ትገፋ tḁgḁ́fã	ትገፍቶ tḁgḁ́ft^{w}o	መገፋት mḁggḁ́fā́t (§ 8)	ትገፊ tḁgḁ́fi (-gā́-)
		ታጥቶ tā́ṭt^{w}o	መታጣት mḁttā́ṭā́t (§ 8)	
ይጣል yí̥ṭṭā́l (§ 8)		ትጥሎ tḁ́ṭi̥l^{w}o (tā́-)	መጣል mḁ́ṭṭā́l (§ 8)	ትጣይ tḁ́ṭā́i̥ (-ā́yy § 6; § 8)

Simp. perf. (§ 25)		Comp. perf. (§ 32)	Contingent (§ 26)	Comp. imperf. (§ 32)
ተጣላ tḁṭā́llā̃	quarrel, i.	ተጣልቷል tḁṭā́ltŏ͡āl	ይጣላ yi̥ṭṭā́llā̃	ይጣላል yi̥ṭṭā́llāl
ተጠመቀ tḁṭḁ́mmḁqḁ	be wrung; be baptized, p.	ተጠምቋል tḁṭḁ́mqŏ͡āl	ይጠመቅ yi̥ṭṭḁ́mmḁq	ይጠመቃል yi̥ṭṭḁ́mmḁ-qāl
ተጠመዘዘ tḁṭḁmḁ́zzḁ-zḁ	be twisted, p.	ተጠምዝዟል tḁṭḁ́mzi̥zŏ͡āl	ይጠመዝዝ yi̥ṭṭḁmḁ́zzḁz	ይጠመዘዛል yi̥ṭṭḁmḁ́zzḁ-zāl
ተጠመደ tḁṭḁ́mmḁdḁ	be yoked, p.	ተጠምዷል tḁṭḁ́mdŏ͡āl	ይጠመድ yi̥ṭṭḁ́mmḁd	ይጠመዳል yi̥ṭṭḁ́mmḁ-dāl
ተጠመጠመ tḁṭḁmḁ́ṭṭḁ-mḁ	be wound, p.	ተጠምጥሟል tḁṭḁ́mṭi̥-mŏ͡āl	ይጠመጠም yi̥ṭṭḁmḁ́ṭ-ṭḁm	ይጠመጠማል yi̥ṭṭḁmḁ́ṭṭḁ-māl
ተጠራ tḁṭḁ́rrā̃	be called, p.	ተጠርቷል tḁṭḁ́rtŏ͡āl (-ṭā́-)	ይጠራ yi̥ṭṭḁ́rrā̃	ይጠራል yi̥ṭṭḁ́rrāl
ተጣራ tḁṭā́rrā̃	summon, t.	ተጣርቷል tḁṭā́rtŏ͡āl	ይጣራ yi̥ṭṭā́rrā̃	ይጣራል yi̥ṭṭā́rrāl
ተጠረገ tḁṭḁ́rrḁgḁ	be cleaned, p.	ተጠርጓል tḁṭḁ́rgŏ͡āl (-ā́r-)	ይጠረግ yi̥ṭṭḁ́rrḁg	ይጠረጋል yi̥ṭṭḁ́rrḁgāl
ተጠረጠረ tḁṭḁrḁ́ṭṭḁrḁ (-ärḁ́ṭṭä-)	be doubted, p.	ተጠርጥሯል tḁṭḁ́rṭi̥rŏ͡āl (-ḁṭā́-)	ይጠረጠር yi̥ṭṭḁrḁ́ṭṭḁr (-ärḁ́ṭṭä-)	ይጠረጠራል yi̥ṭṭḁrḁ́ṭṭḁrāl (-ärḁ́ṭṭä-)

Jussive (§ 27)	Imperative (§ 28)	Gerund (§ 29)	Infinitive (§ 30)	Participle (§ 31)
ይጣላ yi̥ṭṭálã	ተጣላ tḁṭálã	ተጣልቶ tḁṭáltʷo	መጣላት mḁṭṭálất (§ 8)	ተጣይ tḁ́ṭḁ́i̥ (-ấyy §6; §8)
ይጠመቅ yi̥ṭṭḁ́mḁq	ተጠመቅ tḁṭḁ́mḁq	ተጠምቆ tḁṭḁ́mqʷo	መጠመቅ mḁṭṭḁ́mḁq	ተጠማቂ tḁṭḁmmấqi
ይጠምዘዝ yi̥ṭṭḁ́mzḁz		ተጠምዝዞ tḁṭḁ́mzi̥zʷo	መጠምዘዝ mḁṭṭḁ́mzḁz	ተጠምዛዥ tḁṭḁ́mzấž (§ 8)
ይጠመድ yi̥ṭṭḁ́mḁd		ተጠምዶ tḁṭḁ́mdʷo	መጠመድ mḁṭṭḁ́mḁd	ተጠማጅ tḁṭḁ́mmấj (§ 8)
ይጠምጠም yi̥ṭṭḁ́mṭḁm	ተጠምጠም tḁṭḁ́mṭḁm	ተጠምጥሞ tḁṭḁ́mṭi̥mʷo	መጠምጠም mḁṭṭḁ́mṭḁm	ተጠምጣሚ tḁṭḁmṭấmi
ይጠራ yi̥ṭṭḁ́rã (-ṭấ-)		ተጠርቶ tḁṭḁ́rtʷo (-ṭấ-)	መጠራት mḁṭṭḁ́rất (-ṭấ-; § 8)	†ተጠሪ tḁṭḁ́ri (-ṭấ-)
ይጣራ yi̥ṭṭấrã		ተጣርቶ tḁṭấrtʷo	መጣራት mḁṭṭấrất (§ 8)	ተጣሪ tḁṭấri
ይጠረግ yi̥ṭṭḁ́rḁg (-ấr-)		ተጠርጎ tḁṭḁ́rgʷo (-ấr-)	መጠረግ mḁṭṭḁ́rḁg (-ấr-)	
ይጠርጠር yi̥ṭṭḁ́rṭḁr (-ấrṭä-)		ተጠርጥሮ tḁṭḁ́rṭi̥rʷo (-ḁṭấ-)	መጠርጠር mḁṭṭḁ́rṭḁr (-ấrṭä-)	ተጠርጣሪ tḁṭḁrṭấri (-ḁṭä-)

Simp. perf. (§ 25)		Comp. perf. (§ 32)	Contingent (§ 26)	Comp. imperf. (§ 32)
ተጠቀለለ tḁṭḁqḁ́llḁlḁ	be rolled up, p.	ተጠቅልሏል tḁṭḁ́qli̥lŏ͡āl (-ṭắ-) ተጠቅሏል tḁṭḁ́qi̥llŏ͡āl (-ṭắ-)	ይጠቀለል yi̥ṭṭḁqḁ́llḁl (-äl)	ይጠቀለላል yi̥ṭṭḁqḁ́llḁ- lāl
ተጠቃቀሙ tḁṭḁqắq- qḁmu	agree together, i.	ተጠቃቅመዋል tḁṭḁqắq(ĭ̥)- mḁ͡uāl	ይጠቃቀሙ yi̥ṭṭḁqắq- qḁmu	ይጠቃቀማሉ yi̥ṭṭḁqāqqḁ- mállu
ታጠበ tắṭṭḁbḁ (-ỵḁ)	be washed, p.	ታጥቧል tắṭ(ĭ̥)bŏ͡āl (-ỵŏ-)	ይታጠብ yi̥ttắṭṭḁb (-ḁỵ)	ይታጠባል yi̥ttắṭṭḁbāl (-ḁỵ-)
ተጠበሰ tḁṭḁ́bbḁsḁ	be toasted, p.	ተጠብሷል tḁṭḁ́bsŏ͡āl (-ỵs-)	ይጠበስ yi̥ṭṭḁ́bbḁs	ይጠበሳል yi̥ṭṭḁ́bbḁsāl
ተጠበቀ tḁṭḁ́bbḁqḁ	be guarded, p.	ተጠብቋል tḁṭḁ́bbi̥qŏ͡āl	ይጠበቅ yi̥ṭṭḁ́bbḁq	ይጠበቃል yi̥ṭṭḁ́bbḁqāl
ተጣበቀ tḁṭábbḁqḁ	be squeezed, p.	ተጣብቋል tḁṭắbqŏ͡āl (-ỵq-)	ይጣበቅ yi̥ṭṭábbḁq	ይጣበቃል yi̥ṭṭábbḁqāl
ተጠበበ tḁṭḁ́bbḁbḁ (-ỵḁ)	be wise; be in difficulty, i.	ተጠቧል tḁṭḁ́bbŏ͡āl	ይጠበብ yi̥ṭṭḁ́bbḁb (-ḁỵ)	ይጠበባል yi̥ṭṭḁ́bbḁbāl (-ḁỵāl)
ታጠነ tắṭṭḁnḁ	be perfumed, p.	ታጥኗል tắṭ(ĭ̥)nŏ͡āl	ይታጠን yi̥ttắṭṭḁn	ይታጠናል yi̥ttắṭṭḁnāl

Jussive (§ 27)	Imperative (§ 28)	Gerund (§ 29)	Infinitive (§ 30)	Participle (§ 31)
ይጠቅለል yi̥ṭṭḁ́qlḁl (-ắqlä-)	ተጠቅለል tḁṭḁ́qlḁl (-ắqlä-)	ተጠቅልሎ tḁṭḁ́qli̥lʷo (-ṭắ-) ተጠቅሎ tḁṭḁ́qi̥llʷo (-ṭắ-)	መጠቅለል mḁṭṭḁ́qlḁl (-ắqlä-)	ተጠቅላይ tḁṭḁ́qlắi̥ (-ṭắ-; -ắyy § 6; § 8)
ይጠቃቀሙ yi̥ṭṭḁqắqḁ-mu	ተጠቃቀሙ tḁṭḁqắqḁ-mu	ተጠቃቅመው tḁṭḁqắq(i̥)-mḁu	መጠቃቀም mḁṭṭḁqắ-qḁm	ተጠቃቃሚዎች tḁṭḁqāqắ-mʷōč (-čč § 6)
ይታጠብ yi̥ttắṭḁb (-ḁỵ)	ታጠብ tắṭḁb (-ḁỵ)	ታጥቦ tắṭ(i̥)bʷo (-ỵʷo)	መታጠብ mḁttắṭḁb (-ḁỵ)	ታጣቢ tāṭábi (-ỵi)
ይጠበስ yi̥ṭṭḁ́bḁs (-ỵḁs)		ተጠብሶ tḁṭḁ́bsʷo (-ỵs-)	መጠበስ mḁṭṭḁ́bḁs (-ỵḁs)	ተጠባሽ tḁṭḁ́báš (-ḁ́ỵ-; § 8)
ይጠበቅ yi̥ṭṭḁ́bḁq (-ḁ́ỵḁ-)	ተጠበቅ tḁṭḁ́bḁq (-ḁ́ỵḁ-)	ተጠብቆ tḁṭḁ́bbi̥qʷo	መጠበቅ mḁṭṭḁ́bḁq (-ḁ́ỵḁ-)	ተጠባቂ tḁṭḁbbắqi
ይጣበቅ yi̥ṭṭắbḁq (-ỵḁq)		ተጣብቆ tḁṭắbqʷo (-ỵq-)	መጣበቅ mḁṭṭắbḁq (-ỵḁq)	ተጣባቂ tḁṭābắqi (-ỵắ-)
ይጠበብ yi̥ṭṭḁ́bḁb (-ỵḁỵ)	ተጠበብ tḁṭḁ́bḁb (-ỵḁỵ)	ተጠቦ tḁṭḁ́bbʷo	መጠበብ mḁṭṭḁ́bḁb (-ỵḁỵ)	ተጠባቢ tḁṭḁbbábi (-ỵi)
ይታጠን yi̥ttắṭḁn	ታጠን tắṭḁn	ታጥኖ tắṭ(i̥)nʷo	መታጠን mḁttắṭḁn	ታጣኝ tắṭáñ (-ññ § 6; § 8)

Simp. perf. (§ 25)		Comp. perf. (§ 32)	Contingent (§ 26)	Comp. imperf. (§ 32)
ተጠነቀቀ tḁṭḁnḁ́q-qḁqḁ	beware, i.	ተጠንቅቋል tḁṭḁ́ṅqi̥q͡ŏāl	ይጠነቀቅ yi̥ṭṭḁnḁ́q-qḁq	ይጠነቀቃል yi̥ṭṭḁnḁ́q-qḁqāl
ተጠየቀ tḁṭḁ́yyḁqḁ (-äq-)	be asked, p.	ተጠይቋል tḁṭḁ́yyi̥q͡ŏāl	ይጠየቅ yi̥ṭṭḁ́yyḁq (-äq)	ይጠየቃል yi̥ṭṭḁ́yyḁqāl (-äq-)
ተጠጋ tḁṭḁ́ggā̃	lean, i.	ተጠግቷል tḁṭḁ́ggi̥t͡ŏāl	ይጠጋ yi̥ṭṭḁ́ggā̃	ይጠጋል yi̥ṭṭḁ́ggāl
ተጠጣ tḁṭḁ́ṭṭā̃	be drunk, p.	ተጠጥቷል tḁṭḁ́ṭṭi̥t͡ŏāl	ይጠጣ yi̥ṭṭḁ́ṭṭā̃	ይጠጣል yi̥ṭṭḁ́ṭṭāl
ተጣፈ tḁṭáfḁ (-ጸ- -ṣá-)	be written, p.	ተጥፏል tḁ́ṭi̥f͡ŏāl (tá-, -ጽ- -ṣi̥-)	ይጣፍ yi̥ṭṭáf (-ጸ- -ṣṣá-)	ይጣፋል yi̥ṭṭáfāl (-ጸ- -ṣṣá-)
ታጠፈ táṭṭḁfḁ	be folded, p.	ታጥፏል táṭf͡ŏāl	ይታጠፍ yi̥ttáṭṭḁf	ይታጠፋል yi̥ttáṭṭḁfāl
ተጨመረ tḁč̣ḁ́mmḁrḁ (-mä-)	be increased, p.	ተጨምሯል tḁč̣ḁ́mmi̥-r͡ŏāl	ይጨመር yi̥č̣č̣ḁ́mmḁr (-mä-)	ይጨመራል yi̥č̣č̣ḁ́mmḁ-rāl (-mä-)
ተጨረሰ tḁč̣ḁ́rrḁsḁ (-äč̣árrä-)	be finished, p.	ተጨርሷል tḁč̣ḁ́rri̥s͡ŏāl (-äč̣ä-)	ይጨረስ yi̥č̣č̣ḁ́rrḁs (-árrä-)	ይጨረሳል yi̥č̣č̣ḁ́rrḁsāl (-árrä-)
ተጨቈነ tḁč̣ḁ́qqwωnḁ (-č̣ώqqon-)	be pressed, p.	ተጨቍኗል tḁč̣ḁ́qqwŭ-n͡ŏāl (-č̣ώ-)	ይጨቈን yi̥č̣č̣ḁ́qqwωn (-ώqqo-)	ይጨቈናል yi̥č̣č̣ḁ́qqwω-nāl (-ώqqo-)

Jussive (§ 27)	Imperative (§ 28)	Gerund (§ 29)	Infinitive (§ 30)	Participle (§ 31)
ይጠንቀቅ yi̥ṭṭḁ́ṅqḁq	ተጠንቀቅ tḁṭḁ́ṅqḁq	ተጠንቅቆ tḁṭḁ́ṅqi̥q^{w}o	መጠንቀቅ mḁṭṭḁ́ṅqḁq	ተጠንቃቂ tḁṭḁṅqā́qi
ይጠየቅ yi̥ṭṭḁ́yḁq (-ḁ́͡i̥-, -äq)		ተጠይቆ tḁṭḁ́yyi̥q^{w}o	መጠየቅ mḁṭṭḁ́yḁq (-ḁ́͡i̥-, -äq)	ተጠያቂ tḁṭḁyyā́qi
ይጠጋ yi̥ṭṭḁ́gã	ተጠጋ tḁṭḁ́gã	ተጠግቶ tḁṭḁ́ggi̥t^{w}o	መጠጋት mḁṭṭḁ́gā́t (§ 8)	ተጠጊ tḁṭḁ́ggi
ይጠጣ yi̥ṭṭḁ́ṭã		ተጠጥቶ tḁṭáṭṭi̥t^{w}o	መጠጣት mḁṭṭḁ́ṭā́t (§ 8)	ተጠጭ tḁ́ṭḁ́č̣č̣ (-ā́č̣č̣; § 8; -ጪ -č̣č̣i)
ይጣፍ yíṭṭā́f (-ጻ- -ṣṣā́-; § 8)		ተጥፎ tḁ́ṭi̥f^{w}o (tā́-, -ጽ- -ṣi̥-)	መጣፍ mḁ́ṭṭā́f (-ጻ- -ṣṣā́-; § 8)	†ተጣፊ tḁṭā́fi
ይታጠፍ yi̥ttā́ṭḁf		ታጥፎ tā́ṭf^{w}o	መታጠፍ mḁttā́ṭḁf	ታጣፊ tāṭā́fi
ይጨመር yi̥č̣č̣ḁ́mḁr (-mä-)	ተጨመር tḁč̣ḁ́mḁr (-mä-)	ተጨምሮ tḁč̣ḁ́mmi̥r^{w}o	መጨመር mḁč̣č̣ḁ́mḁr (-är)	ተጨማሪ tḁč̣ḁmmā́ri
ይጨረስ yi̥č̣č̣ḁ́rḁs (-ā́rä-)		ተጨርሶ tḁč̣ḁ́rri̥s^{w}o (-äč̣ā́-)	መጨረስ mḁč̣č̣ḁ́rḁs (-ā́rä-)	ተጨራሽ tḁč̣ḁ́rrā́š (-äč̣ā́-; § 8)
ይጨቁን yi̥č̣č̣ḁ́qwωn (-ώqo-)		ተጨቍኖ tḁč̣ḁ́qqwŭn^{w}o (-č̣ώ-)	መጨቁን mḁč̣č̣ḁ́qwωn (-ώqo-)	ተጨቋኝ tḁč̣ḁ́qqwā́ñ (-č̣ώ-; -ññ § 6; § 8)

Simp. perf. (§ 25)		Comp. perf. (§ 32)	Contingent (§ 26)	Comp. imperf. (§ 32)
ተጫነ tḁč̣ā́nḁ	be saddled, p.	ተጭኗል tḁ́č̣i̥nŏ͡āl (tá-)	ይጫን yi̥č̣č̣ā́n	ይጫናል yi̥č̣č̣ā́nāl
ተጫወተ tḁč̣ā́͡uwḁtḁ (-ωt-)	play, i.	ተጫውቷል tḁč̣ā́͡uŭtŏ͡āl (-ā́͡ut-)	ይጫወት yi̥č̣č̣ā́͡uwḁt (-ωt)	ይጫወታል yi̥č̣č̣ā́͡uwḁtāl (-ωt-)
ተፈለገ tḁfḁ́llḁgḁ	be sought, p.	ተፈልጓል tḁfḁ́lli̥gŏ͡āl	ይፈለግ yi̥ffḁ́llḁg	ይፈለጋል yi̥ffḁ́llḁgāl
ተፈረደ tḁfḁ́rrḁdḁ	be decided, p.	ተፈርዷል tḁfḁ́rdŏ͡āl (-fá-)	ይፈረድ yi̥ffḁ́rrḁd	ይፈረዳል yi̥ffḁ́rrḁdāl
ተፋቀ tḁfā́qḁ	be scraped, p.	ተፍቋል tḁ́f(i̥)qŏ͡āl (tá-)	ይፋቅ yi̥ffā́q	ይፋቃል yi̥ffā́qāl
ተፈታ tḁfḁ́ttā̃	be untied, p.	ተፈትቷል tḁfḁ́t(ĭ̥)tŏ͡āl	ይፈታ yi̥ffḁ́ttā̃	ይፈታል yi̥ffḁ́ttāl
ተፈተነ tḁfḁ́ttḁnḁ (-ắttä-)	be tested, p.	ተፈትኗል tḁfḁ́tti̥nŏ͡āl (-fá-)	ይፈተን yi̥ffḁ́ttḁn (-ắttä-)	ይፈተናል yi̥ffḁ́ttḁnāl (-ắttä-)
ተፈወሰ tḁfḁ́͡uwḁsḁ	be cured, p.	ተፈውሷል tḁfḁ́͡uwŭ-sŏ͡āl	ይፈወስ yi̥ffḁ́͡uwḁs	ይፈወሳል yi̥ffḁ́͡uwḁsāl
ተፈገፈገ tḁfḁgḁ́ffḁgḁ	be rubbed, p.	ተፈግፍጓል tḁfḁ́gfi̥gŏ͡āl	ይፈገፈግ yi̥ffḁgḁ́ffḁg	ይፈገፈጋል yi̥ffḁgḁ́ffḁgāl

Jussive (§ 27)	Imperative (§ 28)	Gerund (§ 29)	Infinitive (§ 30)	Participle (§ 31)
ይጫን yi̥č̣č̣ä́n (§ 8)		ተጭኖ tḁ́č̣i̥n^{w}o (tä́-)	መጫን mḁ́č̣č̣ä́n (§ 8)	ተጫኝ tḁ́č̣ä́ñ (tä́-; -ä́ññ § 6; § 8)
ይጫወት yi̥č̣č̣á͡uḁt (-ωt)	ተጫወት tḁč̣á͡uḁt (-ωt)	ተጫውቶ tḁč̣á͡uŭt^{w}o (-á͡ut-)	መጫወት mḁč̣č̣á͡uḁt (-ωt)	ተጫዋች tḁč̣á͡uä́č (§ 8)
ይፈለግ yi̥ffḁ́lḁg		ተፈልጎ tḁfḁ́lli̥g^{w}o	መፈለግ mḁffḁ́lḁg	ተፈላጊ tḁfḁllä́gi
ይፈረድ yi̥ffḁ́rḁd (-fä́-)		ተፈርዶ tḁfḁ́rd^{w}o (-fä́-)	መፈረድ mḁffḁ́rḁd (-fä́-)	ተፈራጅ tḁfḁ́rä́j (-fä́-; § 8)
ይፋቅ yí̥ffä́q (§ 8)		ተፍቆ tḁ́f(i̥)q^{w}o (tä́-)	መፋቅ mḁ́ffä́q (§ 8)	ተፋቂ tḁfä́qi
ይፈታ yi̥ffḁ́tä̃		ተፈትቶ tḁfḁ́t(ĭ̥)t^{w}o	መፈታት mḁffḁ́tä́t (§ 8)	ተፈች tḁ́fḁ́č (-fä́-; § 8; -ቺ -či)
ይፈተን yi̥ffḁ́tḁn (-ä́tä-)	ተፈተን tḁfḁ́tḁn (-ä́tä-)	ተፈትኖ tḁfḁ́tti̥n^{w}o (-fä́-)	መፈተን mḁffḁ́tḁn (-ä́tä-)	ተፈታኝ tḁfḁ́ttä́ñ (-fä́-; -ä́ññ § 6; § 8)
ይፈወስ yi̥ffḁ́͡uḁs		ተፈውሶ tḁfḁ́͡uwŭs^{w}o	መፈወስ mḁffḁ́͡uḁs	ተፈዋሽ tḁfḁ́͡uwä́š (§ 8)
ይፈግፈግ yi̥ffḁ́gfḁg		ተፈግፍጎ tḁfḁ́gfi̥g^{w}o	መፈግፈግ mḁffḁ́gfḁg	

Simp. perf. (§ 25)		Comp. perf. (§ 32)	Contingent (§ 26)	Comp. imperf. (§ 32)
ተፈጀ tḁfḁ́jjä (-fá-) 2nd -ጀህ -jjäh, etc.	be destroyed, p.	ተፈጅቷል tḁfḁ́j(i̥)tŏ͡āl (-fá-)	ይፈጅ yi̥ffḁ́jj (-fá-)	ይፈጃል yi̥ffḁ́jjāl (-fá-)
ተፈጨ tḁfḁ́č̣č̣ä (-fá-)	be ground, p.	ተፈጭቷል tḁfḁ́č̣tŏ͡āl (-fá-)	ይፈጭ yi̥ffḁ́č̣č̣ (-fá-)	ይፈጫል yi̥ffḁ́č̣č̣āl (-fá-)
ቻለ čálḁ	hold, t.	ችሏል či̥lŏ͡āl	ይችል yi̥či̥l	ይችላል yi̥či̥lāl
ቸኰለ čḁ́kkwωlḁ (čώkkolḁ)	hasten, i.	ቸኵሏል čḁ́kkwŭlŏ͡āl (čώ-)	ይቸኵል yi̥čḁ́kkwŭl (-čώ-)	ይቸኵላል yi̥čḁ́kkwŭlāl (-čώ-)
ቸገረው čággḁrḁ͡u (-gä-; §43*a*)	be at a loss, i.	ቸግሮታል čággi̥rʷotāl	ይቸግረው yi̥čággi̥rḁ͡u	ይቸግረዋል yi̥čággi̥rḁ͡uāl
ኖረ nʷṓrḁ	stay, i.	ኑሯል nū́rŏ͡āl ኖሯል Š. nʷṓrŏ͡āl	ይኖር yi̥nʷṓr	ይኖራል yi̥nʷṓrāl
ነሣ nḁ́ssã	take, t.	ነሥቷል nḁ́stŏ͡āl	ይነሣ yi̥nḁ́sã	ይነሣል yi̥nḁ́sāl
ነሰረው nḁ́ssḁrḁ͡u (-sä-; § 43*a*)	bleed at the nose, i.	ነስሮታል nḁ́srʷotāl	ይነስረው yi̥nḁ́srḁ͡u	ይነስረዋል yi̥nḁ́srḁ͡uāl

Jussive (§ 27)	Imperative (§ 28)	Gerund (§ 29)	Infinitive (§ 30)	Participle (§ 31)
ይፈጅ yi̥ffḁ́j (-fä́-; § 8)		ተፈጅቶ tḁfḁ́j(i̥)t^{w}o (-fä́-)	መፈጀት mḁffḁ́jät (-fä́-)	ተፈጅ tḁ́fḁ́j (-fä́-; § 8; -ጂ -ji)
ይፈጭ yi̥ffḁ́č̣ (-fä́-; § 8)		ተፈጭቶ tḁfḁ́č̣t^{w}o (-fä́-)	መፈጨት mḁffḁ́č̣ät (-fä́-)	ተፈጭ tḁ́fḁ́č̣ (-fä́-; § 8; -ጪ -č̣i)
ይቻል yi̥čā́l (§ 8)	ቻል čāl	ችሎ či̥l^{w}o	መቻል mḁ́čā́l (§ 8)	ቻይ čā́i̥ (čāyy § 6)
ይቸኰል yi̥čḁ́kkwŭl (-čώ-)	ቸኰል čḁ́kkwŭl (čώ-)	ቸኰሎ čḁ́kkwŭl^{w}o (čώ-)	መቸኰል mḁčḁ́kkwωl (-čώkkol)	ቸኳይ čḁ́kkwā́i̥ (čώ-; -ā́yy § 6; § 8)
		ቸግሮት čä́ggi̥r^{w}ōt	መቸገር mḁčä́ggḁr (-är)	ቸጋሪ čäggā́ri
ይኑር yi̥nūr	ኑር nūr	ኑሮ nū́r^{w}o ኖሮ Š. n^{w}ṓr^{w}o	መኖር mḁ́n^{w}ṓr (§ 8)	ኗሪ nwā́ri
ይንሣ yi̥nsā̃	ንሣ ni̥sā̃	ነሥቶ nḁ́st^{w}o	መንሣት mḁ́nsā́t (§ 8)	ነሽ nḁš (nä-, -ሺ -ši)
ይንሰረው yi̥nsḁrḁu (-sä-)		ነስሮት nḁ́sr^{w}ōt	መንሰር mḁ́nsḁr (-sä-)	

Simp. perf. (§ 25)		Comp. perf. (§ 32)	Contingent (§ 26)	Comp. imperf. (§ 32)
ነቃ nḁ́qqã	wake, i. split, i.	ነቅቷል nḁ́qtŏ͡āl	ይነቃ yi̥nḁ́qã	ይነቃል yi̥nḁ́qāl
ነቀለ nḁ́qqḁlḁ	uproot, t.	ነቅሏል nḁ́qlŏ͡āl	ይነቅል yi̥nḁ́q(ĭ̥)l	ይነቅላል yi̥nḁ́q(ĭ̥)lāl
ነቀሰ nḁ́qqḁsḁ	comb, t.	ነቅሷል nḁ́qsŏ͡āl	ይነቅስ yi̥nḁ́q(ĭ̥)s	ይነቅሳል yi̥nḁ́q(ĭ̥)sāl
ነቀነቀ nḁqḁ́nnḁqḁ	shake, t.	ነቅንቋል nḁ́qni̥qŏ͡āl (nä́-)	ይነቀንቅ yi̥nḁqḁ́nni̥q	ይነቀንቃል yi̥nḁqḁ́n- ni̥qāl
ነበረ nḁ́bbḁrḁ (-bä-, -በር -bbḁr, -är)	be, i. (§ 33)			
ነካ nḁ́kkã	touch, t.	ነክቷል nḁ́ktŏ͡āl (nä́-)	ይነካ yi̥nḁ́kã (-nä́-)	ይነካል yi̥nḁ́kāl (-nä́-)
ነከረ nḁ́kkḁrḁ (-ä́kkä-)	wet, t.	ነክሯል nḁ́krŏ͡āl (-ä́k-)	ይነክር yi̥nḁ́k(ĭ̥)r (-ä́k-)	ይነክራል yi̥nḁ́k(ĭ̥)rāl (-ä́k-)
ነከሰ nḁ́kkḁsḁ	bite, t.	ነክሷል nḁ́ksŏ͡āl	ይነክስ yi̥nḁ́k(ĭ̥)s	ይነክሳል yi̥nḁ́k(ĭ̥)sāl
ነዳ nḁ́ddã	drive, t.	ነድቷል nḁ́dĭ̥tŏ͡āl (nḁ́rt-, nä́rt- § 7*d*)	ይነዳ yi̥nḁ́dã	ይነዳል yi̥nḁ́dāl

Jussive (§ 27)	Imperative (§ 28)	Gerund (§ 29)	Infinitive (§ 30)	Participle (§ 31)
ይንቃ yı̥́ṅqã̄	**ንቃ** nı̥́qã̄	**ነቅቶ** nḁ́qt^{w}o	**መንቃት** mḁ́ṅqā́t (§ 8)	**ነቂ** nḁ́qi
ይንቀል yı̥́ṅqḁl	**ንቀል** nı̥́qḁl	**ነቅሎ** nḁ́ql^{w}o	**መንቀል** mḁ́ṅqḁl	**ነቃይ** nḁ́qā́i̥ (-ā́yy § 6; § 8)
ይንቀስ yı̥́nqḁs (-ṅq-)	**ንቀስ** nı̥́qḁs	**ነቅሶ** nḁ́qs^{w}o	**መንቀስ** mḁ́nqḁs (-ṅq-)	**ነቃሽ** nḁ́qā́š (§ 8)
ይነቅንቅ yi̥nḁ́qni̥q (-nā́-)	**ነቅንቅ** nḁ́qni̥q (nā́-)	**ነቅንቆ** nḁ́qni̥q^{w}o (nā́-)	**መነቅነቅ** mḁnḁ́qnḁq	**ነቅናቂ** nḁqnā́qi
ይንካ yı̥́ṅkã̄	**ንካ** nı̥́kã̄ [**እንካ** (ı̥)ṅkã̄]	**ነክቶ** nḁ́kt^{w}o (nā́-)	**መንካት** mḁ́ṅkā́t (§ 8)	**ነኪ** nḁ́ki (nā́-)
ይንክር yı̥́ṅkḁr (-kä-)	**ንክር** nı̥́kḁr (-kä-)	**ነክሮ** nḁ́kr^{w}o (-ā́k-)	**መንክር** mḁ́ṅkḁr (-kä-)	**ነካሪ** nḁkā́ri (-äk-)
ይንክስ yı̥́ṅkḁs	**ንክስ** nı̥́kḁs	**ነክሶ** nḁ́ks^{w}o	**መንክስ** mḁ́ṅkḁs	†**ነካሽ** nḁ́kā́š (§ 8)
ይንዳ yı̥́ndã̄	**ንዳ** nı̥́dã̄	**ነድቶ** nḁ́dĭ̥t^{w}o (nḁ́rt-, nā́rt- § 7*d*)	**መንዳት** mḁ́ndā́t (§ 8)	**ነጅ** nḁj (nä-, -**ጂ** -ji)

Simp. perf. (§ 25)		Comp. perf. (§ 32)	Contingent (§ 26)	Comp. imperf. (§ 32)
ነደደ nḁ́ddḁdḁ	burn, i.	ነድዷል nḁ́ddŏ͡āl	ይነድ yi̥nḁ́dd	ይነዳል yi̥nḁ́ddāl
ነደፈ nḁ́ddḁfḁ	sting, t.	ነድፏል nḁ́dfŏ͡āl	ይነድፍ yi̥nḁ́d(ĭ̥)f	ይነድፋል yi̥nḁ́d(ĭ̥)fāl
ነጋ nḁ́ggã	dawn, i.	ነግቷል nḁ́gtŏ͡āl	ይነጋ yi̥nḁ́gã	ይነጋል yi̥nḁ́gāl
ነገረ nḁ́ggḁrḁ (-gä-)	say, t.	ነግሯል nḁ́grŏ͡āl	ይነግር yi̥nḁ́g(ĭ̥)r	ይነግራል yi̥nḁ́grāl
ነገሠ nḁ́ggḁsḁ	reign, i.	ነግሷል nḁ́gsŏ͡āl	ይነግሥ yi̥nḁ́gs	ይነግሣል yi̥nḁ́gsāl
ነገደ nḁ́ggḁdḁ	trade, i.	ነግዷል nḁ́gdŏ͡āl (-ḁ́ggi̥d-)	ይነግድ yi̥nḁ́gd (-ḁ́ggi̥d)	ይነግዳል yi̥nḁ́gdāl (-ḁ́ggi̥d-)
ነጣ nḁ́ṭṭã	be white, i.	ነጥቷል nḁ́ṭ(ĭ̥)tŏ͡āl (nä́-)	ይነጣ yi̥nḁ́ṭã (-nä́-)	ይነጣል yi̥nḁ́ṭāl (-nä́-)
ነጠረ nḁ́ṭṭḁrḁ (-ṭä-)	be clarified, i.	ነጥሯል nḁ́ṭrŏ͡āl	ይነጥር yi̥nḁ́ṭ(ĭ̥)r	ይነጥራል yi̥nḁ́ṭrāl
ነጠቀ nḁ́ṭṭḁqḁ (nä́-)	snatch, t.	ነጥቋል nḁ́ṭ(ĭ̥)qŏ͡āl (nä́-)	ይነጥቅ yi̥nḁ́ṭ(ĭ̥)q (-nä́-)	ይነጥቃል yi̥nḁ́ṭ(ĭ̥)qāl (-nä́-)
ነጠበ nḁ́ṭṭḁbḁ (nä́-, -ḁv̤-)	drip, i.	ነጥቧል nḁ́ṭbŏ͡āl (nä́-, -ṭv̤-)	ይነጥብ yi̥nḁ́ṭ(ĭ̥)b (-nä́-, -v̤)	ይነጥባል yi̥nḁ́ṭ(ĭ̥)bāl (-nä́-, -v̤ā-)

Jussive (§ 27)	Imperative (§ 28)	Gerund (§ 29)	Infinitive (§ 30)	Participle (§ 31)
ይንደድ yí̥ndḁd	ንደድ ní̥dḁd	ነዶ nḁ́dd^{w}o	መንደድ mḁ́ndḁd	ነዳጅ nḁ́dā́j (§ 8)
ይንደፍ yí̥ndḁf	ንደፍ ní̥dḁf	ነድፎ nḁ́df^{w}o	መንደፍ mḁ́ndḁf	ነዳፊ nḁdā́fi
		ነግቶ nḁ́gt^{w}o	መንጋት mḁ́ṅgā́t (§ 8)	
ይንገር yí̥ṅgḁr (-gä-)	ንገር ní̥gḁr (-gä-)	ነግሮ nḁ́gr^{w}o	መንገር mḁ́ṅgḁr (-gä-)	ነጋሪ nḁgā́ri
ይንገሥ yí̥ṅgḁs	ንገሥ ní̥gḁs	ነግሦ nḁ́gs^{w}o	መንገሥ mḁ́ṅgḁs	ነጋሽ nḁ́gā́š (§ 8)
ይንገድ yí̥ṅgḁd [ይነግድ] (yi̥nḁ́ggi̥d)	ንገድ ní̥gḁd [ነግድ] (nḁ́ggi̥d)	ነግዶ nḁ́gd^{w}o (-ḁ́ggi̥d-)	መንገድ mḁ́ṅgḁd [መነገድ] (mḁnḁ́ggḁd)	ነጋጅ nḁ́ggā́j (§ 8)
ይንጣ yí̥nṭã	ንጣ ní̥ṭã	ነጥቶ nḁ́ṭ(i̥)t^{w}o (nā́-)	መንጣት mḁ́nṭā́t (§ 8)	ነጭ nḁč̣č̣ (nä-)
ይንጠር yí̥nṭḁr (-är)		ነጥሮ nḁ́ṭr^{w}o	መንጠር mḁ́nṭḁr (-är)	†ነጣሪ nḁṭā́ri
ይንጠቅ yí̥nṭḁq	ንጠቅ ní̥ṭḁq	ነጥቆ nḁ́ṭ(ĭ̥)q^{w}o (nā́-)	መንጠቅ mḁ́nṭḁq	ነጣቂ nḁṭā́qi (nä-)
ይንጡብ yí̥nṭḁb (-ḁṿ)		ነጥቦ nḁ́ṭb^{w}o (nā́-, -ṭṿ-)	መንጡብ mḁ́nṭḁb (-ḁṿ)	ነጣቢ nḁṭā́bi (nä-, -ṿi)

Simp. perf. (§ 25)		Comp. perf. (§ 32)	Contingent (§ 26)	Comp. imperf. (§ 32)
ነጨ nắč̣č̣ä 2nd ነጨህ nắč̣č̣äh, etc.	pluck out, t.	ነጭቷል nắč̣tŏ͡āl	ይነጭ yi̥nắč̣	ይነጫል yi̥nắč̣āl
ነፋ nḁ́ffã	inflate, t.	ነፍቷል nḁ́ftŏ͡āl (nắ-)	ይነፋ yi̥nḁ́fã (-nắ-)	ይነፋል yi̥nḁ́fāl (-nắ-)
ነፈሰ nḁ́ffḁsḁ	blow, i.	ነፍሷል nḁ́fsŏ͡āl	ይነፍስ yi̥nḁ́fs	ይነፍሳል yi̥nḁ́fsāl
አለ ắlḁ (§ 44*a*)	say, t.	ብሏል bí̥lŏ͡āl	ይል yi̥l	ይላል yí̥lál (§ 8)
አለ állä (§ 32) 2nd አለህ álläh, etc.	be, i.			
አለላከ G. allḁlákḁ	send to and fro, t.	አለልኳል allḁ́l(ĭ̥)kŏ͡āl (-lắl-)	ያለልክ yãllḁ́l(ĭ̥)k (-lắl-)	ያለልካል yãllḁ́l(ĭ̥)kāl (-lắl-)
አላላከ Š. allālákḁ	send to and fro, t.	አላልኳል allál(ĭ̥)kŏ͡āl	ያላልክ yãllál(ĭ̥)k	ያላልካል yãllál(ĭ̥)kāl
አለሰለሰ alḁsḁ́llḁsḁ	soften, t.	አለስልሷል alḁ́sli̥sŏ͡āl	ያለሰልስ yãlḁsḁ́lli̥s	ያለሰልሳል yãlḁsḁ́lli̥sāl
አለቀ állḁqḁ	end, i.	አልቋል ắlqŏ͡āl	ያልቅ yãlq	ያልቃል yắlqāl

Jussive (§ 27)	Imperative (§ 28)	Gerund (§ 29)	Infinitive (§ 30)	Participle (§ 31)
ይንጭ yi̥nč̣	[እ]ንጭ ni̥č̣ (i̥nč̣)	ነጭቶ nä́č̣t^{w}o	መንጨት mḁnč̣ät	ነጭ näč̣ (-ጪ, -č̣i)
ይንፋ yí̥nfã	ንፋ ní̥fã	ነፍቶ nḁ́ft^{w}o (nā́-)	መንፋት mḁ́nfát (§ 8)	ነፊ nḁ́fi (nā́-)'
ይንፈስ yí̥nfḁs		ነፍሶ nḁ́fs^{w}o	መንፈስ mḁ́nfḁs	†ነፋሽ nḁ́fāš (§ 8)
ይበል yí̥bḁl (-í̥y-, -äl)	በል bḁl (bäl)	ብሎ bí̥l^{w}o	ማለት mā́lḁt (-ät)	
ያለልክ yãllḁ́l(i̥)k (-lā́l-)	አለልክ allḁ́l(i̥)k (-lā́l-)	አለልኮ allḁ́l(i̥)k^{w}o (-lā́l-)	ማለላክ mãllḁ́lák (§ 8)	አለላኪ allḁláki
ያላልክ yãllā́l(i̥)k	አላልክ allā́l(i̥)k	አላልኮ allā́l(i̥)k^{w}o	ማላላክ mãllā́lák (§ 8)	አላላኪ allāláki
ያለስልስ yãlḁ́sli̥s	አለስልስ alḁ́sli̥s	አለስልሶ alḁ́sli̥s^{w}o	ማለስለስ mãlḁ́slḁs	
ይለቅ yí̥lḁq	እለቅ í̥lḁq	አልቆ ãlq^{w}o	ማለቅ mā́lḁq	አላቂ ãláqi

Simp. perf. (§ 25)		Comp. perf. (§ 32)	Contingent (§ 26)	Comp. imperf. (§ 32)
አለቀመ aláqqama	take to pasture, t.	አልቅሟል ãlqimŏãl	ያለቅም yãláq(i)m (-lá-)	ያለቅማል yãláq(i)māl (-lá-)
አላቀመ allãqqama	help to reap, t.	አላቅሟል allãq(i)-mŏãl	ያላቅም yãllãqqim	ያላቅማል yãllãqqi-māl
አለቀሰ aláqqasa	weep, i.	አልቅሷል ãlqisŏãl	ያለቅስ yãláqs	ያለቅሳል yãláqsāl
አለቃቀመ alaqãqqa-ma	cause to pick a little, t.	አለቃቅሟል alaqãq(i)-mŏãl	ያለቃቅም yālaqãq-qim	ያለቃቅማል yālaqãqqi-māl
አለቃቀመ allaqãqqa-ma	help to pick, t.	አለቃቅሟል allaqãq(i)-mŏãl	ያለቃቅም yãllaqãq-qim	ያለቃቅማል yãllaqãqqi-māl
አለበ állaba (-ya)	milk, t.	አልቧል ãlbŏãl (-ly-)	ያልብ yãlb (-ly)	ያልባል yálbāl (-ly-)
አለበሰ alábbasa	dress, t.	አልብሷል ãlbisŏãl (-ly-)	ያለብስ yãlábs (-lá-, -ys)	ያለብሳል yãlábsāl (-lá-, -ys-)
አለፈ állafa	pass, t.	አልፏል ãlfŏãl	ያልፍ yãlf	ያልፋል yálfāl
አማ ámmã	slander, t.	አምቷል ãmtŏãl	ያማ yámã	ያማል yámāl

Jussive (§ 27)	Imperative (§ 28)	Gerund (§ 29)	Infinitive (§ 30)	Participle (§ 31)
ያልቅም yā́lqi̥m	አልቅም ā́lqi̥m	አልቅሞ ā́lqi̥mʷo	ማልቀም mā́lqḁm	አልቃሚ alqā́mi
ያላቅም yãllā́qi̥m	አላቅም allā́qi̥m	አላቅሞ allā́q(ĭ̥)mʷo	ማላቀም mãllā́qḁm	አላቃሚ allāqā́mi
ያልቅስ yā́lqi̥s	አልቅስ ā́lqi̥s	አልቅሶ ā́lqi̥sʷo	ማልቀስ mā́lqḁs	አልቃሽ ā́lqā́š (§ 8)
ያለቃቅም yālḁqā́qi̥m	አለቃቅም alḁqā́qi̥m	አለቃቅሞ alḁqā́q(ĭ̥)-mʷo	ማለቃቀም mālḁqā́qḁm	አለቃቃሚ alḁqāqā́mi
ያለቃቅም yãllḁqā́qi̥m	አለቃቅም allḁqā́qi̥m	አለቃቅሞ allḁqā́q(ĭ̥)-mʷo	ማለቃቀም mãllḁqā́-qḁm	አለቃቃሚ allḁqāqā́mi
ይለብ yí̥lḁb (-ḁṿ)	እለብ í̥lḁb (-ḁṿ)	አልቦ ā́lbʷo (-lṿ-)	ማለብ mā́lḁb (-ḁṿ)	አላቢ ãlā́bi (-ṿi)
ያልብስ yā́lbi̥s (-lṿ-)	አልብስ ā́lbi̥s (-lṿ-)	አልብሶ ā́lbi̥sʷo (-lṿ-)	ማልበስ mā́lbḁs (-lṿ-)	አልባሽ ā́lbā́š (-lṿ-; § 8)
ይለፍ yí̥lḁf	እለፍ í̥lḁf	አልፎ ā́lfʷo	ማለፍ mā́lḁf	አላፊ ãlā́fi
ይማ yí̥mã	እማ í̥mã	አምቶ ā́mtʷo	ማማት mā́mā́t (§ 8)	አሚ ā́mi

Simp. perf. (§ 25)		Comp. perf. (§ 32)	Contingent (§ 26)	Comp. imperf. (§ 32)
አመላለሰ ammḁlā́llḁsḁ	fetch and carry, t.	**አመላልሷል** ammḁlā́l(ĭ̥)sŏ͡āl	**የመላልስ** yãmmḁlā́lli̥s	**የመላልሳል** yãmmḁlā́lli̥sāl
አመለከተ amḁlḁ́kkḁtḁ	indicate, t.	**አመልክቷል** amḁ́lki̥tŏ͡āl (-mā́-)	**የመለክት** yāmḁlḁ́kki̥t (-lā́-)	**የመለክታል** yāmḁlḁ́kki̥tāl (-lā́-)
አመመ ámmḁmḁ	ache, i.	**አሟል** ā́mmŏ͡āl	**የምም** yā́mmi̥m [**የም**] (yãmm)	**የማል** yā́mmāl
አማረ amā́rḁ	be pleasant, i.	**አምሯል** ā́mrŏ͡āl	**የምር** yā́m(ĭ̥)r	**የምራል** yā́mrāl
አማሰለ ammássḁlḁ	stir, t.	**አማስሏል** ammā́s(ĭ̥)lŏ͡āl	**የማስል** yãmmássi̥l	**የማስላል** yãmmássi̥lāl
አመሰገነ amḁsḁ́ggḁnḁ	praise, t.	**አመስግኗል** amḁ́sgi̥nŏ͡āl	**የመሰግን** yāmḁsḁ́ggi̥n	**የመሰግናል** yāmḁsḁ́ggi̥nāl
አሞቀ amʷṓqḁ	warm, t.	**አሙቋል** ā́muqŏ͡āl	**የሞቅ** yãmʷṓq	**የሞቃል** yãmʷṓqāl
አምበረከከ ambḁrḁ́kkḁkḁ (-bä-)	cause to kneel, t.	**አምበርክኳል** ambḁ́rki̥kŏ͡āl (-bā́-)	**የምበረክክ** yãmbḁrḁ́kki̥k (-bä-)	**የምበረክካል** yãmbḁrḁ́kki̥kāl (-bä-)
አመነ ámmḁnḁ	believe, t.	**አምኗል** ā́mnŏ͡āl	**የምን** yā́m(ĭ̥)n	**የምናል** yā́m(ĭ̥)nāl

Jussive (§ 27)	Imperative (§ 28)	Gerund (§ 29)	Infinitive (§ 30)	Participle (§ 31)
ያመላልስ yãmmḁlá-l(ĭ̥)s	አመላልስ ammḁlál(ĭ̥)s	አመላልሶ ammḁlál(ĭ̥)-s^{w}o	ማመላለስ mãmmḁlá-lḁs	አመላላሽ ammḁláláš (§ 8)
ያመልክት yãmḁ́lki̥t (-mắ-)	አመልክት amḁ́lki̥t (-mắ-)	አመልክቶ amḁ́lki̥t^{w}o (-mắ-)	ማመልከት mãmḁ́lkḁt (-mắ-, -ät)	አመልካች amḁ́lkắč (-mắ-; § 8)
ይመም yí̥mḁm		አሞ ắmm^{w}o	ማመም mắmḁm	
ይመር yí̥mḁr (-är)		አምሮ ắmr^{w}o	ማማር mắmár (§ 8)	አማሪ ãmắri
ያማስል yãmmắsi̥l	አማስል ammắsi̥l	አማስሎ ammắs(ĭ̥)-l^{w}o	መማሰል mammắsḁl (-äl)	አማሳይ ammắsắi̥ (-ắyy § 6; § 8)
ያመስግን yãmḁ́sgi̥n	አመስግን amḁ́sgi̥n	አመስግኖ amḁ́sgi̥n^{w}o	ማመስገን mãmḁ́sgḁn	አመስጋኝ amḁ́sgắñ (-ññ § 6; § 8)
ያሙቅ yắmuq	አሙቅ ắmuq	አሙቆ ắmuq^{w}o	ማሞቅ mắm^{w}ő̌q (§ 8)	አሟቂ amwắqi
ያምበርክክ yãmbḁ́rki̥k (-bắ-)	አምበርክክ ambḁ́rki̥k (-bắ-)	አምበርክኮ ambḁ́rki̥k^{w}o (-bắ-)	ማምበርከክ mãmbḁ́r-kḁk (-bắ-)	አምበርካኪ ambḁrkắki (-bä-)
ይመን yí̥mḁn	እመን í̥mḁn	አምኖ ắmn^{w}o	ማመን mắmḁn	አማኝ ắmắñ (-ññ § 6; -ắi̥ § 7*d*; § 8)

Simp. perf. (§ 25)		Comp. perf. (§ 32)	Contingent (§ 26)	Comp. imperf. (§ 32)
አሞኘ amʷóññä	deceive, t.	አሞኝቷል amʷóññi̥-tŏ͡āl	ያሞኝ yãmʷóñ (-ññ § 6)	ያሞኛል yãmʷóññāl
አመጠ ámmḁṭḁ	rebel, i.	አምጧል ámmi̥ṭŏ͡āl	ያምጥ yấmmi̥ṭ	ያምጣል yấmmi̥ṭāl
አመጣ amḁ́ṭṭã	bring, t.	አምጥቷል ấmṭi̥tŏ͡āl (-nṭ- § 7*d*)	ያመጣ yãmḁ́ṭã	ያመጣል yãmḁ́ṭāl
አረመ árrḁmḁ	weed, t.	አርሟል árri̥mŏ͡āl	ያርም yấrri̥m	ያርማል yấrri̥māl
አረራቀ G. arrḁrấqḁ (-rär-)	separate, t.	አረርቋል arrḁ́r(i̥)qŏ͡āl (-rấr-)	ያረርቅ yãrrḁ́r(i̥)q (-rấr-)	ያረርቃል yãrrḁ́r(i̥)qāl (-rấr-)
አራራቀ Š. arrārấqḁ	separate, t.	አራርቋል arrấr(i̥)qŏ͡āl	ያራርቅ yãrrấr(i̥)q	ያራርቃል yãrrấr(i̥)qāl
አረሰ árrḁsḁ	plough, t.	አርሷል ấrsŏ͡āl	ያርስ yārs	ያርሳል yấrsāl
አረቀ árrḁqḁ	straighten, t.	አርቋል árri̥qŏ͡āl	ያርቅ yấrri̥q	ያርቃል yấrri̥qāl
አረደ árrḁdḁ	slaughter, t.	አርዷል ấrdŏ͡āl	ያርድ yārd	ያርዳል yấrdāl
አረጀ arấjjä 2nd አረጀሁ arấjjäh, etc.	grow old, i.	አርጅቷል ấrji̥tŏ͡āl	ያረጅ yãráj	ያረጃል yãrájāl

Jussive (§ 27)	Imperative (§ 28)	Gerund (§ 29)	Infinitive (§ 30)	Participle (§ 31)
ያሞኝ yã́mʷoñ (-ññ § 6)	**አሞኝ** ã́mʷoñ (-ññ § 6)	**አሞኝቶ** amʷóññi̥- tʷo	**ማሞኘት** mãmʷóñ- ñät	†**አሞኝ** ã́mʷóñ (§ 8; -ññ § 6) [**አሞኚ**] (amʷóññi)
ያምጥ yã́mmi̥ṭ	**አምጥ** ámmi̥ṭ	**አምጦ** ámmi̥ṭʷo	**ማመጥ** mã́mmḁṭ	**አማጭ** ámmã́č̣ (§ 8)
ያምጣ yã́mṭã (-nṭ-)	**አምጣ** ã́mṭã (-nṭ-)	**አምጥቶ** ã́mṭi̥tʷo (-nṭ-)	**ማምጣት** mã́mṭát (§ 8)	**አምጭ** ã́mč̣ (-ጪ -č̣i)
ያርም yã́rri̥m	**አርም** árri̥m	**አርሞ** árri̥mʷo	**ማረም** mã́rrḁm	**አራሚ** arrã́mi
ያረርቅ yãrrḁ́r(ĭ̥)q (-rã́r-)	**አረርቅ** arrḁ́r(ĭ̥)q (-rã́r-)	**አረርቆ** arrḁ́r(ĭ̥)qʷo (-rã́r-)	**ማረራቅ** mãrrḁ́rã́q (-rã́r-; § 8)	**አረራቂ** arrḁrã́qi (-rär-)
ያራርቅ yãrrã́r(ĭ̥)q	**አራርቅ** arrã́r(ĭ̥)q	**አራርቆ** arrã́r(ĭ̥)qʷo	**ማራራቅ** mãrrã́rã́q (§ 8)	**አራራቂ** arrārã́qi
ይረስ yí̥rḁs	**እረስ** í̥rḁs	**አርሶ** ã́rsʷo	**ማረስ** mã́rḁs	**አራሽ** ã́rã́š (§ 8)
ያርቅ yã́rri̥q	**አርቅ** árri̥q	**አርቆ** árri̥qʷo	**ማረቅ** mã́rrḁq	**አራቂ** arrã́qi
ይረድ yí̥rḁd	**እረድ** í̥rḁd	**አርዶ** ã́rdʷo	**ማረድ** mã́rḁd	**አራጅ** ã́rã́j (§ 8)
		አርጅቶ ã́rji̥tʷo	**ማርጀት** mã́rjät	†**አርጅ** ārj (-ጂ -ji)

Simp. perf. (§ 25)		Comp. perf. (§ 32)	Contingent (§ 26)	Comp. imperf. (§ 32)
አረገበ arrḁ́ggḁbḁ (-ỵḁ)	loosen, t.	አርግቧል árgi̥bŏāl (-i̥ỵ-)	ያረግብ yãrrḁ́g(ĭ̥)b (-(ĭ̥)ỵ)	ያረግባል yãrrḁ́g(ĭ̥)bāl (-(ĭ̥)ỵ-)
አራገበ arrắggḁbḁ (-ỵḁ)	wave, t.	አራግቧል arrắgi̥bŏāl (-i̥ỵ-)	ያራግብ yãrrắggi̥b (-i̥ỵ)	ያራግባል yãrrắggi̥bāl (-i̥ỵ-)
አርገበገበ argḁbḁ́gga-bḁ (-ỵḁ́ggḁỵ-)	flutter, t.	አርገብግቧል argḁ́bgi̥-bŏāl (-ỵgi̥ỵ-)	ያርገበግብ yãrgḁbḁ́g-gi̥b (-ỵḁ́ggi̥ỵ)	ያርገበግባል yãrgḁbḁ́g-gi̥bāl (-ỵḁ́ggi̥ỵ-)
አራገፈ arrắggḁfḁ	unsaddle, t.	አራግፏል arrắg(ĭ̥)fŏāl	ያራግፍ yãrrắggi̥f	ያራግፋል yãrrắggi̥fāl
አረፈ árrḁfḁ	rest, i.	አርፏል ắrfŏāl	ያርፍ yārf	ያርፋል yárfāl
አስለቀመ aslḁ́qqḁmḁ	cause to gather, t.	አስለቅሟል aslḁ́qqi̥-mŏāl	ያስለቅም yãslḁ́qqi̥m	ያስለቅማል yãslḁ́qqi̥-māl
አሰለፈ assḁ́llḁfḁ (-sắ-)	parade, t.	አሰልፏል assḁ́lli̥fŏāl (-sắ-)	ያሰልፍ yãssḁ́lli̥f (-sắ-)	ያሰልፋል yãssḁ́lli̥fāl (-sắ-)
አሳለፈ asállḁfḁ	let pass, t.	አሳልፏል asálli̥fŏāl	ያሳልፍ yãsálli̥f	ያሳልፋል yãsálli̥fāl
አሰማ assḁ́mmã	cause to hear, t.	አሰምቷል assḁ́mmi̥-tŏāl	ያሰማ yãssḁ́mmã	ያሰማል yãssḁ́mmāl

Jussive (§ 27)	Imperative (§ 28)	Gerund (§ 29)	Infinitive (§ 30)	Participle (§ 31)
ያርግብ yárgi̥b (-i̥ỵ)	**አርግብ** árgi̥b (-i̥ỵ)	**አርግቦ** árgi̥b^{w}o (-i̥ỵ-)	**ማርገብ** márgḁb (-ḁỵ)	**አርጋቢ** argábi (-ỵi)
ያራግብ yãrrági̥b (-i̥ỵ)	**አራግብ** arrági̥b (-i̥ỵ)	**አራግቦ** arrági̥b^{w}o (-i̥ỵ-)	**ማራገብ** mãrrágḁb (-ḁỵ)	**አራጋቢ** arrāgábi (-ỵi)
ያርገብግብ yãrgḁ́bgi̥b (-ỵgi̥ỵ)	**አርገብግብ** argḁ́bgi̥b (-ỵgi̥ỵ)	**አርገብግቦ** argḁ́bgi̥b^{w}o (-ỵgi̥ỵ-)	**ማርገብገብ** mãrgḁ́bgḁb (-ỵgḁỵ)	**አርገብጋቢ** argḁbgábi (-ỵgáỵ-)
ያራግፍ yãrrági̥f	**አራግፍ** arrági̥f	**አራግፎ** arrág(i̥)f^{w}o	**ማራገፍ** mãrrágḁf	**አራጋፊ** arrāgáfi
ይረፍ yí̥rḁf	**እረፍ** í̥rḁf	**አርፎ** árf^{w}o	**ማረፍ** márḁf	**አራፊ** ãráfi
ይስለቅም yãslḁ́qqi̥m	**አስለቅም** aslḁ́qqi̥m	**አስለቅሞ** aslḁ́qqi̥m^{w}o	**ማስለቀም** mãslḁ́qqḁm	**አስለቃሚ** aslḁqqámi
ያሰልፍ yãssḁ́lli̥f (-sä́-)	**አሰልፍ** assḁ́lli̥f (-sä́-)	**አሰልፎ** assḁ́lli̥f^{w}o (-sä́-)	**ማሰለፍ** mãssḁ́llḁf (-sä́-)	**አሰላፊ** assḁlláfi (-sä-)
ያሳልፍ yãsálli̥f	**አሳልፍ** asálli̥f	**አሳልፎ** asálli̥f^{w}o	**ማሳለፍ** mãsállḁf	**አሳላፊ** asalláfi
ያሰማ yãssḁ́mmã	**አሰማ** assḁ́mmã	**አሰምቶ** assḁ́mmi̥- t^{w}o	**ማሰማት** mãssḁ́mmát (§ 8)	**አሰሚ** assḁ́mmi

Simp. perf. (§ 25)		Comp. perf. (§ 32)	Contingent (§ 26)	Comp. imperf. (§ 32)
አሳመመ asámmḁmḁ	hurt, t.	አሳምሟል asámmi̥-mŏ͡āl	ያሳምም yā̃sámmi̥m	ያሳምማል yā̃sámmi̥-māl
አሰመረ Š. assḁmḁ́rrḁ 2nd -ረህ -rrḁh (-äh), etc.	take to pasture, t.	አሰመርቷል assḁmḁ́r-tŏ͡āl (-mā̃́-)	ያሰመር yā̃ssḁmḁ́rr	ያሰመራል yā̃ssḁmḁ́r-rāl
አሰማራ G. assḁmā̃́rrā̃	take to pasture, t.	አሰማርቷል assḁmā́r-tŏ͡āl	ያሰማራ yā̃ssḁmā̃́rrā̃	ያሰማራል yā̃ssḁmā̃́r-rāl
አስመሰለ asmḁ́ssḁlḁ	pretend, t.	አስመስሏል asmḁ́ssi̥lŏ͡āl	ያስመስል yā̃smḁ́ssi̥l	ያስመስላል yā̃smḁ́ssi̥lāl
አስመነዘረ asmḁnḁ́z-zḁrḁ (-är-)	cause to change, t.	አስመንዝሯል asmḁ́nzi̥-rŏ͡āl	ያስመነዝር yā̃smḁ-nḁ́zzi̥r	ያስመነዝራል yā̃smḁnḁ́z-zi̥rāl
አሳመጠ asámmḁṭḁ	cause to rebel, t.	አሳምጧል asámmi̥ṭŏ͡āl	ያሳምጥ yā̃sámmi̥ṭ	ያሳምጣል yā̃sámmi̥ṭāl
አስመጣ asmḁ́ṭṭā̃	cause to come, t.	አስመጥቷል asmḁ́ṭṭi̥tŏ͡āl	ያስመጣ yā̃smḁ́ṭṭā̃	ያስመጣል yā̃smḁ́ṭṭāl
አሰረ ássḁrḁ (-sä-)	bind, t.	አስሯል ásrŏ͡āl	ያስር yā́s(ĭ̥)r	ያስራል yā́s(ĭ̥)rāl

Jussive (§ 27)	Imperative (§ 28)	Gerund (§ 29)	Infinitive (§ 30)	Participle (§ 31)
ያሳምም yãsámmi̥m	**አሳምም** asámmi̥m	**አሳምሞ** asám- mi̥mʷo	**ማሳመም** mãsám- mḁm	†**አሳማሚ** asammắmi
ያሰመር yãssḁmḁ́rr	**አሰመር** assḁmḁ́rr	**አሰመርቶ** assḁmḁ́rtʷo (-mắ-)	**ማሰመረት** mãssḁmḁ́r- rḁt (-ät)	**አሰማሪ** assḁmắr(r)i [**አሰምሪ**] (assḁ́mri)
ያሰማራ yãssḁmắrã	**አሰማራ** assḁmắrã	**አሰማርቶ** assḁmắrtʷo	**ማሰማራት** mãssḁmắ- rắt (§ 8)	**አሰማሪ** assḁmắr(r)i
ያስመስል yãsmḁ́ssi̥l	**አስመስል** asmḁ́ssi̥l	**አስመስሎ** asmḁ́ssi̥lʷo	**ማስመሰል** mãsmḁ́ssḁl (-äl)	**አስመሳይ** asmḁ́ssắi̥ (-ắyy § 6; § 8)
ያስመንዝር yãsmḁ́nzi̥r	**አስመንዝር** asmḁ́nzi̥r	**አስመንዝሮ** asmḁ́nzi̥rʷo	**ማስመንዘር** mãsmḁ́nzḁr (-är)	**አስመንዛሪ** asmḁnzắri
ያሳምጥ yãsámmi̥ṭ	**አሳምጥ** asámmi̥ṭ	**አሳምጦ** asámmi̥ṭʷo	**ማሳመጥ** mãsámmḁṭ	**አሳማጭ** asámmắč̣ (§ 8)
ያስመጣ yãsmḁ́ṭṭã	**አስመጣ** asmḁ́ṭṭã	**አስመጥቶ** asmḁ́ṭṭi̥tʷo	**ማስመጣት** mãsmḁ́ṭṭắt (§ 8)	**አስመጭ** ắsmḁ́č̣č̣ (-mắ-; § 8; -ጪ. -č̣č̣i)
ይሰር yí̥sḁr (-sä-)	**እሰር** i̥sḁr (-sä-)	**አስሮ** ắsrʷo	**ማሰር** mắsḁr (-sä-)	**አሳሪ** ãsắri

Simp. perf. (§ 25)		Comp. perf. (§ 32)	Contingent (§ 26)	Comp. imperf. (§ 32)
አሰሩ assḁ́rrā̃ (-sä́-)	employ, t.	**አሰርቷል** assḁ́rri̥tŏ͡āl (-sä́-)	**ያሰሩ** yā̃ssḁ́rrā̃ (-sä́-)	**ያሰሩል** yā̃ssḁ́rrāl (-sä́-)
አሳሰበ asā̃́ssḁbḁ (-ẏḁ)	remind, t.	**አሳስቧል** asā̃́ssi̥bŏ͡āl (-i̥ẏ-)	**ያሳስብ** yā̃sā̃́ssi̥b (-i̥ẏ)	**ያሳስባል** yā̃sā̃́ssi̥bāl (-i̥ẏ-)
አሰሳተ G. assḁsā̃́tḁ	mistake, t.	**አሰስቷል** assḁ́stŏ͡āl	**ያሰስት** yā̃ssḁ́st	**ያሰስታል** yā̃ssḁ́stāl
አሳሳተ Š assā̃sā̃́tḁ	mistake, t.	**አሳስቷል** assā̃́s(ĭ̥)tŏ͡āl	**ያሳስት** yā̃ssā̃́s(ĭ̥)t	**ያሳስታል** yā̃ssā̃́s(ĭ̥)tāl
አሣቀ assā̃́qḁ	amuse, t.	**አሥቋል** ássi̥qŏ͡āl	**ያሥቅ** yā̃́ssi̥q	**ያሥቃል** yā̃́ssi̥qāl
አስቀመጠ asqḁ́mmḁṭḁ	set, t.	**አስቀምጧል** asqḁ́mmi̥- ṭŏ͡āl	**ያስቀምጥ** yā̃sqḁ́mmi̥ṭ	**ያስቀምጣል** yā̃sqḁ́mmi̥- ṭāl
አስቀረ asqḁ́rrḁ 2nd **አስቀረህ** asqḁ́rrḁh (-äh), etc.	delay, t.	**አስቀርቷል** asqḁ́rri̥tŏ͡āl (-qä́-)	**ያስቀር** yā̃sqḁ́rr	**ያስቀራል** yā̃sqḁ́rrāl
አስቀረበ asqḁ́rrḁbḁ (-ẏḁ)	cause to approach, t.	**አስቀርቧል** asqḁ́rri̥bŏ͡āl (-qä́-, -i̥ẏ-)	**ያስቀርብ** yā̃sqḁ́rri̥b (-qä́-, -i̥ẏ)	**ያስቀርባል** yā̃sqḁ́rri̥bāl (-qä́-, -i̥ẏ-)
አስቈረጠ asqwώrrḁṭḁ	cause to cut, t.	**አስቈርጧል** asqwώrri̥- ṭŏ͡āl	**ያስቈርጥ** yā̃sqwώrri̥ṭ	**ያስቈርጣል** yā̃sqwώrri̥- ṭāl

Jussive (§ 27)	Imperative (§ 28)	Gerund (§ 29)	Infinitive (§ 30)	Participle (§ 31)
ያሰራ yãssḁ́rrã (-sắ-)	**አሰራ** assḁ́rrã (-sắ-)	**አሰርቶ** assḁ́rri̥tʷo (-sắ-)	**ማሰራት** mãssḁ́rrắt (-sắ-; § 8)	**አሰሪ** assḁ́rri (-sắ-)
ያሳስብ yãsắssi̥b (-i̥ỵ)	**አሳስብ** asắssi̥b (-i̥ỵ)	**አሳስቦ** asắssi̥bʷo (-i̥ỵ-)	**ማሳሰብ** mãsắssḁb (-ḁỵ)	**አሳሳቢ** asãssắbi (-ỵi)
ያሰስት yãssḁ́st	**አሰስት** assḁ́st	**አሰስቶ** assḁ́stʷo	**ማሰሳት** mãssḁ́sắt (§ 8)	**አሰሳች** assḁ́sắč (§ 8)
ያሳስት yãssắs(ĭ̥)t	**አሳስት** assắs(ĭ̥)t	**አሳስቶ** assắs(ĭ̥)tʷo	**ማሳሳት** mãssắsắt (§ 8)	**አሳሳች** assắsắč (§ 8)
ያሥቅ yắssi̥q	**አሥቅ** ássi̥q	**አሥቆ** ássi̥qʷo	**ማሣቅ** mắssắq (§ 8)	**አሣቂ** assắqi
ያስቀምጥ yãsqḁ́mmi̥ṭ	**አስቀምጥ** asqḁ́mmi̥ṭ	**አስቀምጦ** asqḁ́mmi̥-ṭʷo	**ማስቀመጥ** mãsqḁ́m-mḁṭ	**አስቀማጭ** asqḁ́mmắč̣ (§ 8)
ያስቀር yãsqḁ́rr	**አስቀር** asqḁ́rr	**አስቀርቶ** asqḁ́rri̥tʷo (-qắ-)	**ማስቀረት** mãsqḁ́rrḁt (-ắrrä-)	**አስቀሪ** asqḁ́rri (-qắ-)
ያስቀርብ yãsqḁ́rri̥b (-qắ-, i̥ỵ)	**አስቀርብ** asqḁ́rri̥b (-qắ-, -i̥ỵ)	**አስቀርቦ** asqḁ́rri̥bʷo (-qắ-, -i̥ỵ-)	**ማስቀረብ** mãsqḁ́rrḁb (-ḁỵ)	**አስቀራቢ** asqḁrrắbi (-ỵi)
ያስቈርጥ yãsqwώrri̥ṭ	**አስቈርጥ** asqwώrri̥ṭ	**አስቈርጦ** asqwώrri̥-ṭʷo	**ማስቈረጥ** mãsqwώr-rḁṭ	**አስቈራጭ** asqwώrrắč̣ (§ 8)

Simp. perf. (§ 25)		Comp. perf. (§ 32)	Contingent (§ 26)	Comp. imperf. (§ 32)
አስቀዘነ asqḁ́zzḁnḁ	cause diarrhoea (to) i. & t.	አስቀዝኗል asqḁ́zzi̥nŏ͡āl	ያስቀዝን yãsqḁ́zzi̥n	ያስቀዝናል yãsqḁ́zzi̥nāl
አስቀደመ asqḁ́ddḁmḁ	put in front, t.	አስቀድሟል asqḁ́ddi̥-mŏ͡āl	ያስቀድም yãsqḁ́ddi̥m	ያስቀድማል yãsqḁ́ddi̥-māl
አሰበ ássḁbḁ (-ỵḁ)	suppose, t.	አስቧል ássi̥bŏ͡āl (-i̥ỵ-)	ያስብ yã́ssi̥b (-i̥ỵ)	ያስባል yã́ssi̥bāl (-i̥ỵ-)
አስበራ asbḁ́rrã (-sỵ-)	cause to light, t.	አስበርቷል asbḁ́rri̥tŏ͡āl (-sỵ-, -ã́r-)	ያስበራ yãsbḁ́rrã (-sỵ-)	ያስበራል yãsbḁ́rrāl (-sỵ-)
አሰባበረ assḁbã́b-bḁrḁ (-ỵã́-, -är-)	cause to shatter, t.	አሰባብሯል assḁbã́b(ĭ̥)-rŏ͡āl (-ỵã́ỵ-)	ያሰባብር yãssḁbã́b-bi̥r (-ỵã́-)	ያሰባብራል yãssḁbã́b-bi̥rāl (-ỵã́-)
አሳተ assã́tḁ	cause to err, t.	አስቷል ássi̥tŏ͡āl	ያስት yã́ssi̥t	ያስታል yãssi̥tāl
አስተማረ astḁmã́rḁ	teach, t.	አስተምሯል astḁ́m(ĭ̥)-rŏ͡āl	ያስተምር yãstḁ́m(ĭ̥)r	ያስተምራል yãstḁ́m(ĭ̥)-rāl
አስተኛ astḁ́ññã (-tã́-, -ñä)	send to sleep, t.	አስተኝቷል astḁ́ññi̥tŏ͡āl (-tã́-)	ያስተኛ yãstḁ́ññã (-tã́-, -ñä)	ያስተኛል yãstḁ́ññāl (-tã́-)
አስተከለ astḁ́kkḁlḁ	cause to plant, t.	አስተክሏል astḁ́kki̥lŏ͡āl (-tã́-)	ያስተክል yãstḁ́kki̥l (-tã́-)	ያስተክላል yãstḁ́kki̥lāl (-tã́-)

Jussive (§ 27)	Imperative (§ 28)	Gerund (§ 29)	Infinitive (§ 30)	Participle (§ 31)
		አስቀዝኖ asqḁ́zzi̥nʷo	ማስቀዘን mãsqḁ́zzḁn	አስቀዛኝ asqḁ́zzā́ñ (-ññ § 6; § 8)
ያስቀድም yãsqḁ́ddi̥m	አስቀድም asqḁ́ddi̥m	አስቀድሞ asqḁ́ddi̥mʷo	ማስቀደም mãsqḁ́ddḁm	አስቀዳሚ asqḁddā́mi
ያስብ yā́ssi̥b (-i̥ỵ)	አስብ ássi̥b (-i̥ỵ)	አስቦ ássi̥bʷo (-i̥ỵ-)	ማሰብ mā́ssḁb (-ḁỵ)	አሳቢ assā́bi (-ā́ỵ-)
ያስበራ yãsbḁ́rrã (-sỵ-)	አስበራ asbḁ́rrã (-sỵ-)	አስበርቶ asbḁ́rri̥tʷo (-sỵ-, -ā́r-)	ማስበራት mãsbḁ́rrā́t (-sỵ-; § 8)	አስበሪ asbḁ́rri (-sỵ-, -ā́r-)
ያሰባብር yãssḁbā́b(ĭ̥)r (-ỵā́ỵ-)	አሰባብር assḁbā́b(ĭ̥)r (-ỵā́ỵ-)	አሰባብሮ assḁbā́b(ĭ̥)rʷo (-ỵā́ỵ-)	ማሰባበር mãssḁbā́bḁr (-ỵā́ỵ-, -är)	አሰባባሪ assḁbābā́ri (-ỵāỵ-)
ያስት yā́ssi̥t	አስት ássi̥t	አስቶ ássi̥tʷo	ማሳት mā́ssā́t (§ 8)	አሳች ássā́č (§ 8)
ያስተምር yãstḁ́m(ĭ̥)r	አስተምር astḁ́m(ĭ̥)r	አስተምሮ astḁ́m(ĭ̥)rʷo	ማስተማር mãstḁmā́r (§ 8)	አስተማሪ astḁmā́ri
ያስተኛ yãstḁ́ññã (-tā́-, -ñä)	አስተኛ astḁ́ññã (-tā́-, -ñä)	አስተኝቶ astḁ́ññi̥tʷo (-tā́-)	ማስተኛት mãstḁ́ññā́t (-tā́-; § 8)	
ያስተክል yãstḁ́kki̥l (-tā́-)	አስተክል astḁ́kki̥l (-tā́-)	አስተክሎ astḁ́kki̥lʷo (-tā́-)	ማስተከል mãstḁ́kkḁl	አስተካይ astḁ́kkā́i̥ (-ā́yy § 6; § 8)

Simp. perf. (§ 25)		Comp. perf. (§ 32)	Contingent (§ 26)	Comp. imperf. (§ 32)
አስተካከለ astḁkắkkḁlḁ	equalize, t.	አስተካክሏል astḁkák(i̥)lŏ͡āl	ያስተካክል yãstḁkắkki̥l	ያስተካክላል yãstḁkắkki̥lāl
አስተዋለ astḁwā́lḁ (-tḁ͡uắ-)	notice, t.	አስተውሏል astḁ͡u(ŭ)lŏ͡āl	ያስተውል yãstḁ͡u(ŭ)l	ያስተውላል yãstḁ͡u(ŭ)lāl
አስታወሰ astá͡uwḁsḁ (-wω-)	remind, (of), t.	አስታውሷል astá͡u(ŭ)sŏ͡āl	ያስታውስ yãstá͡u(ŭ)s	ያስታውሳል yãstá͡u(ŭ)sāl
አስታወቀ astá͡uwḁqḁ (-wω-)	inform, t.	አስታውቋል astá͡u(ŭ)qŏ͡āl	ያስታውቅ yãstá͡u(ŭ)q	ያስታውቃል yãstá͡u(ŭ)qāl
አስታየ astắyyä 2nd አስታየህ astắyyäh, etc.	cause to be seen, t.	አስታይቷል astắ͡i̥tŏ͡āl	ያስታይ yãstắ͡i̥ (-ắyy § 6)	ያስታያል yãstắ͡i̥āl (-ắyyā-)
አስቸገረ asčắggḁrḁ (-gä-)	trouble, t.	አስቸግሯል asčắggi̥rŏ͡āl	ያስቸግር yãsčắggi̥r	ያስቸግራል yãsčắggi̥rāl
አስነሣ asnḁ́ssã	rouse, t.	አስነሥቷል asnḁ́ssi̥tŏ͡āl (-nắ-)	ያስነሣ yãsnḁ́ssã	ያስነሣል yãsnḁ́ssāl
አሰናበተ assḁnắbbḁtḁ (-bä-)	dismiss, t.	አሰናብቷል assḁnắbtŏ͡āl (-y̥t-)	ያሰናብት yãssḁnắbbi̥t	ያሰናብታል yãssḁnắbbi̥tāl

Jussive (§ 27)	Imperative (§ 28)	Gerund (§ 29)	Infinitive (§ 30)	Participle (§ 31)
ያስተካክል yãstḁkā́k(ĭ̥)l	**አስተካክል** astḁkā́k(ĭ̥)l	**አስተካክሎ** astḁkā́k(ĭ̥)-l^w^o	**ማስተካከል** mãstḁkā́kḁl	**አስተካካይ** astḁkā́kā͡i̥ (-ā́yy § 6; § 8)
ያስተውል yãstḁ́͡u(ŭ)l	**አስተውል** astḁ́͡u(ŭ)l	**አስተውሎ** astḁ́͡u(ŭ)l^w^o	**ማስተዋል** mãstḁ́wā́l (-tḁ́͡uā́-; § 8)	**አስተዋይ** astḁ́wā͡i̥ (-tḁ́͡uā͡i̥; -ā́yy § 6; § 8)
ያስታውስ yãstá͡u(ŭ)s	**አስታውስ** astá͡u(ŭ)s	**አስታውሶ** astá͡u(ŭ)s^w^o	**ማስታወስ** mãstá͡uḁs (-ωs)	**አስታዋሽ** astá͡uā́š (§ 8)
ያስታውቅ yãstá͡u(ŭ)q	**አስታውቅ** astá͡u(ŭ)q	**አስታውቆ** astá͡u(ŭ)q^w^o	**ማስታወቅ** mãstá͡uḁq (-ωq)	**አስታዋቂ** asta͡uā́qi
ያስታይ yãstā́͡i̥ (-ā́yy § 6)	**አስታይ** astā́͡i̥ (-ā́yy § 6)	**አስታይቶ** astā́͡i̥t^w^o	**ማስታየት** mãstā́͡i̥ät (-tā́ʸät)	
ያስቸግር yãsčā́ggi̥r	**አስቸግር** asčā́ggi̥r	**አስቸግሮ** asčā́ggi̥r^w^o	**ማስቸገር** mãsčā́ggḁr (-är)	**አስቸጋሪ** asčäggā́ri
ያስነሣ yãsnḁ́ssã	**አስነሣ** asnḁ́ssã	**አስነሥቶ** asnḁ́ssi̥t^w^o (-nā́-)	**ማስነሣት** mãsnḁ́ssā́t (§ 8)	**አስነሽ** ā́snḁ́šš (-nā́-; § 8; -ሺ -šši)
ያሰናብት yãssḁnā́bt (-ỵt)	**አሰናብት** assḁnā́bt (-ỵt)	**አሰናብቶ** assḁnā́bt^w^o (-ỵt-)	**ማሰናበት** mãssḁnā́bḁt (-ā́ỵ-, -ät)	**አሰናባች** assḁnā́bā́č (-ā́ỵ-; § 8)

Simp. perf. (§ 25)		Comp. perf. (§ 32)	Contingent (§ 26)	Comp. imperf. (§ 32)
አሰናዳ assḁnā̃́ddā̃	prepare, t.	**አሰናድቷል** assḁnā́d(ĭ̥)- tŏ͡āl (-nā́rt- §7*d*)	**ያሰናዳ** yā̃ssḁnā̃́d- dā̃	**ያሰናዳል** yā̃ssḁnā̃́d- dāl
አሰኘ assā́ññä 2nd **አሰኘህ** assā́ññäh, etc.	cause to be, t.	**አሰኝቷል** assā́ññi̥tŏ͡āl	**ያሰኝ** yā̃ssā́ññ	**ያሰኛል** yā̃ssā́ññāl
አሳከለ asā̃́kkḁlḁ	cause to increase, t.	**አሳክሏል** asā̃́kki̥lŏ͡āl	**ያሳክል** yā̃sā̃́kki̥l	**ያሳክላል** yā̃sḁ̄́kki̥lāl
አስከለከለ askḁlḁ́k- kḁlḁ	cause to hinder, t.	**አስከልክሏል** askḁ́lki̥lŏ͡āl	**ያስከለክል** yā̃skḁlḁ́kki̥l	**ያስከለክላል** yā̃skḁlḁ́kki̥- lāl
አስካካ askā́kkā̃	neigh, i.	**አስካክቷል** askā́ktŏ͡āl	**ያስካክ** yā̃skā́kkā̃	**ያስካካል** yā̃skā́kkāl
አስኬደ Š. askḁ́̃dḁ (-kā̃́-, -dä)	let pass, t.	**አስኬዷል** askḁ́dŏ͡āl (-kā́-)	**ያስኬድ** yā̃skḁ́d (-kā́-)	**ያስኬዳል** yā̃skḁ́dāl (-kā́-)
አስከፈለ askḁ́ffḁlḁ	cause to divide, t.	**አስከፍሏል** askḁ́ffi̥lŏ͡āl	**ያስከፍል** yā̃skḁ́ffi̥l	**ያስከፍላል** yā̃skḁ́ffi̥lāl
አስኼደ G. asχʸḗdä (-sh-[1], -ä̃́d-) [1] not -š-	let pass, t.	**አስኺዷል** ā̃́sχi̥dŏ͡āl (-sh-)	**ያስኼድ** yā̃sχʸḗd (-sh-, -ä̃́d)	**ያስኼዳል** yā̃sχʸḗdāl (-sh-, -ä̃́d-)

Jussive (§ 27)	Imperative (§ 28)	Gerund (§ 29)	Infinitive (§ 30)	Participle (§ 31)
ያሰናዳ yã̄ssḁnã́dã	አሰናዳ assḁnã́dã	አሰናድቶ assḁnã́- d(ĭ̥)tʷo (-nã́rt- § 7*d*)	ማሰናዳት mã̄ssḁnã́- dã́t (§ 8)	አሰናጅ assḁ́nã́j (§ 8; -ጂ -ji)
ያሰኝ yã̄ssã́ññ	አሰኝ assã́ññ	አሰኝቶ assã́ññi̥tʷo	ማሰኘት mã̄ssã́ññät	
ያሳክል yã̄sã́kki̥l	አሳክል asã́kki̥l	አሳክሎ asã́kki̥lʷo	ማሳከል mã̄sã́kkḁl	አሳካይ asã́kkã́i̥ (-ã́yy § 6; § 8)
ያስከልክል yã̄skḁ́lki̥l	አስከልክል askḁ́lki̥l	አስከልክሎ askḁ́lki̥lʷo	ማስከልከል mã̄skḁ́lkḁl	አስከልካይ askḁ́lkã́i̥ (-ã́yy § 6; § 8)
		አስካክቶ askã́ktʷo	ማስካካት mã̄skã́kã́t (§ 8)	
ያስኪድ yã́ski̥d	አስኪድ ã́ski̥d	አስኬዶ askḁ́dʷo (-kã́-)	ማስኬድ mã́skḁ́d (-kã́-; § 8)	አስካጅ ã́skã́j (§ 8; -ጂ -ji)
ያስከፍል yã̄skḁ́ffi̥l	አስከፍል askḁ́ffi̥l	አስከፍሎ askḁ́ffi̥lʷo	ማስከፈል mã̄skḁ́ffḁl (-äl)	አስከፋይ askḁ́ffã́i̥ (-ã́yy § 6; § 8)
ያስኺድ yã́sχi̥d (-sh-)	አስኺድ ã́sχi̥d (-sh-)	አስኺዶ ã́sχi̥dʷo (-sh-)	ማስኼድ mã́sχʸḗd (-sh-, -ä̃́d; § 8)	ያስኺያጅ ã́sχʸã́j (-sh-; -ኻጅ -χã́j, -hã́j; § 8; -ጂ -ji)

Simp. perf. (§ 25)		Comp. perf. (§ 32)	Contingent (§ 26)	Comp. imperf. (§ 32)
አስወሰደ aswḁ́ssḁdḁ (-wώ-)	cause to remove, t.	አስወስዷል aswḁ́ssi̥dŏ͡āl (-wώ-)	ያስወስድ yãswḁ́ssi̥d (-wώ-)	ያስወስዳል yãswḁ́ssi̥dāl (-wώ-)
አሳየ asā́yyä 2nd አሳየህ asā́yyäh, etc.	show, t.	አሳይቷል asā́yyi̥tŏ͡āl	ያሳይ yãsā́yy	ያሳያል yãsā́yyāl
አስያዘ asyā́zḁ	cause to catch, t.	አስይዟል ā́syi̥zŏ͡āl	ያስይዝ yā́syi̥z (§ 8)	ያስይዛል yãsyi̥zāl
አስደረገ asdḁ́rrḁgḁ	cause to do, t.	አስደርጓል asdḁ́rri̥gŏ͡āl (-dā́-)	ያስደርግ yãsdḁ́rri̥g (-dā́-)	ያስደርጋል yãsdḁ́rri̥gāl (-dā́-)
አሳደገ asáddḁgḁ	rear, t.	አሳድጓል asáddi̥gŏ͡āl	ያሳድግ yãsáddi̥g	ያሳድጋል yãsáddi̥gāl
አስገደለ asgḁ́ddḁlḁ (-gā́-)	cause to kill, t.	አስገድሏል asgḁ́ddi̥lŏ͡āl (-gā́-)	ያስገድል yãsgḁ́ddi̥l (-gā́-)	ያስገድላል yãsgḁ́ddi̥lāl (-gā́-)
አስጌጠ asg^{y}éṭḁ	adorn, t.	አስጊጧል ā́sgi̥ṭŏ͡āl	ያስጌጥ yãsg^{y}éṭ	ያስጌጣል yãsg^{y}éṭāl
አሰጣ asḁ́ṭṭã	spread out, t.	አስጥቷል ā́sṭi̥tŏ͡āl	ያሰጣ yãsḁ́ṭã	ያሰጣል yãsḁ́ṭāl
አስጠጋ asṭḁ́ggã	cause to lean, t.	አስጠግቷል asṭḁ́ggi̥tŏ͡āl	ያስጠጋ yãsṭḁ́ggã	ያስጠጋል yãsṭḁ́ggāl

Jussive (§ 27)	Imperative (§ 28)	Gerund (§ 29)	Infinitive (§ 30)	Participle (§ 31)
ያስወስድ yã̄swḁ́ssi̥d (-wώ-)	**አስወስድ** aswḁ́ssi̥d (-wώ-)	**አስወስዶ** aswḁ́ssi̥d^{w}o (-wώ-)	**ማስወሰድ** mã̄swḁ́ssḁd (-wώ-)	**አስወሳጅ** aswḁ́ssã́j (-wώ-; § 8)
ያሳይ yã́sã́͡i̥ (-ã́yy § 6; § 8)	**አሳይ** ã́sã́͡i̥ (-ã́yy § 6; § 8)	**አሳይቶ** asã́yyi̥t^{w}o	**ማሳየት** mã̄sã́yyät	**አሳዪ** asã́yyi
ያስይዝ yã́syi̥z	**አስይዝ** ã́syi̥z	**አስይዞ** ã́syi̥z^{w}o	**ማስያዝ** mã́syã́z (§ 8)	**አስያዥ** ã́syã́ž (§ 8; -ዢ -ži)
ያስደርግ yã̄sdḁ́rri̥g (-dã́-)	**አስደርግ** asdḁ́rri̥g (-dã́-)	**አስደርጎ** asdḁ́rri̥g^{w}o (-dã́-)	**ማስደረግ** mã̄sdḁ́rrḁg	**አስደራጊ** asdḁrrã́gi
ያሳድግ yã̄sáddi̥g	**አሳድግ** asáddi̥g	**አሳድጎ** asáddi̥g^{w}o	**ማሳደግ** mã̄sáddḁg	**አሳዳጊ** asaddã́gi
ያስገድል yã̄sgḁ́ddi̥l (-gã́-)	**አስገድል** asgḁ́ddi̥l (-gã́-)	**አስገድሎ** asgḁ́ddi̥l^{w}o (-gã́-)	**ማስገደል** mã̄sgḁ́ddḁl (-ã́ddä-)	**አስገዳይ** asgḁ́ddã́͡i̥ (-gã́-; -ã́yy § 6; § 8)
ያስጊጥ yã́sgi̥ṭ	**አስጊጥ** ã́sgi̥ṭ	**አስጊጦ** ã́sgi̥ṭ^{w}o	**ማስጌጥ** mã́sg^{y}ẽ́ṭ (§ 8)	
ያስጣ yã́sṭã	**አስጣ** ã́sṭã	**አስጥቶ** ã́sṭi̥t^{w}o	**ማስጣት** mã́sṭã́t (§ 8)	**አስጭ** āsč̣ (-ጪ -č̣i)
ያስጠጋ yã̄sṭḁ́ggã	**አስጠጋ** asṭḁ́ggã	**አስጠግቶ** asṭḁ́ggi̥t^{w}o	**ማስጠጋት** mã̄sṭḁ́ggã́t (§ 8)	**አስጠጊ** asṭḁ́gg^{y}i

Simp. perf. (§ 25)		Comp. perf. (§ 32)	Contingent (§ 26)	Comp. imperf. (§ 32)
አሰፋ asḁ́ffã	extend, t.	አስፍቷል ā́si̥ftŏ͡āl	ያሰፋ yãsḁ́fã	ያሰፋል yãsḁ́fāl
አስፈለገ asfḁ́llḁgḁ	cause to seek, t.	አስፈልጓል asfḁ́lli̥gŏ͡āl	ያስፈልግ yãsfḁ́lli̥g	ያስፈልጋል yãsfḁ́lli̥gāl
አስፈራ asfḁ́rrã (-fä́-)	frighten, t.	አስፈርቷል asfḁ́rri̥tŏ͡āl (-fä́-)	ያስፈራ yãsfḁ́rrã (-fä́-)	ያስፈራል yãsfḁ́rrāl (-fä́-)
አስፈራራ asfḁrã́rrã (-fä-)	threaten, t.	አስፈራርቷል asfḁrártŏ͡āl (-fä-)	ያስፈራራ yãsfḁrã́rrã (-fä-)	ያስፈራራል yãsfḁrã́rrāl (-fä-)
አስፈታ asfḁ́ttã	cause to untie, t.	አስፈትቷል asfḁ́t(i̥)tŏ͡āl	ያስፈታ yãsfḁ́ttã	ያስፈታል yãsfḁ́ttāl
አሸ áššä 2nd አሸሀ áššäh, etc.	seek, t.	uses parts of [እ] ሻ (i̥)šā		
አሸ áššä 2nd አሸሀ áššäh, etc.	rub, t.	አሽቷል ā́štŏ͡āl	ያሽ yāš (yǟš)	ያሻል yā́šāl (yǟ́š-)
አሻቀበ ašā́qqḁbḁ (-yḁ)	turn upwards, i.	አሻቅቧል ašā́qqi̥bŏ͡āl (-i̥y-)	ያሻቅብ yãšā́qqi̥b (-i̥y)	ያሻቅባል yãšā́qqi̥bāl (-i̥y-)
አሸተተ ašḁ́ttḁtḁ (-šä́-)	smell, t.	አሽቷል ā́ši̥ttŏ͡āl	ያሽት yãšḁ́tt (-šä́-)	ያሸታል yãšḁ́ttāl (-šä́-)

Jussive (§ 27)	Imperative (§ 28)	Gerund (§ 29)	Infinitive (§ 30)	Participle (§ 31)
ያስፋ yã́sfã	**አስፋ** ã́sfã	**አስፍቶ** ã́si̥ftʷo	**ማስፋት** mã́sfát (§ 8)	**አስፊ** ã́sfi
ያስፈልግ yãsfḁ́lli̥g	**አስፈልግ** asfḁ́lli̥g	**አስፈልጎ** asfḁ́lli̥gʷo	**ማስፈለግ** mãsfḁ́llḁg	**አስፈላጊ** asfḁllági
ያስፈራ yãsfḁ́rrã (-fä́-)	**አስፈራ** asfḁ́rrã (-fä́-)	**አስፈርቶ** asfḁ́rri̥tʷo (-fä́-)	**ማስፈራት** mãsfḁ́rrát (-fä́-; § 8)	**አስፈሪ** asfḁ́rri (-fä́-)
ያስፈራራ yãsfḁrárã (-fä-)	**አስፈራራ** asfḁrárã (-fä-)	**አስፈራርቶ** asfḁrártʷo (-fä-)	**ማስፈራራት** mãsfḁrárát (-fä-; § 8)	
ያስፈታ yãsfḁ́ttã	**አስፈታ** asfḁ́ttã	**አስፈትቶ** asfḁ́t(i̥)tʷo	**ማስፈታት** mãsfḁ́ttát (§ 8)	**አስፈች** ásfḁ́čč (-fä́-; § 8; -ቺ -čči)
ይሽ yĩš (yĩ̥š)	**እሽ** ĩš (ĩ̥š)	**አሽቶ** ã́štʷo	**ማሽት** mã́šät	
ያሻቅብ yãšã́qqi̥b (-i̥y̥)	**አሻቅብ** ašã́qqi̥b (-i̥y̥)	**አሻቅቦ** ašã́qqi̥bʷo (-i̥y̥-)	**ማሻቀብ** mãšã́qqḁb (-ḁy̥)	**አሻቃቢ** ašãqqábi (-y̥i)
ያሽት yã́ši̥tt	**አሽት** ã́ši̥tt	**አሽቶ** ã́ši̥ttʷo	**ማሽተት** mã́štḁt (-ät)	**አሽታች** ã́štáč (§ 8)

Simp. perf. (§ 25)		Comp. perf. (§ 32)	Contingent (§ 26)	Comp. imperf. (§ 32)
አሸከመ aššḁ́kkḁmḁ (-šắ-)	load, t.	አሸክሟል aššḁ́kki̥- mŏ͡āl (-šắ-)	ያሸክም yãššḁ́kki̥m (-šắ-)	ያሸክማል yãššḁ́kki̥- māl (-šắ-)
አሾከሾከ aššʷokḁ́š- šʷokḁ	talk scan- dal, i.	አሾከሹኳል aššʷokḁ́šŭ- kŏ͡āl [-ሽኳል] (-škŏ͡āl)	ያሾከሹክ yãššʷokḁ́š- šŭk	ያሾከሹካል yãššʷokḁ́š- šŭkāl
አሽካካ aškắkkã	cluck, i.	አሽካክቷል aškắktŏ͡āl	ያሽካካ yãškắkkã	ያሽካካል yãškắkkāl
አሻገረ aššággḁrḁ (-gä-)	take across, t.	አሻግሯል aššágrŏ͡āl	ያሻግር yãššággi̥r	ያሻግራል yãššággi̥rāl
አቈላመጠ aqqwωlắm- mḁṭḁ [እንቈ- G.] (aṅqwω-)	caress, t.	አቈላምጧል aqqwωlắm- ṭŏ͡āl [እንቈ-] (aṅqwω-)	ያቈላምጥ yãqqwω- lắmmi̥ṭ [ያንቈ-] (yãṅqwω-)	ያቈላምጣል yãqqwω- lắmmi̥ṭāl [ያንቈ-] (yãṅqwω-)
አቀለጠ aqḁ́llḁṭḁ	melt, t.	አቅልጧል ắqi̥lṭŏ͡āl (ắqli̥ṭ-)	ያቀልጥ yãqḁ́lṭ	ያቀልጣል yãqḁ́lṭāl
አቆመ aqʷŏ́mḁ	station, t.	አቁሟል ắqumŏ͡āl	ያቆም yãqʷŏ́m	ያቆማል yãqʷŏ́māl
አቅራራ aqrắrrã	chant, i.	አቅራርቷል aqrártŏ͡āl	ያቅራራ yãqrắrrã	ያቅራራል yãqrắrrāl

Jussive (§ 27)	Imperative (§ 28)	Gerund (§ 29)	Infinitive (§ 30)	Participle (§ 31)
ያሸክም yãššḁ́kki̥m (-šắ-)	አሸክም aššḁ́kki̥m (-šắ-)	አሸክሞ aššḁ́kki̥mʷo (-šắ-)	ማሸከም mãššḁ́kkḁm (-šắ-)	አሸካሚ aššḁkkắmi (-šä-)
ያሾክሹክ yãššʷokḁ́- šŭk [-ሽክ] (-šk)	አሾክሹክ aššʷokḁ́šŭk [-ሽክ] [-šk]	አሾክሹኮ aššʷokḁ́šŭ- kʷo [-ሽኮ] (-škʷo)	ማሾክሾክ mãššʷokḁ́- šʷok	አሾክሿኪ aššʷokšwắ- ki
		አሽካክቶ aškắktʷo	ማሽካካት mãškắkắt (§ 8)	
ያሻግር yãššắgi̥r	አሻግር aššắgi̥r	አሻግሮ aššắgrʷo	ማሻገር mãššắgḁr (-är)	አሻጋሪ aššāgắri
ያቈላምጥ yãqqwώ- lắmṭ (§ 8) [ያንቈ-] (yãṅqwώ-)	አቈላምጥ aqqwώ- lắmṭ (§ 8) [አንቈ-] (aṅqwώ-)	አቈላምጦ aqqwω- lắmṭʷo [አንቈ-] (aṅqwω-)	ማቈላመጥ mãqqwω- lắmḁṭ [ማንቈ-] (mãṅqwω-)	አቈላማጭ aqqwωlắ- mắč̣ (§ 8) [አንቈ-] (aṅqwω-)
ያቅልጥ yắqi̥lṭ (yắqli̥ṭ)	አቅልጥ ắqi̥lṭ (ắqli̥ṭ)	አቅልጦ ắqi̥lṭʷo (ắqli̥ṭ-)	ማቅለጥ mắqlḁṭ	አቅላጭ ắqlắč̣ (§ 8)
ያቁም yắqum	አቁም ắqum	አቁሞ ắqumʷo	ማቆም mắqʷōm (§ 8)	አቋሚ ãqwắmi
ያቅራራ yãqrắrã	አቅራራ aqrắrã	አቅራርቶ aqrắrtʷo	ማቅራራት mãqrắrắt (§ 8)	አቅራሪ ãqrắri

Simp. perf. (§ 25)		Comp. perf. (§ 32)	Contingent (§ 26)	Comp. imperf. (§ 32)
አቀራረበ aqqḁrā́rrḁ- bḁ (-ỵḁ)	put close together, t.	አቀራርቧል aqqḁrā́r(ĭ̥)- bŏ͡āl (-ỵŏ-)	ያቀራርብ yãqqḁrā́r- ri̥b (-i̥ỵ)	ያቀራርባል yãqqḁrā́r- ri̥bāl (-i̥ỵ-)
አቀረበ aqḁ́rrḁbḁ (-ỵḁ)	bring near, t.	አቅርቧል ā́qi̥rbŏ͡āl (ā́qri̥-, -ỵŏ-)	ያቀርብ yãqḁ́rb (-qā́-, -rỵ)	ያቀርባል yãqḁ́rbāl (-qā́-, -rỵ-)
አቈሰለ aqwώssḁlḁ	wound, t.	አቍስሏል ā́qwŭs(ĭ̥)lŏ͡āl (ā́qsül-)	ያቈስል yãqwώs(ĭ̥)l	ያቈስላል yãqwώs(ĭ̥)- lāl
አቀና aqḁ́nnã	straighten, t.	አቅንቷል ā́qi̥ntŏ͡āl	ያቀና yãqḁ́nã	ያቀናል yãqḁ́nāl
አቈየ aqwώyyä 2nd አቈየሁ aqwώyyäh, etc.	delay, t.	አቈይቷል ãqwώyyi̥- tŏ͡āl	ያቈይ yãqwώyy	ያቈያል yãqwώyyāl
አቃጠለ a(q)qā́ṭṭḁlḁ	burn, t.	አቃጥሏል a(q)qā́ṭ(ĭ̥)- lŏ͡āl	ያቃጥል yã(q)qā́ṭṭi̥l	ያቃጥላል yã(q)qā́ṭṭi̥- lāl
አቀፈ áqqḁfḁ	embrace, t.	አቅፏል ā́qfŏ͡āl	ያቅፍ yãqf	ያቅፋል yā́qfāl
አበለ ábbḁlḁ	break one's word, i.	አብሏል ā́blŏ͡āl (-ỵl-)	ያብል yā́b(ĭ̥)l (-ā́ỵ-)	ያብላል yā́blāl (-ỵl-)

Jussive (§ 27)	Imperative (§ 28)	Gerund (§ 29)	Infinitive (§ 30)	Participle (§ 31)
ያቀራርብ yãqqḁrắ- r(i̥)b (-(i̥)y̥)	አቀራርብ aqqḁrắr(i̥)b (-(i̥)y̥)	አቀራርቦ aqqḁrắr(i̥)- bʷo (-y̥ʷo)	ማቀራረብ mãqqḁrắ- rḁb (-ḁy̥)	አቀራራቢ aqqḁrārắbi (-y̥i)
ያቅርብ yắqi̥rb (yắqri̥-, -y̥)	አቅርብ ắqi̥rb (ắqri̥-, -y̥)	አቅርቦ ắqi̥rbʷo (ắqri̥-, -y̥ʷo)	ማቅረብ mắqrḁb (-ḁy̥)	አቅራቢ ãqrắbi (-y̥i)
ያቍስል yắqwŭs(i̥)l (yắqsül)	አቍስል ắqwŭs(i̥)l (ắqsül)	አቍስሎ ắqwŭs(i̥)lʷo (ắqsül-)	ማቍሰል mắqwŭsḁl (-äl)	አቍሳይ ắqwŭsắi̥ (-ắyy § 6; § 8)
ያቅና yắq(i̥)nã	አቅና ắq(i̥)nã	አቅንቶ ắqi̥ntʷo	ማቅናት mắqnắt (§ 8)	አቅኝ ắqi̥ñ [አቅኚ] (ắqñi)
ያቄይ yắqwώyy (§ 8)	አቄይ ắqwώyy	አቄይቶ ãqwώyyi̥tʷo	ማቄየት mãqwώy- yät	
ያቃጥል yã(q)qắṭ(i̥)l	አቃጥል a(q)qắṭ(i̥)l	አቃጥሎ a(q)qắṭ(i̥)- lʷo	ማቃጠል mã(q)qắṭḁl (-äl)	አቃጣይ a(q)qắṭắi̥ (-ắyy § 6 ; § 8)
ይቀፍ yi̥qḁf	እቀፍ i̥qḁf	አቅፎ ắqfʷo	ማቀፍ mắqḁf	አቃፊ ãqắfi
neg. አይበል ắi̥bḁl (-i̥y̥-, -äl)	neg. አትበል ãtti̥bḁl (-i̥y̥-, -äl)	አብሎ ắblʷo (-y̥l-)	ማበል mắbḁl (-ắy̥-, -äl)	አባይ ắbắi̥ (ắy̥-; -ắyy § 6; § 8)

Simp. perf. (§ 25)		Comp. perf. (§ 32)	Contingent (§ 26)	Comp. imperf. (§ 32)
አበላ abḁ́llā̃ (aỵ-)	feed, t.	አብልቷል ā́bi̥ltŏ͡āl (ā̃́bli̥t-, ā̃́ỵ-)	ያበላ yā̃bḁ́lā̃ (-ā̃ỵ-)	ያበላል yā̃bḁ́lāl (-ā̃ỵ-)
አበላሸ abbḁlā́ššä 2nd አበላሸህ abbḁlā́ššäh, etc.	spoil, t.	አበላሽቷል abbḁlā́štŏ͡āl	ያበላሽ yā̃bbḁlā́šš	ያበላሻል yā̃bbḁlā́ššāl
አበለጠ abḁ́llḁṭḁ (aỵ-)	increase, t.	አብልጧል ā̃́bli̥ṭŏ͡āl (ā̃́ỵ-, -i̥lṭ-)	ያበልጥ yā̃bḁ́lṭ (-ā̃ỵ-, -ā́l-)	ያበልጣል yā̃bḁ́lṭāl (-ā̃ỵ-, -ā́l-)
አብለጨለጨ abläç̣ā́lläç̣ä (-ỵl-)	glitter, i.		ያብለጨልጭ yā̃bläç̣ā́lli̥ç̣ (-ỵl-)	ያብለጨልጫል yā̃bläç̣ā́l- li̥ç̣āl (-ỵl-)
አበራ abḁ́rrā̃ (aỵ-)	shine, i.	አብርቷል ā́bi̥rtŏ͡āl (ā̃́ỵ-)	ያበራ yā̃bḁ́rā̃ (-ā̃ỵ-, -ā̃́r-)	ያበራል yā̃bḁ́rāl (-ā̃ỵ-, -ā̃́r-)
አበሰ ábbḁsḁ	wipe, t.	አብሷል ábbi̥sŏ͡āl	ያብስ yā̃́bbi̥s	ያብሳል yā̃́bbi̥sāl
አበሰለ abḁ́ssḁlḁ (aỵ-)	cook, t.	አብስሏል ā̃́bsi̥lŏ͡āl (ā̃́ỵ-)	ያበስል yā̃bḁ́s(ĭ̥)l (-ā̃ỵ-)	ያበስላል yā̃bḁ́s(ĭ̥)lāl (-ā̃ỵ-)
አበሰበሰ abḁsḁ́bbḁsḁ (aỵ-)	wet, t.	አበስብሷል abḁ́sbi̥sŏ͡āl (-ỵḁ́sỵ-)	ያበሰብስ yābḁsḁ́bbi̥s (-āỵ-)	ያበሰብሳል yābḁsḁ́bbi̥- sāl (-āỵ-)

Jussive (§ 27)	Imperative (§ 28)	Gerund (§ 29)	Infinitive (§ 30)	Participle (§ 31)
ያ·በላ yã́blã (-ỵl-)	አ·በላ ã́blã (-ỵl-)	አ·በል·ቶ ábi̥lt^{w}o (ã́bli̥t-, ã́ỵ-)	ማ·በላ·ት mã́blã́t (-ỵl-; § 8)	አ·በይ ã́byi (ã́bī, ã́ỵ-)
ያበላሽ yãbbḁlã́š (§ 8)	አበላሽ abbḁlã́š (§ 8)	አበላሽ·ቶ abbḁlã́št^{w}o	ማበላሽ·ት mãbbḁlá- šät	አበላሺ abbḁlã́ši
ያ·በል·ጥ yã́bli̥ṭ (-ã́ỵ-, -i̥lṭ)	አ·በል·ጥ ã́bli̥ṭ (ã́ỵ-, -i̥lṭ)	አ·በል·ጦ ã́bli̥ṭ^{w}o (ã́ỵ-, -i̥lṭ-)	ማ·በለ·ጥ mã́blḁṭ (-ỵl-)	አ·በላ·ጭ ã́blã́č̣ (-ỵl-; § 8)
		አ·በለ·ጭል·ጮ ablã́č̣li̥č̣^{w}o (-ỵl-)	ማ·በለ·ጭለ·ጭ mãblã́č̣läč̣ (-ỵl-)	
ያ·በራ yã́brã (-ỵr-)	አ·በራ ã́brã (-ỵr-)	አ·በር·ቶ ábi̥rt^{w}o (ã́ỵ-)	ማ·በራ·ት mã́brã́t (-ỵr-; § 8)	አ·በሪ ã́bri (-ỵr-)
ይበስ yí̥bḁs (-ỵḁs) ያ·በስ yã́bbi̥s	እበስ í̥bḁs (-ỵḁs) አ·በስ ábbi̥s	አ·በሶ ḁ́bbi̥s^{w}o	ማበስ mã́bbḁs	አባሽ ábbã́š (§ 8)
ያ·በስል yã́bsi̥l (-ỵs-)	አ·በስል ã́bsi̥l (-ỵs-)	አ·በስሎ ã́bsi̥l^{w}o (-ỵs-)	ማ·በሰል mã́bsḁl (-ỵs-, -äl)	አ·በሳይ ã́bsã́i̥ (-ỵs-; -ã́yy § 6; § 8)
ያበስ·በስ yãbḁ́sbi̥s (-ỵḁ́sỵ-)	አበስ·በስ abḁ́sbi̥s (-ỵḁ́sỵ-)	አበስ·በሶ abḁ́sbi̥s^{w}o (-ỵḁ́sỵ-)	ማበስበስ mãbḁ́sbḁs (-ỵḁ́sỵ-)	አበስባሽ abḁ́sbã́š (-ỵḁ́sỵ-; § 8)

Simp. perf. (§ 25)		Comp. perf. (§ 32)	Contingent (§ 26)	Comp. imperf. (§ 32)
አበቃ abḁ́qqā̃ (aỵ-, -ắq-)	finish, i. & t.	አብቅቷል ắbqi̥tŏ͡āl (-ỵq-)	ያበቃ yā̃bḁ́qā̃ (-ā̃ỵ-, -ắq-)	ያበቃል yā̃bḁ́qāl (-ā̃ỵ-, -ắq-)
አበበ ábbḁbḁ (-ỵḁ)	bloom, i.	አብቧል ábbi̥bŏ͡āl (-ỵŏ-)	ያብብ yắbbi̥b (-i̥ỵ)	ያብባል yắbbi̥bāl (-i̥ỵ-)
አበደ ábbḁdḁ	be mad, i.	አብዷል ắbdŏ͡āl (-ỵd-)	ያብድ yā̃bd (-ỵd)	ያብዳል yắbdāl (-ỵd-)
አበደረ abḁ́ddḁrḁ (aỵ-, -ắddä-)	lend, t.	አበድሯል abḁ́ddi̥rŏ͡āl (aỵ-, -ắdd-)	ያበድር yā̃bḁ́ddi̥r (-ā̃ỵ-, -ắdd-)	ያበድራል yā̃bḁ́ddi̥rāl (-ā̃ỵ-, -ắdd-)
አበጀ abḁ́jjä (aỵ-, -ắj-) 2nd -ጀህ -jjäh, etc.	make, t.	አበጅቷል abḁ́jji̥tŏ͡āl (aỵ-, -ắj-)	ያበጅ yā̃bḁ́jj (-ā̃ỵ-, -ắj-)	ያበጃል yā̃bḁ́jjāl (-ā̃ỵ-, -ắj-)
አበጠ ábbḁṭḁ	swell, i.	አብጧል ắbṭŏ͡āl (-ỵṭ-)	ያብጥ yā̃bṭ (-ỵṭ)	ያብጣል yắbṭāl (-ỵṭ-)
አበጠረ abḁ́ṭṭḁrḁ (aỵ-, -ắṭṭä-)	winnow, t.	አበጥሯል abḁ́ṭṭi̥rŏ͡āl (aỵ-, -ắṭ-)	ያበጥር yā̃bḁ́ṭṭi̥r (-ā̃ỵ-, -ắṭ-)	ያበጥራል yā̃bḁ́ṭṭi̥rāl (-ā̃ỵ-, -ắṭ-)
አታለለ attắllḁlḁ	deceive, t.	አታሏል attắllŏ͡āl	ያታልል yā̃ttắlli̥l	ያታልላል yā̃ttắlli̥lāl

Jussive (§ 27)	Imperative (§ 28)	Gerund (§ 29)	Infinitive (§ 30)	Participle (§ 31)
ያብቃ yã́bqã (-ṿq-)	**አብቃ** ã́bqã (-ṿq-)	**አብቅቶ** ã́bqi̥t^{w}o (-ṿq-)	**ማብቃት** mã́bqát (-ṿq- ; § 8)	**†አብቂ** ã́bqi (-ṿq-)
ያብብ yã́bbi̥b (-i̥ṿ)		**አብቦ** ábbi̥b^{w}o (-ṿ^{w}o)	**ማበብ** mã́bbḁb (-ḁṿ)	**አባቢ** abbã́bi (-ṿi)
		አብዶ ã́bd^{w}o (-ṿd-)	**ማበድ** mã́bḁd (-ṿḁ-)	**አባጅ** áb(b)ã́j (§ 8)
ያበድር yãbḁ́ddi̥r (-ãṿ-, -ã́dd-)	**አበድር** abḁ́ddi̥r (aṿ-, -ã́dd-)	**አበድሮ** abḁ́ddi̥r^{w}o (aṿ-, -ã́dd-)	**ማበደር** mãbḁ́ddḁr (-ãṿ-, -ã́ddä-)	**አበዳሪ** abḁddã́ri (aṿ-, -ädd-)
ያብጅ yábi̥jj (-ã́ṿ-)	**አብጅ** ã́bi̥jj (ã́ṿ-)	**አበጅቶ** abḁ́jji̥t^{w}o (aṿ-, -ã́j-)	**ማበጀት** mãbḁ́jjät (-ãṿ-, -ã́j-)	
ይበጥ yí̥bḁṭ (-ṿḁ-)	**እበጥ** í̥bḁṭ (-ṿḁ-)	**አብጦ** ã́bṭ^{w}o (-ṿṭ-)	**ማበጥ** mábḁṭ (-ṿḁ-)	**አባጭ** ã́bã́č̣ (ã́ṿ- ; § 8)
ያበጥር yãbḁ́ṭṭi̥r (-ãṿ-, -ã́ṭ-)	**አበጥር** abḁ́ṭṭi̥r (aṿ-, -ã́ṭ-)	**አበጥሮ** abḁ́ṭṭi̥r^{w}o (aṿ-, -ã́ṭ-)	**ማበጠር** mãbḁ́ṭṭḁr (-ãṿ-, -ã́ṭṭä-)	**አበጣሪ** abḁṭṭã́ri (aṿ-, -äṭṭ-)
ያታልል yãttã́li̥l	**አታልል** attã́li̥l	**አታሎ** attã́ll^{w}o	**ማታለል** mãttálḁl (-äl)	**አታላይ** attã́lá͡i̥ (-ã́yy § 6; § 8)

Simp. perf. (§ 25)		Comp. perf. (§ 32)	Contingent (§ 26)	Comp. imperf. (§ 32)
አተመ áttḁmḁ	seal, t. (= ኀተመ)	አትሟል átti̥mŏ͡āl	ያትም yắtti̥m	ያትማል yắtti̥māl
አተረፈ atḁ́rrḁfḁ (-tắ-)	earn, t.	አትርፏል ắti̥rfŏ͡āl	ያተርፍ yãtḁ́rf (-tắ-)	ያተርፋል yãtḁ́rfāl (-tắ-)
አኖረ anʷŏ́rḁ	put, t.	አኑሯል ắnurŏ͡āl	ያኖር yãnʷŏ́r	ያኖራል yãnʷŏ́rāl
አነሰ ánnḁsḁ	diminish, i.	አንሷል ắnsŏ͡āl	ያንስ yãns	ያንሳል yắnsāl
አነሣ anḁ́ssã	raise, t.	አንሥቷል ắnsi̥tŏ͡āl	ያነሣ yãnḁ́sã	ያነሣል yãnḁ́sāl
አንሾካሾከ Š. anšʷokáš- šʷokḁ	whisper, t.	አንሾካሹኳል anšʷokắšŭ- kŏ͡āl [-ሽኳል] (-škŏ͡āl)	ያንሾካሹክ yãnšʷokáš- šŭk	ያንሾካሹካል yãnšʷokáš- šŭkāl
አነቃ anḁ́qqã	wake, t.	አንቅቷል ắṅqi̥tŏ͡āl	ያነቃ yãnḁ́qã	ያነቃል yãnḁ́qāl
አንቀላፋ aṅqḁlắffã	doze, i.	አንቀላፍቷል aṅqḁlắftŏ͡āl	ያንቀላፋ yãṅqḁlắffã	ያንቀላፋል yãṅqḁlắffāl
አንቀሳቀሰ aṅqḁsắq- qḁsḁ	move, t.	አንቀሳቅሷል aṅqḁsắq(i̥)- sŏ͡āl	ያንቀሳቅስ yãṅqḁsắq- qi̥s	ያንቀሳቅሳል yãṅqḁsắq- qi̥sāl
አነበበ anḁ́bbḁbḁ (-ṿḁ)	read, t.	አንብቧል ắnbi̥bŏ͡āl (ắmb-, -i̥ṿ-)	ያነብ yãnḁ́bb	ያነባል yãnḁ́bbāl

Jussive (§ 27)	Imperative (§ 28)	Gerund (§ 29)	Infinitive (§ 30)	Participle (§ 31)
ያትም yā́ttịm	አትም áttịm	አትሞ áttịmʷo	ማትም mā́ttạm	አታሚ attā́mi
ያትርፍ yā́tịrf	አትርፍ ā́tịrf	አትርፎ ā́tịrfʷo	ማትረፍ mā́trạf	አትራፊ ãtrā́fi
ያኑር yā́nur	አኑር ā́nur	አኑሮ ā́nurʷo	ማኖር mā́nʷṓr (§8)	አኗሪ anwā́ri
ይነስ yịnạs		አንሶ ā́nsʷo	ማነስ mā́nạs	አናሽ ā́nā́š (§ 8)
ያንሣ yā́nsã	አንሣ ā́nsã	አንሥቶ ā́nsịtʷo	ማንሣት mā́nsā́t (§8)	አንሽ ānš (-ሺ -ši)
ያንሾካሹክ yãnšʷokā́- šŭk	አንሾካሹክ anšʷokā́- šŭk	አንሾካሹኮ anšʷokā́- šŭkʷo [-ሽኮ] (-škʷo)	ማንሾካሾክ mãnšʷo- kā́šʷok	አንሾካሿኪ anšʷokā- šwā́ki
ያንቃ yā́ṅqã	አንቃ ā́ṅqã	አንቅቶ ā́ṅqịtʷo	ማንቃት mā́ṅqā́t(§8)	አንቂ ā́ṅqi
ያንቀላፋ yãṅqạlā́fã	አንቀላፋ aṅqạlā́fã	አንቀላፍቶ aṅqạlā́ftʷo	ማንቀላፋት mãṅqạlā́fā́t (§ 8)	አንቀላፊ aṅqạlā́fi
ያንቀሳቅስ yãṅqạsā́- q(ị)s	አንቀሳቅስ aṅqạsā́q(ị)s	አንቀሳቅሶ aṅqạsā́- q(ị)sʷo	ማንቀሳቀስ mãṅqạsā́- qạs	
ያንቡብ yā́nbịb (-ā́mb-, -ịy̥)	አንቡብ ā́nbịb (ā́mb-, -ịy̥)	አንቡቦ ā́nbịbʷo (ā́mb-, -ịy̥-)	ማንበብ mā́nbạb (-ā́mb-, -ạy̥)	አንባቢ anbā́bi (amb-, -y̥i)

Simp. perf. (§ 25)		Comp. perf. (§ 32)	Contingent (§ 26)	Comp. imperf. (§ 32)
አንኳረፈ aṅkwā́rrḁfḁ	snore, purr, i.	አንኳርፏል aṅkwā́r(i̥)-fo͡āl	ያንኳርፍ yãṅkwā́rri̥f	ያንኳርፋል yãṅkwā́rri̥-fāl
አነከሰ anḁ̆kkḁsḁ	be lame, i.	አንክሷል ā́ṅki̥so͡āl	ያነክስ yãnḁ̆kki̥s	ያነክሳል yãnḁ̆kki̥sāl
አንኰሻኰሸ aṅkwωšák-kwωšḁ	cause to rustle, t.	አንኰሻኵሿል aṅkwωšā́-kwŭšo͡āl	ያንኰሻኵሽ yãṅkwωšák-kwŭš	ያንኰሻኵሻል yãṅkwωšák-kwŭšāl
አንከባለለ aṅkḁbállḁlḁ (-y̥á-)	roll, t.	አንከባሏል aṅkḁbállo͡āl (-y̥á-)	ያንከባልል yãṅkḁbálli̥l (-y̥á-)	ያንከባልላል yãṅkḁbálli̥-lāl (-y̥á-)
አንኳኳ aṅkwā́kkwã	clatter, i.	አንኳኵቷል aṅkwā́kwŭ-to͡āl (-ákt-)	ያንኳኳ yãṅkwā́k-kwã	ያንኳኳል yãṅkwā́k-kwāl
አናወጠ annā́͡uwḁṭḁ (-wω-)	disturb, t.	አናውጧል annā́͡uŭṭo͡āl	ያናውጥ yãnnā́͡uwŭṭ	ያናውጣል yãnnā́͡uwŭ-ṭāl
አነደደ anḁ̆ddḁdḁ	kindle, t.	አንድዷል ā́ndi̥do͡āl	ያነድድ yãnḁ̆ddi̥d ያነድ yãnḁ̆dd	ያነድዳል yãnḁ̆ddi̥dāl ያነዳል yãnḁ̆ddāl
አንጐራጐረ aṅgwωrág-gwωrḁ	hum, i.		ያንጐራጕር yãṅgwωrág-gwŭr	ያንጐራጕራል yãṅgwωrág-gwŭrāl
አነገተ anḁ̆ggḁtḁ	sling over the shoulder, t.	አንግቷል ā́ngi̥to͡āl	ያነግት yãnḁ̆ggi̥t	ያነግታል yãnḁ̆ggi̥tāl

Jussive (§ 27)	Imperative (§ 28)	Gerund (§ 29)	Infinitive (§ 30)	Participle (§ 31)
ያንኳርፍ yãṅkwā́rĭ̥f (yā́ṅkwā́rf § 8)	አንኳርፍ aṅkwā́rĭ̥f (áṅkwā́rf § 8)	አንኳርፎ aṅkwā́r(ĭ̥)-fʷo	ማንኳረፍ mãṅkwā́rḁf	አንኳራፊ aṅkwārā́fi
		አንክሶ ā́ṅki̥sʷo	ማንከስ mā́ṅkḁs	አንካሽ ā́ṅkā́š (§ 8)
ያንኰሻኵሽ yãṅkwωšā́-kwŭ́š	አንኰሻኵሽ aṅkwωšā́-kwŭ́š	አንኰሻኵሾ aṅkwωšā́-kwŭ́šʷo	ማንኰሻኰሽ mãṅkwωšā́-kwωš	አንኰሻኳሽ aṅkwωšā́-kwā́š (§ 8)
ያንከባልል yãṅkḁbā́lĭ̥l (-ỵā́-)	አንከባልል aṅkḁbā́lĭ̥l (-ỵā́-)	አንከባሎ aṅkḁbállʷo (-ỵá-)	ማንከባለል mãṅkḁbā́lḁl (-ỵā́-, -äl)	አንከባላይ aṅkḁbálā́i̥ (-ỵá-; -ā́yy § 6; § 8)
ያንኳኳ yãṅkwā́kwã	አንኳኳ aṅkwā́kwã	አንኳኵቶ aṅkwā́kwŭ́-tʷo (-ā́kt-)	ማንኳኳት mãṅkwā́-kwā́t (§ 8)	
ያናውጥ yãnnā́uŭ́ṭ	አናውጥ annā́uŭ́ṭ	አናውጦ annā́uŭ́ṭʷo	ማናወጥ mãnnā́uḁṭ (-ωṭ)	አናዋጭ annā́uā́č̣ (§ 8)
ያንድድ yā́ndi̥d	አንድድ ā́ndi̥d	አንድዶ ā́ndi̥dʷo	ማንደድ mā́ndḁd	አንዳጅ ā́ndáj (§ 8)
ያንጐራጕር yãṅgwωrā́-gwŭ́r	አንጐራጕር aṅgwωrā́-gwŭ́r	አንጐራጕሮ aṅgwωrā́-gwŭ́rʷo	ማንጐራጐር mãṅgwωrā́-gwωr	አንጐራጓሪ aṅgwωrā-gwā́ri
ያንግት yā́ṅgi̥t	አንግት ā́ṅgi̥t	አንግቶ ā́ṅgi̥tʷo	ማንገት mā́ṅgḁt	አንጋች ā́ṅgā́č (§ 8)

Simp. perf. (§ 25)		Comp. perf. (§ 32)	Contingent (§ 26)	Comp. imperf. (§ 32)
አነጠ ánnḁṭḁ	fashion, t.	አንጧል ánni̥ṭŏ͡āl	ያንጥ yã́nni̥ṭ	ያንጣል yã́nni̥ṭāl
አንጠለጠለ anṭḁlḁ́ṭṭḁlḁ	hang, t.	አንጠልጥሏል anṭḁ́lṭi̥lŏ͡āl (-ṭá-)	ያንጠለጥል yãnṭḁlḁ́ṭṭi̥l	ያንጠለጥላል yãnṭḁlḁ́ṭṭi̥- lāl
አነጠሰ anḁ́ṭṭḁsḁ	sneeze, i.	አንጥሷል ã́nṭi̥sŏ͡āl	ያነጥስ yãnḁ́ṭṭi̥s	ያነጥሳል yãnḁ́ṭṭi̥sāl
አነጠፈ anḁ́ṭṭḁfḁ	spread, t.	አንጥፏል ã́nṭi̥fŏ͡āl	ያነጥፍ yãnḁ́ṭṭi̥f	ያነጥፋል yãnḁ́ṭṭi̥fāl
አከለ ákkḁlḁ	amount to, i.	አክሏል ákki̥lŏ͡āl	ያክል yã́kki̥l ያኽል [ያህል] yã́k(i̥)l (yã́χ-, yã́h-)	ያክላል yã́kki̥lāl ያኽላል [ያህ-] yã́k(i̥)lāl (yã́χ-, yã́h-)
አከራየ akkḁrã́yyä (-kä-) 2nd -ራየህ -rã́yyäh, etc.	let on hire, t.	አከራይቷል akkḁráyi̥- tŏ͡āl (-kä-, -á͡i̥t-)	ያከራይ yãkkḁrã́yy (-kä-)	ያከራያል yãkkḁrã́y- yāl (-kä-)
አከበረ akḁ́bbḁrḁ (-bä-)	honour, t.	አክብሯል ã́kbi̥rŏ͡āl (-kẏ-, -ki̥br-, -ẏr-)	ያክብር yãkḁ́b(ĭ̥)r (-ḁ́ẏ-)	ያከብራል yãkḁ́b(i̥)rāl (-ḁ́ẏ-)
አከከ ákkḁkḁ	scratch, t.	አኳል ã́kkŏ͡āl	ያክ yãkk	ያካል yã́kkāl
አካፈለ akkã́ffḁlḁ	distribute, t.	አካፍሏል akkã́flŏ͡āl	ያካፍል yãkkã́ffi̥l	ያካፍላል yãkkã́ffi̥lāl

Jussive (§ 27)	Imperative (§ 28)	Gerund (§ 29)	Infinitive (§ 30)	Participle (§ 31)
ያንጥ yä́nni̥ṭ	አንጥ ánni̥ṭ	አንጦ ánni̥ṭʷo	ማንጥ mä́nnḁṭ	አናጢ an(n)ä́ṭi (§ 7*b*)
ያንጠልጥል yäntạ̊lti̥̣l (-ṭä́-)	አንጠልጥል anṭḁlṭi̥l (-ṭä́-)	አንጠልጥሎ anṭḁlṭi̥lʷo (-ṭä́-)	ማንጠልጠል mänṭḁlṭḁl (-ä́lṭä-)	አንጠልጣይ anṭḁlṭä́i̥ (-ṭä́- ; -ä́yy § 6; § 8)
ያንጥስ yä́nṭi̥s	አንጥስ ä́nṭi̥s	አንጥሶ ä́nṭi̥sʷo	ማንጠስ mä́nṭḁs	አንጣሽ ä́nṭä́š (§ 8)
ያንጥፍ yä́nṭi̥f	አንጥፍ ä́nṭi̥f	አንጥፎ ä́nṭi̥fʷo	ማንጠፍ mä́nṭḁf	አንጣፊ anṭä́fi
ያክል yä́kki̥l	አክል ákki̥l	አክሎ ákki̥lʷo	ማከል mä́kkḁl ማህል máhal	አካይ ákkä́i̥ (-ä́yy § 6; § 8)
ያከራይ yäkkḁrái̥ (-kä-)	አከራይ akkḁrái̥ (-kä-)	አከራይቶ akkḁrá- yi̥tʷo (-kä-, -ái̥t-)	ማከራየት mäkkḁráyät (-kä-, -ái̥ät)	
ያክብር yákbi̥r (-kỵ̈-, -ki̥br, -ỵ̈r)	አክብር ä́kbi̥r (-kỵ̈-, -ki̥br, -ỵ̈r)	አክብሮ ä́kbi̥rʷo (-kỵ̈-, -ki̥br-, -ỵ̈r-)	ማክበር mákbḁr (-kỵ̈-, -är)	አክባሪ äkbä́ri (-kỵ̈-)
ይከክ yí̥kḁk	እከክ í̥kḁk	አኮ ä́kkʷo	ማከክ mákḁk	አካኪ äkä́ki
ያካፍል yäkkä́fi̥l	አካፍል akkä́fi̥l	አካፍሎ akkä́flʷo	መካፈል mäkkä́fḁl (-äl)	አካፋይ akkä́fä́i̥ (-ä́yy § 6; § 8)

Simp. perf. (§ 25)		Comp. perf. (§ 32)	Contingent (§ 26)	Comp. imperf. (§ 32)
አወለቀ awḁ́llḁqḁ (a͡uḁ́-, -ώl-)	take off, t.	**አውልቋል** á͡uli̥qŏ͡āl	**ያወልቅ** yãwḁ́lq (ya͡uḁ́-, -ώlq)	**ያወልቃል** yãwḁ́lqāl (ya͡uḁ́-, -ώlq-)
አወረደ awώrrḁdḁ (a͡uώ-)	unload, t.	**አውርዷል** ấwŭrdŏ͡āl (á͡uŭ-)	**ያወርድ** yãwώrd (ya͡uώ-)	**ያወርዳል** yãwώrdāl (ya͡uώ-)
አዋሰ awấsḁ (a͡uấ-)	bring as guarantor, t.	**አውሷል** ấwi̥sŏ͡āl (á͡uŭs-)	**ያውስ** yấwi̥s (yá͡uŭs)	**ያውሳል** yấwi̥sāl (yá͡uŭs-)
አወቀ á͡uwḁqḁ (-wω-)	know, t.	**አውቋል** á͡u(ŭ)qŏ͡āl	**ያውቅ** yá͡u(ŭ)q	**ያውቃል** yá͡u(ŭ)qāl
አወዛወዘ a͡uwḁzá͡u-wḁzḁ (-ωzá͡uwω-)	shake, t.	**አወዛውዟል** a͡uwḁzá͡uŭ-zŏ͡āl (a͡uwωz-)	**ያወዛውዝ** ya͡uwḁzá͡u-wŭz (ya͡uwωz-)	**ያወዛውዛል** ya͡uwḁzá͡u-wŭzāl (ya͡uwωz-)
አውደለደለ a͡udḁlḁ́d-dḁlḁ (-älấddä-)	be idle, i.	**አውደልድሏል** a͡udḁ́ldi̥lŏ͡āl (-dấ-)	**ያውደለድል** ya͡udḁlḁ́d-di̥l (-älấ-)	**ያውደለድላል** ya͡udḁlḁ́d-di̥lāl (-älấ-)
አወጣ awώṭṭã (a͡uώ-)	expel, t.	**አውጥቷል** á͡uṭtŏ͡āl	**ያወጣ** yãwώṭã (ya͡uώ-)	**ያወጣል** yãwώṭāl (ya͡uώ-)
አዘመተ azzḁ́mmḁtḁ	send on a campaign, t.	**አዘምቷል** azzḁ́mmi̥-tŏ͡āl	**ያዘምት** yãzzḁ́mmi̥t	**ያዘምታል** yãzzḁ́mmi̥-tāl

Jussive (§ 27)	Imperative (§ 28)	Gerund (§ 29)	Infinitive (§ 30)	Participle (§ 31)
ያውልቅ yá͡uli̥q	**አውልቅ** á͡uli̥q	**አውልቆ** á͡uli̥qʷo	**ማውለቅ** má͡ulḁq	
ያውርድ yã́wŭrd (yá͡uŭ-)	**አውርድ** ã́wŭrd (á͡uŭ-)	**አውርዶ** ã́wŭrdʷo (á͡uŭ-)	**ማውረድ** má͡urḁd	**አውራጅ** á͡urã́j (§ 8)
ያውስ yã́wi̥s (yá͡uŭs)	**አውስ** ã́wi̥s (á͡uŭs)	**አውሶ** ã́wi̥sʷo (á͡uŭsʷo)	**ማዋስ** mã́wã́s (má͡uã́s; §8)	**አዋሽ** ã́wã́š (á͡uã́š ; § 8 ; -**ሺ** -ši)
ይወቅ yí̥wḁq (yúḁ-, -ωq)	**እወቅ** í̥wḁq (-ωq)	**አውቆ** á͡u(ŭ)qʷo	**ማወቅ** mã́wḁq (mã́͡uḁ-, -ωq)	**አዋቂ** ãwã́qi (a͡uã́-)
ያወዛውዝ ya͡uwḁzá͡uŭz (ya͡uwωz-)	**አወዛውዝ** a͡uwḁzá͡uŭz (a͡uwωz-)	**አወዛውዞ** a͡uwḁzá͡u- ŭzʷo (a͡uwωz-)	**ማወዛወዝ** ma͡uwḁzá͡uḁz (ma͡uwω-, -zá͡uωz)	**አወዛዋዥ** a͡uwḁzá͡uã́ž (a͡uwω- ; § 8)
ያውደልድል ya͡udḁ́ldi̥l (-dã́-)	**አውደልድል** a͡udḁ́ldi̥l (-dã́-)	**አውደልድሎ** a͡udḁ́ldi̥lʷo (-dã́-)	**ማውደልደል** ma͡udḁ́ldḁl (-ã́ldä-)	**አውደልዳይ** a͡udḁ́ldã́͡i̥ (-dã́- ; -ã́yy § 6 ; § 8)
ያውጣ yá͡uṭã	**አውጣ** á͡uṭã	**አውጥቶ** á͡uṭtʷo	**ማውጣት** má͡uṭã́t (§ 8)	**አውጭ** a͡učˌ (-**ጪ** -čˌi)
ያዘምት yãzzḁ́mmi̥t	**አዘምት** azzḁ́mmi̥t	**አዘምቶ** azzḁ́m- mi̥tʷo	**ማዘመት** mãzzḁ́m- mḁt (-ät)	**አዝማች** ázmã́č (§ 8)

Simp. perf. (§ 25)		Comp. perf. (§ 32)	Contingent (§ 26)	Comp. imperf. (§ 32)
አዞረ azʷŏ́rạ	turn round, t.	አዙሯል ấzurŏ͡āl	ያዞር yãzʷŏ́r	ያዞራል yãzʷŏ́rāl
አዘነ ázzạnạ	grieve, i.	አዝኗል ấznŏ͡āl	ያዝን yấz(ị)n	ያዝናል yấznāl
አዘዘ ázzạzạ	order, t.	አዟል ấzzŏ͡āl	ያዝ yãzz	ያዛል yấzzāl
አዛጋ azzấggã	yawn, i.	አዛግቷል azzấgtŏ͡āl	ያዛጋ yãzzấggã	ያዛጋል yãzzấggāl
አየ ấyyä (§ 44*b*) 2nd አየህ ấyyäh, etc.	see, t.	አይቷል ấ͡ịtŏ͡āl	ያይ yấ͡ị	ያያል yấ͡ịāl (yấʸāl)
አደላ adạ́llã (-dấ-)	show favour, i.	አድልቷል ấdịltŏ͡āl (§ 8)	ያደላ yãdạ́lã (-dấ-)	ያደላል yãdạ́lāl (-dấ-)
አደመጠ adạ́mmạṭạ	listen to, t.	አድምጧል ấdịmṭŏ͡āl	ያደምጥ yãdạ́mṭ (-dấ-)	ያደምጣል yãdạ́mṭāl (-dấ-)
አደረ áddạrạ (-dä-)	pass the night, i.	አድሯል ấdrŏ͡āl	ያድር yấd(ị)r	ያድራል yấdrāl
አደረገ adạ́rrạgạ	do, t.	አድርጓል ấdrịgŏ͡āl (ấrg- § 7*d*)	ያደርግ yãdạ́rg (-dấ-)	ያደርጋል yãdạ́rgāl (-dấ-)

Jussive (§ 27)	Imperative (§ 28)	Gerund (§ 29)	Infinitive (§ 30)	Participle (§ 31)
ያዙር yã́zur	አዙር ázur	አዙሮ ã́zur^{w}o	ማዞር máz^{w}ṍr (§ 8)	አዟሪ azwã́ri
ይዘን yi̥zḁn	እዘን i̥zḁn	አዝኖ ã́zn^{w}o	ማዘን mã́zḁn	አዛኝ ã́zã́ñ (-ññ § 6; § 8)
ይዘዝ yi̥zḁz	እዘዝ i̥zḁz	አዞ ã́zz^{w}o	ማዘዝ mã́zḁz	አዛዥ ázzã́ž (§ 8)
ያዛጋ yãzzã́gã	አዛጋ azzã́gã	አዛግቶ azzã́gt^{w}o	ማዛጋት mãzzã́gã́t (§ 8)	አዛጊ azzã́gi
ይይ yi̥y (yī̥, yī)	እይ i̥y (ī̥, ī)	አይቶ ã́i̥t^{w}o	ማየት mã́i̥ät (mã́^{y}ät)	†አዪ ã́yyi
ያድላ yã́d(i̥)lã	አድላ ã́d(i̥)lã	አድልቶ ã́di̥lt^{w}o	ማድላት mã́d(i̥)lã́t (§ 8)	አድሊ ã́d(i̥)li [አድይ] (ã́di)
ያድምጥ yã́di̥mṭ	አድምጥ ã́di̥mṭ	አድምጦ ã́di̥mṭ^{w}o	ማድመጥ mã́d(ī̥)mḁṭ	አድማጭ ã́d(ī̥)mã́č̣ (§ 8)
ይደር yi̥dḁr (-är)	እደር i̥dḁr (-är)	አድሮ ã́dro	ማደር mã́dḁr (-är)	አዳሪ ãdã́ri
ያድርግ yã́dri̥g (yārg)	አድርግ ã́dri̥g (ārg)	አድርጎ ã́dri̥g^{w}o (ã́rg^{w}o)	ማድረግ mã́drḁg (mã́r-)	አድራጊ adrã́gi

Simp. perf. (§ 25)		Comp. perf. (§ 32)	Contingent (§ 26)	Comp. imperf. (§ 32)
አደሰ áddḁsḁ	renew, t.	አድሷል áddi̥sŏāl	ያድስ yā̃́ddi̥s	ያድሳል yā̃́ddi̥sāl
አደባ adḁ́bbā̃	ambush, t.	አድብቷል ā̃́di̥btŏāl (-y̥t-, -dbi̥t-, -dy̥-)	ያደባ yā̃dḁ́bā̃ (-dá-, -y̥ā̃)	ያደባል yā̃dḁ́bāl (-dá-, -y̥āl)
አደነ áddḁnḁ	hunt, t.	አድኗል áddi̥nŏāl	ያድን yā̃́ddi̥n	ያድናል yā̃́ddi̥nāl
አዳነ adā́nḁ	save, t.	አድኗል ā́di̥nŏāl	ያድን yā́di̥n	ያድናል yā́di̥nāl
አደከመ adā́kkḁmḁ	tire, t.	አድክሟል ā̃́dki̥mŏāl	ያደክም yā̃dā́k(i̥)m	ያደክማል yā̃dā́k(i̥)māl
አደገ áddḁgḁ	grow, i.	አድጓል ā̃́dgŏāl	ያድግ yā̃́di̥g	ያድጋል yā̃́d(i̥)gāl
አደፈ áddḁfḁ	be dirty, i.	አድፏል ā̃́d(i̥)fŏāl	ያድፍ yā̃́d(i̥)f	ያድፋል yā̃́d(i̥)fāl
አገለባበጠ aggḁlḁbā̃́bbḁṭḁ (-y̥ā̃́-)	completely disarrange, t.	አገለባብጧል aggḁlḁbā́bṭŏāl (-y̥ā́y̥-)	ያገለባብጥ yā̃ggḁlḁbā̃́bbi̥ṭ (-y̥ā̃́-)	ያገለባብጣል yā̃ggḁlḁbā̃́bbi̥ṭāl (-y̥ā̃́-)
አገለገለ agḁlḁ́ggḁlḁ	serve, t.	አገልግሏል agḁ́lgi̥lŏāl	ያገለግል yā̃gḁlḁ́ggi̥l	ያገለግላል yā̃gḁlḁ́ggi̥lāl

Jussive (§ 27)	Imperative (§ 28)	Gerund (§ 29)	Infinitive (§ 30)	Participle (§ 31)
ያድስ yã́ddi̥s	አድስ áddi̥s	አድሶ áddi̥sʷo	ማደስ mã́ddḁs	አዳሽ áddã́š (§ 8)
ያድባ yã́d(i̥)bã (-ỵã)	አድባ ã́d(i̥)bã (-ỵã)	አድብቶ ádi̥btʷo (-ỵt-, -dbi̥t-, -dỵ-)	ማድባት mã́d(i̥)bã́t (-ỵã́t; § 8)	አድቢ ã́d(i̥)bi (-ỵi)
ያድን yã́ddi̥n	አድን áddi̥n	አድኖ áddi̥nʷo	ማደን mã́ddḁn	አዳኝ áddã́ñ (-ññ § 6; § 8)
ያድን yã́di̥n	አድን ã́di̥n	አድኖ ádi̥nʷo	ማዳን mã́dã́n (§ 8)	†አዳኝ ã́dã́ñ (-ññ § 6; § 8)
ያድክም yã́dki̥m	አድክም ã́dki̥m	አድክሞ ã́dki̥mʷo	ማድከም mã́dkḁm	አድካሚ ãdkã́mi
ይደግ yi̥dḁg	እደግ i̥dḁg	አድጎ ã́dgʷo	ማደግ mã́dḁg	†አዳጊ ãdã́gi
ይደፍ yi̥dḁf		አድፎ ã́d(i̥)fʷo	ማደፍ mã́dḁf	አዳፊ ãdã́fi
ያገለባብጥ yãggḁlḁ- bã́b(i̥)ṭ (-ỵã́ỵ-)	አገለባብጥ aggḁlḁbã́- b(i̥)ṭ (-ỵã́ỵ-)	አገለባብጦ aggḁlḁbã́b- ṭʷo (-ỵã́ỵ-)	ማገለባበጥ mãggḁlḁ- bã́bḁṭ (-ỵã́ỵ-)	አገለባባጭ aggḁlḁbã́- bã́č̣ (-ỵã́ỵ-)
ያገልግል yãgḁ́lgi̥l	አገልግል agḁ́lgi̥l	አገልግሎ agḁ́lgi̥lʷo	ማገልገል mãgḁ́lgḁl	አገልጋይ agḁ́lgã́i̥ (-ã́yy § 6; § 8)

Simp. perf. (§ 25)		Comp. perf. (§ 32)	Contingent (§ 26)	Comp. imperf. (§ 32)
—	—	—	—	—
አጕረበ agwώrrḁbḁ (-ẏḁ)	be blistered, i.	አጕርቧል ágwŭrbŏ͡āl (-rẏ-)	ያጕርብ yã̄gwώrb (-rẏ)	ያጕርባል yã̄gwώrbāl (-rẏ-)
አገረገረ agḁrḁ́ggḁrḁ (-ärḁ́ggä-)	shy, i.	አገርግሯል agḁ́rgi̥rŏ͡āl (agá̃-)	ያገረግር yã̄gḁrḁ́ggi̥r (-ärḁ́-)	ያገረግራል yã̄gḁrḁ́ggi̥-rāl (-ärḁ́-)
አገሣ agḁ́ssã	roar, i.	አግሥቷል ấgi̥stŏ͡āl	ያገሣ yã̄gḁ́sã	ያገሣል yã̄gḁ́sāl
አገባ agḁ́bbã	cause to enter, marry, t.	አግብቷል ấgi̥btŏ͡āl (-ẏt-)	ያገባ yã̄gḁ́bã (-ẏã)	ያገባል yã̄gḁ́bāl (-ẏāl)
አጋባ aggấbbã	give in marriage, t.	አጋብቷል aggấbtŏ͡āl (-ẏt-)	ያጋባ yã̄ggấbbã	ያጋባል yã̄ggấbbāl
አጐነበሰ agwωnḁ́b-bḁsḁ	be bent, i.	አጐንብሷል agwώmbi̥-sŏ͡āl	ያጐነብስ yã̄gwωnḁ́b-bi̥s	ያጐነብሳል yã̄gwωnḁ́b-bi̥sāl
አገናኘ aggḁnấññä 2nd -ኘህ -ññäh, etc.	cause to meet, t.	አገናኝቷል aggḁnấñ-tŏ͡āl	ያገናኝ yã̄ggḁnấñ (-ññ § 6)	ያገናኛል yã̄ggḁnấñ-ñāl
አገኘ agḁ́ññä (-gấ-) 2nd -ኘህ -ññäh, etc.	find, t.	አግኝቷል ấgi̥ñtŏ͡āl 1st አግኝቻለሁ agi̥ñ(i̥č)čál-lḁu͡^{h}	ያገኝ yã̄gḁ́ñ (-gấ-; -ññ § 6)	ያገኛል yã̄gḁ́ññāl (-gấ-)
አገደደ agḁ́ddḁdḁ	cause a lack of, t.	አግዷል ấgi̥ddŏ͡āl	ያገድ yã̄gḁ́dd	ያገዳል yã̄gḁ́ddāl

Jussive (§ 27)	Imperative (§ 28)	Gerund (§ 29)	Infinitive (§ 30)	Participle (§ 31)
ያጕርብ yắgwŭrb (-rỵ)		**አጕርቦ** ắgwŭrb^{w}o (-rỵ-)	**ማጕረብ** mắgwŭrḁb (-ḁỵ)	**አጕራቢ** ãgwŭrắbi (-ỵi)
ያገርግር yãgḁ́rgi̥r (-gắ-)		**አገርግሮ** agḁ́rgi̥r^{w}o (-gắ-)	**ማገርገር** mãgḁ́rgḁr (-ắrgä-)	**አገርጋሪ** agḁrgắri (agä-)
ያግሣ yắgsã	**አግሣ** ắgsã	**አግሥቶ** ắgi̥st^{w}o	**ማግሣት** mắgsắt(§8)	
ያግባ yắgbã (-ỵã)	**አግባ** ắgbã (-ỵã)	**አግብቶ** ắgi̥bt^{w}o (-ỵt-)	**ማግባት** mắgbắt (-gỵ- ; § 8)	**አግቢ** ắgbi (-gỵ-)
ያጋባ yãggắbã (-ỵã)	**አጋባ** aggắbã (-ỵã)	**አጋብቶ** aggắbt^{w}o (-ỵt-)	**ማጋባት** mãggắbắt (-ỵắt ; § 8)	
ያጐንብስ yãgwώmbi̥s	**አጐንብስ** agwώmbi̥s	**አጐንብሶ** agwώm- bi̥s^{w}o	**ማጐንበስ** mãgwώm- bḁs	†**አጐንባሽ** agwώmbắš (§ 8)
ያገናኝ yãggḁnắñ (-ññ § 6; § 8)	**አገናኝ** aggḁnắñ (-ññ § 6; §8)	**አገናኝቶ** aggḁnắñ- t^{w}o	**ማገናኘት** mãggḁnắñ- (ñ)ät	
ያግኝ yắgi̥ñ (-ññ § 6)	**አግኝ** ắgi̥ñ (-ññ § 6)	**አግኝቶ** ắgi̥ñt^{w}o 1st **አግኝቼ** ắgi̥ñ(i̥č)č^{y}e	**ማግኘት** mắg(i̥)ñät	†**አግኝ** ắgi̥ñ (-ññ § 6)
ያግድ yắgi̥dd	**አግድ** ắgi̥dd	**አግዶ** ắgi̥dd^{w}o	**ማግደድ** mắgdḁd	**አግዳጅ** ắgdắj (§ 8)

Simp. perf. (§ 25)		Comp. perf. (§ 32)	Contingent (§ 26)	Comp. imperf. (§ 32)
አጌጠ ag^{y}éṭḁ	be ornamental, i.	አጊጧል ắgi̥ṭŏ͡āl	ያጌጥ yãg^{y}éṭ	ያጌጣል yãg^{y}éṭāl
አጣ áṭṭã	lack, t.	አጥቷል ắṭtŏ͡āl (áṭṭi̥t-)	ያጣ yáṭã	ያጣል yáṭāl
አጠለቀ aṭḁ́llḁqḁ	deepen, t.	አጥልቋል ắṭi̥lqŏ͡āl (ắṭli̥q-)	ያጠልቅ yãṭḁ́lq (-ṭắ-)	ያጠልቃል yãṭḁ́lqāl (-ṭắ-)
አጠመመ aṭḁ́mmḁmḁ	bend, t.	አጠሟል aṭḁ́mmŏ͡āl	ያጠምም yãṭḁ́mmi̥m	ያጠምማል yãṭḁ́mmi̥- māl
አጠመደ aṭḁ́mmḁdḁ	set (a trap), t.	አጥምዷል ắṭi̥mdŏ͡āl (ắṭmi̥d-)	ያጠምድ yãṭḁ́md	ያጠምዳል yãṭḁ́mdāl
አጠረ áṭṭḁrḁ (-är-)	be short, i.	አጥሯል ắṭrŏ͡āl	ያጥር yáṭ(i̥)r	ያጥራል yáṭrāl
አጠራ aṭḁ́rrã	purify, t.	አጥርቷል ắṭi̥rtŏ͡āl	ያጠራ yãṭḁ́rã (-ắr-)	ያጠራል yãṭḁ́rāl (-ắr-)
አጠበ áṭṭḁbḁ (-ṿḁ)	wash, t.	አጥቧል ắṭbŏ͡āl (-ṭṿ-)	ያጥብ yáṭ(i̥)b (-ṭ(i̥)ṿ)	ያጥባል yáṭbāl (-ṭṿ-)
አጣበቀ aṭṭábbḁqḁ	squeeze, t.	አጣብቋል aṭṭábqŏ͡āl (-ṿq-)	ያጣብቅ yãṭṭábbi̥q	ያጣብቃል yãṭṭábbi̥qāl

Jussive (§ 27)	Imperative (§ 28)	Gerund (§ 29)	Infinitive (§ 30)	Participle (§ 31)
ያጊጥ yã́gi̥ṭ	አጊጥ ági̥ṭ	አጊጦ ági̥ṭ^{w}o	ማጌጥ mã́g^{y}ḗṭ (§ 8)	
ይጣ yí̥ṭã	እጣ í̥ṭã	አጥቶ ã́ṭt^{w}o (áṭṭi̥t^{w}o)	ማጣት mã́ṭát (§ 8)	አጭ āč̣ (-ጪ -č̣i)
ያጥልቅ yáṭi̥lq (yã́ṭli̥q)	አጥልቅ ã́ṭi̥lq (ã́ṭli̥q)	አጥልቆ ã́ṭi̥lq^{w}o (ã́ṭli̥q-)	ማጥለቅ mã́ṭlḁq	አጥላቂ ãṭlã́qi
ያጠም yã́ṭḁ́mm (§ 8)	አጠም áṭḁ́mm (§ 8)	አጠሞ aṭḁ́mm^{w}o	ማጠመም mãṭḁ́mḁm	አጠማሚ aṭḁmã́mi
ያጥምድ yã́ṭi̥md (yã́ṭmi̥d)	አጥምድ ã́ṭi̥md (ã́ṭmi̥d)	አጥምዶ ã́ṭi̥md^{w}o (ã́ṭmi̥d^{w}o)	ማጥመድ mã́ṭmḁd	አጥማጅ ã́ṭmã́j (§ 8)
ይጠር yí̥ṭḁr (-är)		አጥሮ ã́ṭr^{w}o	ማጠር mã́ṭḁr (-är)	አጣሪ ãṭári
ያጥሩ yã́ṭrã	አጥሩ ã́ṭrã	አጥርቶ ã́ṭi̥rt^{w}o	ማጥሩት mã́ṭrát (§ 8)	አጥሪ ã́ṭri
ይጠብ yí̥ṭḁb (-ḁy̦)	እጠብ í̥ṭḁb (-ḁy̦)	አጥቦ ã́ṭb^{w}o (-ṭy̦-)	ማጠብ mã́ṭḁb (-ḁy̦)	አጣቢ ãṭábi (-y̦i)
ያጣብቅ yãṭṭáb(ĭ̥)q (-y̦(ĭ̥)q)	አጣብቅ aṭṭáb(ĭ̥)q (-y̦(ĭ̥)q)	አጣብቆ aṭṭábq^{w}o	ማጣበቅ mãṭṭábḁq (-y̦ḁq)	አጣባቂ aṭṭābã́qi (-āy̦ã́-)
		(-y̦q-)		

Simp. perf. (§ 25)		Comp. perf. (§ 32)	Contingent (§ 26)	Comp. imperf. (§ 32)
አጠበበ aṭḁ́bbḁbḁ (-ṿḁ)	make narrow, t.	አጥብቧል ã́ṭbi̥bŏ͡āl (-ṿi̥ṿ-)	ያጠብ yãṭḁ́bb	ያጠባል yãṭḁ́bbāl
አጠነ áṭṭḁnḁ	perfume, t.	አጥኗል ã́ṭnŏ͡āl	ያጥን yá̃ṭ(i̥)n	ያጥናል yá̃ṭnāl
አጠጣ aṭḁ́ṭṭã	water, give drink to, t.	አጠጥቷል aṭḁ́ṭṭi̥tŏ͡āl	ያጠጣ yãṭḁ́ṭṭã	ያጠጣል yãṭḁ́ṭṭāl
አጠፈ áṭṭḁfḁ	fold, t.	አጥፏል ã́ṭ(i̥)fŏ͡āl	ያጥፍ yá̃ṭ(i̥)f	ያጥፋል yá̃ṭ(i̥)fāl
አጠፋ aṭḁ́ffã	extinguish, lose, t.	አጥፍቷል á̃ṭi̥ftŏ͡āl	ያጠፋ yãṭḁ́fã	ያጠፋል yãṭḁ́fāl
አጫወተ ač̣č̣á͡uwḁtḁ (-wωt-)	converse with, t.	አጫውቷል ač̣č̣á͡u(ŭ)-tŏ͡āl	ያጫውት yãč̣č̣á͡uwŭt	ያጫውታል yãč̣č̣á͡uwŭ-tāl
አጨደ áč̣č̣ḁdḁ (-ädä)	reap, t.	አጭዷል á̃č̣i̥dŏ͡āl	ያጭድ yá̃č̣i̥d	ያጭዳል yá̃č̣i̥dāl
አፈላ afḁ́llã	boil, t.	አፍልቷል á̃fi̥ltŏ͡āl	ያፈላ yãfḁ́lã	ያፈላል yãfḁ́lāl
አፈረ áffḁrḁ (-fä-)	be ashamed, i.	አፍሯል á̃frŏ͡āl	ያፍር yá̃f(i̥)r	ያፍራል yá̃frāl

Jussive (§ 27)	Imperative (§ 28)	Gerund (§ 29)	Infinitive (§ 30)	Participle (§ 31)
ያጥቢብ yã́ṭbi̥b (-ỵi̥ỵ)	**አጥቢብ** ã́ṭbi̥b (-ỵi̥ỵ)	**አጥቢቦ** ã́ṭbi̥bʷo (-ỵi̥ỵ-)	**ማጥበብ** mã́ṭbḁb (-ỵḁỵ)	**አጥባቢ** ãṭbábi (-ỵáỵ-)
ይጠን yi̥ṭḁn	**እጠን** i̥ṭḁn	**አጥኖ** ã́ṭnʷo	**ማጠን** mã́ṭḁn	**አጣኝ** ã́ṭáñ (-ññ § 6; § 8)
ያጣጣ yãṭḁ́ṭṭã	**አጣጣ** aṭḁ́ṭṭã	**አጠጥቶ** aṭḁṭṭi̥tʷo	**ማጣጣት** mãṭḁ́ṭṭát (§ 8)	**አጠጭ** ã́ṭḁčč̣ (-ṭá-; § 8; -ጪ -č̣či)
ይጠፍ yi̥ṭḁf	**እጠፍ** i̥ṭḁf	**አጥፎ** ã́ṭ(i̥)fʷo	**ማጠፍ** mã́ṭḁf	**አጣፊ** ãṭáfi
ያጥፋ yáṭfã	**አጥፋ** ã́ṭfã	**አጥፍቶ** áṭi̥ftʷo	**ማጥፋት** máṭfát (§ 8)	**አጥፊ** áṭfi
ያጪውት yãč̣č̣á͡uŭt (yã́č̣č̣a͡ut)	**አጪውት** ač̣č̣á͡uŭt (áč̣č̣a͡ut)	**አጪውቶ** ač̣č̣á͡u(ŭ)- tʷo	**ማጪወት** mãč̣č̣á͡uḁt (-á͡uωt)	**አጪዋች** ač̣č̣á͡uáč (§ 8)
ይጨድ yi̥č̣ḁd (-äd)	**እጨድ** i̥č̣ḁd (-äd)	**አጭዶ** áč̣i̥dʷo	**ማጨድ** máč̣ḁd (-äd)	**አጪጅ** áč̣áj (§ 8)
ያፍላ yáflã	**አፍላ** áflã	**አፍልቶ** áfi̥ltʷo	**ማፍላት** máflát (§ 8)	**አፍሊ** áfli [**አፍይ**] (áfi)
ይፈር yi̥fḁr (-fä-)	**እፈር** i̥fḁr (-fä-)	**አፍሮ** áfrʷo	**ማፈር** máfḁr (-fä-)	**አፋሪ** ãfári

Simp. perf. (§ 25)		Comp. perf. (§ 32)	Contingent (§ 26)	Comp. imperf. (§ 32)
—	—	—	—	—
አፈረሰ afḁ́rrḁsḁ	destroy, t.	አፍርሷል ã́fi̥rsŏ͡āl	ያፈርስ yãfḁ́rs (-fã́-)	ያፈርሳል yãfḁ́rsāl (-fã́-)
አፈሰ áffḁsḁ	gather up, t.	አፍሷል ã́fsŏ͡āl	ያፍስ yāfs	ያፍሳል yā́fsāl
አፈሰሰ afḁ́ssḁsḁ	pour, t.	አፍስሷል ã́fsi̥sŏ͡āl አፍሷል ã́fi̥ssŏ͡āl	ያፈስ yãfḁ́ss	ያፈሳል yãfḁ́ssāl
አፈነዳ afḁnḁ́ddã	burst, t.	አፈንድቷል afḁ́ndi̥tŏ͡āl	ያፈነዳ yāfḁnḁ́ddã	ያፈነዳል yāfḁnḁ́ddāl
አፎኘ Š. af^wṓññä 2nd -ኘህ -ññäh, etc.	hiss, i.	አፎኝቷል af^wṓññi̥tŏ͡āl	ያፎኝ yãf^wṓññ	ያፎኛል yãf^wṓññāl
አፈጠነ afḁ́ṭṭḁnḁ (-ã́ṭṭä-)	hasten, t.	አፍጥኗል ã́fṭi̥nŏ͡āl	ያፈጥን yãfḁ́ṭ(i̥)n (-fã́-)	ያፈጥናል yãfḁ́ṭ(i̥)nāl (-fã́-)
አፏጨ afwã́čč̣ä 2nd -ጨህ -čč̣äh, etc.	whistle, i.	አፏጭቷል afwã́č̣tŏ͡āl (-fwáyyt- § 7*d*)	ያፏጭ yãfwã́čč̣	ያፏጫል yãfwã́čč̣āl
ከለከለ kḁlḁ́kkḁlḁ	hinder, t.	ከልክሏል kḁ́lki̥lŏ͡āl	ይከለክል yi̥kḁlḁ́kki̥l	ይከለክላል yi̥kḁlḁ́kki̥- lāl
ከመረ kḁ́mmḁrḁ (-mär-)	pile, t.	ከምሯል kḁ́mmi̥rŏ͡āl	ይከምር yi̥kḁ́mmi̥r	ይከምራል yi̥kḁ́mmi̥- rāl

Jussive (§ 27)	Imperative (§ 28)	Gerund (§ 29)	Infinitive (§ 30)	Participle (§ 31)
ያፍርስ yā́fi̥rs	አፍርስ ā́fi̥rs	አፍርሶ ā́fi̥rsʷo	ማፍረስ mā́frḁs	አፍራሽ ā̃frā́š (§ 8)
ይፈስ yí̥fḁs	እፈስ í̥fḁs	አፍሶ ā́fsʷo	ማፈስ mā́fḁs	አፋሽ ā́fā́š (§ 8)
ያፍስስ yā́fsi̥s	አፍስስ ā́fsi̥s	አፍስሶ ā́fsi̥sʷo	ማፍሰስ mā́fsḁs	አፍሳሽ ā́fsā́š (§ 8)
ያፍስ yā́fi̥ss	አፍስ ā́fi̥ss	አፍሶ ā́fi̥ssʷo		
ያፈንዳ yā̃fḁ́ndā̃	አፈንዳ afḁ́ndā̃	አፈንድቶ afḁ́ndi̥tʷo	ማፈንዳት mā̃fḁ́ndā́t (§ 8)	†አፈንጅ ā́fḁ́nj (§ 8; -ጂ -ji)
ያፎኝ yā́fʷóññ (§ 8)	አፎኝ ā́fʷóññ (§ 8)	አፎኝቶ afʷóññi̥tʷo	ማፎኘት mā̃fʷóññät	
ያፍጥን yā́fṭi̥n	አፍጥን ā́fṭi̥n	አፍጥኖ ā́fṭi̥nʷo	ማፍጠን mā́fṭḁn	አፍጣኝ ā́fṭā́ñ (-ññ § 6; § 8)
ያፏጭ yā́fwā́č̣ (-č̣č̣ Š.; § 8)	አፏጭ ā́fwā́č̣ (-č̣č̣ Š.; § 8)	አፏጭቶ afwā́č̣tʷo (-fwáyyt- § 7*d*)	ማፏጨት mā̃fwā́č̣ät (-č̣č̣- Š.)	
ይከልክል yi̥kḁ́lki̥l	ከልክል kḁ́lki̥l	ከልክሎ kḁ́lki̥lʷo	መከልከል mḁkḁ́lkḁl	ከልካይ kḁ́lkā́i̥ (-ā́yy § 6; § 8)
ይከምር yi̥kḁ́mmi̥r	ከምር kḁ́mmi̥r	ከምሮ kḁ́mmi̥rʷo	መከመር mḁkḁ́mmḁr (-mär)	ከማሪ kḁmmā́ri

Simp. perf. (§ 25)		Comp. perf. (§ 32)	Contingent (§ 26)	Comp. imperf. (§ 32)
ኰረኰረ kwωrḁ́k-kwωrḁ (-rώ-)	spur, t.	ኰርኵሯል kwώrkwŭ-rŏ͡āl	ይኰረኵር yi̥kwωrḁ́k-kwŭr (-rώ-)	ይኰረኵራል yi̥kwωrḁ́k-kwŭrāl (-rώ-)
ከሳ kḁ́ssā̃	become thin, i.	ከስቷል kḁ́stŏ͡āl	ይከሳ yi̥kḁ́sā̃	ይከሳል yi̥kḁ́sāl
ከሰሰ kḁ́ssḁsḁ	accuse, t.	ከሷል kḁ́ssŏ͡āl	ይከስ yi̥kḁ́ss	ይከሳል yi̥kḁ́ssāl
ከበረ kḁ́bbḁrḁ (-bä-)	be honoured, i.	ከብሯል kḁ́brŏ͡āl (-ỵr-)	ይከብር yi̥kḁ́b(ĭ̥)r (-ḁ́ỵ-)	ይከብራል yi̥kḁ́b(ĭ̥)rāl (-ḁ́ỵ-)
ከበደ kḁ́bbḁdḁ	be heavy, i.	ከብዷል kḁ́bdŏ͡āl (-ỵd-)	ይከብድ yi̥kḁ́bd (-ỵd)	ይከብዳል yi̥kḁ́bdāl (-ỵd-)
ከተተ kḁ́ttḁtḁ	pack, t.	ከቷል kḁ́ttŏ͡āl	ይከት yi̥kḁ́tt	ይከታል yi̥kḁ́ttāl
ከዳ kḁ́ddā̃	run away, i.	ከድቷል kḁ́d(ĭ̥)tŏ͡āl (-ḁ́rt-, -ắrt- § 7*d*)	ይከዳ yi̥kḁ́dā̃	ይከዳል yi̥kḁ́dāl
ካደ kắdḁ	renounce, t.	ክዷል kí̥dŏ͡āl	ይክድ yi̥kí̥d	ይክዳል yi̥kí̥dāl
ከደነ kḁ́ddḁnḁ	cover, t.	ከድኗል kḁ́dnŏ͡āl	ይከድን yi̥kḁ́d(ĭ̥)n	ይከድናል yi̥kḁ́d(ĭ̥)nāl

Jussive (§ 27)	Imperative (§ 28)	Gerund (§ 29)	Infinitive (§ 30)	Participle (§ 31)
ይኰርኵር yi̥kwώr- kwŭr	ኰርኵር kwώrkwŭr	ኰርኵሮ kwώrkwŭ- rʷo	መኰርኰር mḁkwώr- kwωr	ኰርኳሪ kwωrkwā́ri
ይክሳ yí̥ksã		ክስቶ kḁ́stʷo	መክሳት mḁ́ksā́t (§ 8)	ክሽ kḁ́š (käš, -ሺ -ši)
ይክሰስ yí̥ksḁs	ክሰስ kí̥sḁs	ክሶ kḁ́ssʷo	መክሰስ mḁ́ksḁs	ክሳሽ kḁ́sā́š (§ 8)
ይክበር yí̥kbḁr (-kỵ-, -är)	ክበር kí̥bḁr (-í̥ỵ-, -är)	ክብሮ kḁ́brʷo (-ỵr-)	መክበር mḁ́kbḁr (-kỵ-, -är)	ክባሪ kḁbā́ri (-ỵā́-)
ይክበድ yí̥kbḁd (-kỵ-)		ክብዶ kḁ́bdʷo (-ỵd-)	መክበድ mḁ́kbḁd (-kỵ-)	ክባጅ kḁ́bā́j (-ỵā́-; § 8)
ይክተት yí̥ktḁt (-ät)	ክተት kí̥tḁt (-ät)	ክቶ kḁ́ttʷo	መክተት mḁ́ktḁt (-ät)	ክታች kḁ́tā́č (§ 8)
ይክዳ yí̥kdã	ክዳ kí̥dã	ክድቶ kḁ́d(i̥)tʷo (-ḁ́rt-, -ā́rt- § 7*d*)	መክዳት mḁ́kdā́t (§ 8)	ክጅ kḁj (käj, -ጂ -ji)
ይካድ yí̥kā́d (§ 8)	ካድ kād	ክዶ kí̥dʷo	መካድ mḁ́kā́d (§ 8)	ካጅ kāj (-ጂ -ji)
ይክደን yí̥kdḁn	ክደን kí̥dḁn	ክድኖ kḁ́dnʷo	መክደን mḁ́kdḁn	ክዳኝ kḁ́dā́ñ (-ññ § 6; § 8)

Simp. perf. (§ 25)		Comp. perf. (§ 32)	Contingent (§ 26)	Comp. imperf. (§ 32)
ከፋ kḁ́ffã	be bad, i.	ከፍቷል kḁ́ftŏ͡āl	ይከፋ yi̥kḁ́fã	ይከፋል yi̥kḁ́fāl
ከፈለ kḁ́ffḁlḁ	divide, t.	ከፍሏል kḁ́flŏ͡āl (kắ-)	ይከፍል yi̥kḁ́f(ĭ̥)l (-kắ-)	ይከፍላል yi̥kḁ́flāl (-kắ-)
ከፈተ kḁ́ffḁtḁ	open, t.	ከፍቷል kḁ́ftŏ͡āl	ይከፍት yi̥kḁ́ft	ይከፍታል yi̥kḁ́ftāl
ከፈከፈ kḁfḁ́kkḁfḁ	sprinkle, t.	ከፍክፏል kḁ́fki̥fŏ͡āl	ይከፈክፍ yi̥kḁfḁ́kki̥f	ይከፈክፋል yi̥kḁfḁ́kki̥fāl
ዋለ wā́lḁ	spend noon, i.	ውሏል wí̥lŏ͡āl (wŭ́l-)	ይውል yi̥wí̥l (yi̥wŭ́l, yūl)	ይውላል yi̥wí̥lāl (yi̥wŭ́l-, yū́l-)
ወለቀ wḁ́llḁqḁ (wώ-)	get dislocated, i.	ወልቋል wḁ́lqŏ͡āl (wώ-)	ይወልቅ yi̥wḁ́lq (yuḁ́-, -ώl-)	ይወልቃል yi̥wḁ́lqāl (yuḁ́-, -ώl-)
ወለወለ wḁlḁ́͡uwḁlḁ	wipe, t.	ወልውሏል wḁ́lwi̥lŏ͡āl (-lwŭ́l-)	ይወለውል yi̥wḁlḁ́͡uwi̥l (yuḁ-, -wŭ́l)	ይወለውላል yi̥wḁlḁ́͡uwi̥lāl (yuḁ-, -wŭ́lāl)
ወለደች wḁ́llḁdäč (wắ-, wώ-; -čč̆ § 6)	bear, t.	ወልዳለች wḁldállăč (wä-, wω-; -čč̆ § 6)	ትወልድ ti̥wḁ́ld (-wắ-, -wώ-)	ትወልዳለች ti̥wḁldálläč (-wä-, -wω-; -čč̆ § 6)
ወረሰ wώrrḁsḁ	inherit, t.	ወርሷል wώrsŏ͡āl	ይወርስ yi̥wώrs (yuώ-)	ይወርሳል yi̥wώrsāl (yuώ-)

Jussive (§ 27)	Imperative (§ 28)	Gerund (§ 29)	Infinitive (§ 30)	Participle (§ 31)
ይክፉ yí̥kfä̃	ክፉ kí̥fä̃	ክፍቶ kḁ́ftʷo	መክፋት mḁ́kfā́t (§ 8)	ክፊ kḁ́fi (kā́-)
ይክፈል yí̥kfḁl (-äl)	ክፈል kí̥fḁl (-äl)	ክፍሎ kḁ́flʷo (kā́-)	መክፈል mḁ́kfḁl (-äl)	ክፋይ kḁ́fā́͡i̥ (-ā́yy § 6; §8)
ይክፈት yí̥kfḁt (-ät)	ክፈት kí̥fḁt (-ät)	ክፍቶ kḁ́ftʷo	መክፈት mḁ́kfḁt (-ät)	ክፋች kḁ́fā́č (§ 8)
ይክፍክፍ yi̥kḁ́fki̥f	ክፍክፍ kḁ́fki̥f	ክፍክፎ kḁ́fki̥fʷo	መክፍክፍ mḁkḁ́fkḁf	ክፍካፊ kḁfkā́fi
ይዋል yí̥wā́l (yúā́l; § 8)	ዋል wāl	ውሎ wí̥lʷo (wŭ́lʷo)	መዋል mḁ́wā́l (mḁ́͡uā́l; § 8)	ዋይ wā́͡i̥ (wāyy § 6)
ይውለቅ yí̥wŭlḁq (yŭ́l-)		ወልቆ wḁ́lqʷo (wώ-)	መውለቅ mḁ́wŭlḁq (mḁ́͡ul-)	
ይወልውል yi̥wḁ́lwi̥l (yuḁ́-, -wŭ́l)	ወልውል wḁ́lwi̥l (-wŭ́l)	ወልውሎ wḁ́lwi̥lʷo (-lwŭ́l-)	መወልወል mḁwḁ́lwḁl (mḁ͡uḁ́-)	ወልዋይ wḁ́lwā́͡i̥ (-ā́yy § 6; § 8)
ትውለድ tí̥wŭlḁd	ውለጅ wŭ́lḁj (-lä-, -ጂ, -ji)	ወልዳ wḁ́ldä̃ (wā́-, wώ-)	መውለድ mḁ́wŭlḁd (mḁ́͡ul-)	ወላጅ wḁ́lā́j (wā́-, wώ-; § 8)
ይውረስ yí̥wŭrḁs (yŭ́r-)	ውረስ wŭ́rḁs	ወርሶ wώrsʷo	መውረስ mḁ́wŭrḁs (mḁ́͡ur-)	ወራሽ wώrā́š (§ 8)

Simp. perf. (§ 25)		Comp. perf. (§ 32)	Contingent (§ 26)	Comp. imperf. (§ 32)
ወረወረ wḁrḁ́͡uwḁrḁ	throw, t.	ወርውሯል wḁ́rwŭrŏ͡āl	ይወረውር yi̥wḁrḁ́͡u-wŭr (yuḁ-)	ይወረውራል yi̥wḁrḁ́͡uwŭ-rāl (yuḁ-)
ወረደ wώrrḁdḁ	descend, i.	ወርዷል wώrdŏ͡āl	ይወርድ yi̥wώrd (yuώ-)	ይወርዳል yi̥wώrdāl (yuώ-)
ወሰነ wώssḁnḁ	define, t.	ወስኗል wώssi̥nŏ͡āl	ይወስን yi̥wώssi̥n (yuώ-)	ይወስናል yi̥wώssi̥nāl (yuώ-)
ወሰደ wḁ́ssḁdḁ (wώ-)	remove, t.	ወስዷል wḁ́s(ĭ̥)dŏ͡āl (wώ-)	ይወስድ yi̥wḁ́s(ĭ̥)d (yuḁ́-, -ώs-)	ይወስዳል yi̥wḁ́s(ĭ̥)dāl (yuḁ́-, -ώs-)
ዋሸ wā́ššä 2nd ዋሸህ wā́ššäh, etc.	tell a lie, i.	ዋሽቷል wā́štŏ͡āl	ይዋሽ yi̥wā́šš (yuā́-)	ይዋሻል yi̥wā́ššāl (yuā́-)
ወሸመ wḁ́ššḁmḁ (wώ-)	commit adultery, i.	ወሽሟል wḁ́šši̥mŏ͡āl (wώ-)	ይወሽም yi̥wḁ́šši̥m (yuḁ́-, -ώš-)	ይወሽማል yi̥wḁ́šši̥māl (yuώ-, -ώš-)
ወቀጠ wώqqḁṭḁ	crush, t.	ወቅጧል wώqṭŏ͡āl	ይወቅጥ yi̥wώqṭ (yuώ-)	ይወቅጣል yi̥wώqṭāl (yuώ-)
ዋኘ wā́ññä 2nd ዋኘህ wā́ññäh, etc.	swim, i.	ዋኝቷል wā́ñtŏ͡āl	ይዋኝ yi̥wā́ññ (yuā́-)	ይዋኛል yi̥wā́ññāl (yuā́-)

Jussive (§ 27)	Imperative (§ 28)	Gerund (§ 29)	Infinitive (§ 30)	Participle (§ 31)
ይወርውር yi̥wḁ́rwŭr (yuḁ́-)	ወርውር wḁ́rwŭr	ወርውሮ wḁ́rwŭr^{w}o	መወርወር mḁwḁ́rwḁr (mḁuḁ́-)	ወርዋሪ wḁrwā́ri
ይውረድ yí̥wŭrḁd (yū́r-)	ውረድ wū́rḁd	ወርዶ wώrd^{w}o	መውረድ mḁ́wŭrḁd (mḁ́ur-)	ወራጅ wώrā́j (§ 8)
ይወስን yi̥wώssi̥n (yuώ-)	ወስን wώssi̥n	ወስኖ wώssi̥n^{w}o	መወሰን mḁwώssḁn (mḁuώ-)	ወሳኝ wώssā́ñ (-ññ § 6; § 8)
ይውሰድ yí̥wŭsḁd (yū́s-)	ውሰድ wí̥sḁd (wū́s-, ús-)	ወስዶ wḁ́s(ĭ̥)d^{w}o (wώ-)	መውሰድ mḁ́wŭsḁd (mḁ́us-)	ወሳጅ wḁ́sā́j (wώ- ; § 8)
ይዋሽ yí̥wā́š (yúā́š ; § 8)	ዋሽ wāš	ዋሽቶ wā́št^{w}o	መዋሸት mḁwā́šät (mḁuá-)	ዋሽ wāš (-ሺ. -ši)
ይወሽም yi̥wḁ́šši̥m (yuḁ́-, -ώš-)	ወሽም wḁ́šši̥m (wώ-)	ወሽሞ wḁ́šši̥m^{w}o (wώ-)	መወሸም mḁwḁ́ššḁm (mḁuḁ́-, -ώš-, -äm)	ወሻሚ wḁššā́mi (wω-)
ይውቀጥ yí̥wŭqḁṭ (yū́q-)	ውቀጥ wū́qḁṭ	ወቅጦ wώqṭ^{w}o	መውቀጥ mḁ́wŭqḁṭ (mḁ́uq-)	ወቃጭ wώqā́č̣ (§ 8)
ይዋኝ yí̥wā́ñ (yúā́- ; § 8 ; -ññ Š.)	ዋኝ wāñ (-ññ Š.)	ዋኝቶ wā́ñt^{w}o	መዋኘት mḁwā́ñät (mḁuá-; -ññ- Š.)	ዋኝ wā́ñ (-ññ § 6 ; -ኚ -ññi)

Simp. perf. (§ 25)		Comp. perf. (§ 32)	Contingent (§ 26)	Comp. imperf. (§ 32)
ወዛ wḁ́zzã (wώ-)	sweat, i.	ወዝቷል wḁ́ztŏ͡āl (wώ-)	ይወዛ yi̥wḁ́zã (yuḁ́-, -ώz-)	ይወዛል yi̥wḁ́zāl (yuḁ́-, -ώz-)
ወዘወዘ wḁzḁ́͡uwḁzḁ (-ωzḁ́͡uwω-)	shake, t.	ወዝውዟል wḁ́zwŭzŏ͡āl (wώ-)	ይወዘውዝ yi̥wḁzḁ́͡uwŭz (yuḁ-, -ωzḁ́͡u-)	ይወዘውዛል yi̥wḁzḁ͡uwŭ-zāl (yuḁ-, -ωzḁ́͡u-)
ወደቀ wώddḁqḁ	fall, i.	ወድቋል wώd(i̥)qŏ͡āl	ይወድቅ yi̥wώd(i̥)q (yuώ-)	ይወድቃል yi̥wώd(i̥)qāl (yuώ-)
ወደደ wώddḁdḁ	love, t.	ወዷል wώddŏ͡āl	ይወድ yi̥wώdd (yuώ-)	ይወዳል yi̥wώddāl (yuώ-)
ወጋ wώggã (ʷώg-)	prick, t.	ወግቷል wώgtŏ͡āl (ʷώg-)	ይወጋ yi̥wώgã (yuώ-)	ይወጋል yi̥wώgāl (yuώ-)
ወጣ wώṭṭã	come out, i.	ወጥቷል wώṭ(i̥)tŏ͡āl	ይወጣ yi̥wώṭã (yuώ-)	ይወጣል yi̥wώṭāl (yuώ-)
ዋጠ wā́ṭḁ	swallow, t.	ውጧል wŭ́ṭŏ͡āl	ይውጥ yi̥wŭ́ṭ (yuŭ́ṭ)	ይውጣል yi̥wŭ́ṭāl (yuŭ́ṭ-)
ወጠረ wώṭṭḁrḁ (-är-)	stretch, t.	ወጥሯል wώṭṭi̥rŏ͡āl	ይወጥር yi̥wώṭṭi̥r (yuώ-)	ይወጥራል yi̥wώṭṭi̥rāl (yuώ-)

Jussive (§ 27)	Imperative (§ 28)	Gerund (§ 29)	Infinitive (§ 30)	Participle (§ 31)
ይውዛ yí̥wŭzã (yŭ́z-)	**ውዛ** wŭ́zã	**ወዝቶ** wḁ́zt^{w}o (wώ-)	**መውዛት** mḁ́wŭzắt (mḁ́͡uz-; § 8)	**ወዥ** wḁž (wω-, -ዢ -ži)
ይወዝውዝ yi̥wḁ́zwŭz (yuḁ́-, -ώzw-)	**ወዝውዝ** wḁ́zwŭz (wώ-)	**ወዝውዞ** wḁ́zwŭz^{w}o (wώ-)	**መወዝወዝ** mḁwḁ́zwḁz (mḁ͡uḁ́-, -ώzwω-)	**ወዝዋዥ** wḁ́zwắž (wώ-; § 8)
ይውደቅ yí̥wŭdḁq (yŭ́d-)	**ውደቅ** wŭ́dḁq	**ወድቆ** wώd(ı̥̆)q^{w}o	**መውደቅ** mḁ́wŭdḁq (mḁ́͡ud-)	**ወዳቂ** wωdắqi
ይውደድ yí̥wŭdḁd (yŭ́d-)	**ውደድ** wŭ́dḁd	**ወዶ** wώdd^{w}o	**መውደድ** mḁ́wŭdḁd (mḁ́͡ud-)	**ወዳጅ** wώdắj (§ 8)
ይውጋ yí̥wŭgã (yŭ́g-)	**ውጋ** wŭ́gã (^{w}úg-)	**ወግቶ** wώgt^{w}o (^{w}ώg-)	**መውጋት** mḁ́wŭgắt (mḁ́͡ug-; § 8)	**ወጊ** wḁ́gi (wώ-, ^{w}ώ-)
ይውጣ yí̥wŭṭã (yŭ́ṭã)	**ውጣ** wí̥ṭã (wŭ́ṭã)	**ወጥቶ** wώṭ(ı̥̆)t^{w}o	**መውጣት** mḁ́wŭṭát (mḁ́͡uṭ-; § 8)	**ወጭ** wḁč̣ (wω-, -ጪ -č̣i)
ይዋጥ yí̥wắṭ (yúắṭ; § 8)	**ዋጥ** wāṭ	**ውጦ** wŭ́ṭ^{w}o	**መዋጥ** mḁ́wắṭ (mḁ́͡uắṭ; § 8)	**ዋጭ** wāč̣ (-ጪ -č̣i)
ይወጥር yi̥wώṭṭi̥r (yuώ-)	**ወጥር** wώṭṭi̥r	**ወጥሮ** wώṭṭi̥r^{w}o	**መወጠር** mḁwώṭṭḁr (mḁ͡uώ-, -är)	**ወጣሪ** wωṭṭắri

Simp. perf. (§ 25)		Comp. perf. (§ 32)	Contingent (§ 26)	Comp. imperf. (§ 32)
ወፈረ wǿffḁrḁ (-är-)	be thick, i.	ወፍፏል wǿffi̥rŏ͡āl	ይወፍር yi̥wǿffi̥r (yuǿ-)	ይወፍራል yi̥wǿffi̥rāl (yuǿ-)
ዘለለ zḁ́llḁlḁ	jump, t.	ዘሏል zḁ́llŏ͡āl	ይዘል yi̥zḁ́ll	ይዘላል yi̥zḁ́llāl
ዘመረ zḁ́mmḁrḁ (-är-)	chant, t.	ዘምሯል zḁ́mmi̥rŏ͡āl	ይዘምር yi̥zḁ́mmi̥r	ይዘምራል yi̥zḁ́mmi̥rāl
ዘመተ zḁ́mmḁtḁ	go on a campaign, i.	ዘምቷል zḁ́mtŏ͡āl	ይዘምት yi̥zḁ́mt	ይዘምታል yi̥zḁ́mtāl
ዘራ zḁ́rrā̃ (zấ-)	sow, t.	ዘርቷል zḁ́rtŏ͡āl (zấ-)	ይዘራ yi̥zḁ́rā̃ (-zấ-)	ይዘራል yi̥zḁ́rāl (-zấ-)
ዞረ zʷŏ́rḁ	revolve, i.	ዞሯል zúrŏ͡āl ዞ- zʷŏ́- Š.	ይዞር yi̥zʷŏ́r	ይዞራል yi̥zʷŏ́rāl
ዘረጋ zḁrḁ́ggā̃ (zä-)	stretch, t.	ዘርግቷል zḁ́rgi̥tŏ͡āl (zấ-)	ይዘረጋ yi̥zḁrḁ́ggā̃ (-zä-)	ይዘረጋል yi̥zḁrḁ́ggāl (-zä-)
ዘረፈ zḁ́rrḁfḁ (zấ-)	loot, t.	ዘርፏል zḁ́rfŏ͡āl (zấ-)	ይዘርፍ yi̥zḁ́rf (-zấ-)	ይዘርፋል yi̥zḁ́rfāl (-zấ-)
ዘቀዘቀ zḁqḁ́zzḁqḁ	incline, t.	ዘቅዝቋል zḁ́qzi̥qŏ͡āl	ይዘቀዝቅ yi̥zḁqḁ́zzi̥q	ይዘቀዝቃል yi̥zḁqḁ́zzi̥qāl

Jussive (§ 27)	Imperative (§ 28)	Gerund (§ 29)	Infinitive (§ 30)	Participle (§ 31)
ይወፍር yi̥wώffi̥r (yuώ-)		**ወፍሮ** wώffi̥r^{w}o	**መወፈር** mḁwώffḁr (mḁ͡uώ-, -är)	**ወፋሪ** wωffā́ri
ይዝለል yí̥zlḁl (-äl)	**ዝለል** zí̥lḁl (-äl)	**ዘሎ** zḁ́ll^{w}o	**መዝለል** mḁ́zlḁl (-äl)	**ዘላይ** zḁ́lā́͡i̥ (-ā́yy §6; §8)
ይዘምር yi̥zḁ́mmi̥r	**ዘምር** zḁ́mmi̥r	**ዘምሮ** zḁ́mmi̥r^{w}o	**መዘመር** mḁzḁ́mmḁr (-är)	**ዘማሪ** zḁmmā́ri
ይዝመት yí̥zmḁt (-ät)	**ዝመት** zí̥mḁt (-ät)	**ዘምቶ** zḁ́mt^{w}o	**መዝመት** mḁ́zmḁt (-ät)	**ዘማች** zḁ́mā́č (§ 8)
ይዝሩ yí̥zrã	**ዝሩ** zí̥rã	**ዘርቶ** zḁ́rt^{w}o (zā́-)	**መዝሩት** mḁ́zrā́t (§ 8)	**ዘሪ** zḁ́ri (zā́-)
ይዙር yí̥zur	**ዙር** zur	**ዙሮ** zúr^{w}o ዘ- z^{w}ṓ- Š.	**መዙር** mḁ́z^{w}ṓr (§ 8)	**ዟሪ** zwā́ri
ይዘርጋ yi̥zḁ́rgã (-zā́-)	**ዘርጋ** zḁ́rgã (zā́-)	**ዘርግቶ** zḁ́rgi̥t^{w}o (zā́-)	**መዘርጋት** mḁzḁ́rgā́t (-zā́-; § 8)	**ዘርጊ** zḁ́rgi (zā́-)
ይዝረፍ yí̥zrḁf	**ዝረፍ** zí̥rḁf	**ዘርፎ** zḁ́rf^{w}o (zā́-)	**መዝረፍ** mḁ́zrḁf	**ዘራፊ** zḁrā́fi (zä-)
ይዘቅዝቅ yi̥zḁ́qzi̥q	**ዘቅዝቅ** zḁ́qzi̥q	**ዘቅዝቆ** zḁ́qzi̥q^{w}o	**መዘቅዘቅ** mḁzḁ́qzḁq	**ዘቅዛቂ** zḁqzā́qi

Simp. perf. (§ 25)		Comp. perf. (§ 32)	Contingent (§ 26)	Comp. imperf. (§ 32)
ዘባ zḁ́bbã	warp, i.	ዘብቷል zḁ́btŏ͡āl (-ỵt-)	ይዘባ yi̥zḁ́bã (-ḁ́ỵ-)	ይዘባል yi̥zḁ́bāl (-ḁ́ỵ-)
ዘነበ zḁ́nnḁbḁ (zä́-, -ỵḁ)	rain, i.	ዘንቧል zḁ́n(ĭ̥)bŏ͡āl (zä́-, -ỵŏ-)	ይዘንብ yi̥zḁ́n(ĭ̥)b (-zä́-, -ỵ)	ይዘንባል yi̥zḁ́n(ĭ̥)bāl (-zä́-, -ỵāl)
ዘወረ zḁ́͡uwḁrḁ	turn round, t.	ዘውሯል zḁ́͡uwŭrŏ͡āl	ይዘውር yi̥zḁ́͡uwŭr	ይዘውራል yi̥zḁ́͡uwŭrāl
ዘጋ zḁ́ggã	shut, t.	ዘግቷል zḁ́gtŏ͡āl	ይዘጋ yi̥zḁ́gã	ይዘጋል yi̥zḁ́gāl
ዘገየ zḁgḁ́yyä 2nd ዘገየህ zḁgḁ́yyäh, etc.	be late, i.	ዘግይቷል zḁ́gyi̥tŏ͡āl (zä́-)	ይዘገይ yi̥zḁgḁ́yy	ይዘገያል yi̥zḁgḁ́yyāl
ዘፈነ zḁ́ffḁnḁ (zä́-)	dance, i.	ዘፍኗል zḁ́f(ĭ̥)nŏ͡āl (zä́-)	ይዘፍን yi̥zḁ́f(ĭ̥)n (-zä́-)	ይዘፍናል yi̥zḁ́f(ĭ̥)nāl (-zä́-)
ያዘ yázḁ (§ 44*c*)	hold, t.	ይዟል yí̥zŏ͡āl	ይይዝ yi̥(y)í̥z [ዪዝ] (yī̥z)	ይይዛል yi̥(y)í̥zāl [ዪዛል] (yí̥zāl)

Jussive (§ 27)	Imperative (§ 28)	Gerund (§ 29)	Infinitive (§ 30)	Participle (§ 31)
ይዝባ yí̥zbā̃ (-zẏ-)		**ዘብቶ** zḁ́btʷo (-ẏt-)	**መዝባት** mḁ́zbā́t (-zẏ-; § 8)	**ዘቢ** zḁ́bi (zā̈́-, -ẏi)
ይዝነብ yí̥znḁb (-ḁẏ)		**ዘንቦ** zḁ́n(ĭ̥)bʷo (zā̈́-, -ẏʷo)	**መዝነብ** mḁ́znḁb (-ḁẏ)	
ይዘውር yi̥zḁ́͡uwŭr	**ዘውር** zḁ́͡uwŭr	**ዘውሮ** zḁ́͡uwŭrʷo	**መዘወር** mḁzḁ́͡uwḁr	**ዘዋሪ** zḁ͡uwā́ri
ይዝጋ yí̥zgā̃	**ዝጋ** zí̥gā̃	**ዘግቶ** zḁ́gtʷo	**መዝጋት** mḁ́zgā́t (§ 8)	**ዘጊ** zḁ́gi (zā̈́-)
ይዘገይ Š. yi̥zḁ́gḁ́͡i̥ (-ḁ́yy § 6; § 8; pl. -**ገዩ** -gḁ́yyu) **ይዘግይ** G. yi̥zḁ́gyi̥(-zā́-; pl. -**ግዩ**-gyu)	**ዘገይ** Š. zḁ́gḁ́͡i̥ (-ḁ́yy § 6; § 8; pl. -**ገዩ** -gḁ́yyu) **ዘግይ** G. zḁ́gyi̥ (zā́-; pl. -**ግዩ**-gyu)	**ዘግይቶ** zḁ́gyi̥tʷo (zā̈́-)	**መዘገየት** Š. mḁzḁgḁ́yyät **መዘግየት** G. mḁzḁ́gyät (-zā̈́-)	
ይዝፈን yí̥zfḁn	**ዝፈን** zí̥fḁn	**ዘፍኖ** zḁ́f(ĭ̥)nʷo (zā̈́-)	**መዝፈን** mḁ́zfḁn	**ዘፋኝ** zḁ́fā́ñ (zā̈́-; -ññ § 6; § 8)
ይያዝ yí̥(y)ā̃́z (§ 8)	**ያዝ** yā̃z	**ይዞ** yí̥zʷo	**መያዝ** mḁ́yā̃́z (mḁ́͡i̥ā́z, mḁ́ʸā̃z; § 8)	**ያዥ** yāž (-**ዢ** -ži)

Simp. perf. (§ 25)		Comp. perf. (§ 32)	Contingent (§ 26)	Comp. imperf. (§ 32)
ደለደለ dḁlḁ́ddḁlḁ (-äläddä-)	level, t.	ደልድሏል dḁ́ldi̥lŏ͡āl (dá̈-)	ይደለድል yi̥dḁlḁ́ddi̥l (-älá̈-)	ይደለድላል yi̥dḁlḁ́ddi̥- lāl (-älá̈-)
ደማ dḁ́mmã (dá̈-)	bleed, i.	ደምቷል dḁ́mtŏ͡āl (dá̈-)	ይደማ yi̥dḁ́mã (-dá̈-)	ይደማል yi̥dḁ́māl (-dá̈-)
ዳመጠ dámmḁṭḁ	gin, t.	ዳምጧል dá̈mṭŏ͡āl	ይዳምጥ yi̥dámmi̥ṭ	ይዳምጣል yi̥dámmi̥ṭāl
ደረሰ dḁ́rrḁsḁ	arrive, i.	ደርሷል dḁ́rsŏ͡āl (dá̈-)	ይደርስ yi̥dḁ́rs (-dá̈-)	ይደርሳል yi̥dḁ́rsāl (-dá̈-)
ደረቀ dḁ́rrḁqḁ	dry, i.	ደርቋል dḁ́rqŏ͡āl (dá̈-)	ይደርቅ yi̥dḁ́rq (-dá̈-)	ይደርቃል yi̥dḁ́rqāl (-dá̈-)
ዳሰሰ dá̈ssḁsḁ	handle, t.	ዳሷል dá̈ssŏ͡āl	ይዳስስ yi̥dá̈ssi̥s	ይዳስሳል yi̥dá̈ssi̥sāl
ደበለቀ dḁbḁ́llḁqḁ (-ḁẏḁ́-)	mix, t.	ደብልቋል dḁ́bli̥qŏ͡āl (dá̈-, -ẏl-)	ይደበልቅ yi̥dḁbḁ́lli̥q (-dä-, -ḁẏḁ́-, -á̈ll-)	ይደበልቃል yi̥dḁbḁ́lli̥qāl (-dä-, -ḁẏḁ́-, -á̈ll-)
ዳነ dá̈nḁ	recover, i.	ድኗል dí̥nŏ͡āl	ይድን yi̥dí̥n	ይድናል yi̥dí̥nāl
ደነቀው dḁ́nnḁqḁ͡u (§ 43*a*)	wonder, i.	ደንቆታል dḁ́ṅqʷotāl (dá̈-)	ይደንቀው yi̥dḁ́ṅqḁ͡u (-dá̈-)	ይደንቀዋል yi̥dḁ́ṅqḁ͡uāl (-dá̈-)

Jussive (§ 27)	Imperative (§ 28)	Gerund (§ 29)	Infinitive (§ 30)	Participle (§ 31)
ይደልድል yi̥dḁ́ldi̥l (-dấ-)	**ደልድል** dḁ́ldi̥l (dấ-)	**ደልድሎ** dḁ́ldi̥lʷo (dấ-)	**መደልደል** mḁdḁ́ldḁl (-ấldä-)	**ደልዳይ** dḁ́ldấi̥ (dấ-; -ấyy § 6; § 8)
ይድማ yí̥dmã		**ደምቶ** dḁ́mtʷo (dấ-)	**መድማት** mḁ́dmất (mấ-; § 8)	
ይዳምጥ yí̥dấmṭ (§ 8)	**ዳምጥ** dāmṭ	**ዳምጦ** dấmṭʷo	**መዳመጥ** mḁdấmḁṭ	**ዳማጭ** dấmấč̣ (§ 8)
ይድረስ yí̥drḁs	**ድረስ** dí̥rḁs	**ደርሶ** dḁ́rsʷo (dấ-)	**መድረስ** mḁ́drḁs	**ደራሽ** dḁ́rấš (dấ-; § 8)
ይድረቅ yí̥drḁq	**ድረቅ** dí̥rḁq	**ደርቆ** dḁ́rqʷo (dấ-)	**መድረቅ** mḁ́drḁq	**ደራቂ** dḁrấqi (dä-)
ይዳስ yí̥dấss (§ 8)	**ዳስ** dấss	**ዳሶ** dấssʷo	**መዳሰስ** mḁdấsḁs	**ዳሳሽ** dấsấš (§ 8)
ይደብልቅ yi̥dḁ́bli̥q (-dấ-, -ỵl-)	**ደብልቅ** dḁ́bli̥q (dấ-, -ỵl-)	**ደብልቆ** dḁ́bli̥qʷo (dấ-, -ỵl-)	**መደብለቅ** mḁdḁ́blḁq (-dấ-, -ỵl-)	**ደብላቂ** dḁblấqi (dä-, -ỵl-)
ይዳን yí̥dấn (§ 8)		**ድኖ** dí̥nʷo	**መዳን** mḁ́dấn (§ 8)	
		ደንቆት dḁ́ṅqʷṓt (dấ-; § 8)		

Simp. perf. (§ 25)		Comp. perf. (§ 32)	Contingent (§ 26)	Comp. imperf. (§ 32)
ደነበረ dḁnḁ́bbḁrḁ (-är-)	bolt, i.	ደንብሯል dá̄mbi̥rŏ͡āl	ይደነብር yi̥dḁnḁ́bbi̥r	ይደነብራል yi̥dḁnḁ́b- bi̥rāl
ደነገጠ dḁnḁ́ggḁṭḁ	be horrified, i.	ደንግጧል dḁ́ṅgi̥ṭŏ͡āl (dá̄-)	ይደነግጥ yi̥dḁnḁ́ggi̥ṭ	ይደነግጣል yi̥dḁnḁ́ggi̥- ṭāl
ዳኘ dá̄ññä 2nd ዳኘህ dá̄ññäh, etc.	arbitrate, i.	ዳኝቷል dá̄ñtŏ͡āl	ይዳኝ yi̥dá̄ññ	ይዳኛል yi̥dá̄ññāl
ደከመ dá̄kkḁmḁ	be tired, i.	ደክሟል dá̄k(ĭ̥)mŏ͡āl	ይደክም yi̥dá̄k(ĭ̥)m	ይደክማል yi̥dá̄k(ĭ̥)māl
ደወለ dḁ́͡uwḁlḁ (-wω-)	ring, t.	ደውሏል dḁ́͡uwŭlŏ͡āl	ይደውል yi̥dḁ́͡uwŭl	ይደውላል yi̥dḁ́͡uwŭlāl
ደገመ dḁ́ggḁmḁ (dá̄-)	repeat, t.	ደግሟል dḁ́gmŏ͡āl (dá̄-)	ይደግም yi̥dḁ́g(ĭ̥)m (-dá̄-)	ይደግማል yi̥dḁ́g(ĭ̥)māl (-dá̄-)
ደገፈ dḁ́ggḁfḁ	support, t.	ደግፏል dḁ́ggi̥fŏ͡āl (dá̄-)	ይደግፍ yi̥dḁ́ggi̥f (-dá̄-)	ይደግፋል yi̥dḁ́ggi̥fāl (-dá̄-)
ዳጠ dá̄ṭḁ	slip, i.	ዲጧል dí̥ṭŏ͡āl	ይዲጥ yi̥dí̥ṭ	ይዲጣል yi̥dí̥ṭāl
ጃለ já̄lḁ	be ugly, i.	ጃሏል já̄lŏ͡āl [ጂሏል] (jí̥lŏ͡āl)		

Jussive (§ 27)	Imperative (§ 28)	Gerund (§ 29)	Infinitive (§ 30)	Participle (§ 31)
ይደንብር yi̥dä́mbi̥r	ደንብር dä́mbi̥r	ደንብሮ dä́mbi̥rʷo	መደንበር mḁdä́mbḁr (-är)	ደንባሪ dämbä́ri
ይደንግጥ yi̥dḁ́ṅgi̥ṭ (-dä́-)		ደንግጦ dḁ́ṅgi̥ṭʷo (dä́-)	መደንገጥ mḁdḁ́ṅgḁṭ (-ä́ṅgä-)	ደንጋጭ dḁ́ṅgä́č̣ (dä́-; § 8)
ይዳኝ yí̥dä́ñ (-ññ § 6; § 8)	ዳኝ dāñ (-ññ § 6)	ዳኝቶ dä́ñtʷo	መዳኘት mḁdä́ñ(ñ)ät	ዳኝ dāñ (-ññ § 6; -ኚ -ññi)
ይድክም yí̥dkḁm		ደክሞ dä́k(ĭ̥)mʷo	መድክም mḁ́dkḁm	ደካሚ däkä́mi
ይደውል yi̥dḁ́uwŭl	ደውል dḁ́uwŭl	ደውሎ dḁ́uwŭlʷo	መደወል mḁdḁ́uwḁl (-ωl)	ደዋይ dḁ́uwä́i̥ (-ä́yy § 6; § 8)
ይድገም yí̥dgḁm	ድገም dí̥gḁm	ደግሞ dḁ́gmʷo (dḁ́mmʷo, dä́-)	መድገም mḁ́dgḁm	ደጋሚ dḁgä́mi (dä-)
ይደግፍ yi̥dḁ́ggi̥f (-dä́-)	ደግፍ dḁ́ggi̥f (dä́-)	ደግፎ dḁ́ggi̥fʷo (dä́-)	መደገፍ mḁdḁ́ggḁf	
ይዳጥ yí̥dä́ṭ (§ 8)	ዳጥ dāṭ	ድጦ dí̥ṭʷo ጀሎ jä́lʷo [ጅሎ] (jí̥lʷo)	መዳጥ mḁ́dä́ṭ (§ 8)	

Simp. perf. (§ 25)		Comp. perf. (§ 32)	Contingent (§ 26)	Comp. imperf. (§ 32)
ጀመለ jḁ́mmḁlḁ	add, t.	ጀምሏል jḁ́mmi̥lŏ͡āl	ይጀምል yi̥jḁ́mmi̥l	ይጀምላል yi̥jḁ́mmi̥lāl
ጀመረ jḁ́mmḁrḁ (-är-)	begin, t.	ጀምሯል jḁ́mmi̥rŏ͡āl	ይጀምር yi̥jḁ́mmi̥r	ይጀምራል yi̥jḁ́mmi̥rāl
ጋለበ gā́llḁbḁ (-ỵḁ)	gallop, i. & t.	ጋልቧል gā́l(ĭ̥)bŏ͡āl (-ỵ^{w}ŏ-)	ይጋልብ yi̥gā́lli̥b (-i̥ỵ)	ይጋልባል yi̥gā́lli̥bāl (-i̥ỵ-)
ገለባበጠ gḁlḁbā́b-bḁṭḁ (-ỵä́-)	invert completely, t.	ገለባብጧል gḁlḁbábṭŏ͡āl (-ỵä́ỵ-)	ይገለባብጥ yi̥gḁlḁbā́b-bi̥ṭ (-gä-, -ỵä́-)	ይገለባብጣል yi̥gḁlḁbā́b-bi̥ṭāl (-gä-, -ỵä́-)
ገለበጠ gḁlḁ́bbḁṭḁ	invert, t.	ገልብጧል gā́lbi̥ṭŏ͡āl (-ỵi̥-)	ይገለብጥ yi̥gḁlḁ́bbi̥ṭ (-gä-)	ይገለብጣል yi̥gḁlḁ́bbi̥-ṭāl (-gä-)
ገመሰ gḁ́mmḁsḁ	plough, t.	ገምሷል gḁ́msŏ͡āl	ይገምስ yi̥gḁ́ms	ይገምሳል yi̥gḁ́msāl
ገራ gḁ́rrā̃	tame, t.	ገርቷል gḁ́rtŏ͡āl (gä́-)	ይገራ yi̥gḁ́rā̃ (-gä́-)	ይገራል yi̥gḁ́rāl (-gä́-)
ገረመ gḁ́rrḁmḁ	astonish, t.	ገርሟል gḁ́rmŏ͡āl (gä́-)	ይገርም yi̥gḁ́rm (-gä́-)	ይገርማል yi̥gḁ́rmāl (-gä́-)
ገረመ gḁ́rrḁmḁ	be tame, i.	ገርሟል gḁ́rri̥mŏ͡āl (gä́-)	ይገርም yi̥gḁ́rri̥m (-gä́-)	ይገርማል yi̥gḁ́rri̥māl (-gä́-)

Jussive (§ 27)	Imperative (§ 28)	Gerund (§ 29)	Infinitive (§ 30)	Participle (§ 31)
ይጀምል yi̥jḁ́mmi̥l	ጀምል jḁ́mmi̥l	ጀምሎ jḁ́mmi̥lʷo	መጀመል mḁjḁ́mmḁl (-äl)	ጀማይ jḁ́mmā́i̥ (-ā́yy §6; § 8)
ይጀምር yi̥jḁ́mmi̥r	ጀምር jḁ́mmi̥r	ጀምሮ jḁ́mmi̥rʷo	መጀመር mḁjḁ́mmḁr (-är)	ጀማሪ jḁmmā́ri
ይጋልብ yi̥gā́lb (-lỵ; § 8)	ጋልብ gālb (-lỵ)	ጋልቦ gā́l(ĭ̥)bʷo (-ỵʷo)	መጋለብ mḁgā́lḁb (-ḁỵ)	ጋላቢ gālā́bi (-ỵi)
ይገለባብጥ yi̥gḁ́lḁbā́bṭ (-gā́-, -ỵā́ỵ-; § 8)	ገለባብጥ gḁ́lḁbā́bṭ (gā́-, -ỵā́ỵ-; § 8)	ገለባብጦ gḁlḁbā́bṭʷo (-ỵā́ỵ-)	መገለባበጥ mḁgḁlḁbā́- bḁṭ (-ỵā́ỵ-)	ገለባባጭ gḁlḁbā́bā́č̣ (-ỵā́ỵ-; § 8)
ይገልብጥ yi̥gā́lbi̥ṭ (-ỵi̥-)	ገልብጥ gā́lbi̥ṭ (-ỵi̥-)	ገልብጦ gā́lbi̥ṭʷo (-ỵi̥-)	መገልበጥ mḁgā́lbḁṭ (-lỵ-, -äṭ)	ገልባጭ gā́lbā́č̣ (-lỵ-; § 8)
ይግመስ yí̥gmḁs	ግመስ gí̥mḁs	ገምሶ gḁ́msʷo	መግመስ mḁ́gmḁs	ገማሽ gạmā́š (§ 8)
ይግራ yí̥grā̃	ግራ gí̥rā̃	ገርቶ gḁ́rtʷo (gā́-)	መግራት mḁ́grā́t (§ 8)	ገሪ gḁ́ri (gā́-)
ይግረም yí̥grḁm		ገርሞ gḁ́rmʷo (gā́-)	መግረም mḁ́grḁm	
ይገርም yi̥gḁ́rri̥m (-gā́-)		ገርሞ gḁ́rri̥mʷo (gā́-)	መገረም mḁgḁ́rrḁm	

Simp. perf. (§ 25)		Comp. perf. (§ 32)	Contingent (§ 26)	Comp. imperf. (§ 32)
ገረገረ gḁrḁ́ggḁrḁ (-ärḁ́ggä-)	stop short, i.	ገርግሯል gḁ́rgi̥rŏ͡āl (gắ-)	ይገረግር yi̥gḁrḁ́ggi̥r (-ärḁ́-)	ይገረግራል yi̥gḁrḁ́ggi̥-rāl (-ärḁ́-)
ጐረጐረ gwωrḁ́g-gwωrḁ (-rώgg-)	inspect, t.	ጐርጕሯል gwώrgwi̥-rŏ͡āl (-wŭrŏ-)	ይጐረጕር yi̥gwωrḁ́g-gwi̥r (-rώggwŭr)	ይጐረጕራል yi̥gwωrḁ́g-gwi̥rāl (-rώggwŭr-)
ገረፈ gḁ́rrḁfḁ (gắ-)	beat, t.	ገርፏል gḁ́rfŏ͡āl (gắ-)	ይገርፍ yi̥gḁ́rf (-gắ-)	ይገርፋል yi̥gḁ́rfāl (-gắ-)
ገሰገሰ gḁsḁ́ggḁsḁ	travel fast, i.	ገስግሷል gḁ́sgi̥sŏ͡āl (gắ-)	ይገሰግስ yi̥gḁsḁ́ggi̥s (-sắg-)	ይገሰግሳል yi̥gḁsḁ́ggi̥-sāl (-sắg-)
ገባ gḁ́bbā̃	enter, i.	ገብቷል gḁ́btŏ͡āl (-y̥t-)	ይገባ yi̥gḁ́bā̃ (-y̥ā̃)	ይገባል yi̥gḁ́bāl (-y̥āl)
ገበረ gḁ́bbḁrḁ (-bä-)	pay tribute, i.	ገብሯል gḁ́bbi̥rŏ͡āl	ይገብር yi̥gḁ́bbi̥r	ይገብራል yi̥gḁ́bbi̥rāl
ጋተ gắtḁ	give to drink, t.	ግቷል gí̥tŏ͡āl	ይግት yi̥gí̥t	ይግታል yi̥gí̥tāl
ገነነ gḁ́nnḁnḁ	increase, i.	ገኗል gḁ́nnŏ͡āl	ይገን yi̥gḁ́nn	ይገናል yi̥gḁ́nnāl
ገዛ gḁ́zzā̃	buy, t.	ገዝቷል gḁ́ztŏ͡āl	ይገዛ yi̥gḁ́zā̃	ይገዛል yi̥gḁ́zāl

Jussive (§ 27)	Imperative (§ 28)	Gerund (§ 29)	Infinitive (§ 30)	Participle (§ 31)
ይገርግር yi̥gḁ́rgi̥r (-i̥gá̈-)		ገርግሮ gḁ́rgi̥rʷo (gá̈-)	መገርገር mḁgḁ́rgḁr (-á̈rgä-)	ገርጋሪ gḁrgá̈ri (gä-)
ይጐርጕር yi̥gwώrgwi̥r (-gwŭr)	ጐርጕር gwώrgwi̥r (-gwŭr)	ጐርጕሮ gwώrgwi̥rʷo (-gwŭrʷo)	መጐርጐር mḁgwώr- gwωr	ጐርጓሪ gwωrgwá̈ri
ይግረፍ yí̥grḁf	ግረፍ gí̥rḁf	ገርፎ gḁ́rfʷo (gá̈-)	መግረፍ mḁ́grḁf	ገራፊ gḁrá̈fi (gä-)
ይገስግስ yi̥gḁ́sgi̥s (-gá̈-)	ገስግስ gḁ́sgi̥s (gá̈-)	ገስግሶ gḁ́sgi̥sʷo (gá̈-)	መገስገስ mḁgḁ́sgḁs	ገስጋሽ gḁ́sgá̈š (§ 8)
ይግባ yí̥gbã (-ṿã)	ግባ gí̥bã (-ṿã)	ገብቶ gḁ́btʷo (-ṿt-)	መግባት mḁ́gbá̈t (-gṿ- ; § 8)	ገቢ gḁ́bi (gá̈-, -ṿi)
ይገብር yi̥gḁ́bbi̥r	ገብር gḁ́bbi̥r	ገብሮ gḁ́bbi̥rʷo	መገበር mḁgḁ́bbḁr (-är)	ገባሪ gḁbbá̈ri
ይጋት yí̥gá̈t (§ 8)	ጋት f. ጋች gāt, f. gāč	ግቶ gí̥tʷo	መጋት mḁ́gá̈t (§ 8)	ጋች gāč
ይግነን yí̥gnḁn	ግነን gí̥nḁn	ገኖ gḁ́nnʷo	መግነን mḁ́gnḁn	ገናኝ gḁ́ná̈ñ (-ññ §6; §8)
ይግዛ yí̥gzã	ግዛ gí̥zã	ገዝቶ gḁ́ztʷo	መግዛት mḁ́gzá̈t (§ 8)	ገዥ gḁž (gä-, -ገዢ -ži)

Simp. perf. (§ 25)		Comp. perf. (§ 32)	Contingent (§ 26)	Comp. imperf. (§ 32)
ጐዳ gwώddã̄	injure, t.	ጐድቷል gwώd(ĭ̥)tŏ͡āl (-ώrt- § 7*d*)	ይጐዳ yi̥gwώdã̄	ይጐዳል yi̥gwώdāl
ገደለ gḁ́ddḁlḁ (gắ-)	kill, t.	ገድሏል gḁ́dlŏ͡āl (gḁ́llŏ-, gắ-)	ይገድል yi̥gḁ́dl (-gḁ́ll, -gắ-)	ይገድላል yi̥gḁ́dlāl (-gḁ́ll-, -gắ-)
ጐደለ gwώddḁlḁ	be lacking, i.	ጐድሏል gwώdlŏ͡āl	ይጐድል yi̥gwώdl	ይጐድላል yi̥gwώdlāl
ገደበ gḁ́ddḁbḁ (-ỵḁ)	dam, t.	ገድቧል gḁ́ddi̥bŏ͡āl (gắ-, -i̥ỵ-)	ይገድብ yi̥gḁ́ddi̥b (-gắ-, -i̥ỵ)	ይገድባል yi̥gḁ́ddi̥bāl (-gắ-, -i̥ỵ-)
ገደደ gḁ́ddḁdḁ	be wanting, i.	ገዷል gḁ́ddŏ͡āl	ይገድ yi̥gḁ́dd	ይገዳል yi̥gḁ́ddāl
ገደፈ gḁ́ddḁfḁ	break (a fast), t.	ገድፏል gḁ́dfŏ͡āl (gắ-)	ይገድፍ yi̥gḁ́df (-gắ-)	ይገድፋል yi̥gḁ́dfāl (-gắ-)
ገደፈ gḁ́ddḁfḁ	support, t.	ገድፏል gḁ́ddi̥fŏ͡āl (gắ-)	ይገድፍ yi̥gḁ́ddi̥f (-gắ-)	ይገድፋል yi̥gḁ́ddi̥fāl (-gắ-)
ጋጠ gắṭḁ	gnaw, t.	ግጧል gí̥ṭŏ͡āl	ይግጥ yi̥gí̥ṭ	ይግጣል yi̥gí̥ṭāl
ገጠመ gḁ́ṭṭḁmḁ	meet, i.	ገጥሟል gḁ́ṭmŏ͡āl	ይገጥም yi̥gḁ́ṭ(ĭ̥)m	ይገጥማል yi̥gḁ́ṭ(ĭ̥)māl

Jussive (§ 27)	Imperative (§ 28)	Gerund (§ 29)	Infinitive (§ 30)	Participle (§ 31)
ይጐዳ yí̥gwŭdã	ጐዳ gwŭ́dã	ጎድቶ gwǿd(i̥)t^{w}o (-ǿrt- § 7*d*)	መጐዳት mḁ́gwŭdắt (§ 8)	ጎጅ gwωj (-ጂ -ji)
ይግደል yí̥gdḁl (-äl)	ግደል gí̥dḁl (-äl)	ገድሎ gḁ́dl^{w}o (gḁ́ll^{w}o, gắ-)	መግደል mḁ́gdḁl (-äl)	ገዳይ gḁ́dắi̥ (gắ-; -ắyy § 6; § 8)
ይጐደል yí̥gwŭdḁl (-äl)	ጐደል gwŭ́dḁl (-äl)	ጎድሎ gwǿdl^{w}o	መጐደል mḁ́gwŭdḁl (-äl)	ጎዳይ gwǿdắi̥ (-ắyy § 6; § 8)
ይገድብ yi̥gḁ́ddi̥b (-gắ-, -i̥ṿ)	ገድብ gḁ́ddi̥b (gắ-, -i̥ṿ)	ገድቦ gḁ́ddi̥b^{w}o (gắ-, -i̥ṿ^{w}o)	መገደብ mḁgḁ́ddḁb (-gắ-, -ḁṿ)	ገዳቢ gḁddắbi (gä-, -ṿi)
ይግደድ yí̥gdḁd		ገዶ gḁ́dd^{w}o	መግደድ mḁ́gdḁd	†ገዳጅ gḁ́dắj (§ 8)
ይግደፍ yí̥gdḁf	ግደፍ gí̥dḁf	ገድፎ gḁ́df^{w}o (gắ-)	መግደፍ mḁ́gdḁf	ገዳፊ gḁdắfi
ይገድፍ yi̥gḁ́ddi̥f (-gắ-)	ገድፍ gḁ́ddi̥f (gắ-)	ገድፎ gḁ́ddi̥f^{w}o (gắ-)	መገደፍ mḁgḁ́ddḁf	
ይጋጥ yí̥gắṭ (§ 8)	ጋጥ gāṭ f. ጋጭ gāč̣	ግጦ gí̥ṭ^{w}o	መጋጥ mḁ́gắṭ (§ 8)	ጋጭ gāč̣
ይግጠም yí̥gṭḁm	ግጠም gí̥ṭḁm	ገጥሞ gḁ́ṭm^{w}o	መግጠም mḁ́gṭḁm	ገጣሚ gḁṭắmi

Simp. perf. (§ 25)		Comp. perf. (§ 32)	Contingent (§ 26)	Comp. imperf. (§ 32)
ገጨ gḁ́č̣č̣ä 2nd ገጨህ gḁ́č̣č̣äh, etc.	knock, t.	ገጭቷል gḁ́č̣tŏ͡āl (gắ-)	ይገጭ yi̥gḁ́č̣ (-gắ-)	ይገጫል yi̥gḁ́č̣āl (-gắ-)
ጋጨ Š. gắč̣ä	abuse, t.	ግጯል gí̥č̣ŏ͡āl	ይግጭ yi̥gí̥č̣	ይግጫል yi̥gí̥č̣āl
ጋጨ G. gắč̣č̣ä 2nd ጋጨህ gắč̣č̣äh, etc.	sling, t.	ጋጭቷል gắč̣(ĭ̥)tŏ͡āl	ይጋጭ yi̥gắč̣č̣	ይጋጫል yi̥gắč̣č̣āl
ገፋ gḁ́ffā̃	push, t.	ገፍቷል gḁ́ftŏ͡āl	ይገፋ yi̥gḁ́fā̃	ይገፋል yi̥gḁ́fāl
ጠላ ṭḁ́llā̃	hate, t.	ጠልቷል ṭḁ́ltŏ͡āl	ይጠላ yi̥ṭḁ́lā̃	ይጠላል yi̥ṭḁ́lāl
ጣለ ṭắlḁ	throw, t.	ጥሏል ṭí̥lŏ͡āl	ይጥል yi̥ṭí̥l	ይጥላል yi̥ṭí̥lāl
ጠለቀ ṭḁ́llḁqḁ	dive, i.	ጠልቋል ṭḁ́lqŏ͡āl (ṭắ-)	ይጠልቅ yi̥ṭḁ́lq (-ṭắ-)	ይጠልቃል yi̥ṭḁ́lqāl (-ṭắ-)
ጠለየ ṭḁ́llḁyä (-l͡ḁi̥ä) 2nd ጠለይህ ṭḁ́llḁyi̥h (-l͡ḁi̥h), etc.	pray, i.	ጠልይዋል ṭḁ́llyĭ̥wāl (-lyuā-)	ይጠልይ yi̥ṭḁ́llyi̥ (-li)	ይጠልያል yi̥ṭḁ́ll(ĭ̥)yāl

Jussive (§ 27)	Imperative (§ 28)	Gerund (§ 29)	Infinitive (§ 30)	Participle (§ 31)
ይግጭ yi̥gč̣	ግጭ gi̥č̣	ገጭቶ gḁ́č̣tʷo (gā́-)	መግጨት mḁ́gč̣ät	ገጭ gḁč̣ (gäč̣) [ገጪ] (gḁ́č̣i, gā́-)
ይጋጭ yi̥gā́č̣ (§ 8)	ጋጭ gāč̣	ግጮ gi̥č̣ʷo	መጋጭ mḁ́gā́č̣ (§ 8)	ጋጪ gā́č̣i
ይጋጭ yi̥gā́č̣ (§ 8)	ጋጭ gāč̣	ጋጭቶ gā́č̣(ĭ̥)tʷo	መጋጨት mḁgā́č̣ät	
ይግፋ yí̥gfā̃	ግፋ gí̥fā̃	ገፍቶ gḁ́ftʷo	መግፋት mḁ́gfā́t (§ 8)	ገፊ gḁ́fi (gā́-)
ይጥላ yí̥ṭlā̃	ጥላ ṭí̥lā̃	ጠልቶ ṭḁ́ltʷo	መጥላት mḁ́ṭlā́t (§ 8)	ጠይ ṭḁ́i̥ (ṭḁ́yy § 6)
ይጣል yí̥ṭā́l (§ 8)	ጣል ṭāl	ጥሎ ṭí̥lʷo	መጣል mḁ́ṭā́l (§ 8)	ጣይ ṭā́i̥ [ጣዪ] (ṭā́yi)
ይጥለቅ yí̥ṭlḁq	ጥለቅ ṭí̥lḁq	ጠልቆ ṭḁ́lqʷo (ṭā́-)	መጥለቅ mḁ́ṭlḁq	ጠላቂ ṭḁlā́qi
ይጠልይ yi̥ṭḁ́llyi̥ (-li)	ጠልይ ṭḁ́llyi̥ (-li)	ጠልዮ ṭḁ́llyĭ̥ʷo (-yo)	መጠለይ mḁṭḁ́llḁi̥	ጠላዪ ṭḁ́llā́i (-lā́i̥ ; -lā́yy § 6 ; § 8)

Simp. perf. (§ 25)		Comp. perf. (§ 32)	Contingent (§ 26)	Comp. imperf. (§ 32)
ጣመ ṭā́mḁ	taste pleasant, i.	ጥሟል ṭi̥mŏ͡āl	ይጥም yi̥ṭí̥m	ይጥማል yi̥ṭí̥māl
ጦመ ṭʷṓmḁ	fast, i.	ጡሟል ṭúmŏ͡āl	ይጦም yi̥ṭʷṓm	ይጦማል yi̥ṭʷṓmāl
ጠመመ ṭḁ́mmḁmḁ	be bent, i.	ጠሟል ṭḁ́mmŏ͡āl	ይጠም yi̥ṭḁ́mm	ይጠማል yi̥ṭḁ́mmāl
ጠመቀ ṭḁ́mmḁqḁ	wring, t.	ጠምቋል ṭḁ́mqŏ͡āl	ይጠምቅ yi̥ṭḁ́mq	ይጠምቃል yi̥ṭḁ́mqāl
ጠማው ṭḁ́mma͡u (§ 43*a*)	be thirsty, i.	ጠምቶታል ṭḁ́mtʷotāl	ይጠማው yi̥ṭḁ́ma͡u	ይጠማዋል yi̥ṭḁ́ma͡uāl
ጠመዘዘ ṭḁmḁ́zzḁzḁ	twist, t.	ጠምዝዟል ṭḁ́mzi̥zŏ͡āl	ይጠመዝዝ yi̥ṭḁmḁ́zzi̥z	ይጠመዝዛል yi̥ṭḁmḁ́zzi̥-zāl
ጠመደ ṭḁ́mmḁdḁ	yoke, t.	ጠምዷል ṭḁ́mdŏ͡āl	ይጠምድ yi̥ṭḁ́md	ይጠምዳል yi̥ṭḁ́mdāl
ጠመጠመ ṭḁmḁ́ṭṭḁmḁ	wind, t.	ጠምጥሟል ṭḁ́mṭi̥mŏ͡āl	ይጠመጥም yi̥ṭḁmḁ́ṭṭi̥m	ይጠመጥማል yi̥ṭḁmḁ́ṭṭi̥-māl
ጠራ ṭḁ́rrā̃	(*a*) call, t. (*b*) be pure, i.	ጠርቷል ṭḁ́rtŏ͡āl (tā́-)	ይጠራ yi̥ṭḁ́rā̃	ይጠራል yi̥ṭḁ́rāl
ጠረበ ṭḁ́rrḁbḁ (-y̥ḁ)	hew, t.	ጠርቧል ṭḁ́rbŏ͡āl (ṭā́-, -ry̥-)	ይጠርብ yi̥ṭḁ́rb (-ṭā́-, -ry̥)	ይጠርባል yi̥ṭḁ́rbāl (-ṭā́-, -ry̥-)

Jussive (§ 27)	Imperative (§ 28)	Gerund (§ 29)	Infinitive (§ 30)	Participle (§ 31)
ይጣም yi̥ṭám (§ 8)		ጥሞ ṭi̥mʷo	መጣም mḁṭám (§ 8)	
ይጡም yi̥ṭum	ጡም ṭum	ጡሞ ṭúmʷo	መጦም mḁṭʷṓm (§ 8)	ጧሚ ṭŏ͡ámi
ይጥመም yi̥ṭmḁm	ጥመም ṭi̥mḁm	ጠሞ ṭḁmmʷo	መጥመም mḁṭmḁm	ጠማሚ ṭḁmámi
ይጥመቅ yi̥ṭmḁq	ጥመቅ ṭi̥mḁq	ጠምቆ ṭḁmqʷo	መጥመቅ mḁṭmḁq	ጠማቂ ṭḁmáqi
ይጥማው yi̥ṭma͡u		ጠምቶት ṭḁmtʷõt	መጥማት mḁṭmát (§ 8)	
ይጠምዝዝ yi̥ṭḁmzi̥z	ጠምዝዝ ṭḁmzi̥z	ጠምዝዞ ṭḁmzi̥zʷo	መጠምዝዝ mḁṭḁmzḁz	ጠምዛዥ ṭḁmzá̃ž (§ 8)
ይጥመድ yi̥ṭmḁd	ጥመድ ṭi̥mḁd	ጠምዶ ṭḁmdʷo	መጥመድ mḁṭmḁd	ጠማጅ ṭḁmáj (§ 8)
ይጠምጥም yi̥ṭḁmṭi̥m	ጠምጥም ṭḁmṭi̥m	ጠምጥሞ ṭḁmṭi̥mʷo	መጠምጠም mḁṭḁmṭḁm	ጠምጣሚ ṭḁmṭámi
ይጥራ yi̥ṭrã	ጥራ ṭi̥rã	ጠርቶ ṭḁrtʷo (ṭá-)	መጥራት mḁṭrát (§ 8)	(*a*) ጠሪ ṭḁri (ṭá-)
ይጥረብ yi̥ṭrḁb (-ḁy̭)	ጥረብ ṭi̥rḁb (-ḁy̭)	ጠርቦ ṭḁrbʷo (ṭä-, -ry̭-)	መጥረብ mḁṭrḁb (-ḁy̭)	ጠራቢ ṭḁrábi (ṭä-, -y̭i)

Simp. perf. (§ 25)		Comp. perf. (§ 32)	Contingent (§ 26)	Comp. imperf. (§ 32)
ጠረገ ṭḁ́rrḁgḁ	clean, t.	ጠርጓል ṭḁ́rgŏ͡āl (ṭā́-)	ይጠርግ yi̥ṭḁ́rg (-ṭā́-)	ይጠርጋል yi̥ṭḁ́rgāl (-ṭā́-)
ጠረጠረ ṭḁrḁ́ṭṭḁrḁ (-ärḁ́ṭṭä-)	doubt, t.	ጠርጥሯል ṭḁ́rṭi̥rŏ͡āl (ṭā́-)	ይጠረጥር yi̥ṭḁrḁ́ṭṭi̥r (-i̥ṭä-)	ይጠረጥራል yi̥ṭḁrḁ́ṭṭi̥rāl (-i̥ṭä-)
ጤሰ ṭʸḗsḁ	smoke, i. be enraged, i.	ጢሷል ṭísŏ͡āl (ṭí̥-) ጤሷል Š. ṭʸḗsŏ͡āl	ይጤስ yi̥ṭʸḗs	ይጤሳል yi̥ṭʸḗsāl
ጠቀለለ ṭḁqḁ́llḁlḁ	roll up, t.	ጠቅልሏል ṭḁ́qli̥lŏ͡āl (ṭā́-) ጠቅሏል ṭḁ́qi̥llŏ͡āl (ṭā́-)	ይጠቀልል yi̥ṭḁqḁ́lli̥l	ይጠቀልላል yi̥ṭḁqḁ́lli̥lāl
ጠቀመ ṭḁ́qqḁmḁ (ṭā́-)	be useful, i. sew, t.	ጠቅሟል ṭḁ́qmŏ͡āl (ṭā́-)	ይጠቅም yi̥ṭḁ́q(ĭ̥)m (-ṭā́-)	ይጠቅማል yi̥ṭḁ́q(ĭ̥)māl (-ṭä́-)
ጠቈመ ṭḁ́qqwωmḁ (ṭώ-)	betray, t.	ጠቍሟል ṭḁ́qqwŭ-mŏ͡āl	ይጠቍም yi̥ṭḁ́qqwŭm	ይጠቍማል yi̥ṭḁ́qqwŭ-māl
ጠቀሰ ṭḁ́qqḁsḁ	beckon, i.	ጠቅሷል ṭḁ́qsŏ͡āl	ይጠቅስ yi̥ṭḁ́q(ĭ̥)s	ይጠቅሳል yi̥ṭḁ́q(ĭ̥)sāl
ጠባ ṭḁ́bbā̃	suck, t. dawn, i.	ጠብቷል ṭḁ́btŏ͡āl (-ẏt-)	ይጠባ yi̥ṭḁ́bā̃ (-ẏā̃)	ይጠባል yi̥ṭḁ́bāl (-ḁ́ẏ-)

Jussive (§ 27)	Imperative (§ 28)	Gerund (§ 29)	Infinitive (§ 30)	Participle (§ 31)
ይጥረግ yí̥ṭrḁg	ጥረግ ṭí̥rḁg	ጠርጎ ṭḁ́rg^{w}o (ṭắ-)	መጥረግ mḁ́ṭrḁg	ጠራጊ ṭḁrắgi (ṭä-)
ይጠርጥር yi̥ṭḁ́rṭi̥r (-ṭắ-)	ጠርጥር ṭḁ́rṭi̥r (ṭắ-)	ጠርጥሮ ṭḁ́rṭi̥r^{w}o (ṭắ-)	መጠርጠር mḁṭḁ́rṭḁr (-ắrṭä-)	ጠርጣሪ ṭḁrṭắri (ṭä-)
ይጢስ yí̥ṭis (-i̥s)	ጢስ ṭis (ṭi̥s)	ጢሶ ṭís^{w}o (ṭí̥-) ጤሶ Š. ṭ^{y}ḗs^{w}o	መጤስ mḁ́ṭ^{y}ḗs (§ 8)	ጢያሽ ṭyāš (ṭāš)
ይጠቅልል yi̥ṭḁ́qli̥l (-ṭắ-)	ጠቅልል ṭḁ́qli̥l (ṭắ-)	ጠቅልሎ ṭḁ́qli̥l^{w}o (ṭắ-) ጠቅሎ ṭḁ́qi̥ll^{w}o (ṭắ-)	መጠቅለል mḁṭḁ́qlḁl (-ắqlä-)	ጠቅላይ ṭḁ́qlắi̥ (ṭắ-; -ắyy § 6; § 8)
ይጥቀም yí̥ṭqḁm	ጥቀም ṭí̥qḁm	ጠቅሞ ṭḁ́qm^{w}o (ṭắ-)	መጥቀም mḁ́ṭqḁm	ጠቃሚ ṭḁqắmi (ṭä-)
ይጠቊም yi̥ṭḁ́qqwŭm	ጠቊም ṭḁ́qqwŭm	ጠቍሞ ṭḁ́qqwŭ- m^{w}o	መጠቈም mḁṭḁ́q- qwωm (-ṭώ-)	ጠቋሚ ṭḁqqwắmi (ṭω-)
ይጥቀስ yí̥ṭqḁs	ጥቀስ ṭí̥qḁs	ጠቅሶ ṭḁ́qs^{w}o	መጥቀስ mḁ́ṭqḁs	ጠቃሽ ṭḁ́qắš (§ 8)
ይጥባ yí̥ṭbā̃ (-ṭy̥-)	ጥባ ṭí̥bā̃ (-y̥ā̃)	ጠብቶ ṭḁ́bt^{w}o (-y̥t-)	መጥባት mḁ́ṭbắt (-ṭy̥-; § 8)	ጠቢ ṭḁ́bi (ṭắ-, -y̥i)

Simp. perf. (§ 25)		Comp. perf. (§ 32)	Contingent (§ 26)	Comp. imperf. (§ 32)
ጠበሰ ṭḁ́bbḁsḁ	grill, t.	ጠብሷል ṭḁ́bsŏ͡āl (-ỵs-)	ይጠብስ yi̥ṭḁ́bs (-ỵs)	ይጠብሳል yi̥ṭḁ́bsāl (-ỵs-)
ጠበቀ ṭḁ́bbḁqḁ	be tied tight, i.	ጠብቋል ṭḁ́bqŏ͡āl (-ỵq-)	ይጠብቅ yi̥ṭḁ́bq (-ỵq)	ይጠብቃል yi̥ṭḁ́bqāl (-ỵq-)
ጠበቀ ṭḁ́bbḁqḁ	guard, t.	ጠብቋል ṭḁ́bbi̥qŏ͡āl	ይጠብቅ yi̥ṭḁ́bbi̥q	ይጠብቃል yi̥ṭḁ́bbi̥qāl
ጠበበ ṭḁ́bbḁbḁ (-ỵḁ)	be narrow, i.	ጠቧል ṭḁ́bbŏ͡āl	ይጠብ yi̥ṭḁ́bb	ይጠባል yi̥ṭḁ́bbāl
ጠነቈለ ṭḁnḁ́qqwω- lḁ	prick, t.	ጠንቍሏል ṭḁ́ṅqwŭlŏ͡āl	ይጠነቍል yi̥ṭḁnḁ́q- qwŭl	ይጠነቍላል yi̥ṭḁnḁ́q- qwŭlāl
ጠየቀ ṭḁ́yyḁqḁ (-yä-)	ask, t.	ጠይቋል ṭḁ́yyi̥qŏ͡āl	ይጠይቅ yi̥ṭḁ́yyi̥q	ይጠይቃል yi̥ṭḁ́yyi̥qāl
ጣደ ṭā́dḁ	bake, t.	ጥዷል ṭí̥dŏ͡āl	ይጥድ yi̥ṭí̥d	ይጥዳል yi̥ṭí̥dāl
ጠገበ ṭḁ́ggḁbḁ (-ỵḁ)	have enough (food, etc.), i.	ጠግቧል ṭḁ́g(ĭ̥)bŏ͡āl (ṭä́-, -ỵŏ-)	ይጠግብ yi̥ṭḁ́g(ĭ̥)b (-ṭä́-, -ỵ)	ይጠግባል yi̥ṭḁ́g(ĭ̥)bāl (-ṭä́-, -ỵā-)
ጠጣ ṭḁ́ṭṭã	drink, t.	ጠጥቷል ṭḁ́ṭṭi̥tŏ͡āl	ይጠጣ yi̥ṭḁ́ṭṭã	ይጠጣል yi̥ṭḁ́ṭṭāl

Jussive (§ 27)	Imperative (§ 28)	Gerund (§ 29)	Infinitive (§ 30)	Participle (§ 31)
ይጥበስ yí̥ṭbḁs (-ṭʏ̣-)	ጥበስ ṭí̥bḁs (-ʏ̣ḁ-)	ጠብሶ ṭḁ́bs^{w}o (-ʏ̣s-)	መጥበስ mḁ́ṭbḁs (-ṭʏ̣-)	ጠባሽ ṭḁ́bā́š (-ḁ́ʏ̣- ; § 8)
ይጥበቅ yí̥ṭbḁq (-ṭʏ̣-)		ጠብቆ ṭḁ́bq^{w}o (-ʏ̣q-)	መጥበቅ mḁ́ṭbḁq (-ṭʏ̣-)	ጠባቂ ṭḁbā́qi (-ḁʏ̣-)
ይጠብቅ yi̥ṭḁ́bbi̥q	ጠብቅ ṭḁ́bbi̥q	ጠብቆ ṭḁ́bbi̥q^{w}o	መጠበቅ mḁṭḁ́bbḁq	ጠባቂ ṭḁbbā́qi
ይጥበብ yí̥ṭbḁb (-ṭʏ̣ḁʏ̣)		ጠቦ ṭḁ́bb^{w}o	መጥበብ mḁ́ṭbḁb (-ṭʏ̣ḁʏ̣)	ጠባቢ ṭḁbā́bi (-ʏ̣ā́ʏ̣-)
ይጠንቍል yi̥ṭḁ́ṅqwŭl	ጠንቍል ṭḁ́ṅqwŭl	ጠንቍሎ ṭḁ́ṅqwŭl^{w}o	መጠንቈል mḁṭḁ́ṅqwḁl (-wωl)	ጠንቋይ ṭḁ́nqwā́i̥ (-ā́yy § 6; § 8)
ይጠይቅ yi̥ṭḁ́yyi̥q	ጠይቅ ṭḁ́yyi̥q	ጠይቆ ṭḁ́yyi̥q^{w}o	መጠየቅ mḁṭḁ́yyḁq (-äq)	ጠያቂ ṭḁyyā́qi
ይጣድ yí̥ṭā́d (§ 8)	ጣድ ṭād	ጥዶ ṭí̥d^{w}o	መጣድ mḁ́ṭā́d (§ 8)	ጣጅ ṭāj (-ጂ -ji)
ይጥገብ yí̥ṭgḁb (-ʏ̣)	ጥገብ ṭí̥gḁb (-ʏ̣)	ጠግቦ ṭḁ́g(ĭ̥)b^{w}o (ṭä́-, -ʏ̣^{w}o)	መጥገብ mḁ́ṭgḁb (-ʏ̣)	ጠጋቢ ṭḁgā́bi (-ʏ̣i)
ይጠጣ yi̥ṭḁ́ṭṭã	ጠጣ ṭḁ́ṭṭã	ጠጥቶ ṭḁ́ṭṭi̥t^{w}o	መጠጣት mḁṭḁ́ṭṭát (§ 8)	ጠጭ ṭḁč̣č̣ (ṭä-, -ጪ -č̣č̣i)

Simp. perf. (§ 25)		Comp. perf. (§ 32)	Contingent (§ 26)	Comp. imperf. (§ 32)
ጠፋ ṭḁffã	be extinguished, p.	ጠፍቷል ṭḁftŏ͡āl	ይጠፋ yi̥ṭḁ́fã	ይጠፋል yi̥ṭḁ́fāl
ጣፈ ṭā́fḁ	write, t.	ጥፏል ṭí̥fŏ͡āl	ይጥፍ yi̥ṭí̥f	ይጥፋል yi̥ṭí̥fāl
ጣፈጠ ṭā́ffḁṭḁ	be sweet, i.	ጣፍጧል ṭā́fṭŏ͡āl	ይጣፍጥ yi̥ṭā́ffi̥ṭ	ይጣፍጣል yi̥ṭā́ffi̥ṭāl
ጨለመ č̣ǟ́llämḁ	be dark, i.	ጨልሟል č̣ǟ́lli̥mŏ͡āl	ይጨልም yi̥č̣ǟ́lli̥m	ይጨልማል yi̥č̣ǟ́lli̥māl
ጨመረ č̣ḁ́mmḁrḁ (-är-)	increase, t.	ጨምሯል č̣ḁ́mmi̥rŏ͡āl	ይጨምር yi̥č̣ḁ́mmi̥r	ይጨምራል yi̥č̣ḁ́mmi̥rāl
ጨረሰ č̣ḁ́rrḁsḁ (-ǟ́rrä-)	finish, t.	ጨርሷል č̣ḁ́rri̥sŏ͡āl (č̣ǟ́-)	ይጨርስ yi̥č̣ḁ́rri̥s (-č̣ǟ́-)	ይጨርሳል yi̥č̣ḁ́rri̥sāl (-č̣ǟ́-)
ጨቈነ č̣ḁ́qqwωnḁ (č̣ώqqonḁ)	press, t.	ጨቍኗል č̣ḁ́qqwŭnŏ͡āl (č̣ώ-)	ይጨቍን yi̥č̣ḁ́qqwŭn (-č̣ώ-)	ይጨቍናል yi̥č̣ḁ́qqwŭ- nāl (-č̣ώ-)
ጫነ č̣ā́nḁ	saddle, t.	ጭኗል č̣í̥nŏ͡āl	ይጭን yi̥č̣í̥n	ይጭናል yi̥č̣í̥nāl
ጮኸ č̣ʷóhḁ (§ 7*d*)	shout, i.	ጩኋል č̣úhŏ͡āl ጮ- č̣ʷó- Š.	ይጮኽ yi̥č̣ʷóh	ይጮኻል yi̥č̣ʷóhāl

Jussive (§ 27)	Imperative (§ 28)	Gerund (§ 29)	Infinitive (§ 30)	Participle (§ 31)
ይጥፋ yı̥ṭfã̈		ጠፍቶ ṭḁ́ftʷo	መጥፋት mḁ́ṭfát (§ 8)	ጠፊ ṭḁ́fi (ṭá-)
ይጣፍ yı̥ṭáf (§ 8)	ጣፍ ṭāf	ጥፎ ṭı̥́fʷo	መጣፍ mḁ́ṭáf (§ 8)	ጣፊ ṭáfi
ይጣፍጥ yı̥ṭáfṭ (§ 8)	ጣፍጥ ṭāfṭ	ጣፍጦ ṭáfṭʷo	መጣፈጥ mḁṭáfḁṭ	ጣፋጭ ṭáfáč̣ (§ 8)
ይጨልም yi̥č̣állı̥m		ጨልሞ č̣állı̥mʷo	መጨለም mḁč̣álläm	
ይጨምር yi̥č̣ḁ́mmı̥r	ጨምር č̣ḁ́mmı̥r	ጨምሮ č̣ḁ́mmı̥rʷo	መጨመር mḁč̣ḁ́mmḁr (-är)	ጨማሪ č̣ḁmmári
ይጨርስ yi̥č̣ḁ́rrı̥s (-č̣á-)	ጨርስ č̣ḁ́rrı̥s (č̣á-)	ጨርሶ č̣ḁ́rrı̥sʷo (č̣á-)	መጨረስ mḁč̣ḁ́rrḁs (-árrä-)	ጨራሽ č̣ḁ́rráš (č̣á-; § 8)
ይጨቍን yi̥č̣ḁ́qqwŭn (-č̣ώ-)	ጨቍን č̣ḁ́qqwŭn (č̣ώ-)	ጨቍኖ č̣ḁ́qqwŭnʷo (č̣ώ-)	መጨቈን mḁč̣ḁ́qqwωn (-ώqqo-)	ጨቋኝ č̣ḁ́qqwáñ (č̣ώ-; -ññ § 6; § 8)
ይጫን yı̥č̣án (§ 8)	ጫን č̣ān	ጭኖ č̣ı̥́nʷo	መጫን mḁ́č̣án (§ 8)	ጫኝ č̣āñ (-ññ § 6; -ኚ -ññi)
ይጩኽ yı̥č̣uh	ጩኽ č̣uh	ጩኾ č̣úhʷo ጮ- č̣ʷó- Š.	መጮኽ mḁ́č̣ʷóh (§ 8)	ጯኺ č̣ŏáhi

Simp. perf. (§ 25)		Comp. perf. (§ 32)	Contingent (§ 26)	Comp. imperf. (§ 32)
ጻፈ ṣáfḁ	write, t.	ጽፏል ṣi̥fŏ͡āl	ይጽፍ yi̥ṣí̥f	ይጽፋል yi̥ṣí̥fāl
ፈላ fḁ́llā̃	boil, i.	ፈልቷል fḁ́ltŏ͡āl (fä́-)	ይፈላ yi̥fḁ́lā̃	ይፈላል yi̥fḁ́lāl
ፈላለገ fḁlā́llḁgḁ	make a slightsearch for, t.	ፈላልጓል fḁlál(ĭ̥)gŏ͡āl	ይፈላልግ yi̥fḁlā́lli̥g	ይፈላልጋል yi̥fḁlā́lli̥gāl
ፈለገ fḁ́llḁgḁ	seek, t.	ፈልጓል fḁ́lli̥gŏ͡āl	ይፈልግ yi̥fḁ́lli̥g	ይፈልጋል yi̥fḁ́lli̥gāl
ፈራ fḁ́rrā̃ (fä́-)	fear, t.	ፈርቷል fḁ́rtŏ͡āl (fä́-)	ይፈራ yi̥fḁ́rā̃ (-fä́-)	ይፈራል yi̥fḁ́rāl (-fä́-)
ፈረሰ fḁ́rrḁsḁ	be ruined, i.	ፈርሷል fḁ́rsŏ͡āl (fä́-)	ይፈርስ yi̥fḁ́rs (-fä́-)	ይፈርሳል yi̥fḁ́rsāl (-fä́-)
ፈረደ fḁ́rrḁdḁ	judge, i.	ፈርዷል fḁ́rdŏ͡āl (fä́-)	ይፈርድ yi̥fḁ́rd (-fä́-)	ይፈርዳል yi̥fḁ́rdāl (-fä́-)
ፈሰሰ fḁ́ssḁsḁ	leak, i.	ፈሷል fḁ́ssŏ͡āl	ይፈስ yi̥fḁ́ss	ይፈሳል yi̥fḁ́ssāl
ፋቀ fā́qḁ	scrape, t.	ፍቋል fí̥qŏ͡āl	ይፍቅ yi̥fí̥q	ይፍቃል yi̥fí̥qāl
ፈቀደ fḁ́qqḁdḁ	allow, t.	ፈቅዷል fḁ́q(ĭ̥)dŏ͡āl (fä́-)	ይፈቅድ yi̥fḁ́q(ĭ̥)d (-fä́-)	ይፈቅዳል yi̥fḁ́q(ĭ̥)dāl (-fä́-)

Jussive (§ 27)	Imperative (§ 28)	Gerund (§ 29)	Infinitive (§ 30)	Participle (§ 31)
ይጻፍ yí̥ṣā́f (§ 8)	ጻፍ ṣāf	ጽፎ ṣí̥fʷo	መጻፍ mḁ́ṣā́f (§ 8)	ጻፊ ṣā́fi
ይፍላ yí̥flā̃	ፍላ fí̥lā̃	ፈልቶ fḁ́ltʷo (fā́-)	መፍላት mḁ́flā́t (§ 8)	†ፈይ fḁ́i̥͡ (fḁyy § 6)
ይፈላልግ yi̥fḁlā́li̥g	ፈላልግ fḁlā́li̥g	ፈላልጎ fḁlā́l(ĭ̥)gʷo	መፈላለግ mḁfḁlā́lḁg	ፈላላጊ fḁlālā́gi
ይፈልግ yi̥fḁ́lli̥g	ፈልግ fḁ́lli̥g	ፈልጎ fḁ́lli̥gʷo	መፈለግ mḁfḁ́llḁg	ፈላጊ fḁllā́gi
ይፍራ yí̥frā̃	ፍራ fí̥rā̃	ፈርቶ fḁ́rtʷo (fā́-)	መፍራት mḁ́frā́t (§ 8)	ፈሪ fḁ́ri (fā́-)
ይፍረስ yí̥frḁs		ፈርሶ fḁ́rsʷo (fā́-)	መፍረስ mḁ́frḁs	ፈራሽ fḁ́rā́š (fā́- ; § 8)
ይፍረድ yí̥frḁd	ፍረድ fí̥rḁd	ፈርዶ fḁ́rdʷo (fā́-)	መፍረድ mḁ́frḁd	ፈራጅ fḁ́rā́j (fā́- ; § 8)
ይፍሰስ yí̥fsḁs		ፈሶ fḁ́ssʷo	መፍሰስ mḁ́fsḁs	ፈሳሽ fḁ́sā́š (§ 8)
ይፋቅ yí̥fā́q (§ 8)	ፋቅ fāq	ፍቆ fí̥qʷo	መፋቅ mḁ́fā́q (§ 8)	ፋቂ fā́qi
ይፍቀድ yí̥fqḁd	ፍቀድ fí̥qḁd	ፈቅዶ fḁ́q(ĭ̥)dʷo (fā́-)	መፍቀድ mḁ́fqḁd	ፈቃጅ fḁ́qā́j (§ 8)

Simp. perf. (§ 25)		Comp. perf. (§ 32)	Contingent (§ 26)	Comp. imperf. (§ 32)
ፈታ fḁ́ttã	untie, t.	ፈትቷል fḁ́t(i̥)tŏ͡āl	ይፈታ yi̥fḁ́tã	ይፈታል yi̥fḁ́tāl
ፈተነ fḁ́ttḁnḁ (-ắttä-)	test, t.	ፈትኗል fḁ́tti̥nŏ͡āl (fắ-)	ይፈትን yi̥fḁ́tti̥n (-fắ-)	ይፈትናል yi̥fḁ́tti̥nāl (-fắ-)
ፈነቀለ fḁnḁ́qqḁlḁ	move, t.	ፈንቅሏል fḁ́ṅqi̥lŏ͡āl	ይፈነቅል yi̥fḁnḁ́qqi̥l	ይፈነቅላል yi̥fḁnḁ́qqi̥- lāl
ፈነዳ fḁnḁ́ddã	burst, i.	ፈንድቷል fḁ́ndi̥tŏ͡āl	ይፈነዳ yi̥fḁnḁ́ddã	ይፈነዳል yi̥fḁnḁ́ddāl
ፈከረ fḁ́kkḁrḁ (-är-)	boast, i.	ፈክሯል fḁ́kki̥rŏ͡āl	ይፈክር yi̥fḁ́kki̥r	ይፈክራል yi̥fḁ́kki̥rāl
ፈወሰ fḁ́͡uwḁsḁ	cure, t.	ፈውሷል fḁ́͡uwŭsŏ͡āl	ይፈውስ yi̥fḁ́͡uwŭs	ይፈውሳል yi̥fḁ́͡uwŭsāl
ፈጀ fḁ́jjä (fắ-) 2nd -ጀህ -jjäh, etc.	destroy, t.	ፈጅቷል fḁ́j(i̥)tŏ͡āl (fắ-)	ይፈጅ yi̥fḁ́j (-fắ-)	ይፈጃል yi̥fḁ́jāl (-fắ-)
ፈጃጀ fḁjắjjä (fä-) 2nd -ጀህ -jjäh, etc.	destroy utterly, t.	ፈጃጅቷል fḁjáj(i̥)tŏ͡āl (fä-)	ይፈጃጅ yi̥fḁjắjj (-fä-)	ይፈጃጃል yi̥fḁjắjjāl (-fä-)

Jussive (§ 27)	Imperative (§ 28)	Gerund (§ 29)	Infinitive (§ 30)	Participle (§ 31)
ይፍታ y̥íftã̈	ፍታ f̥ítã̈	ፈትቶ fḁ́t(ĭ̥)tʷo	መፍታት mḁ́ftä́t (§ 8)	ፈች fḁč (fä-, -ቺ -či)
ይፈትን y̥ifḁ́ttịn (-fä́-)	ፈትን fḁ́ttịn (fä́-)	ፈትኖ fḁ́ttịnʷo (fä́-)	መፈተን mḁfḁ́ttạn (-ä́ttä-)	ፈታኝ fḁ́ttä́ñ (fä́-; -ññ § 6; § 8)
ይፈንቅል y̥ifḁ́ṅqil̥	ፈንቅል fḁ́ṅqil̥	ፈንቅሎ fḁ́ṅqil̥ʷo	መፈንቀል mḁfḁ́ṅqḁl	ፈንቃይ fḁ́ṅqä́i̥ (-ä́yy § 6; § 8)
ይፈንዳ y̥ifḁ́ndã̈		ፈንድቶ fḁ́ndịtʷo	መፈንዳት mḁfḁ́ndä́t (§ 8)	†ፈንጅ fḁ́nj (fä́-, -ጂ -ji)
ይፈክር y̥ifḁ́kkịr	ፈክር fḁ́kkịr	ፈክሮ fḁ́kkịrʷo	መፈከር mḁfḁ́kkḁr (-är)	ፈካሪ fḁkkä́ri
ይፈውስ y̥ifḁ́͡uwŭ́s	ፈውስ fḁ́͡uwŭ́s	ፈውሶ fḁ́͡uwŭ́sʷo	መፈወስ mḁfḁ́͡uwḁs	ፈዋሽ fḁ́͡uwä́š (§ 8)
ይፍጅ y̥íf̥íj (§ 8)	ፍጅ fi̥j	ፈጅቶ fḁ́j(ĭ̥)tʷo (fä́-)	መፍጀት mḁ́fjät	†ፈጅ fḁj (fä-, -ጂ -ji)
ይፈጃጅ y̥ifḁ́jä́j (-fä́-; § 8)	ፈጃጅ fḁ́jä́j (fä́-; § 8)	ፈጃጅቶ fḁjä́j(ĭ̥)tʷo (fä-)	መፈጃጀት mḁfḁjä́jät (-fä-)	ፈጃጅ fḁ́jä́j (fä́-; § 8; -ጂ -ji)

Simp. perf. (§ 25)		Comp. perf. (§ 32)	Contingent (§ 26)	Comp. imperf. (§ 32)
ፈገፈገ fḁgḁ́ffḁgḁ	rub, t.	ፈግፍጓል fḁ́gfi̥gŏ͡āl	ይፈገፍግ yi̥fḁgḁ́ffi̥g	ይፈገፍጋል yi̥fḁgḁ́ffi̥gāl
ፈጠነ fḁ́ṭṭḁnḁ (-ä́ṭṭä-)	hasten, i.	ፈጥኗል fḁ́ṭ(ĭ̥)nŏ͡āl (fä́-)	ይፈጥን yi̥fḁ́ṭ(ĭ̥)n (-fä́-)	ይፈጥናል yi̥fḁ́ṭ(ĭ̥)nāl (-fä́-)
ፈጨ fḁ́č̣č̣ä (fä́-) 2nd -ጨህ -č̣č̣äh, etc.	grind, t.	ፈጭቷል fḁ́č̣tŏ͡āl (fä́-)	ይፈጭ yi̥fḁ́č̣ (-fä́-)	ይፈጫል yi̥fḁ́č̣āl (-fä́-)

Jussive (§ 27)	Imperative (§ 28)	Gerund (§ 29)	Infinitive (§ 30)	Participle (§ 31)
ይፈግፍግ yi̥fḁ́gfi̥g	**ፈግፍግ** fḁ́gfi̥g	**ፈግፍጎ** fḁ́gfi̥g^{w}o	**መፈግፈግ** mḁfḁ́gfḁg	**ፈግፋጊ** fḁgfä́gi
ይፍጠን yí̥fṭḁn	**ፍጠን** fí̥ṭḁn	**ፈጥኖ** fḁ́ṭ(ĭ̥)n^{w}o (fä́-)	**መፍጠን** mḁ́fṭḁn	**ፈጣኝ** fḁ́ṭä́ñ (fä́-; -ññ § 6; § 8)
ይፍጭ yi̥fč̣	**ፍጭ** fi̥č̣	**ፈጭቶ** fḁ́č̣t^{w}o (fä́-)	**መፍጨት** mḁ́fč̣ät	**ፈጭ** fḁč̣ (fä-, -ጪ -č̣i)

INDEX.

(The numbers refer to the paragraphs.)